AA

explorer

JAPAN

David Scott

AA Publishing

Written by David Scott
Original photography by Jim Holmes
Edited, designed and produced by AA Publishing
Maps © The Automobile Association 1996

Distributed in the United Kingdom by AA Publishing, Norfolk House, Priestley Road, Basingstoke, Hampshire RG24 9NY.

A CIP catalogue record for this book is available from the British Library.
ISBN 0 7495 1032 3

Published by AA Publishing (a trading name of Automobile Association Developments Limited, whose registered office is Norfolk House, Priestley Road, Basingstoke, Hampshire RG24 9NY. Registered number 1878835).

Colour separation by Fotographics
Printed in Italy by Printer SRL, Trento

Cover picture: Zen garden. Page 2a: the art of *Kamakura-bori* (finely chiselled wood). Page 4: the Fujiyama building, Ginza, Tokyo. Page 5a: Shinto prayer boards. Page 5b: the *torii* gate entrance 'tunnel' to the Taiko dani-Inari Shrine, Tsuwano, Western Honshu. Page 5c: cherry blossom, Ueno Park, Tokyo. Page 6: street market near Yoyogi-koen Park, Tokyo. Page 7: harvesting sugar cane on Miyako-jima. Page 9: Sanja Matsuri festival (May), Asakusa, Tokyo. Page 33a: courtesan. Page 33b: detail, Byodoin Temple, near Kyoto. Page 49: paper lantern. Page 95b: silk seller. Page 121: *geisha* girls. Page 155: detail, Kotohiragu Shrine, Skikoku Island. Page 187: an old woman on Irimote Island, Okinawa. Page 208: Takayama Morning Market. Page 209: Matsumoto farmer. Page 231: Abashiri fisherwoman. Page 247a: Ginza Corner, Tokyo. Page 247b: rice planting.

Saké *barrels*

David Scott is a restaurateur and an internationally published writer specialising in Japan, food and travel writing. He has written or co-authored a number of highly successful titles, including *Middle Eastern Vegetarian Cooking, Japanese Cooking, Elements of Zen, Samurai and Cherry Blossom*, a book focusing on Japanese life and culture, *AA Essential Japan* and *Fighting Arts*, a guide to the martial arts. He is a founder of the Uechi-Ryu Karate Association (Great Britain) and presently ranked Renshi (sixth Dan). David Scott is a long-standing member of the Kanzeon Zen Buddhist Sangha.

How to use this book

This book is divided into five main sections:

- ❑ Section 1: ***Japan Is***
  discusses aspects of life and living today, from salarymen and the economic miracle to religion and entertainment

- ❑ Section 2: ***Japan Was***
  places the country in its historical context and explores those past events whose influences are felt to this day

- ❑ Section 3: ***A to Z Section***
  is broken down into seven regional chapters, and covers places to visit, including walks. Within this section fall the Focus-on articles, which consider a variety of topics in greater detail

- ❑ Section 4: ***Travel Facts***
  contains the strictly practical information that is vital for a successful trip

- ❑ Section 5: ***Hotels and Restaurants***
  lists recommended establishments in Japan, giving a brief résumé of what they offer

How to use the star rating
Most places described in this book have been given a separate rating:

▶▶▶ **Do not miss**

▶▶ **Highly recommended**

▶ **Worth seeing**

Not essential viewing

Map references
To make the location of a particular place easier to find, every main entry in this book is given a map reference, such as 176B3. The first number (176) indicates the page on which the map can be found, the letter (B) and the second number (3) pinpoint the square in which the main entry is located. The maps on the inside front cover and inside back cover are referred to as IFC and IBC respectively.

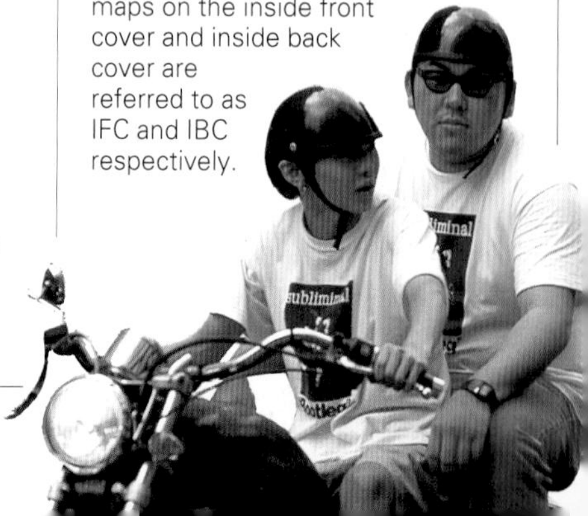

Contents

Quick reference

This quick-reference guide highlights the elements of the book you will use most often: the maps; the introductory features; the Focus-on articles and the walks.

Maps and plans

Japan Is

Takako Nishizaki
Takako Nishizaki is one of Japan's finest violinists. After studying with her father, Shinji Nishizaki, she became the first student of Shinichi Suzuki, the creator of the Suzuki Method of Violin tuition for children, and subsequently studied at the Toho and Julliard schools of music. A prolific recording artist, she has recorded much of the major solo repertoire, including concertos by Bach, Vivaidi, Mozart, Beethoven, Tchaikovsky and Brahms.

My Japan

by Takako Nishizaki

As a musician I travel a lot and cannot help remarking, whenever I return home, how different Japan still is from the rest of the world. Although, on the surface, Japanese cities resemble other modern cities, there are many differences. There are well-maintained temples and shrines in every little suburb, even though many Japanese rarely, if ever, attend them. Tiny old houses sit among towering skyscrapers, because the owners don't want to sell out to developers. The people are honest and polite, even though many Japanese feel awkward when dealing with foreigners. There are the department stores with their huge variety of merchandise and invariably polite and helpful sales ckerks – not to mention the welcoming ladies at the door or escalator bowing to every potential customer.

The streets are clean and I never worry when returning home late at night. Public transport, if sometimes overcrowded, is efficient and reliable. And then there is the food – the numerous noodle shops and speciality restaurants where you can eat 30 different styles of pork cutlet, 40 different oyster dishes or 30 or 40 different types of *sushi*. Many of the best eating places are hidden away in the older parts of the big cities, known only to local gourmets.

The essence of Japan, at least for me, is the contrast between old and new, the traditional and the ultra-modern, because it reflects my own upbringing...a citizen of the world on the surface, but a traditional Japanese at heart.

Katsuhiko Kashiwazaki
The 1981 world lightweight judo champion, Katsuhiko Kashiwazaki is a well-known figure in international judo circles, both through his teaching and his numerous technical books. He is professor of judo at the Kokusai Budo Gaigaku (International Budo University, Katsura), where he directs one of the largest judo faculties in Japan. He also practises Shodo (Japanese calligraphy).

My Japan

by Katsuhiko Kashiwazaki

In recent years Japan has followed the road of the modern nation. High-rise buildings dominate the skylines of the major cities of Tokyo or Osaka. All the other familiar accoutrements of high-tech life impinge on the eye – neon lights flashing the messages of Sony, National and Hitachi 24 hours a day; the latest cars, sleek and polished, cramming the roads and highways. But I know that this is just one side of Japan. Even in the last decade of the 20th century, modern culture and traditional culture exist side by side. The real heart of the Japanese people is to be found in the *dojo*, the training halls, where, every day, people tread the paths of the traditional arts. These include *Ikebana*, the art of flower arrangement, *Chado*, the Way of Tea, *Shodo*, the Way of the Pen, and, of course, *Budo*, the Martial Way, which includes *Judo*, *Kendo* and *Karatedo*.

For the Japanese these Ways are not just of historical interest, they are a training for life itself. Through the intense and detailed study of one Way, the personality is changed and honed, and the joys and frustrations of life given a deeper, richer perspective. That is why the written character *Do* is added to the word for the discipline – *Do* means The Way. You will find a *dojo* for each of these Ways, even in small towns. There you will find men and women of all ages practising their Way. This is the Japan I love.

JAPAN IS

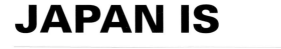

Violent and gentle

■ The *samurai* warriors of old Japan saw the cherry blossom, with its beautiful but short life, as a symbol of their own lives, which could end violently at any moment. It is in this oscillation between beauty and ugliness, tenderness and violence, delicacy and coarseness that many people find the source of their fascination for the Japanese and Japan. The natural physical expression of this union of extremes, and perhaps a potent force in forming the Japanese character, is found in the violence and gentleness of the landscape and the climate of the Japanese islands......■

The islands – Kyushu, Shikoku, Honshu and Hokkaido – may be thought of as the peaks of a deeply submerged mountain range and the seas off the coasts plunge to great depths. These peaks are themselves mountainous and even outside mountain regions the Japanese countryside is often exceptionally hilly. The land is either flat or rises sharply and as a result the population is largely and densely confined to the coastal plains or the occasional small areas of flat land found in the mountain ranges. Together they cover less than one fifth of the land surface.

❑ The southern peak of Sakurajima volcano, which is sited on its own broad patch of land across the bay from the city of Kagoshima, still erupts quite regularly. During eruptions, clouds of black ash from the mountain cover Kagoshima in a fine coating of dust and collect in drifts along the shop fronts. ❑

Ibukushima shrine, Hiroshima

Many of the mountains within the various mountain chains are volcanic: there are 50 active or semi-active volcanoes scattered throughout Japan. Mount Fuji, Japan's highest peak, last erupted in the 18th century, but Mount Asama, nearby, frequently rumbles and belches smoke. Other active volcanic areas are found in southern Hokkaido, central Honshu and Kyushu.

The Japan coastline is immensely varied in its topography and long in relation to the country's land area. The Japan Sea coast runs smoothly from south to north in an extended line of beaches and wide banks of sand dunes. In contrast, the wind- and tide-beaten Pacific coast is rugged with jutting peninsulas, such as Izu, and deep bays, such as those of Sendai and Tokyo. The Inland Sea coast is different again. Constant sea erosion, matched by land-forming alluvial mud deposits brought down by the rivers, has formed a flat plain hinterland that is nowadays the region of Japan's most extensive industrial zone.

Japan lies directly along a fault line marking the juxtaposition between the Pacific and Asian Plates, which grind against each other and cause earthquakes. The major cities most at risk are Tokyo and Osaka, and the foundations of all their newer buildings are designed to allow them to sway without cracking. Earthquakes under the sea also produce tidal waves (*tsunami*), which regularly pound the coasts of Japan.

Add to these perils the typhoon winds that occasionally savage the land, heavy snowfalls in the north, torrential summer rainstorms in the south, the heavy humid heat of central and western Honshu and Kyushu, and one could be forgiven for being nervous of a visit to Japan.

❑ Over 20 serious earthquakes have struck Japan during the past century, including the catastrophic Great Kanto Earthquake of 1 September 1923, which hit the country's most densely populated area, including the cities of Tokyo and Yokohama. More than 100,000 people were killed, over 60,000 in Tokyo alone, mainly as a result of the ensuing fires. ❑

Fortunately, Japanese inventiveness, foresight and long experience of natural phenomena have allowed them to adapt to and cope with these forces, and in most cases one need have no fears.

The gentle beauty of Japan: Mount Fuji framed by cherry blossom

■ For a demonstration of the Japanese approach to business, visit a gasoline station. A team of attendants runs across the forecourt to meet the car. One fills the tank, another cleans the headlights, windscreen and mirrors, a third empties the ashtrays and cleans the mats and a fourth takes the money. One of the team then stops the flow of traffic outside the garage, guides the car into the passing stream of vehicles and finally waves goodbye......■

Eagerness and enthusiasm for business are important factors in Japanese commercial success in world markets. Another is the long-term view taken by Japanese businessmen. Competition is fierce in Japan, but it is founded on long-term objectives rather than quick money schemes. First and foremost, customers must be provided with what they want and with the best service possible. Customer loyalty is carefully nurtured and from this base the business and profits can grow.

Post-war success After World War II the Japanese were economically and spiritually broken by their first military defeat in history and by the horrific way in which the war was finally ended, with the destruction of two major cities by atomic bombs. A new start was required and a re-examination of national values was undertaken at every level. As a result, radical changes were made, such as the constitutional principle forbidding the formation of armed services other than for defence. These changes, together with certain qualities inherent in the nature of Japanese society, provided the structure for their future success.

The Japanese work force demonstrated a sense of mutual responsibility and competitiveness together with an unquestioned acceptance of long working hours and commitment to job and employer. Managers developed a keen understanding of the needs of specific home and overseas markets and the skills needed to fulfil them. By a combination of good marketing, an eye and an ear

Symbol of new prosperity: Bay Bridge, Yokohama

Business on the march in Tokyo

for what people wanted, the application of new technology and the ability to produce high-quality goods quickly and economically, the Japanese learned how to dominate world markets. At home the Japanese government protected its own markets from foreign competitors by imposing rigorous import quotas and duties. International pressure is now changing this situation, but the problem for importers is that the Japanese simply prefer to buy Japanese goods.

Future prospects Despite their achievements, the Japanese are worried about the future. Widespread conformity to the norm, such an advantage in the past, may become an obstacle to the diversity and creativity needed to maintain economic success in the future. There is growing concern that the very long hours worked by most men and the shortage of holidays are becoming counterproductive in terms of efficiency, and are posing a threat to the family life that underpins Japanese society. Less economic success and a happier home life may be the aspirations of the future. By then the Japanese may be the richest people on earth, and well able to afford more leisure.

❑ Company managements in Japan try to control all aspects of their employees' lives. To help workers to escape the employer's eagle eye, a Tokyo department store has set up telephone alibi booths. Callers can select a tape with a suitable background – a hospital, railway station or airport, perhaps – and then phone the boss to make an excuse for being late or taking the day off. There are also `kitchen sounds' for the absent housewife who wishes to convince her husband that she is happily at home getting on with her chores. ❑

Assembly-line technology – the way ahead for Japan's economy

Salarymen

■ **On the street of any Japanese city the man walking past in a white shirt and blue suit, indistinguishable from other men around him, is probably a salaryman. A salaryman enjoys lifelong employment with the same company, which he joins in his early 20s. The expectation on both sides is that he will remain there until he retires. Anyone leaving a company position would be considered unreliable, and would find re-employment difficult......** ■

Life style Apart from job security, companies also provide salaried employees and their families with health care, housing and leisure facilities. Managers even arrange their staff's holidays. This system is accepted by most Japanese employees, who like conformity and the security of a rigid social structure.

Salarymen nearly always work late. This is expected and, indeed, essential if they are to be promoted.

Salarymen are always on call – even when they're on the road

❏ Wages are calculated on the basis of a salaryman's expected day-to-day domestic expenses, which depend on his job status. Added to this is a twice-yearly bonus for holidays, cars, luxury items and any other expenses relating to a person's position in the company, such as membership in a golf club for upper management. ❏

They may even waste time during the day to be sure of work in the evening. After work, salarymen usually go out to drink with their colleagues. This, too, is expected. The tradition is catered for by numerous bars and restaurants, found in the business areas of all large cities. A salaryman's wife expects her husband home late, and may even worry that he is not advancing at work if he gets home early each evening.

In the office Salarymen expect their bosses to trust them and to leave the responsibility of day-to-day matters solely in their hands. A boss who makes decisions about mundane matters would lose respect. Once employees have grown to trust their managers, their loyalty is total and good relationships between management and staff are normal in Japanese business. Both parties are usually on close terms and will go out drinking together. However, even outside work, company status is recognised and deferred to.

Strikes do take place but they are normally only ritualised stoppages. Every year, during the second week in April, salarymen go on strike for one or two days to support their yearly wage claim; during this time they wear red armbands to signify that they are on strike. Many even stay on the company premises during the day, but they do not work, and do not go out drinking with the management.

Stresses There is a heavy price to pay for Japan's economic prosperity. Salarymen work long hours, often under competitive and stressful conditions; Sunday is the only day they have to spend with their wives and children. This can put marriages under strain and prevent close relationships from developing between fathers and children, as well as giving all the responsibility for their upbringing to the mother. As a group, salarymen are great cigarette consumers; the incidence of lung cancer and of stress-related illnesses is high and rising.

Relaxation after the stresses of office life: a picnic in Nara (below) and (right) a drink with the lads

■ Japan is a newly self-confident country, a hothouse where the wealth created by the world's most dynamic economy is being diverted into an unprecedented consumer boom. Anything is possible – even airports in the sea – and cities such as Tokyo and Osaka have become a mecca for the world's most talented artists and designers......■

Communication The futuristic Kansai International Airport opened in the summer of 1994 on a huge, man-made island in Osaka Bay, and handles over half a million passengers each week. An access bridge carries road and rail transportation directly to and from Osaka to the passenger terminal building. From the Shin-Osaka station 'bullet trains' leave for destinations throughout Japan. There is sea access to the airport and fast, direct air connections to all major Japanese cities. For the Japanese, speed of communication is an intrinsic and vital part of the future.

Future cities For the visitor, the changes brought about by Japan's international commercial success and the influences of the West are most clearly seen in urban landscapes. In the major cities individually designed, chrome, marble and glass apartment blocks are replacing the old multi-storey box flats with their balconies hung with drying clothes and airing futons. Architecturally adventurous office buildings rise in the business districts, while environmentally controlled glass-domed shopping arcades shut out the noise and fumes of traffic in the city centres. Carefully sculpted and tended Zen gardens are still found in the grounds of city temples, but they may now be

❑ A new hi-tech toilet on the Japanese market is fitted with a pulse and blood pressure indicator, and a sensor in the bowl analyses the user's urine. The results are relayed to a computer into which the user has already punched personal details. By installing this 'thinking' toilet, employers are able to monitor their employees' health on a regular basis. ❑

Train of the future, landscape of the past: a bullet train races past Mount Fuji

overlooked by the razor-sharp images of video advertising screens or the hi-tech dazzle of neon billboards. Joggers in expensive designer wear can be seen running in city parks among the falling cherry blossom while, overhead, helicopters whirl past and away in the distance jumbo jets rise into the sky.

Future doubts To maintain the wealth for their present and proposed spending, the Japanese work extremely long hours and holidays are pitiably brief. The big question for the future is whether the workforce will continue to endure these conditions or whether the often-voiced fear that they are becoming tainted by 'Western idleness' will prove true. Many Japanese worry that they will then be overtaken by the Koreans and Taiwanese; and there is the additional problem, faced by all the world's developed nations, of an ageing population and a low birth rate.

❑ In 1992 the Central Japan Railway Company launched a new Shinkansen bullet train that is even faster than the original. The "Nozomi", which operates on the Tokaido line, runs at almost 170mph (270kph). It reduces the standard three-hour journey time between Tokyo and Osaka by 30 minutes. ❑

Kansai International Airport, Osaka Bay, Japan's latest monumental engineering project

Robots The solution to all these difficulties may be provided by the robot. Already Japan far surpasses the rest of the world in the number of robots in use and in the application of such technology. Robots can now paint, dance, speak, play golf and even arrange flowers. It is hoped that their exploitation will provide the answer to labour shortages, and Japanese mass-production techniques are already well suited to their use. These may well ensure Japan's continued economic successes and innovatory future.

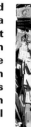

Shinto and Zen

■ **Shinto, a religion unique to Japan, and Zen Buddhism, practised for over a thousand years, have exerted a significant influence on Japanese history. Known by the Japanese as *Kami-No-Michi*, 'The Way Of The Gods', Shinto has its origins in the myths of ancient Japan. Zen is perhaps best known in the West for the inspiration it has provided for Japanese martial arts......** ■

Shinto beliefs and rituals Followers of Shinto worship the spirit god Kami, whose nature is manifested in all the things around them – rivers, mountains, trees, rocks and animals. Each deity has a place in a hierarchy of power which culminates in the sun goddess Amaterasu, worshipped at the imperial shrines of Ise, on the Ise-Shima Peninsula of Honshu (see pages 106–7). The local *kami* are lesser deities, who look after just one village or one family's fields.

There are no fixed scriptures in Shinto. Its rituals and ceremonies, a daily part of Japanese life, are directed at receiving a blessing from the gods for a particular function or event. Shinto priests, wearing long, flowing robes and tall, lacquered silk hats, officiate at all manner of occasions: blessing babies, marriages, children starting school, new construction sites and even new cars.

Confucianism, brought to Japan by Chinese merchants in AD400, had an important influence on Shinto beliefs, still evident in contemporary society. It emphasised loyalty to the family, with the father as patriarchal head, and demanded reverence and respect for the memory of ancestors.

Offerings are made at Shinto shrines, or *jinja*, either to ancestors or to the guardian spirits of the shrine. Before making an offering the worshipper pours water from a trough by the inner shrine over his hands and rinses his mouth. He then attracts the gods by clapping his hands three times and pulling on a rope attached to a wooden clapper. A silent prayer is then given and an offering of fruit, money, incense or *fuda* (strips of paper symbolising purity, sold at the entrance) is made.

With its emphasis on the basic purity of all things, Shinto was fertile ground for the assimilation of Buddhist and especially Zen Buddhist beliefs. The two schools of thought

Above and opposite: many faces of Buddhism in Japan

have never merged, but the majority of Japanese Buddhists subscribe to a mixture of both.

Zen beliefs and rituals There are two main branches of Zen: the Rinzai school, founded by Eisai in 1191, and the Soto school, founded by Dogen in 1244. Both traditions developed out of the Chinese Buddhist school of Ch'an.

The warriors' Zen The Rinzai school placed emphasis on sudden enlightenment, using meditation and *koan*, questions not soluble by logical thinking (for example: 'What is the sound of one hand clapping?'). This attracted the warrior classes of 12th-century Japan, who liked the idea that sudden inspiration, quick intuition and intense concentration were the predominant values, rather than learning. Eisai opened a temple in Kamakura, the site of the new warrior capital; descendants of the warrior class ruled Japan for the following six centuries and Zen became the religion espoused by the ruling classes.

Samurai warriors used Zen meditation to prepare for battle, but their interest in the spiritual essence of Zen increased during the Tokugawa era (1603–1867) and martial arts gradually became a vehicle for expressing Zen ideals.

The people's Zen Dogen believed that everyone is enlightened, but ignorant of this fact. He placed great emphasis on the detail of daily activities and saw each moment as an opportunity to express gratitude for our 'Buddha nature'. Now revered as one of Japan's greatest historical figures, Dogen avoided the military and aristocratic power struggles of his day, creating in Soto Zen a 'people's faith'. Soto Zen now has a much larger number of temples and followers than Rinzai.

Taikodani Shrine, Tsuwano

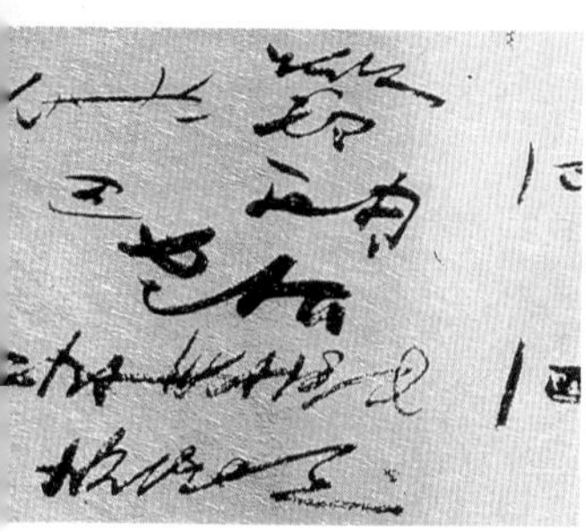

■ From the age of three or four, most Japanese children start to attend kindergarten. The choice of a good school is crucial since, even from this early age, university entrance is the focus of the child's education, and there is intense pressure to do well. This heavy burden that is placed on the shoulders of Japanese youth, especially on young men, of whom most is expected, sometimes has disastrous consequences...... ■

Reading and writing Despite having the highest literacy rate in the world, problems for the nation's children begin with the Japanese language. Schoolchildren must master four ways of writing: *Kanji*, *Hiragana*, *Katakana* and *Romaji*. *Kanji* are Chinese characters, *Hiragana* are Japanese characters used to link *Kanji* ideograms, *Katakana* is used to write foreign words and *Romaji* uses the Roman alphabet to write Japanese. It is estimated that Japanese students need two years more of schooling than their Western counterparts just to overcome the complications of their own writing system.

Educational pressures start early

❑ There are over 40,000 *Kanji* Japanese characters but nowadays only about 3,000 are taught in schools. *Toyo-kanji* are the 2,000 most common *Kanji* characters which are chosen by the Japanese government for use in popular written books and newspapers. ❑

The education race If a child is to do well, from the time he or she starts kindergarten (which usually charges tuition), his or her parents need to save money to pay for private tutoring and later, possibly, for private college and university. Education is the key to upward social and

❏ *Ronin* was a term originally applied to free-roaming *samurai* warriors without a master and consequently without status. Today it refers to high-school graduates who have failed their university entrance exams. *Ronin* cram for a year or even two or three in an attempt to gain entrance at their next attempt. ❏

economic mobility. The importance given to it in this status-conscious country is enormous. This, of course, creates intense competition for good results, a process which itself devalues qualifications thereby increasing the competition even more.

At the age of six a child goes to elementary school, which he or she attends from Monday to Friday, 8:40am to 4:30pm, and Saturday mornings. At the age of 12, the child moves to *chugakko*, middle school, for the final three years of compulsory education. Here the pressure really begins and many students attend expensive *juku*, or private tutoring schools, where classes are conducted before and after school and on Sundays.

From *chugakko* over 90 per cent of students attempt the difficult entrance examinations for *kotogakko*, senior high school; if they are unsuccessful, students aim for a less demanding, private college. Once in senior high school they generally work themselves close to a nervous breakdown in preparation for the forthcoming arduous university entrance examinations. Some go over the edge, and suicide is not uncommon. To fail is to fail one's family and to lose social credibility.

Fortunately, once in university, the young men and scarcer women can relax for four years. A final degree and employment is almost guaranteed and their time there can be an oasis between past pressures to succeed and those yet to come.

Women students Most female students are not expected to aspire to a university place, but to attend a two-year junior college course,

Schoolchildren in orderly ranks

where they study subjects such as education, social sciences and home economics. Even today, women students are considered to be biding their time until marriage.

Young women are not expected to pursue an academic life

The role of women

■ From a Western perspective, of all the developed nations Japan is the country where the question of rights for women has been least addressed. Traditional attitudes are being modified by pressure from women and by wider changes in society as a whole. But the slow pace of change reflects a value system deeply rooted in Japanese history and traditions......■

A woman's role The traditional role of the Japanese woman has been that of the dutiful wife. Her job was to bring up her husband's children, look after his home and, among the poorer classes, help in his business. By law the home and children were his, not hers. Women from every background were expected to be obedient, humble and to complement their menfolk. To fail in these roles was to risk divorce. Men from the merchant and common classes could divorce their wives very easily – and life for a divorced woman was hard.

A well-brought-up young woman was taught to control her emotions, to be diligent in household duties and to be attractive and pleasing to men. Jealousy was considered to be ugly and egotistical, and even to this day, in the Shinto marriage ceremony, the bride wears on her head a *tsunokakushi*, a folded white cloth which symbolises her intention of concealing the horns of jealousy.

Power at home Before the birth of her first baby a daughter-in-law living with her husband's family had the lowest status in the family unit, but her power in the family increased as the years passed. Her first change in status came with the birth of her first male child: through his success she could exercise influence within the family and the community. This also ensured the traditionally strong bond

Two faces of the Japanese woman: at a traditional wedding...

between Japanese mother and son. A wife's influence would also increase as she and her husband grew older. Husbands who, from a young age, have all their needs catered for by their wives often become dependent, and in private the wife may well have been making the important family decisions.

Women today In modern Japan women are often still in charge of household finances. The husband gives his wife his wage packet and she gives him pocket money. At a restaurant after a family meal, the wife pays the bill – but during the meal she serves the rice, pours the tea, orders the beer for her husband and keeps his glass topped up.

In general, Japanese women have little political or commercial power, except as voters and consumers. Despite making up 40 per cent of the Japanese workforce, most women hold low-status jobs, and even in jobs equivalent to men's, women receive only 60 per cent of the men's take-home pay.

Women's views about their roles in contemporary Japan largely depend

...and doing a sharp deal

on their age group. Elderly women tend to think that radical changes in women's attitudes will lead to a breakdown in society. Middle-aged women are often caught between reactionary husbands and daughters who expect equality with their brothers. Young, married mothers are perhaps the most confused group. Their homes, with many labour-saving devices, may be easy to run but are usually small and cramped. Their children and husbands are out at school and work six days a week and often late into the evening. In these circumstances it is difficult to sustain the roles of home-maker and mother. Young, unmarried Japanese women are the group who, to the visitor, seem to most clearly enjoy themselves in modern Japan. They do not have equal opportunity in the work place but employment with good wages is assured and they have considerably more free time than their male colleagues. Many seem to actively prefer this to a company career and want nothing to do with the company rat race.

Sumo wrestling

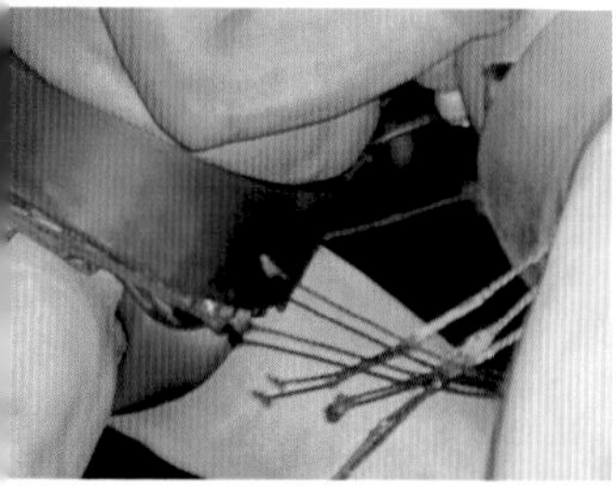

■ *Sumo* is Japan's national sport and an integral part of the country's cultural fabric. It can also lay strong claims to being the world's oldest sport: its roots lie in the realms of mythology, and it is said to have been popular with the gods. Before becoming a sport in the 6th century, *sumo* was practised as a form of divination and as a way of invoking the goodwill of the spirits......■

The ritual Once started, *sumo* techniques are executed with great speed, and each bout is over quickly. The *rikishi* (wrestlers) move with consummate skill and their expertise can easily be misjudged by a casual observer. The fight is the core of *sumo*, but its attractions for the *cognoscenti* are the pre-fight rituals, drawn in part from the battlefield. These rituals demonstrate the Shinto origins of *sumo* and serve to raise the psychological tension between the fighters to fever pitch.

Careful preparing of a sumo *star for the forthcoming show*

The rules The *dohyo*, or wrestling area, is a circular clay ring surrounded by rice-straw bales. The rules of the sport are simple: the first wrestler to set a foot or any other part of his body outside the ring, or to touch the ground inside the ring with anything but the sole of his foot, is the loser. There is no classification by weight; lighter men try to overcome their handicap by making use of superior speed and agility.

Ranking is based on a pyramid system, with teenage beginners (*jonokuchi*) at the bottom and grand champions (*yokozuna*) at the top. Surprisingly, juniors start their training with the same build as ordinary mortals. They then steadily put on weight by eating large quantities of rice and c*hanko-nabe*, a hearty stew of meat, fish and vegetables, washed down by large quantities of beer and *sake*. Their life style is hard and strict, and dictated by their stable master.

The fight Once in the ring the *rikishi* loosen up with a movement called *shiko*: they raise each leg sideways to waist height and then bring it down with a formidable stamp (this movement is said to drive out stray devils). Salt is then thrown into the air by each man to purify the ring after the last bout's loss. The wrestlers face each other in a low squat in the middle of the ring, each trying to stare the other down. Finally, at a word from the referee, they squat, lean forward, touch hands on the ground and then crash into each other at full force.

The changes *Sumo* is steeped in tradition and ritual but it is also about professionalism and winning. Of the many hundreds of wrestlers, few become nationally known, but Western attitudes to the sport are beginning to influence age-old traditions. Even the legendary inscrutability of the competitors has now been breached. Nowadays, winners are sometimes even known to allow themselves a smile in victory and losers a frown in defeat.

In the past the rigorous discipline of a *sumo* wrestler's training deterred most foreigners from trying to join their ranks, but this situation is now changing. At the time of writing the only foreign *rikishi* considered by the Japanese to be both a good enough wrestler and an embodiment of the spirit of *sumo* is Akebono, who is of Irish-Polynesian descent. *Sumo* wrestling, which to diehard traditionalists represents the quintessential Japan, may no longer be the last bastion of their struggle to curtail Western influence.

❏ Top *sumo* wrestlers have the status, media attention and riches of Hollywood stars, and are treated with the respect and deference normally only accorded to royalty. They have private fan clubs, corporate sponsors and, it is said, the pick of Japanese womanhood; apparently these enormous men are irresistible to some women. ❏

Crowds enjoy the sumo *spectacle at a Tokyo arena*

■ The Japanese have a rich and varied cultural history, and classical performing arts such as *noh* and *kabuki* and the elegant pleasures of pastimes such as the tea ceremony continue to flourish. However, the principal source of Japanese entertainment and nightlife is the network of bars, restaurants, coffee shops, tea houses and cocktail lounges that are an integral part of even the smallest Japanese town......■

Work and pleasure Entertainment is a key component of the world of business deals, and corporate entertainment, which is said to drive the economy, always appears as a large (sometimes hidden) debit in the accounts of any successful Japanese company. Company employees usually meet after work for drinks and perhaps to eat, and on these occasions it is quite acceptable, after a fair amount of alcohol, to criticise a superior or colleague (or foreign guest) in a manner that would be inappropriate in the formal atmosphere of work. Tomorrow it will be forgotten.

❑ The Japanese home is a wife's domain, and Japanese men entertain their friends, business colleagues and acquaintances away from the house, at a favourite bar or restaurant. If they invite you out, they expect to pick up the bill – just as though you were a house guest for dinner. ❑

Outrageous façades adorn street food and karaoke *venues of Osaka*

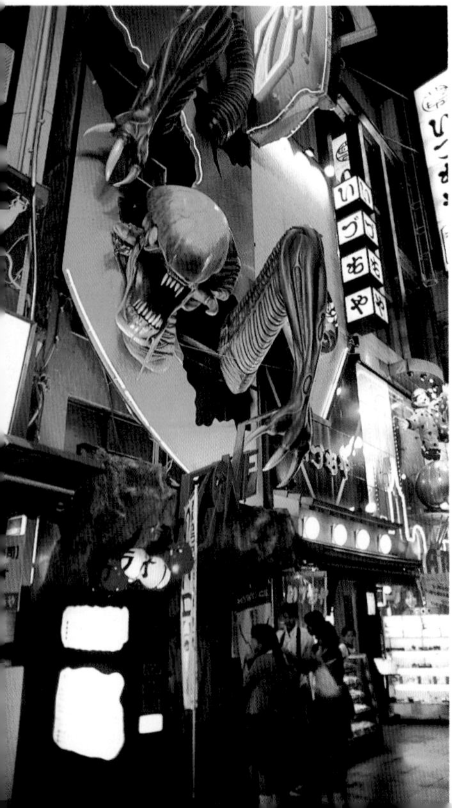

Sex and drink Movie theatres, discotheques and intimate clubs are to be found in downtown areas alongside 'Soapland' districts, where striptease and massage parlours rub shoulders with street food kiosks and fast food restaurants. Historically sex and eroticism played an important role in the nightlife of male-dominated Japan, both as a sexual outlet for men and as a way for independent women to make a living. Paid-for sex is very expensive, and prices rise rapidly as the customer's requirements move onward from a basic massage. Many of the clubs in Soapland areas are owned by the Yakuza (the Japanese mafia).

Prices in restaurants and bars vary widely and they are usually high in establishments that do not display a price list. The cost of drinks in any bar is high; the cheapest are those frequented by young men and women, office workers and college students. Those that employ hostesses to fill your glass and to make idle chat can be prohibitively expensive. *Geisha* bars, where expertly trained women entertain with witty conversation, traditional dancing, music and food (but not sex) are not generally open to foreigners – nor within their price range.

Simple and refined pleasures
Japanese coffee shops (*kissaten*) are one of the country's best discoveries. They pride themselves on serving exquisite coffee and on providing a first-class sound system, playing jazz, classical, rock or other music. A cup of coffee is relatively expensive but once you have ordered you can sit for as long as you wish reading, writing or looking at the magazines and comics always available. (Early in the day, *kissaten* frequently offer a good breakfast for the price of a coffee; ask for 'morning service' in English.)

Noh theatre, *bunraku* (puppet theatre – see page 88) and *kabuki* (see pages 58–9) are available in the major cities and although alien in format to most Westerners, they are usually worth seeing both for the spectacle and the insight they give into the nature of the Japanese.

Tokyo's dazzling nightlife

■ **Traditional meals are cooked and presented with the intention of inspiring the spirit as well as the senses. The ingredients and menu are chosen to take into account the season, region and occasion. Tableware is selected to harmonise with the texture and appearance of the food which, according to the Japanese, must be tasted with the tongue, the heart and the eye to be truly enjoyed......**■

The Buddhist influence Japanese cuisine developed in a state of isolation and its style is quite unique. Buddhist beliefs, which forbade the eating of flesh, together with the nature of the landscape and climate restricted the choice of food, and the main ingredients of the Japanese diet were rice, noodles, vegetables, pickles, seafood, soy-bean products and fruit. To some degree this remains the case today but ironically, now that such ingredients are highly recommended by nutritionists, the Japanese are eating more and more meat and dairy products.

Cooking categories At a Japanese meal individual dishes are served in small amounts but in a greater variety than in the West. They are all served at the same time, rather than in courses, and the order in which they are eaten is a matter of personal choice. Each dish is classified according to the way it is cooked, rather than by the main ingredient. For example, *yakimono* are grilled foods and the most popular way of cooking fish. *Agemono* are deep-fried dishes, of which *tempura* is the best known and loved. *Nimono*, such as the dish *shabu-shabu*, is food simmered in water or some other liquid such as sake. Diners pick out cooked morsels with their chopsticks and later sip the cooking liquor out of a bowl like soup.

Other categories are *sashimi*, in which pieces of very fresh raw fish are served with *wasabi*, a green Japanese mustard; *sushi*, vinegared rice patties topped with a variety of foods, particularly raw fish, and *nabemono*, one-pot meals such as the well known *sukiyaki* (pronounced 'ski-yaki').

Basic foods Rice is eaten with every meal, including breakfast. *Han*, the Japanese word for rice, is given the honourable prefix *go*, so that rice is referred to as *go-han*, or 'honourable rice'. The rice at a meal is usually eaten last, rather than as an accompaniment to other foods. It is the

❑ In Japan the use of seaweed as a foodstuff is commonplace. *Kombu* seaweed is packaged in fancy boxes and given as presents by dinner guests. Unusually rich in vitamins and minerals, it has nutritional value and is generally used as a seasoning. ❑

A food stall in Hokkaido

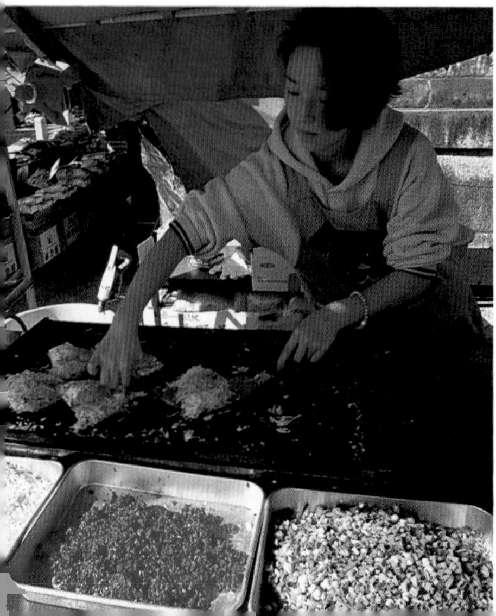

Minshuku-*style breakfast*

core of the meal, and the Japanese usually eat two or three bowls of it at a time.

Noodles are eaten almost as often as rice. One of the great delights of being in Japan is to eat a bowl of noodles in one of the inexpensive noodle restaurants found in even the smallest village. The Japanese eat their noodles quickly, with lots of sucking and slurping noises and 'aahs' of contentment.

Surprisingly few seasonings and condiments are used; the cuisine depends as much on the natural flavour of the ingredients, their aroma and visual beauty as on added flavourings. Apart from soya sauce, *miso* (a soya-bean paste) and seaweed, the most commonly used flavourings are: *goma*, a mixture of toasted and crushed sesame seeds and salt; *mirin*, a sweet fortified wine similar to sherry; ginger root; *toga-rashi*, a blend of several spices tasting like a combination of black pepper and cayenne; and *wasabi*.

O-cha, or green tea is the usual offering with food in Japanese homes and restaurants. In the latter tea is served to guests on their arrival and at the end of the meal, and is always provided free of charge.

An elegant display of tempura, *the popular deep-fried dish*

Festivals and events

■ Japan is a land of festivals and celebratory events and even the smallest villages have their own calendars of activities. Most have some kind of historical or religious significance, but they are generally boisterous affairs providing an excuse for lots of noise, merrymaking, eating and drinking and spectator participation......■

It is very possible, particularly in the summer months, that you will accidentally come across a local festival in progress but for more specific information contact the Tourist Information Centres in Tokyo and Kyoto (see page 264), who publish monthly bulletins of events. The larger, better-known festivals mentioned here are always very popular with the Japanese and if you plan to visit one it is wise to book accommodation and transport well in advance.

Summer O-Bon **(13–16 August):** at this time of the year the Japanese like to return to their home towns or villages to take part in the O-Bon ceremonies that mark the return to earth of all departed ancestors. At the end of the rituals, candlelit paper lanterns are set to float down rivers and out to sea, to mark the return of the spirits to their own world. Yasukuni Shrine in Tokyo and Nachi Shrine in Katsuura, Wakayama prefecture hold large ceremonies.
Gion Matsuri **(16–17 July):** this is perhaps the best known of all Japanese festivals. It takes place in Kyoto, and events span a month. The highlight is a huge procession of floats on 17 July. The ceremony is over 1,000 years old and began as a purification ritual to rid the city of plague. Each of Kyoto's 29 neighbourhoods builds its own elaborately decorated float.

Dressed up for Tokyo's White Heron festival

Autumn Jidai Matsuri **(22 October):** the Imperial Palace in Kyoto is the start of a large procession to mark the founding of the city. Thousands of people dressed in the costumes of different historical eras march along in this noisy, happy event, finishing at the Heian Shrine.
Shichi-Go-San **(15 November):** on this day girls aged between three and seven and five-year-old boys are dressed in their best clothes and taken to city and village shrines and temples, where prayers are offered up for their good health.

Winter Joya-No-Kane and Ganjitsu **(31 December–1 January):** on New Year's Eve everybody stays up until midnight, when temple bells ring out 108 times. New Year's Day is seen as an opportunity for renewal: debts are paid and arguments settled. Festivities go on for seven days and most businesses come to a halt. On 2 January the Imperial Family appears at the Imperial Palace in Tokyo and huge crowds gather to greet them.

Spring Cherry Blossom Viewing **(March to May):** at this time of the year cherry blossom viewing parties take place all over Japan. The exact date depends on the ripening of the blossom in a particular region. Local television station weather forecasts give updates on the state of the blossom ripeness in each area of Japan.

Kodomo-no-Hi (Children's Day, May 5): this national holiday centres around the nation's children, with a special emphasis on young boys (it is sometimes known as Boys' Day). Families fly giant paper *koi* (carp) from their homes to symbolise the strength of manhood: the larger examples represent the eldest sons and the increasingly smaller ones the younger children.

National Holidays

January 1 New Year's Day; **January 15** Coming of Age Day; **February 11** Founding of the Nation Day; **March 21** Vernal Equinox Day (varies); **April 29** Greenery Day; **May 3** Constitution Day; **May 5** Children's Day (the period from April 29 to May 6, called 'Golden Week', is essentially a national week off, and is not a good time for visitors to travel); **September 15** Respect for the Aged Day; **September 23** Autumn Equinox Day (varies); **October 10** Health–Sports Day; **November 3** Culture Day; **November 23** Labour Thanksgiving Day; **December 23** Emperor's Birthday.

Karatsu festival, Kyushu Island

■ Shinto, the ancient religion of Japan, lays great emphasis on purification and cleanliness. Partly because of this, bathing and the rituals surrounding it are very much a part of the Japanese culture. No other country in the world boasts more natural hot springs, and the popular custom of bathing in them for physical and spiritual regeneration dates from the distant past......■

Private bathing At home the Japanese find two Western habits particularly difficult to comprehend. The first is that we wear shoes in the house and the second is that we sit in the dirty water in which we wash. In Japan the bather sits outside the tub on a small stool, scoops water over him or herself, washes, rinses off the soap and only then, with a clean body, climbs into the tub to soak and relax in the very hot water.

Public bathing Communal bathing is also popular and *sento*, public bath houses, are places to meet friends, share gossip and jokes and to soak away aches, pains and worries. For the independent traveller they are worth visiting not just to get clean but to see the Japanese at their ribald best in their natural habitat. *Sento* are found in most cities and small towns and come in a variety of shapes and forms varying from Gothic exaggeration to Zen simplicity. They have recently enjoyed a revival in popularity among young people, and many are being renovated in their original style.

Onsen Tourist accommodation is available around most of Japan's *onsen* (hot springs). At spas such as Beppu, large commercial resorts of many hotels have developed, where the emphasis for visitors is on group togetherness (a sacred concept in Japan). At other, more isolated *onsen*, there may be only two or three thatched-roof cottages with a single outdoor bath (a *rotemburo*). Here the visitor comes to seek spiritual rather than material solace.

The bliss of an open-air onsen

JAPAN WAS

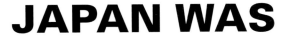

Prehistory

■ The prehistoric era of Japan's history usually refers to the age before the first writing system and the Buddhist religion were introduced, in the 6th century AD. Japan's earliest settlers, who arrived in about 100,000BC, are a mystery. They were probably not the ancestors of the predominantly Mongoloid modern Japanese, nor of the Ainu, the earliest known native people of Japan (see pages 236–7). A possible similarity in language may be the only link between these original inhabitants and present-day Japanese......■

A Jomon clay facemask, now in Tokyo National Museum

The near prehistoric era may be divided into three distinct periods. The Jomon age (*c* 10,000–300BC) was one in which pottery-making (without a wheel) and other crude technical skills emerged. During the Yayoi era (300BC–AD300) immigrants and invaders from mainland Asia brought agricultural and military knowledge. The third age, the Kofun period (AD300–700), was marked by the construction of *kofun* (large earthen tombs) throughout Japan and the growing influence of Chinese culture.

Jomon era The Jomon people were hunters and gatherers. They lived in small communities, primarily in central Honshu, and had a well-developed religion of nature worship, deifying the sun and moon. During this period, according to Japanese mythology, the sun goddess Amaterasu sent one of her descendants to the island of Kyushu to establish order and to unify the people of Japan. This aim was later partly realised by Jimmu, the great grandson of the emissary and the half-legendary first emperor of Japan.

The sun-goddess Amaterasu

❏ A Chinese traveller in south-west Japan in about AD200 described what he saw as follows: 'The people live on raw vegetables and go about barefooted. They smear their bodies with pink and scarlet. They serve food on bamboo and wooden trays, helping themselves with their fingers. Whenever they undertake an enterprise or a journey and discussion arises, they bake bones and divine in order to tell whether fortune will be good or bad…If the lowly meet important men on the road, they stop and withdraw to the roadside.' ❏

Yayoi era During the 2nd and 1st centuries BC craftsmen and warriors, driven from Korea and China by political turmoil, crossed the Korean Straits to Japan in large numbers. They brought with them mining and metal-working skills, pottery-making with a wheel, cloth-weaving techniques and rice cultivation in flooded paddies. In their turn they took up many of the customs and the language of the indigenous people. Japan flourished as a country of many small states, some of which were ruled by women; rule by women continued in outlying regions until almost the 9th century AD.

Kofun era A later development of the Yayoi era was the formation of powerful clans and the development of a military elite skilled in horsemanship and weapons. At the beginning of the Kofun period, clan chiefs fought to maintain or expand control of their independent kingdoms. By AD300, however, the chieftain of the Yamato clan, based in the Yamato lowlands, south of Kyoto, had brought many of them under his command. Over the next 250 years, by intermarriage and the exercise of political and military skills, the Yamato unified Japan under a succession of single leaders. It was for the burial of such powerful men that the huge *kofun* burial mounds were created. This era also saw the introduction of Buddhism into Japan and the formation of close cultural links with China, marking a new period in Japanese history.

❑ *Kofun* were often encircled with *haniwa*, clay figures of warriors and servants; inside the mounds were bronze mirrors, glass beads and other objects that would be needed by the dead in their next life. Numerous *kofun* mounds and *haniwa* may be seen at Saitobaru, north of Miyazaki in Kyushu. ❑

A replica Kofun figure, in Kyushu

The classical period

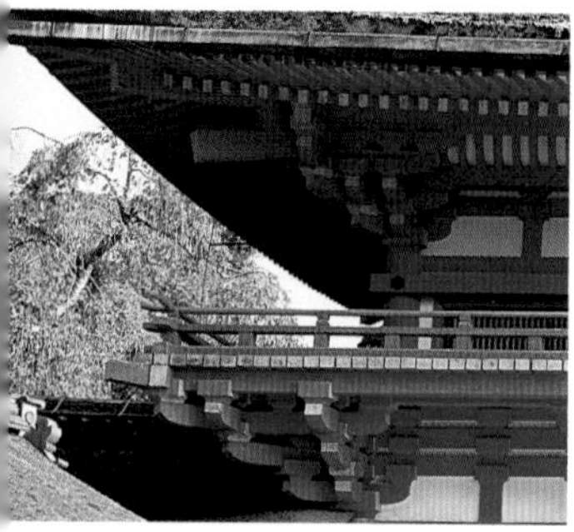

■ With the introduction in the 6th century of Buddhism and the use of Chinese characters for writing, Japan entered its classical period (710–1185). During this time the first permanent capital was established at Nara and later at Heian-kyo (Kyoto). Early in the classical period the Japanese were influenced on a large scale by Chinese cultural and scholarly ideals, but by the 10th century they had evolved a unique and sophisticated culture of their own......■

Prince Shotoku Buddhism was already known in 6th-century Japan, but it was first properly introduced to the Japanese court by the king of a minor Korean state. In 553 he sent the Emperor Buddhist images, vestments, incense, sutras (scriptures) and other ritual objects as part of a petition seeking Japanese military aid. Some influential members of the court found the new religion attractive while others remained loyal to their native Shinto (see pages 40–1). Those in favour of Buddhism eventually won the struggle for power and in 604 Shotoku (574–622), prince regent to an infant empress, drafted a document, greatly influenced by Buddhist and Confucian principles, calling for political and constitutional reforms. Shotoku founded many Buddhist temples and monasteries, including the famous Horyuji Temple at Nara.

Taika reform Shotoku's vision was overtaken by political events and in 645 Emperor Kotoku, backed by traditionalist Japanese nobles, instituted the Taika Reform. All land was declared the property of the throne and its administration was to be controlled by officials appointed by the Emperor or his ministers. The reforms were not strictly enforced, but they did eventually create a hierarchical system that became the basis of the feudal system later to dominate Japanese life.

A clay farmer, made in the 6th century

Nara period In 710 Japan's first permanent capital was established at Nara (see pages 114–15). It was built on the pattern of Ch'ang-an (Xian), the famous capital city of the Chinese Tang Dynasty. With its green-roofed, red-painted buildings, Nara became the focus of courtly and religious life, and this period saw a huge expansion of Buddhist temple construction. Much of the nation's

❑ The conflict between Buddhism and Shinto was reconciled by the Buddhist monk Gyogi. In 740 he was requested to visit Ise, location of the most important of Shinto shrines (see pages 106–7), to meditate on the propriety of the Emperor's plans to erect a giant statue of the Buddha. Gyogi received a message from Amaterasu, the sun goddess, that the two religions were just different forms of the same path. This was widely accepted and, to this day, both religions are practised side by side. ❑

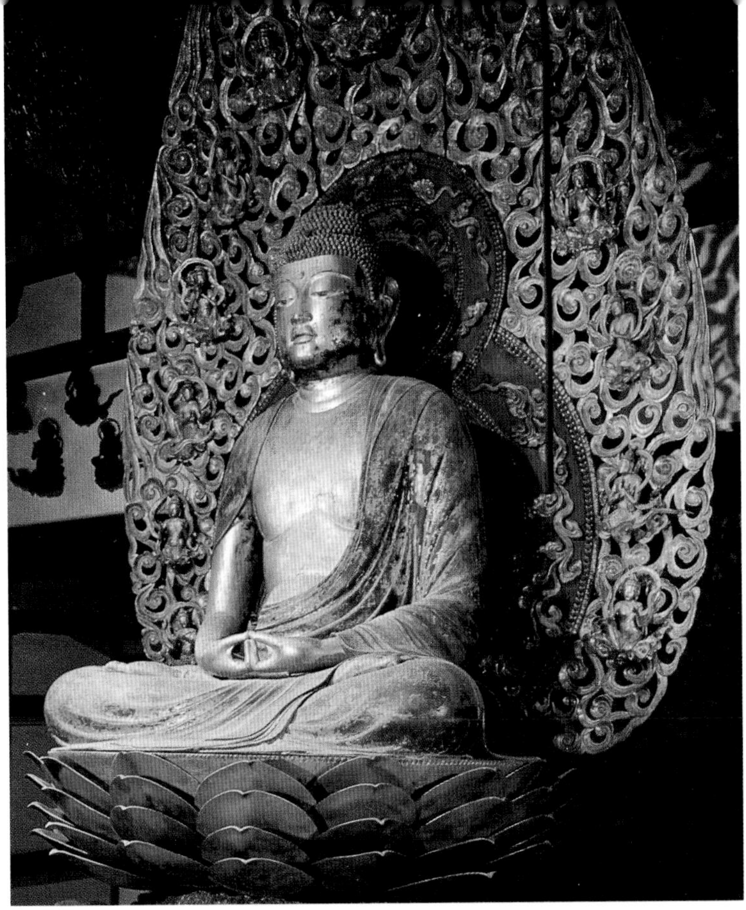

Amitabha, from the Heian period

wealth was spent on sculptures, paintings, books, lacquerware and other art work to grace these sacred buildings.

As temples and monasteries continued to expand, the power of the clergy increased. In 784 Emperor Kammu decided to move the capital to avoid this influence and increase the authority of the secular government. Supported by the powerful Fujiwara clan, members of which ruled as regents for the Emperor, he moved to what became an even grander capital at Heian-Kyo (Kyoto).

Heian period Between 794 and 1156 Japan was peaceful and prosperous and enjoyed one of the most culturally fruitful periods in its history. This was partly as a result of the imperial court's decision in 894 to end all official communication with the now failing Tang Dynasty in China. Japan once again became inward-looking and over the next 300 years a specifically Japanese culture evolved. Towards the end of the Heian period the influence of the Fujiwara family waned while other provincial warrior clans grew in military power. Meanwhile the imperial family and their noble courtiers lost touch with the affairs of the country and were finally ignored by the warrior families. The Taira and Minamoto clans engaged in a fierce civil war for control of the nation before Minamoto Yoritomo eventually led his side to victory. He subsequently established a new capital in Kamakura, leaving the imperial court in Kyoto, and formed a military government, becoming the nation's first *shogun* (see pages 38–9). This was the system of government that was destined to rule Japan for the following 700 years.

Shogun and samurai

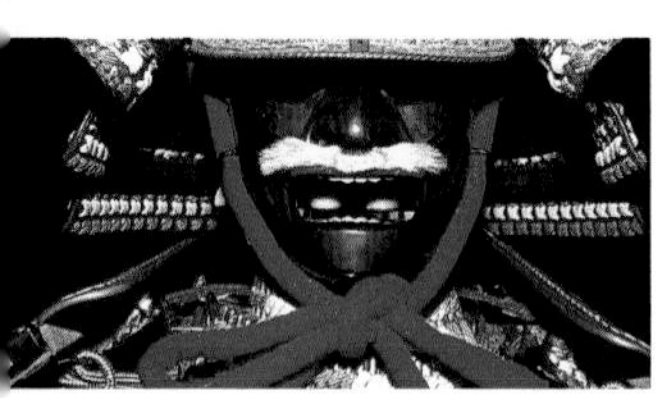

■ **Throughout Japanese history the Emperor, although spiritually venerated, has rarely had any political power. Overall control was always held by the clan leader (*daimyo*) with the strongest army. Such leaders became known as the *shogun*; their warrior soldiers were called *samurai*......** ■

The way of the warrior In the late 9th century Japan broke off all relations with the rest of the world and embarked on 300 years of isolation. It was during this time that the *samurai* developed as a distinct warrior class and the ethics of the *bushido* (the Way of the Warrior) evolved. *Samurai* literally means 'one who serves' and each soldier owed total allegiance to his *daimyo*.

The formidable foe: a full set of samurai *warrior armour*

Samurai were divided into three groups. At the top were those who served the *shogun*, second were the *samurai* of ordinary *daimyo* and at the bottom were those called *ronin*, who had lost their masters through war or politics. *Ronin* roamed the land, some working as mercenaries, others turning to crime. Their exploits feature in many Japanese stories, films and plays.

Civil War From the 12th until the 16th century, Japan suffered almost continuous civil war. Battles were fought between opposing clans seeking overall power or by emperors trying to gain political control to match their spiritual rule of the land. The situation improved in the late 16th century, when General Oda Nobunaga defeated the other most powerful *daimyo* in the country, General Imagawa, to become ruler of virtually all Japan. Nobunaga was both a ruthless soldier and a devotee of the arts. Under his guidance there was a renaissance of interest in poetry,

❏ During the Kamakura period (1192–1333) there were women among the *samurai*. Tomoe, a member of the Minamoto, is described in records of the period as having long, black hair and a fair complexion; her face was very lovely and she was a fearless rider, whom neither the fiercest horse nor the roughest ground could dismay. So dextrously did she handle sword and bow, according to the chronicler, that she was a match for a thousand warriors and fit to meet either god or devil. ❏

theatre, dancing and fashion, which flourished in the relative peace of his reign. He also encouraged trade with the outside world, and European arts and Christianity became fashionable.

Isolation Toyotomi Hideyoshi succeeded Nobunaga in 1582. His was a different outlook: he believed that foreign influences were weakening Japan, and introduced laws forbidding the Japanese to leave the country and reducing the influx of foreign goods and people, while at the same time reinforcing the traditional feudal patterns of society.

Hideyoshi died in 1598 and was succeeded by Tokugawa Ieyasu, who moved his headquarters from Kyoto to Edo (now Tokyo). From here the Tokugawa family dominated Japanese life for the next 250 years.

A samurai *on horseback, armed with bow and arrows*

One after another, the Tokugawa *shogun* maintained hostility to all foreign religions and secular influences and carried out a determined policy of national seclusion.

Shogunate outdated The Tokugawa system of government finally broke down in the mid-19th century. The *samurai* had been emasculated by lack of battle opportunity, and had become as interested in the arts of the tea ceremony and calligraphy as in sword-fighting, losing their authoritarian grip on the country. Both they and the peasants had grown very poor, while a newly prosperous merchant class had emerged as a force of change. Outgunned by Western powers, the Shogunate was forced to sign treaties and Western explorers and traders were again allowed to enter Japan. In 1868, after fighting off Tokugawa loyalists, Emperor Meiji took power and ended shogunate rule for ever.

JAPAN WAS *Feudal*

■ **The feudalism that is to some degree still manifested in Japanese society and the Japanese language has its origins in the laws enacted by the Tokugawa *shogun*. It was their intention to control every aspect of Japanese life, in every corner of the land. The place in which a person lived, what he ate, the type of clothes he wore, even the posture he adopted and the way he slept were all dictated by the state......** ■

At the top of the ladder, emperors and their courts were restricted to Kyoto, their duties confined to the ceremonial. The Tokugawa family maintained the emperor in his position but only to confer the title of *shogun* (full title: 'Commander-in-Chief for Quelling the Barbarians') on whomever the family nominated.

Like the emperor's, the affairs of military lords were closely monitored by the *shogun*. They were controlled by the allotment or dispossession of the territories from which they were entitled to collect taxes. Rights to land were given only in exchange for oaths of allegiance. The number of armed men they had, the types of fortifications around their castles and even their social contacts were controlled. Government inspectors ensured that they upheld their agreements, and if they broke any they were punished by loss of land or exile to a distant part of the country. As an extra safety measure the Tokugawa *shogun* maintained control of the three largest cities – Edo (now Tokyo), Kyoto and Osaka – and gave the lands around them to close relatives and loyal allies.

After the emperor and noble lords, the Buddhist and Shinto clergy were the groups most likely to make trouble for the *shogun*. They were thus split up under the Tokugawa regime into individual sects, which were themselves divided into separate independent units. No co-operation or joint decisions were allowed between sects, and rivalry for land and income was encouraged: a perfect

❑ The *samurai* class enjoyed many privileges and during the Tokugawa years (1603–1867) had little to do since there were few battles to fight. They were, however, expected to set a good example to the rest of society and to lead sober and honest lives. In two centuries of relative peace the *samurai* brought the art of fighting to a high point of ceremonial and ritual skill, although expertise in real battle fighting and war tactics diminished. Nevertheless, it was *samurai* from the southern domains of Satsuma and Choshu who carried out the *coup d'état* of 1867 that brought along the Meiji Restoration of 1868. ❑

Two powerful feudal leaders: Ieyasu...

example of 'divide and rule'.

The rest of society was split into four groups. In descending order of status they were *samurai*, farmers, craftsmen and merchants. Women belonged to the same class as their fathers or husbands. Membership of a particular class was hereditary and fixed. The *samurai* did not work as such and they considered the pursuit of money as dishonourable. They were supported by taxes from the farming class, who suffered considerable hardship maintaining the top-heavy warrior class.

Farmers, the main bulk of the population, although not at the bottom of the social order, were the most exploited of the classes. Upon them depended the rice harvest and thus the *samurai*'s and the *shogun*'s prosperity. They had to work hard and were not allowed to leave the vicinity of their birthplace; most lived in considerable poverty.

Craftsmen had lower status than farmers but had more mobility and freedom in the way they led their lives. Master craftsmen, particularly sword-makers, were valued for their skills and lived in the security of their lord's protection.

...and Hideyoshi. These great warriors ruled Japan in the 16th and 17th centuries.

Merchants were at the bottom of the social ladder, since they produced nothing, were motivated by profit and dealt with money. In spite of their lowly position in the social order, the merchants later became the main beneficiaries of the Tokugawa era and as a group they were responsible for later changes in cultural and social attitudes.

Courtesans of the 18th century

■ **During the long Tokugawa era (1603–1867), Japanese were prohibited from travelling outside the country and foreigners were not allowed in. In contrast, during the Meiji era (1868–1912), all things Japanese were despised and many historical buildings and relics were destroyed, while American and European cultures were admired. During this period there was even a cult for marrying Western women to 'improve' the nation's bloodstock......** ■

Open and closed There has been a cyclic character to the history of Japanese culture which follows a three-phase pattern. In the first phase, the country opens itself to outside influences, such as those from China between the 6th and 9th centuries and the West between the 16th and 17th centuries. During these periods the Japanese tend to underrate traditional Japanese values and qualities, although never completely letting go of them. This phase is followed by a period of reassessment and consolidation, during which some imported notions are jettisoned and others are subtly altered, acquiring a distinctly Japanese feel. The third stage is a withdrawal from the outside world. The Japanese shut themselves off from the rest of the world and settle down to a life of regularity and security, safe from the risks created by foreign influences. This cycle has repeated itself throughout Japanese history and has continued into our own time.

Chinese influences The first major influence on Japanese thought and culture, and perhaps the most important in its history, came from China. During the 6th and 9th centuries

Left and below: Commodore Perry and his US Navy ships

Emperor Meiji and his empress

there was active contact with the Chinese governments of the Tang Dynasty and tradesmen, craftsmen, artists and scholars regularly crossed the waters between the two countries. Confucian principles were introduced into Japanese government and Buddhism, brought from China, enjoyed a time of great popularity and prosperity. Nara, the first permanent Japanese capital city, was modelled on Ch'ang-an (Xian), the gracious seat of the Tang Dynasty, characterised, like Nara, by green-roofed buildings with red wooden walls. During this time contact was also made with countries further afield than China, and Shoso-in museum, in the present grounds of the Todaiji Temple, Nara (see pages 114–15), contains beautiful artefacts of the period from Persia, India, Greece and Korea.

Isolation In the 9th century Japan broke off all relations with the rest of the world and underwent 300 years of isolation. It was during this time that Kublai Khan made his unsuccessful attempt to invade Japan with over 100,000 Mongol soldiers. The country was saved by a typhoon wind, which swept away the enemy fleet and earned the name *kamikaze* – 'the Divine Wind'. Japan was not invaded again until the end of World War II.

The Tokugawa *shoguns* (1603–1868) also enforced a policy of national seclusion and it was not until Commodore Perry and his US Navy ships arrived in 1853, demanding that Japan open to overseas trade, that relations with the West were restored.

Expansion During his 44-year reign (1868–1912), Emperor Meiji led Japan from being an isolated, agriculturally based, feudal society to a powerful nation with a modern navy and army, railways, a parliament and an industrial base. However, by the beginning of the 1930s Japan's industrial economy needed overseas markets and new sources of raw materials. At the same time there was an upsurge of nationalism and a growing sense that Japan was the natural leader of mainland Asia and the Pacific basin. Both factors led to the decision to invade Manchuria in 1931, followed by a full-scale invasion of China in 1937. Japan withdrew from the League of Nations, and totalitarian politics and militarism grew in popularity. The movement was unlike Italian or German fascism, since the emperor remained the secular and spiritual head of the state, and the focus of a consensus form of government. The Japanese did, however, join forces with Hitler, and on 7 December 1941, with the bombing of Pearl Harbor, they entered World War II.

■ Shinto teachings that the emperor was a living *kami* (sacred spirit) and that the spirits of the dead were alive contributed towards the development of the patriarchal, ancestor-worshipping culture of traditional Japan. The emperor, as a living god, was seen as the symbolic and literal father of the family of the Japanese people. Such beliefs lived on in World War II, when Japanese suicide squads sacrificed their lives for the emperor......■

Ancient history Before the 4th century AD Japan was a collection of independent states rather than a single nation. In time the various ruling families made alliances, one of them, the Yamato, gradually gaining precedence over the others and winning paramount control. From this background emerged the forebears of today's imperial family. Contemporary knowledge of this period is vague, but all lineal ancestors of the present emperor are said to have descended from the same blood line. Whatever the truth, the Japanese imperial dynasty is generally acknowledged as the longest-reigning in world history.

In Japanese mythology the origins of the imperial family are much more glamorous. The emperor is believed to be a direct descendant of the sun goddess Amaterasu. As such, he is a divine being who has the power to intercede with heaven on behalf of mankind.

Emperor Hirohito

❑ Emperor Meiji was succeeded by his son Yoshito, renamed Emperor Taisho, in 1912. Not much is known about Taisho; he suffered from mental illness and was kept out of the public eye. The illness is said to have been caused by lead poisoning; apparently his wet-nurse had used white lead to whiten her breasts, a common practice of the day. ❑

The emperor as figurehead In more recent times the emperor did not, despite his divine status, have real political power; this was in the hands of the *shogun*. During the Edo period (1603–1867) the emperors' upkeep and that of their courtiers was maintained by grants from the *shogun* of land, from which they kept the income. This maintained them in a respectable, rather than a luxurious life style. An emperor's activities were supervised by government officials and limited to cultural pursuits. However, although he was only a figurehead, his title was hereditary and the line of succession had to be maintained. This was a potential danger to the Tokugawa shogunate – and it did, in fact lead, to its downfall.

Power regained By the late 18th century the emasculation of the *samurai* and poverty of the peasants had weakened the Tokugawa regime, and in 1867 the young Emperor Meiji was put forward as the country's leader. After fighting off Tokugawa loyalists he attained full power in 1868 and began his revolutionary reign, the Meiji Restoration.

Emperor Meiji for the first time formally instigated Shinto as the official state religion. Since the Shinto belief is that the emperor is of divine lineage and a living god, this new ruling gave him total power over the nation. He used it primarily to abolish the old class system and to institute new laws and reforms that were intended to give more human rights to all Japanese.

Modern times Emperor Hirohito (b. 1901) died in 1989 and his son Akihito ascended to the Chrysanthemum Throne in 1990. The protracted enthronement ceremonies culminated in the Daijosai, the Great Food Offering Rite, when, in the dead of night, freshly harvested sacred rice and *sake* were offered to the gods and other ancient fertility rites were performed. The emperor was transmuted into a 'living god' behind drawn curtains where, alone except for two attendant shrine virgins, he awaited the arrival of the sun goddess Amaterasu.

Emperor Meiji

In 1946 Emperor Hirohito declared that he was not a god. For some Japanese the fact that his son has not followed this lead by diluting the Daijosai ceremony is a disappointment.

Courtesans walking to view cherry blossom, by Kunisada Utagawa

■ **Japan signed the Anti-Comintern Pact with Germany in 1936 and with Italy in 1937, a union which grew into the Tripartite Pact signed in 1940. By forming these alliances, Japan made obvious its hostility to Great Britain and to the US, the only country strong enough to prevent Japanese expansion in the Pacific......■**

Pearl Harbor Tension between Japan and the US was increased in 1940 when the US banned the sale of fuel, iron and steel to Japan, extending this to a total ban on all exports in 1941. The loss of oil was particularly severe, leading the Japanese Navy General Staff to predict that Japan's oil reserves would only last two years.

As far as the Japanese military were concerned, the survival of their country was at stake. Prime Minister Konoe was replaced by General Tojo Hideki, and the decision was taken to go to war. On 7 December 1941 the Japanese attacked the US fleet at Pearl Harbor, Hawaii. Within days they attacked the Philippine Islands and sank two British battleships.

Japanese forces seemed unstoppable, and by 1942 Japan controlled a vast empire reaching 6,400km southwards from Sakhalin and 7,600km eastwards from Burma to the Gilbert and Ellice islands (modern Tuvalu and Kiribati). However, national resentments, caused by the economic exploitation of the areas under Japanese control, coupled with the brutal treatment of their civilian populations, meant that Japanese plans for a 'New Order' in the Far East never had support.

Japanese losses The turning point in the war came at the Battle of Midway, 3–6 June 1942. A powerful Japanese naval force attempted to destroy the US Pacific Fleet, but US cryptoanalysts had broken the Japanese naval codes, and the Americans were waiting. During the battle American planes sank four Japanese aircraft carriers. The disastrous loss of its major striking force meant that the Japanese Navy was forced on to the defensive, and slowly but inexorably the Allies moved towards the main Japanese Islands.

The Japanese lost almost all of their merchant fleet to Allied aircraft and submarines, which starved Japan of raw materials. The Allied

American marines watch as shells explode on Japanese troops dug into the hills in southern Okinawa

The battleship *West Virginia* burning in Pearl Harbor, Hawaii, after the attack by Japanese planes

policy of bombing the mainland added to the hardships, but the tenacity and stubborn courage of civilians and troops in defence of their bases meant that the Allies, even in the face of heavy Japanese losses, could never presume they would surrender. When American forces attacked Okinawa over 260,000 Japanese soldiers and civilians died, and over 50,000 American troops were either killed or wounded before the island was taken.

❑ As pressure increased on the Japanese Imperial forces, special attack units known as *kamikaze* were formed. Named after the 'divine wind' which saved Japan from invasion by the Mongols, these manned planes, boats or flying bombs loaded with explosives, crashed into enemy ships. Over 1,500 planes and flying bombs were used, sanking 34 Allied ships and damaging 288. ❑

The atom bomb In July 1945 the Potsdam Declaration was issued, calling for the unconditional surrender of Japan. The Japanese refused. Rather than accept the enormous casualties they expected if forced to invade the Japanese mainland, the Allies attacked Hiroshima with an atomic bomb on 6 August 1945, destroying most of the city and killing 80,000 people. On 9 August a second bomb hit Nagasaki. Faced with such devastation the Japanese government surrendered on 14 August 1945. Foreign forces occupied the country until 1952, when, under a democratic constitution, Japan regained its independence.

Sugamo
Rikugien Garden
Ikebukuro
Ōtsuka
Higashi-Ikebukuro
Hon-Komagor
HAKUSAN-DORI
Sunshine City
YAMATE-DORI
SHINOBAZU-DORI
Minami-Ikebukuro
5
TOSHIMA-KU
Gokokuji Temple
Koishikawa Botanical Gardens
Mejiro
MEJIRO-DORI
SHIN-MEJIRO-DORI
SHUTO EXPRESSWAY NO 5
BUNKYŌ-K
Takadanobaba
St Mary's Cathedral
KASUGA-DORI
Takadanobaba
WASEDA-DORI
Theatre Museum
Yamanote Line
MEIJI-DORI
Korakuen Garden
Tōkyō Dome
4
ŌKUBO-DORI
Shin-Ōkubo
Iidabashi
Suidōbashi
Iidabashi
Ōkubo
ŌKUBO-DORI
SHINJUKU-KU
MEJIRO-DORI
Fujimi
Kabukichō
ŌME-KAIDO
Yasukuni Shrine
Nishi-Shinjuku
YASUKUNI-DORI
Shinjuku
Ichigaya
Sanbanchō
Kitanomaru Park
Shinjuku Central Park
SHINJUKU-DORI
National Museum of Modern Art
KŌSHŪ-KAIDŌ
Shinjuku-Imperial Gardens
Yotsuya
Yoyogi
CHIYODA-KU
3
Sendagaya
Kioichō
National Theatre
Imperial Palace
Shinanomachi
Japanese Sword Museum
Meiji Shrine Treasure House
SHUTO EXPRESSWAY NO 4
Akasaka Palace
Nijūbashi Bridge
Yoyogi
National Noh Theatre
National Stadium
National Diet Building
Meiji Shrine
Suntory Museum of Art
YAMATE-DORI
Yoyogi Park
Jingu Baseball Stadium
Nagatachō
Kasumigaseki
Hibiya Park
Harajuku
Ota Memorial Museum of Art
AOYAMA-DORI
GAIEN-HIGASHI-DORI
Akasaka
SHIBUYA-KU
Jingūmae
SAKURADA-DORI
Nogi Shrine
Jinnan
Olympic Stadium
Kita-Aoyama
Aoyama
Suntory Hall
Minami-Aoyama
Toranomon
HIBIYA-DORI
2
Udagawachō
Roppongi
Azabudai
Japan Folk Crafts Museum
Nezu Institute of Fine Arts
Tōkyō Tower
Komaba
Dōgenzaka
SHUTO EXPRESSWAY NO 3
Shibuya
GAIEN-NISHI-DORI
Shiba-Park
Zojōji Temple
MEGURO-KU
Yamanote Line
MINATO-KU
SAKURADA-DORI
Shiba
MEIJI-DORI
DAIICHI-KEIHIN
Mita
1
SHUTO EXPRESSWAY NO 2
Shibaura
YAMATE-DORI
Ebisu
Tamachi
National Park for Nature Study
Tōkyō Metropolitan Teien Art Museum
Sengakuji Temple
Meguro Museum of Art
A
B
C

A to Z

TOKYO

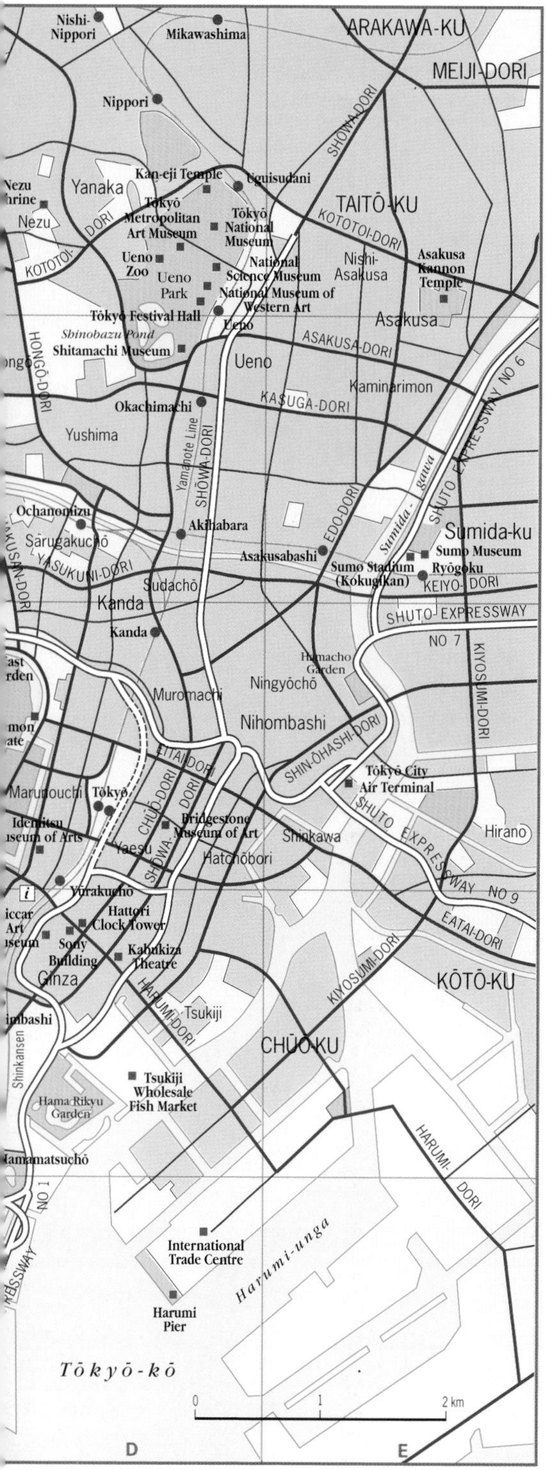
Nishi-Nippori
Mikawashima
ARAKAWA-KU
MEIJI-DORI
Nippori
SHOWA-DORI
Nezu Shrine
Yanaka
Kan-eji Temple
Uguisudani
Tōkyō Metropolitan Art Museum
Tōkyō National Museum
TAITŌ-KU
KOTOTOI-DORI
Nezu
DORI
KOTOTOI-
Ueno Zoo
Ueno Park
National Science Museum
Nishi-Asakusa
Asakusa Kannon Temple
National Museum of Western Art
Tōkyō Festival Hall
Ueno
Asakusa
Shinobazu Pond
Shitamachi Museum
ASAKUSA-DORI
HONGŌ-DORI
Ueno
Kaminarimon
Okachimachi
KASUGA-DORI
SHUTO EXPRESSWAY NO 6
Yushima
Yamanote Line
SHŌWA-DORI
Sumida-gawa
EDO-DORI
Ochanomizu
Akihabara
Sumida-ku
Sarugakuchō
Asakusabashi
Sumo Museum
YASUKUNI-DORI
Sumo Stadium (Kokugikan)
Ryōgoku
KEIYO-DORI
Sudachō
Kanda
SHUTO EXPRESSWAY NO 7
Kanda
KIYOSUMI-DORI
Hamacho Garden
Ningyōchō
Muromachi
Nihombashi
SHIN-ŌHASHI-DORI
EITAI-DORI
Tōkyō City Air Terminal
Marunouchi
Tōkyō
CHŪŌ-DORI
SHUTO EXPRESSWAY NO 9
Bridgestone Museum of Art
Shinkawa
Hirano
Yaesu
SHŌWA-DORI
Hatchōbori
Yūrakuchō
Hattori Clock Tower
EATAI-DORI
Sony Building
Kabukiza Theatre
KIYOSUMI-DORI
Ginza
KŌTŌ-KU
HARUMI-DORI
Tsukiji
CHŪŌ-KU
Shinkansen
Tsukiji Wholesale Fish Market
Hama Rikyu Garden
HARUMI-DORI
NO 1
International Trade Centre
Harumi-unga
Harumi Pier
Tōkyō-kō
0
1
2 km
D
E

Harajuku district
Every Sunday, along the avenue south of Yoyogi Koen Park, near JR Harajuku station, dozens of Japanese rock bands give free open-air concerts, accompanied by rock-and-roll fans with greased hair, wearing crepe-soled shoes and drain-pipe jeans, and young girls with bouffant hairstyles and short, flared skirts, who dance in sequence. Food stalls and traditional drummers add to the fun.

Tokyo's Stark Building

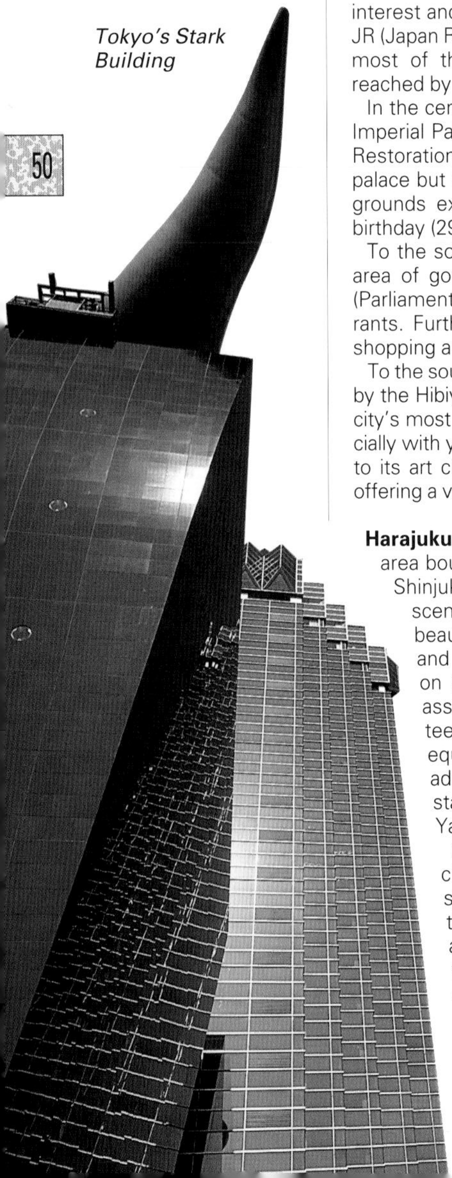

Tokyo One quarter of all Japanese live within a 50km radius of the Imperial Palace, Tokyo. Over 12 million live in Tokyo itself, one of the world's largest cities and the political, economic and cultural capital of Japan. Unlike the historic cities of Kyoto and Nara, Tokyo is not a place of classic sights and traditional charms; few buildings survived both the great earthquake of 1923 and the bombing of the war, but it is a powerhouse of creative energy, global influence and wealth.

For the first-time visitor, Tokyo may appear as a disappointing jumble of high-rise buildings, concrete flyovers and crowded sidewalks. However, any exploration on foot, away from modern thoroughfares, reveals it to be a complex metropolis of interconnected towns, each with its own neighbourhoods of individual character.

For tourists with limited time the area of Tokyo of most interest and most easily explored is that bounded by the JR (Japan Railways) Yamanote loop line. Within this circle most of the places you will wish to visit are easily reached by subway or taxi or on foot.

In the centre of Tokyo is the monumental 19th-century Imperial Palace, the seat of the emperor since the Meiji Restoration of 1868. There are good walks near the palace but the public is not allowed access to the actual grounds except on 2 January and the late Emperor's birthday (29 April).

To the southwest of the palace is Akasaka district, an area of government buildings which includes the Diet (Parliament), large expensive hotels and luxurious restaurants. Further east is the Ginza, Tokyo's world-famous shopping and expense account entertainment district.

To the south of Akasaka is Roppongi, an area served only by the Hibiya line but which has nonetheless become the city's most cosmopolitan and popular nightlife area, especially with young people and foreigners, who are attracted to its art cinemas, experimental theatre and restaurants offering a variety of ethnic cuisines.

Harajuku and Shinjuku On the western edge of the area bounded by the Yamanote line are Harajuku and Shinjuku. Harajuku is the centre of the teen fashion scene and the site of the historically important and beautiful Meiji Shrine. Omotesando-dori Avenue and Yoyogi-koen Park are popular meeting places on Sundays for rock bands, street dancers and assorted punks and rockers (unaggressive teenage rebels). Aoyama district, nearby, is equally fashion-conscious but the mood is more adult; the shops of Tokyo's fashion design superstars, such as Issey Miyake and Yohji Yamamoto, are found here.

Shinjuku started life as a characterless satellite city within a city and gained a reputation for sleazy nightlife. It has, in the main, outgrown this image and outside the incredibly complex and seemingly chaotic Shinjuku subway station are good department stores and gift shops and respectable restaurants and bars. However, the Kabukicho area, within Shinjuku district, is still the place to go for seedy massage parlours and cheap dives.

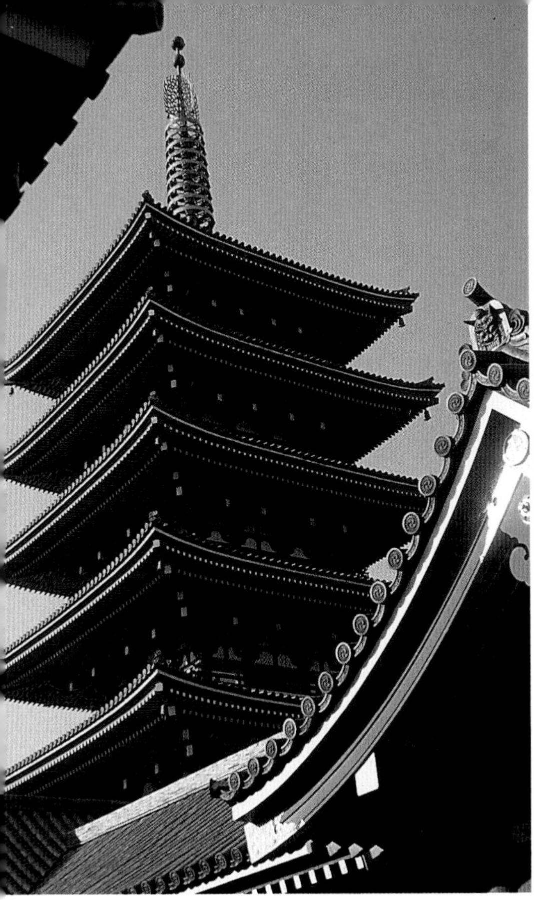

Ancient Japan survives in Asakusa

Finding an address
It is extremely difficult even for local people and taxi drivers to find a place in Japan, and especially in Tokyo, just by its address. There is no logical system of house numbers and streets do not have names, although some major roads and avenues do. Instead, addresses are by district, and within each district each building has a one- or two-digit (hyphenated) number. The best way to locate an address is to find it on a map of the vicinity. This is made easier by the practice of printing small maps on the back of business cards, restaurant match-packets and so on. Otherwise, travel to the general vicinity by bus or train and then take a cab for the final part of the journey.

Ueno and Asakusa A flavour of old Japan can be experienced in the Ueno and Asakusa districts, in the northeast of the city. Ueno Park is the cultural heart of Tokyo and most of the nation's major art galleries and museums are found in its grounds, as well as the zoo that houses Japan's prized giant pandas. Asakusa is a temple town and home of the famous Kannon Temple, a popular visiting place during holidays and festivals. North of Ueno is Yanaka, where flimsy wooden houses and temples have somehow escaped the bulldozer in old streets that are a favourite haunt of photographers and artists.

Traditional culture in Tokyo: Kabuki theatre in performance

Temple origins
According to legend, the Asakusa Kannon Temple was established in the 7th century, when two local fishermen discovered in their nets a statue of Kannon, the Buddhist Goddess of Mercy. Originally built on this site to house the statue, the temple has been rebuilt and enlarged many times over the intervening centuries. The original image of Kannon found by the fisherman is said to be buried beneath the gold-plated inner shrine found beyond the main altar in the Main Hall, but this has never been verified.

▶▶▶ Asakusa Kannon Temple (Sensoji Temple) 49E5

2-3-1 Asakusa, Taito-ku
Subway: Asakusa

Asakusa district forms part of the old downtown or *shitamachi* section of Tokyo. Settled by merchants, artisans and craftsmen during the Edo period (1600–1868), Asakusa is still an area associated with popular Japanese culture. The Asakusa Kannon Temple in the heart of the district, the oldest temple in Tokyo, is a place of worship held in particular affection.

The Kaminarimon or the Gate of the God of Thunder, hung with a huge red paper lantern, marks the main entrance to the temple. Nakamise-dori Street begins inside the gate and leads to the temple compound. Invariably crowded, the street is lined with small stalls selling snack foods, traditional gifts and souvenirs.

At the end of the street the smaller Hozomon gateway opens on to a five-storey pagoda, the temple landmark, and the Main Hall. Both buildings are post-war concrete replicas of original wooden structures. The Main Hall has little architectural merit but the constant stream of visitors gives it life and energy. At its entrance stands a large bronze incense burner. Worshippers wave the billowing incense smoke over their hands and heads, a charm to heal or prevent illness, before climbing the steps to offer prayers to Kannon (Goddess of Mercy). Inside the rather dimly lit interior is a collection of huge 18th- and 19th-century votive paintings on wood (*ema*), donated to the temple by leading artists of the Edo period. The great dragon painting on the ceiling is by Kawabata Ryushi, a famous 20th-century painter. Three immense red paper lanterns hanging from the ceiling were given by local *geisha* associations. Another measure of Asakusa's *shitamachi* origins is the popularity of the temple with *kabuki* actors and *sumo* wrestlers, who traditionally make offerings there before the start of a theatre season or tournament.

Asakusa Kannon Temple: detail...

...and façade

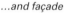

Picasso, at the Bridgestone Museum of Art

The streets and covered passageways surrounding the temple are teeming with shops, restaurants, tea houses and a great variety of nightlife (see pages 68–9).
Open: 24 hours.

Dembo-in (Abbot's Residence)►► is in the grounds of the Asakusa Kannon Temple but permission to enter must be obtained from the Dembo-in temple offices, near the foot of the pagoda. Simply sign the visitors book and obtain a ticket; then walk back down Nakamise-dori Street, past the closed front entrance of Dembo-in. Turn right at the next corner and walk down Dembo-in dori Street to the entrance gate opposite Asakusa Public Hall. Inside the peaceful temple grounds is a stroll garden, designed by the tea ceremony master Enshu Kobori (1579–1647). The garden pond contains carp and turtles and from one angle the Asakusa Kannon pagoda is clearly reflected on its surface. The wooden abbot's residence and guest hall were built in the mid-18th century and the bronze bell at the main entrance dates from 1387.

►► Bridgestone Museum of Art *49D3*

1-10-1 Kyobashi, Chuo-ku
Subway: Kyobashi; JR: Tokyo
On the second floor of the Bridgestone building, the Museum of Art displays one of Japan's best private collections of painting and sculpture, mainly of the Impressionist school and the Ecole de Paris. It includes works by Rodin, Moore, Giacometti, Picasso, Rembrandt, Utrillo and Modigliani, as well as some fascinating post-Meiji Japanese paintings in highly derivative Western styles.
Open: 10–5:30 (last entrance 5pm). Closed: Monday and 20 December–6 January.

Temple festivals
Major festivals are regularly held at the Asakusa Kannon Temple. The most popular attractions are the Setsubun ceremony (3 February); the Kinryu-No-mai (Golden Dragon Dance) on 18 March and 18 October; the Sanja festival of Asakusa Shrine on 17 and 18 May; the Shirasagi-No-mai (White Crane Dance) on 3 November; and the year-end Hagoita-ichi market between 17 and 18 December, when stalls sell *hagoita* (paddles) richly decorated with portraits of famous figures from *kabuki*. The paddle is used with a shuttlecock to play a traditional game, similar to badminton, during the New Year Festival.

▶▶▶ Ginza *49D2*

Subway: Ginza (exit for the 4 *chome* intersection)
The most famous shopping and entertainment district in Japan, Ginza contains Tokyo's largest concentration of department stores, expensive boutiques, galleries, coffee shops, bars and restaurants. It is also an important commercial centre, home to some of Japan's foremost companies, as well as the location of several hotels.

Ginza's most famous landmark is the Hattori Clock Tower, which stands at the top of the Wako department store at the intersection of Harumi-dori street and Ginza-dori street. The clock was first installed in 1894; many of the nearby shops are as old or older. The Kimuraya bakery shop, next door to Wako, opened in 1874 and is still very popular, especially for its beancurd bread. Mikimoto (4-5-5 Ginza) sells cultured pearls and was, perhaps, the first shop in the world to do so, having opened in 1899.

The **Sony Building▶▶**, 5-3-1 Ginza, Chuo-ku contains restaurants and boutiques, in addition to three Sony showrooms (first, third and fourth floors), where new products and developments are displayed to the public (open 11–8).

Ginza traffic

►► Idemitsu Museum of Arts 49D3

Kokusai Building, 9th Floor, 3-1-1 Marunouchi, Chiyoda-ku
Subway: Hibiya
Located on the ninth floor of the Kokusai Building, the Idemitsu is one of the largest and best designed private museums in Tokyo. It contains an excellent collection of Zen calligraphy and ink paintings (some by the famous Zen monk Sengai), fine examples of Chinese porcelain of the Tang and Song dynasties and Japanese ceramics. There is a Japanese-style tea room open to the public.
Open: 10–5. Closed: Monday (and Tuesday if Monday is a national holiday) and Sunday.

►► Kabukiza Theatre 49D2

4-12-5 Ginza, Chuo-ku
Subway: Higashi-Ginza
Tokyo's best known *kabuki* theatre sits at the intersection of two main streets in Ginza: Harumi-dori and Showa-dori. It first opened its doors in 1889, but was rebuilt in 1924 during a period of Japanese revivalism, in a baroque style inspired by castle architecture of the 16th century. The present building is a 1951 reconstruction of this structure. This is one of the best places to see the fun spectacle of *kabuki* (see pages 58–9). English programme notes and an earphone system are available, and there are daily matinée and evening performances all year except August and December. It is possible to pay to see just one act.

►► Kokuritsu Hakubutsukan (Tokyo National Museum) 49D5

13-9 Ueno-koen, Taito-ku
JR: Ueno (exit via Ueno-koen)
The National Museum covers the whole history of Japan and Japanese art from the earliest periods on record. Its collection of archaeology, sculpture, painting, lacquer work, ceramics and armour make it the most complete collection of its kind anywhere in the world. Architecturally, the museum is a mish-mash of buildings of opposing styles and periods, but the treasures on view are remarkable.

There are four main exhibition areas. Honkan, the main hall, directly facing the front gate, is rather gloomy, but a wander through the 25 rooms of ancient Japanese sculpture, textiles, metalwork, armour and swords, ceramics, paintings, lacquerware and calligraphy is well worthwhile. Hyokeikan, to the left of the main entrance, was constructed in 1909 to celebrate the marriage of the future Emperor Taisho, and houses important Japanese archaeological exhibits. The third exhibition space is the Horyuji Treasure House, open only on Thursday (closed even then if it is heavily raining or very humid). It contains rare and priceless Buddhist artefacts and works of art from the Horyuji Temple in Nara, said to be the birthplace of Japanese Buddhism. Finally, the Toyokan Gallery of Oriental Antiques specialises in archaeological, historical and cultural objects from China, southeast Asia and India.
Open: Tuesday to Sunday 9–4:30. Closed: Monday and 25 December–3 January.

Money-making
The name Ginza means 'place where silver is minted' and refers to the government mint established in the area in 1612 on land reclaimed from the sea. Ginza in its present role was created in the latter half of the 19th century to serve as a model of the Western-style culture the Japanese were embracing at the time. Its stores were the first in Japan to employ window displays, and window shopping is still one of Ginza's attractions. It has given rise to the common phrase *Gin-bura* – to stroll aimlessly through Ginza (or any shopping district). A more recent pastime is *depato meguri*, or hopping from one department store to the next.

Armour, Tokyo National Museum

Imperial lineage
Although some women held imperial power in ancient Japan, from the Nara era (710–794) until the present only males have been allowed to sit on the imperial throne. Except for the crown prince and his oldest son, who may not refuse the throne, it is possible for other descendants of the Emperor to give up their imperial status and become commoners through marriage.

The Imperial Palace

►►► Kokyo (Imperial Palace) *48C3*

Subway: Otemachi
The residence of the reigning Emperor of Japan and his family is set in extensive grounds right in the heart of Tokyo's business centre, on the former site of Edo Castle, the home of the Tokugawa *shogun* (1603–1867). Construction of the palace began after the Meiji Restoration of 1868, when the Emperor moved from Kyoto to Tokyo. Most of the main buildings were destroyed in World War II, but rebuilding was completed in 1968. The actual palace is closed to the public and the private palace grounds are open only twice a year, on the Emperor's birthday and 2 January. Access on these days is via the Nijubashi Bridge, a double-arched stone bridge of German design, one of Tokyo's most familiar sights (reached from Nijubashi-mae subway station).

The Imperial Palace East Garden, formerly at the heart

of Edo Castle and making up one third of the palace grounds, is open to the public. Popular with Japanese and foreign tourists, and with Tokyoites keen for air and a stroll in the sunlight, the garden is a welcome oasis in the noise and fumes of downtown Tokyo. The most convenient entrance is via the Otemon Gate, once the principal gate to Edo Castle and an impressive example of a *masugata* (defensive) gate.

To the north of the palace lies Kitanomaru-koen Park, formerly the private grounds of the Imperial Guard but now open to the public and the home of several museums (access via Kudanshita subway station).
Open (East Garden): 9–4 (enter by 3pm). Closed: Monday, Friday and 25 December–3 January.

▶▶▶ Meiji Jingu (Meiji Shrine) *48A3*

1-1 Yoyogi, Kamizono-cho, Shibuya-ku
Subway: Meijijingumae. JR: Harajuku and Yoyogi
This Shinto shrine and its large park are dedicated to the spirit of Emperor Meiji (1852–1912) and his wife, Empress Shoken (1850–1914). Emperor Meiji reigned during Japan's transformation from an isolated nation, unchanged for many hundreds of years, into a modern world power. He and Empress Shoken are buried near Kyoto, but this shrine was completed in his memory in 1920 with labour volunteered by over 100,000 Japanese. It was destroyed in an air raid in 1945 and rebuilt in 1958. The grounds are thickly wooded (planted with many trees and shrubs donated by the various provinces of Japan) and contain a famous iris garden, once frequented by the Emperor and his consort. It is a beautiful and cool retreat, even during Tokyo's hot, humid summer months. The approach to the shrine itself is spanned by a huge *torii* gate (see panel), made of cypress wood over 1,700 years old. Behind the shrine is the Treasure House, in which articles used by Emperor Meiji are exhibited.

The shrine is very popular during the New Year festival, and on New Year's Eve, trains run to the nearest JR station throughout the night. It is also particularly busy on Sundays, and on Thursdays young couples come here to present their newborn babies in a ceremony known as *miya mairi*; the babies and their mothers are often dressed in traditional robes and kimonos.
Open: shrine and inner garden every day sunrise to sunset, except the third Friday of each month. Iris garden 1 March–3 November 9–4:30, otherwise 9–4.

Torii gates
Torii, the large gates that stand at the entrances to Shinto shrines, are made of wood, either plain or painted red. Each gate has two round, upright columns and two crossbeams. The purest and most primitive style of *torii* is made of logs with their bark intact. The red *torii* rising out of the sea at Itsukushima Shrine on Miyajima Island is one of the most famous symbols of Japan.

At the Meiji Shrine

■ *Kabuki*, literally 'song, dance, act', is said to have been created at the beginning of the 17th century by Okuni, a temple priestess who was also a skilled Buddhist dancer and a great beauty. She fell in love with a *ronin* (a masterless *samurai*) and fled with him, finally settling in Edo (Tokyo), where she founded a theatre and began recruiting actors......■

Sword-free theatre
A government edict of 1631, forbidding the wearing of swords in the theatre, had the effect of excluding the *samurai*, who refused to relinquish their weapons. The nobility abandoned the theatre, which became the pastime of the commercial and lower classes. By attending the theatre himself in 1887, the Emperor Meiji rehabilitated *kabuki* among the higher social echelons.

The audience
Despite the slow action, a Japanese *kabuki* theatre audience takes great delight in a performance, hissing the villain and appreciating a well-delivered speech. Theatregoers may skip boring acts and return for those they enjoy. In the foyer they can meet friends, chat, drink and buy food from a variety of restaurants and stalls.

Kabuki *has villains...*

Larger than life From its early beginnings, only two different sorts of plays have been performed in *kabuki*: historical dramas and plays about everyday life. Whatever the subject, however, the sets and acting are always flamboyant and exaggerated, with the passions, lusts and violence of life amply portrayed. Animals with human speech arrive in clouds of smoke and dance magically; rivers of blood flow from the heads of soldiers fallen to vengeful armies; victories and defeats are interlaced with the tender tragedies of failed love affairs or the triumphant reunion of lost lovers. In a society in which social and private lives were rigidly controlled, *kabuki* gave actors and their audience room to vent emotions they could not normally express.

Men as women In time, women were expelled from *kabuki* and men were required to play their roles. Since then, *onnagata*, men who specialise in female roles, have striven to present the perfect idealised version of universal woman. To play their roles well they study and practise female characteristics, even in their daily lives. Yoshisawa Ayame, an early and great *kabuki* artist, said that the ideal woman could only be expressed by an actor; he called it 'the synthetic ideal'. This admiration of the synthetic is frequently encountered in Japan, perhaps because the Japanese are able to judge the artificial and plastic substitute as a thing in its own right rather than as a copy of something 'real'. For this reason, although transvestite clubs and performers are popular all over Japan, they never have the camp overtones of their Western equivalents.

Costumes, music *Kabuki* actors wear wigs, heavy make-up and elaborate costumes. The plays unfold very slowly in a succession of tableaux; tension is maintained by the powerfully contained emotions of the actors. The orchestra, composed of traditional instruments, underlines the action and adds to the charged atmosphere. As a performance, the *kabuki* is a mix of classical theatre, opera and music hall.

The 47 *ronin* One of the plays that is most popular with *kabuki* theatre-goers is *The Adventure of the 47 ronin*. Its story (outlined below) contains two of the classic ingredients of a *kabuki* play: satisfaction of honour and suicide. In 1701, in the *shogun*'s palace, Lord Kira insulted Lord Asano. Asano drew his sword and sprang at Kira, who

fled. Unable to avenge his honour, Asano had no alternative but to commit *seppuku* (suicide by the sword). His vassals thus became *ronin* or wandering, masterless *samurai.* They swore to avenge their lord, and spent two years waiting for their moment. Eventually, one snowy night, they entered Kira's castle and cut off his head. They carefully washed the severed head, for an inferior must appear clean before his superior and Kira had become Asano's inferior. Then they took the head, together with the sword that had been used and a letter recounting what they had done, and placed them all on Asano's grave. Finally, no longer having any aim in life, and to avoid punishment for their crime, all 47 *ronin* committed *seppuku* and were buried beside their lord.

This *kabuki* plot is based on a true story – the graves of the 47 *ronin* are in the Sengakuji Temple in Tokyo (see page 61).

...and heroines – all played by men

Transvestism
The Tokugawa era government took strong measures against any trend that threatened class boundaries. In 1667, to prevent what was seen as overfamiliarity between male and female actors, and the appearance in their ranks of prostitutes, the state banned them from appearing on stage together. This gave rise to the tradition of transvestism in Japanese theatre.

Quiet streets around Sengakuji Temple

Hiroshige
Hiroshige (1797–1858), now one of Japan's most famous woodblock print (*ukiyo-e*) artists, was considered eccentric in his day. Rather than portraying orthodox themes in the conventional symbolic manner, his work dealt with the lives of ordinary people, presented in a realistic manner. His prints were sold in teahouses or shops and popular editions were published many times. By the time he was 35 Hiroshige was a well-known artist in the Tokyo area. In the late 19th century Europe began to discover Japanese art and Hiroshige's work was recognised for its extraordinary composition, colour and freshness. His influence can be seen in paintings by Manet, Toulouse Lautrec and van Gogh. News of Hiroshige's reception in the West increased interest at home and, by the turn of the century, he had become a nationally known figure.

Nizaemon VII in the role of Ki-no-Natora, *by Toshusai Sharaku, Ota Memorial Museum of Art*

►► Nihon Mingeikan (Japan Folk Crafts Museum) *48A2*

4-3-33 Komaba, Meguro-ku
Subway: Komabatodaimae
At the turn of the century Soetsu Yanagi was one of Japan's leading philosophers and critics, and wrote prolifically on Western art, literature and philosophy. He and his circle of friends published a monthly arts magazine with the aim of introducing European culture to Japan, but gradually his interest switched from European to Asiatic art. He became distressed that the folk art of his own country was swiftly disappearing. Yanagi embarked on a campaign to preserve *mingei* – the term he coined to describe this 'art of the people' – and to increase national

Within three decades he had founded this museum, dedicated not to the fine arts but to the intrinsic beauty of crafts made for daily use. Items are displayed in a replica farmhouse from Tochigi prefecture, north of Tokyo, and include Soetsu Yanagi's own large collection. Exhibitions are rotated four times a year to allow all the examples of pottery, textiles, carvings, furniture, kitchen equipment and so on to be shown.
Open: 10–5 (last entry 4pm). Closed: Monday and 22 December – 3 January and while changing exhibitions.

▶▶ Ota Memorial Museum of Art *48A2*

1-10-10 Jingumae, Shibuya-ku
Subway: Meijijingumae. JR: Harajuku
The late Seizo Ota, former Chairman of Tokyo Mutual Life, left a formidable bequest of over 12,000 woodblock prints (*ukiyo-e*) and, in the tradition of successful Japanese entrepreneurs, the money to construct this small, purpose-built museum to display them. The galleries are well lit and the prints expertly displayed on a rotating basis, representing most of Japan's best-known print artists. There is a coffee shop in the basement.

Opposite the museum entrance is Omotesando Avenue, busy with shoppers and, particularly on Sundays, the young and fashion-conscious. The Ota is in a small side street near Meiji-dori Avenue – a haven of peace among the trendy streets of Harajuku.
Open: 10:30–5:30. Closed: Monday and from the 24th to the end of every month and 20 December – 3 January.

▶▶ Sengakuji Temple *48C1*

2-11-1 Takanawa, Minato-ku (turn right from the station and walk up the hill; the entrance is past the traffic lights on the left)
Subway: Sengakuji
The 47 *ronin* buried in this temple are revered by the Japanese as examples of truly loyal men (see pages 58–9). An English-language version of the story of their sacrifice for their master, Lord Asano, who had been wrongly obliged to commit *seppuku* (ritual suicide), is available at the shops near the temple entrance.

To the right of the entrance is a statue of Yoshio Oishi, leader of the *ronin* and Lord Asano's chief retainer. Beyond the main inner gate and to the left is the cemetery. On the way you will pass a well where the *ronin* washed the severed head of Lord Kira (Asano's betrayer) before laying it on their master's grave. The head was eventually given back to Kira's family and in the small museum in the temple grounds a receipt issued by a temple priest for 'one head' is on display in one of the dusty cabinets. The tombs of the 47 *ronin* are blackened with the smoke from sticks of incense burnt in tribute.
Open: 9–4.

Seppuku

In the feudal era in Japan suicide was often required of *samurai*. When defeated in battle, *samurai* took their own lives to save their honour. The method of committing suicide was known as *seppuku* or by the more vulgar term *harakiri*, 'belly-slitting'. A man who had to or wanted to commit suicide would put on the appropriate ceremonial kimono, go to a specially designated pavilion, greet any witnesses, and sit down in front of a tray bearing a nine-inch dagger, wrapped in white paper so that only the point of it showed. The suicide would then grasp the dagger by the middle of the blade and plunge it into his stomach, cutting across horizontally. Then a designated second would immediately decapitate him, with one blow of his own sword.

Sengakuji Temple

Shinjuku frontier town
Shinjuku was originally a small post town on the Koshu-kaido highway providing horses, brothels, inns and teahouses for passing travellers. It became a boom town with the building of a railway station in 1885 and earned a reputation as a brash, free and easy area. A frontier feel is still associated with eastern Shinjuku. Having been spared by the 1923 Kanto earthquake, the district expanded at a faster pace than the rest of the city. The present Shinjuku station was opened in 1964.

The modern face of Japan at Shinjuku

▶▶▶ Shinjuku 48A4

Subway: Shinjuku (Marunouchi line (red) at the north end of the station, on the east side; Toei–Shinjuku line (green) at the south end, on the west side)

Shinjuku district has the largest, busiest and most chaotic railway station in Japan (see pages 92–3). Railway lines divide Shinjuku into two very different areas. The eastern side is a busy shopping district, with a warren of underground shopping arcades and a lively entertainment district at night. Kabuki-cho area, on the east side, is notorious for its sex establishments (see pages 244–5). The unplanned, vibrant quality of the east is in fine contrast to the ordered development of the west side, where sleek, high-rise office buildings and modern luxury hotels have earned the nickname 'Skyscraper City'. The city government recently moved there, into the Tokyo Metropolitan Government offices designed by Kenzo Tange. See also page 70.

Shinjuku Gyoen▶▶ (the Shinjuku Imperial Gardens), an 80-hectare park at Naito-cho (subway: Shinjuku Gyoenmae), belonged first to a family of feudal lords, then to Emperor Meiji. The gardens were opened to the public after World War II. The northern end of the park is given over to large expanses of greenery, and in the east there is a garden in 19th-century French style. Famous for its spring cherry blossoms and autumn chrysanthemums, the park is treasured by residents of crowded Shinjuku (open 9–4:30; closed Mon). South of Shinjuku Gyoen are the beautiful National *Noh* Theatre and gardens, where English-language guides to *noh* theatre are on sale.

A statue of warrior Saigo Takemori in Ueno

▶▶ Shitamachi Museum 49D4

2-1 Ueno-Koen, Taito-ku
Subway: Ueno, Yushima
Shitamachi translates as 'town below the castle', and refers to the district in a town where the merchant and artisan classes lived and worked. Asakusa and Ueno in Tokyo were such areas. These closely built, densely populated districts developed their own popular culture, customs and social habits – such as being quick to help a neighbour or to argue and working hard. After World War II the characteristic nature of these areas started to disappear and this museum was constructed to record their heritage. There are reconstructions of an ordinary merchant's house (look out for the bamboo basket hanging from the ceiling, in which valuables were packed and carried in the event of a fire), an old schoolhouse, a tenement house with a copper-smith's workshop and a small sweet-shop. English-speaking guests are well catered for. Open: Tuesday to Sunday 9:30–4:30. Closed: Mondays and 29 December–3 January.

▶▶ Ueno District and Zoo 49D5

Ueno station is the gateway from Tokyo to northern Japan. Department stores, shopping centres, restaurants and bars cluster around the station, and behind it is Ueno Park, Japan's first and largest public park. Within the park are several museums, including the Tokyo National Museum (see page 55) and the Shitamachi Museum (see above), and Shinobazu Pond. The **National Museum of Western Art▶▶▶** (open 9:30–5; closed Monday), designed by Le Corbusier, houses the Matsukata Collection of 19th- and 20th-century French art; the **Tokyo Metropolitan Art Museum▶▶▶** (open 9–5; closed every third Monday) exhibits modern Japanese art and the **National Science Museum▶▶▶** (open 9–4:30; closed Monday) houses displays on science, technology and traditional crafts. **Ueno Zoo** (open 9:30–4:30; closed Monday) opened in 1882; crowds flock there to see the two giant pandas given by the People's Republic of China.

Doll Temple
Kaneiji Kiyomizudo Temple, in the grounds of Ueno Park, was built in imitation of the famous Kiyomizudera Temple in Kyoto (see page 129). Mothers leave dolls around the altar of the temple to protect the health of their babies. The dolls are collected throughout the year and ritually burned in a rather macabre ceremony every 25 September.

Ueno Park

Tsukiji

■ Tsukiji is Tokyo's wholesale seafood distribution centre and perhaps the biggest, most colourful and most exciting fish market in the world. The market opens before dawn, and as business is virtually over by 9:30am, many tourists miss the opportunity of seeing this Japanese institution......■

The outer market
In the outer, smaller area of the market are stalls and shops providing everything for the catering trade from *bonito* fish flakes to personalised toothpicks. There are also small cafés, bars and coffee shops serving the fish-sellers, buyers and truckmen. They are the places to go for breakfast after a visit to the inner market.

To get to Tsukiji market, take a cab from your hotel or a train on the Hibiya subway line to Tsukiji station, two stops past Ginza station. Turn left out of the station, walk down Shin Ohashi-dori Avenue past two sets of traffic lights, turn left again and you will find yourself in the outer market. Cross the blue iron bridge that leads across a small canal to the sheds of the wholesale market. Walk past the lines of vans, piles of polystyrene boxes and small boxwood fires, built by the truckmen to keep warm while they wait to return home. Soon you will come upon the frantic bustle of the market, where over a thousand fish stalls and streams of buyers and sellers compete for space in a maze of alleyways, while men push and pull carts loaded with huge tuna fish or stacks of polystyrene boxes full of ice and wriggling fish.

Tuna fish auction The market specialises in *maguro* (tuna fish), sometimes brought to the market straight from the fishing boats that tie up at the dock behind it, though most are flown in from all over Japan and from London, Boston and Africa. The *maguro*, some of them weighing over 300kg, are auctioned every morning and then pushed on carts to the buyers' stalls. There they are put on marble slabs and sliced into sections with an electric saw; the sections are then cut into smaller pieces with a long and very sharp knife. Only at this stage does the buyer know if the fish has the desired high fat content

Seafood for sale before the sun is up

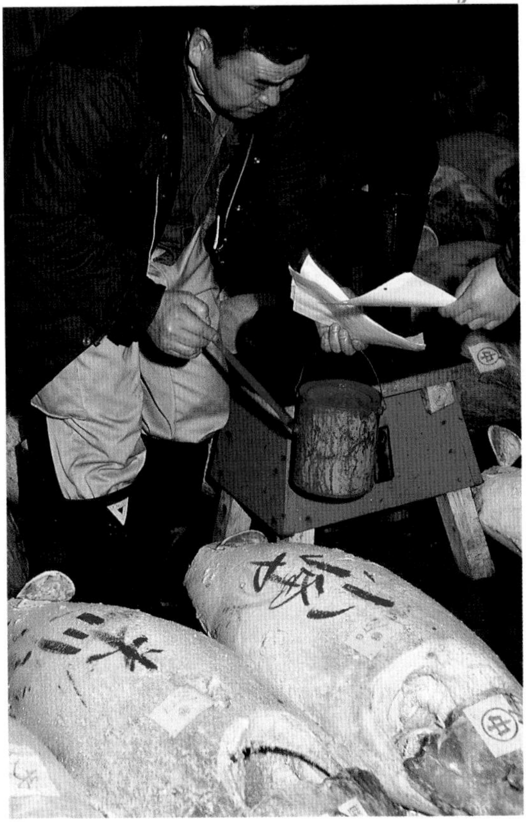

Sushi and knives

At lunchtime the *sushi* bars around the market sell the freshest *sushi* you are ever likely to taste. These vinegared rice patties can be topped with a variety of food but in Tsukiji they are prepared by the *sushi-san* with raw fish bought that morning. In the winter *sushi* is eaten with a hot *saké* for a perfect lunch. The outer market also has several stalls selling Japanese cooking knives, among the best in the world, beautifully made with plain wooden handles. Blades are marked with the maker's trademark in *kanji.*

Marking tuna with the buyer's sign

and thus whether he has paid a good or bad price for it.

Late at night, trucks from village co-operatives all over Japan start to arrive with their loads of fresh fish. They reach the market and queue to be unloaded between midnight and 4am. Trucks carrying water tanks full of live fish go to the south end of the market, where their catch is transferred to aerated holding tanks to await the auction. At around 4am the trucks leave the auctioneers, and wholesale buyers arrive to look at the produce. The buyers examine the tuna for fat content and take a good look inside the boxes of other fish to make sure they are fresh. What they buy and the prices they pay are crucial to the profits they will make later in the day.

At 5:20am the auction begins. Tuna fish are auctioned on the ground floor and other fish and seafood on the first floor. Meanwhile, at the market stalls, buyers' assistants are clearing up, getting boxes of fresh ice ready, sharpening knives and preparing for the arrival of the stevedores with the morning purchases. Between 6 and 9am, the retailers, restaurateurs and *sushi-san* (see panel) arrive to buy fish and to catch up on the day's news. By 9:30am the pace in the market is slower and it is time to leave.

At the entrance to the blue iron bridge leading to the market is the Namiyoke Temple, a Shinto shrine dedicated to the safety of seamen. A stall at its gate sells delicious, freshly baked cakes filled with red-bean jam.

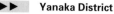

A kamikaze flying *bomb on display at Yasukuni Shrine*

►► Yanaka District *49D5*

This neighbourhood, north of the Shitamachi Museum (see page 63) was one of the few in Tokyo to escape most of the destruction of the 1923 Kanto earthquake and World War II bombing. With its narrow streets and old shops and houses, it preserves much of the flavour of a Shitamachi area, and is worth exploring on foot – if you do not mind the risk of getting lost. JR Nippori station, on the Yamanote line, is a good starting point.

►► Yasukuni Shrine *48C4*

3-1-1 Kudankita, Chiyoda-ku
Subway: Kudanshita

This Shinto shrine, a national monument in Japan, was built at the request of Emperor Meiji in honour of Japanese who had died in the battle to reinstate his imperial authority in the Meiji Restoration of 1868. Since then it has been dedicated to the spirits of all Japanese soldiers and civilians who gave their lives in the 'defence' of the Japanese Empire. Many of the 2.5 million souls honoured at the shrine died in imperialistic wars – and as such their enshrinement is out of step with the post-war Japanese constitution, which renounces militarism and separates the state from religion. As a result of this contradiction the shrine has been at the centre of a number of political controversies. The official visit of Japan's Prime Minister in 1985 created an outcry from the government of China and a torrent of protest from Japanese opposition parties, who saw the visit as sanctifying war criminals. Nevertheless, the shrine is regularly visited by many thousands of Japanese, who go simply to pay their respects to lost relatives and friends and to pray for 'the repose of their souls'.

Yasukuni is a complex of buildings that include the Main Hall, the Hall of Worship, a museum called the Yushukan, a *noh* theatre and a *sumo* wrestling ring. The Main Hall and Hall of Worship are built in the primitive unadorned *shinmei* style of the ancient shrines at Ise (see pages 106–7). The Yushukan is essentially a military museum with exhibits such as a tank, a naval gun and the Human Torpedo (*Kaiten*), the submarine equivalent of a *kamikaze* plane. The most recent addition is a steam locomotive from the Thai–Burma 'Death Railway', built by Allied prisoners of war. The museum's contents in the context of the shrine are, to say the least, disquieting.

Look for the huge steel *torii* gate which stands at the entrance of an avenue, lined with stone lanterns, cherry and *ginko* trees; this leads to another enormous *torii* and, finally, the main gate to the inner sanctuary.

Open: shrine 24 hours, Main Hall and Museum 9:30–4:30.

***Sumo* at Yasukuni Shrine**

Between 21 and 23 April, open-air *sumo* matches are held every afternoon at the Yasukuni Shrine. The event marks the end of a Shinto spring festival and traditionally the best *sumo* men in Japan dedicate their services freely. Pre-match rituals are shortened but otherwise the contests are conducted with the usual ceremony. Each *sumo* stable has its own open marquee, where the wrestlers prepare themselves before entering the ring. Visitors can wander freely among the enormous men. Look out for top wrestlers arriving in black stretch limousines, a single man filling the whole back seat.

► Yoyogi-koen Park *48A2*

Subway: Omotesando. JR: Harajuku
Once a Japanese army drilling ground, this area was requisitioned by the US Army after World War II, when it became known as Washington Heights. In 1964 the land was used for the construction of the athletes' Olympic Village before its final conversion to public parkland. The park is a welcome open space but its real interest to visitors is on Sundays, when rock-and-roll fans take over (see panel, page 50). Takeshita-dori, nearby, is a cramped alleyway where cheap boutiques and stall-holders sell sunglasses, posters, badges and cut-rate fashion clothes: a young teenager's dream.

Rockers at Yoyogi-koen Park

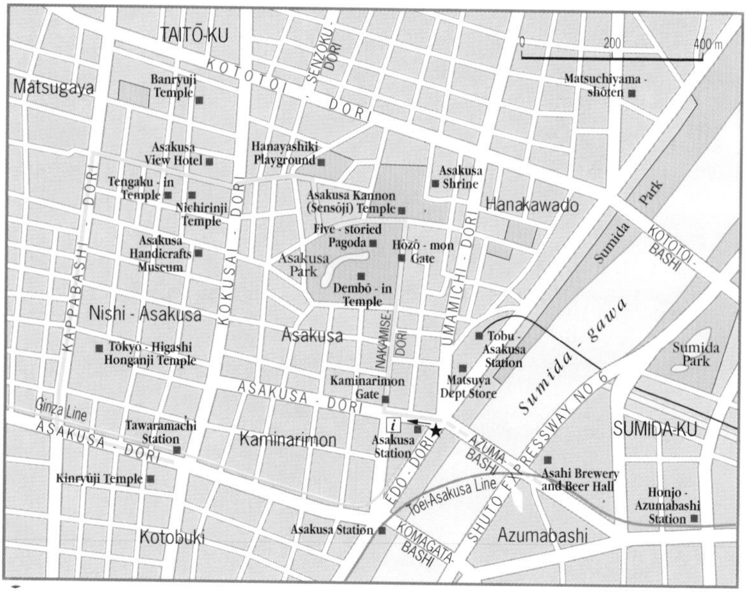

Walk Asakusa

Distance: 2.5km; time: one hour. Tokyo's 'downtown' shopping and entertainment district, on the banks of the Sumida River, is the spiritual home of the *Edokko*, Tokyo's equivalent of London's cockneys. Asakusa is a great place for inexpensive souvenir shopping, or for the serious cook to look for additions to the *batterie de cuisine*.

On leaving Asakusa subway station, Ginza line, pause to look across the Sumida river. To the left of the bridge stand the **Asahi Brewery Company**'s headquarters and the **Asahi Beer Hall**▶, both landmarks of the Tokyo 1980s style, designed by the Frenchman, Philippe Starck. The brewery building is said to represent a glass of beer, complete with a head of foam, while the strange golden object atop the Beer Hall represents a flame.

Turning around, walk two blocks away from the river to find the **Kaminarimon** or Thunder Gate, marking the entry to the precincts of **Sensoji Temple**, better known as the **Asakusa Kannon Temple** (see page 52). The approach to the temple, the Nakamise-dori, is lined with stalls selling all manner of traditional souvenirs and sweetmeats, plus some more

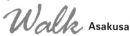

way-out articles: 50m along on the left-hand side, a corner stall has an intriguing line in canine formal wear. In common with even the most modest of neighbourhood shopping streets in Tokyo, Nakamise-dori's decorations change with the seasons.

After visiting the temple, walk round and to the west for three minutes to reach the **Hanayashiki playground▶**, a children's small funfair. Between Hanayashiki and the tower of the Asakusa View Hotel is a group of theatres and cinemas, heart of the Asakusa entertainment district, with a distinctly different, more homely atmosphere to fashionable Shibuya and Shinjuku. Continue walking along the street to the left of the Asakusa View Hotel, until you meet **Kappabashidori Avenue▶▶**, the heart of the catering trade wholesale district and the place to go for excellent knives, exotic kitchen utensils and also the lurid plastic food replicas that grace so many restaurant and cafeteria window displays.

To end the walk, continue south down Kappabashi until you reach Tawaramachi subway station, Ginza line. Carry on south to reach the tourist information office.

Above: the Sumida River
Below: Asakusa Kannon Temple

Walk Shinjuku

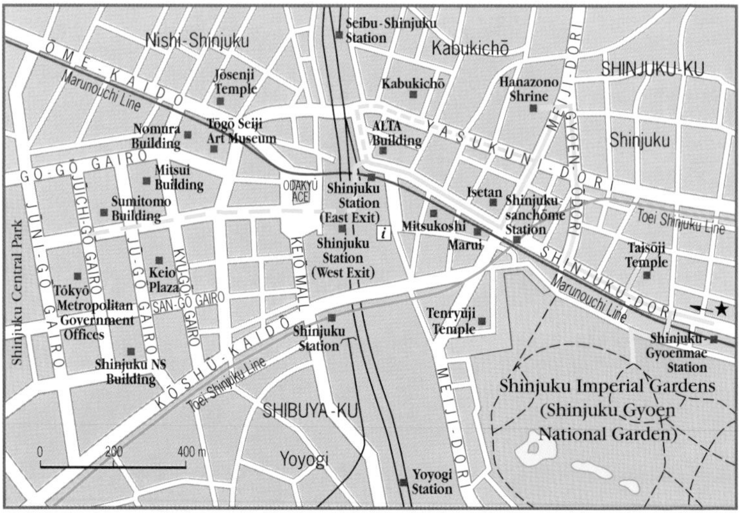

Distance: 3.5km; time: one and a half to two hours.
Relax in the Shinjuku Gyoen Park before encountering Tokyo's busiest shopping and entertainment district.

Start at Shinjuku-Gyoenmae subway station, Marunouchi line and walk one block to the **Shinjuku Gyoen Park**. This broad, pleasantly landscaped park offers good views of the cluster of skyscrapers to the northwest in Tokyo's new administrative and business district. Leaving the park, walk back past the subway station, and across the main road, Shinjuku-dori, to find the entrance to the **Taisoji Temple►►**, originally built in the 17th century and housing a large statue of Yama, king of the Buddhist hell.

Continue west along Shinjukudori, then turn right into Meiji-dori and head north, crossing the wide Yasukuni-dori Avenue, to find the entrance to the **Hanazono Shrine►►►**, bright with scarlet *torii* gates. The shrine is famous for its annual *Tori-no-Ichi*, held each November, a market for lavishly decorated bamboo rakes sold as good luck charms. After visiting the shrine, go back across Yasukuni to rejoin Shinjuku-dori and then turn right, towards Shinjuku station. Here are the department stores, **Isetan**, **Marui** and **Mitsukoshi**. Alternatively, turn right along Yasukuni and approach Shinjuku station. The streets to the right make up **Kabuki-cho►**, the city's largest nightlife area.

Either way leads to Shinjuku station. Opposite the east exit stands the **ALTA Building** with a giant TV screen, a popular meeting point. Follow the signs through the station ticket hall to the west exit. On the lower level, the walkway leads to the right, to an underground link with the business district. Walk to ground level to see the marble twin towers of the **Tokyo Metropolitan Government offices►**, a vast and expensive show of architectural bravura.

Return by underground walkway to Shinjuku station.

Metropolitan Government offices

Walk Shibuya and Harajuku

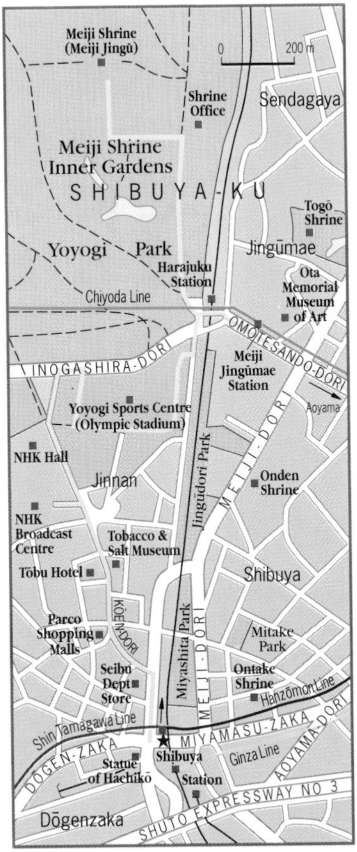

Distance: 2.5km; time: at least one and a half hours.

This walk leads through one of Tokyo's most fashionable districts to the sombre beauty of the Meiji Shrine, then back into the mixture of tacky and high fashion in Harajuku.

Start at the north exit of JR Shibuya station, JR Yamanote line, subway Hanzomon and Ginza lines, by the statue of **Hachiko**▶, a dog owned by a university professor, who met his master at Shibuya station every day, and continued to wait for him at the same time for seven years after his master's death in 1935.

Walk north from the statue of Hachiko, along Koen-dori (Park Street), lined with boutiques and restaurants. Continue up the slope, past the **Parco shopping malls** and the **Tobu Hotel** to the **NHK (Japan Broadcasting System) Broadcast Center** and the **NHK Hall**▶▶, one of Tokyo's largest venues for classical music performances.

Walk northeast to the entrance to Yoyogi Park (see page 67). The **Yoyogi Sports Centre** ▶ was one of three arenas for the 1964 Olympic Games, designed by Kenzo Tange.

Skirt the Sports Centre and cross the JR railtracks by the bridge alongside JR Harajuku station. To the left is the entrance to the **Meiji Shrine** (see page 57). A gravel walk, lined with lanterns, leads to the main buildings.

Walk back to JR Harajuku station and cross into Omotesando Avenue and down the slope to the intersection with Meiji-dori. The streets around this crossroads are the youth fashion centre of Japan. Note the specialist condom store on the corner of Omotesando and Meiji-dori, and the tiny, enclosed basketball court on the opposite corner. Tucked in behind, off Omotesando, is the Ota Memorial Museum of Art (see page 61).

End the walk at Harajuku, or continue up Omotesando to the up-market residential district of Aoyama.

Modern buildings at Shibuya

Excursions

▶▶▶ Kamakura

95D3

About 50km south of Tokyo

Between 1192 and 1333 Kamakura was the capital city of Japan (see panel). Today it is one of the most interesting places in Japan, with 65 Buddhist temples and 19 Shinto shrines. It is also an attractive and prosperous residential town in its own right. Being much smaller than Kyoto, Japan's other religious centre, Kamakura is easier to negotiate. The local tourist office (left of the main JR Kamakura station entrance) publishes a map of footpath routes that link the best-known temples. Paths are signposted in English as well as Japanese.

Getting there JR's Yokosuka line connects Tokyo with Kamakura. Trains run about every 10 to 15 minutes and stop at Tokyo, Shinbashi and Shinagawa stations on Tokyo's Yamanote loop line. A more interesting route, though longer, is to take the Odakyu line from Tokyo station to Fujisawa and change for the Enoden narrow-gauge train, which pulls three wooden carriages through small villages to Kamakura station. *En route*, it passes Hase station, the location of The Great Buddha and Hasedera Temple. Either station is a good starting point for a day's walking tour, the best way to explore Kamakura.

Among the temples and shrines worth visiting in Kamakura, the following are particularly interesting.

Engakuji Temple▶▶ was built in the 13th century by the Zen warrior Tokimune Hojo, to commemorate the deaths of both Japanese and Mongolian soldiers killed during the Mongols' attempted invasion of Japan, and to mark his gratitude to Zen for the calm it had given him during the campaign. Engakuji has extensive gardens and grounds and numerous sub-temples, but Shari-den, the Shrine of the Sacred Tooth of the Buddha, is perhaps the most interesting to visit, built in the Chinese style popular during the Kamakura era, 1192–1333 (open 8–5, till 4 November–March).

New capital
In the 12th century the military leader of Japan, Minamoto Yoritomo, moved the seat of military government away from Kyoto to the isolated village of Kamakura, and established there Japan's first *shogun*-controlled military government. Over the next two centuries a number of Japan's most important temples and shrines were built there, as the military and the clergy influenced each other to create a new breed of Zen warriors and warrior monks.

Shopping
Kamakura-bori, or finely chiselled wood, is the speciality of this area. Once finished, every item, such as a jewellery box, is painted, usually red and black, and then lacquered to a glossy finish.

Making offerings at the Zeniarai Benten Shrine, Kamakura

Temple for battered wives
Tokeiji Temple (near Engakuji Temple) became famous during the Tokugawa era as the only legal refuge for women who had left their husbands. Women who managed to reach the safety of the temple grounds escaped the jurisdiction of their husbands and could seek a divorce. Those caught before they reached the temple could be legally punished and even executed by their husbands.

Hase Kannon Temple (Hasedera)►►, close to Hase station, is set on a hill with fine views of the open sea. The main sanctuary houses the famous 11-headed gilt statue of Kannon, over 9m high and carved from a single log of camphorwood. The many faces of the goddess symbolise various stages of enlightenment. The most beguiling sight in Hase temple is the thousands of tiny statues of Jizo, the guardian deity of children, dressed in tiny clothes and surrounded with children's toys as offerings. Once symbolising parents' hopes for their children, these Jizo statues now mainly represent aborted children (open 7–5, till 4:40 November–March).

Above and below: Buddhas at the Great Buddha Shrine

Kamakura's best-known sight is the **Great Buddha►►►**, in the grounds of the Kotokuin Temple. This bronze figure of a seated Buddha, the Daibutsu, over 10m high, was cast in the 13th century and housed in a massive wooden temple building. One hundred and forty years later the temple and Kamakura were flattened by a huge tidal wave that swept inland. The structure that housed the Buddha was washed away, but the Buddha itself remained unmoved and for the last six centuries it has stood in the open air (open 7–5:45).

The **Zeniarai Benten Shrine►►►**, also known as the Money-Washing Shrine, is reached through a stone tunnel cut into a steep rock face. Once inside the temple grounds, you pass through a guard of honour of *torii* gates, erected so close together that they almost form a tunnel. Off the main temple is a cave, into which flows a mountain spring, directed into a channel running around the walls. Here is where the money-washing takes place: put several coins in a wicker basket, swirl them under the water and wish for financial success (open 7–5:45).

Toshogu Shrine: an elaborate tower...

▶▶▶ Nikko

209C2

140km north of Tokyo

Nikko town, at the centre of the much visited 1,407 sq km Nikko National Park, has been a religious centre since the 8th century. The park's numerous volcanic mountains and lakes include the sacred mountain Nantaisan, at the base of which lies the ravishing Lake Chuzenji and Kegon Waterfall, the highest in Japan. Nikko is a two-hour train journey from Tokyo or Ueno stations; Lake Chuzenji is a bus ride away from Nikko along a winding mountain road. To get to Nikko take the Tohoku Shinkansen line from Tokyo or Ueno stations to Utsonomiya, then change for the local line. Alternatively, take the Tobu line limited express from Matsuzukaya department store in Tokyo's Asakusa district. To reach Lake Chuzenji take any bus from platforms 1, 2 or 3 of the bus terminal near Nikko station to Chuzenji town, at the east end of the lake.

Toshogu Shrine▶▶▶, ornately decorated in vibrant colours, was begun in 1634 by the grandson of Tokugawa Ieyasu (see panel). A mixture of Shinto and Buddhist elements and elaborate carvings give it a Chinese flavour; over 2 million sheets of gold leaf were used in the gilding that covers it. A Shinto *torii* gate and a Buddhist pagoda stand together in front of the black lacquer and gold-leaf adorned Nio Mon front gate, which bears animal and plant motifs. Near by, on the lintel of the Sacred Stable for White Horse, is the carving of three monkeys, 'Hear No Evil, See No Evil, Speak No Evil', produced by local craftsmen who regarded them as guardian spirits. Further into the shrine's compound is Yomei Mon, Gate of Sunlight, the lavishly adorned entrance to the inner sanctum and once the limit for lower ranked *samurai* (ordinary people

One hundred Toshogu shrines
The Tokugawa shogunate encouraged the worship of Ieyasu's spirit and eventually more than 100 Toshogu branch shrines were built throughout Japan. In 1873, Toshogu Shrine was dedicated to two other great warlords: Toyotomi Hideyoshi (1536–98) and Minamoto no Yoritomo (1147–99).

...and a gate figure

were not allowed past the front gate). A succession of chambers leads to the Gokuden (Sacred Palace), which houses the gold lacquer shrine dedicated to the great warriors and leaders Toyotomi Hideyoshi, Tokugawa Ieyasu and Minamoto Yoritomo (see panel).

The entrance to Toshogu Shrine is along the broad Ote-dori Avenue, easily found from Nikko station, and up the Thousand Person stone steps that lead to the front gate. It is part of the **Rinnoji Temple▶▶** complex. The best way to see the shrine and other sites in Rinnoji is by buying a strip of tickets from the Rinnoji Temple gatehouse, on the right-hand side of Ote-dori Avenue before you reach Toshogu Shrine (open 8–5, till 4 November–March). The **Daiyuin Mausoleum▶▶**, ornate but smaller than Toshogu, is generally considered to be the most aesthetically pleasing of the two.

Across the road from the steps to the entrance of Rinnoji Temple, the arched red **Shinkyo (Sacred Bridge)▶▶** spans the Daiyagawa river. Originally reserved for the exclusive use of the *shogun* and imperial envoys, it can now be crossed by anyone willing to pay the fee (9–4). This is where the priest Shodo (see panel) was said to have been carried across the river on two giant serpents in his quest to reach the summit of sacred Mount Nantai.

The bus to **Lake Chuzenji▶▶** climbs to 1,270m up a winding road (there is another route for the descent). Near the bus station in Chuzenji town is Kegon Waterfall, where an elevator carries visitors to the bottom of the river gorge. To the right of the lake, Futaarasan Shrine takes the old name of Mount Nantai, the volcanic cone (2,482m) rising above it. Each August pilgrims climb to the inner Futaara Shrine, on the edge of the summit crater. In Chuzenji Temple, on the left shore of the lake, the main treasure is a statue of a thousand-handed Kannon, said to have been carved from a tree by priest Shodo himself.

The Kegon Waterfall, at Lake Chuzenji

Nikko and the Toshogu Shrine

Nikko was founded in AD782, when a Buddhist temple was erected there by the priest Shodo (735–817). However, the town, although known for its religious pilgrims, did not attract prominent national attention until after the death of Ieyasu, founder of the Tokugawa shogunate in 1616. He left instructions in his will that his remains were to be interred in Nikko. The Toshogu Shrine was built as his mausoleum and as a memorial to his achievements in unifying and governing Japan. It is thus as much a secular as a religious monument and the shrine is a major tourist attraction, especially on 17 May, the main shrine festival date, highlighted by a procession of hundreds of men in authentic *samurai* costume.

■ *Samurai* from the ruling class were apprenticed to masters of archery and swordmanship, and demanded equipment to match the skills they developed. As a result there emerged a group of artist craftsmen who manufactured swords and armour combining beauty and function to the highest degree. They developed a technical mastery that far surpassed Western methods of the day, and their swords became renowned throughout the world......■

Sword power
A story is told of two famous competing swordsmiths – Muramasa and Masamune – who were almost equal in skill. When a sword made by Muramasa was held upright in a running stream every dead leaf that drifted against its edge was cut in two. However, when Masamune's sword was put to the same test, the floating leaves passed either side of its edge, remaining uncut. Masamune's sword was judged the superior for its spiritual power over the leaves.

Making the sword For the main core of the blade the swordsmith used a soft, laminated steel, which was flexible and tough. The exterior was made of a combination of hard steels which were hammered together, folded over, hammered again and so on, many times over. This technique formed a skin over the inner blade that was composed of thousands upon thousands of layers of different grades of hard steel welded together. The blade was then hardened even more by heating and cooling. Finally it was coated with clay, leaving only the cutting edge exposed. The clay-coated blade was then heated to the correct temperature and plunged into a tub of cold water. Cooling instantly, the cutting edge became so hard that, once honed, it retained its razor sharpness despite repeated use. The part of the blade covered in clay cooled at a slower rate and retained a perfect degree of softness and flexibility necessary to give the blade 'feel' and durability.

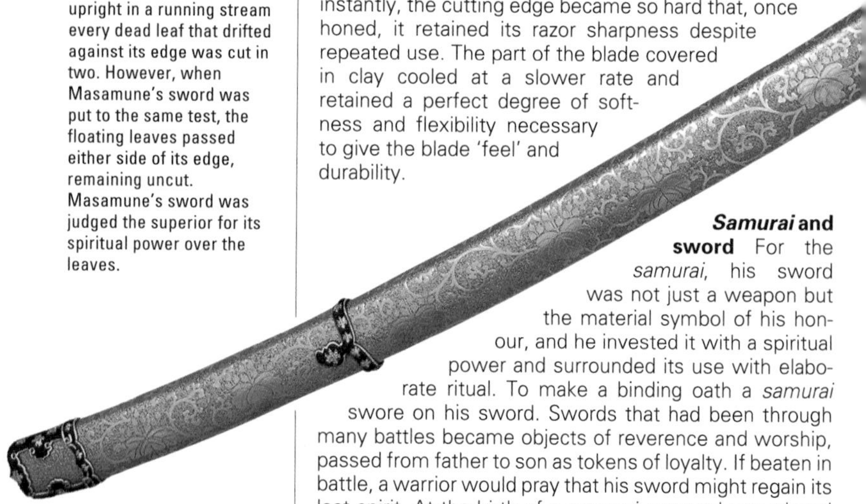

***Samurai* and sword** For the *samurai*, his sword was not just a weapon but the material symbol of his honour, and he invested it with a spiritual power and surrounded its use with elaborate ritual. To make a binding oath a *samurai* swore on his sword. Swords that had been through many battles became objects of reverence and worship, passed from father to son as tokens of loyalty. If beaten in battle, a warrior would pray that his sword might regain its lost spirit. At the birth of a *samurai*, a sword was placed beside the newborn baby and at his death a sword was laid by his corpse.

Sword and spirit Because a *samurai* sword was held to have such spiritual significance, the task of making swords was given mystical importance. The sword-maker occupied an honoured place in society and was required to undergo both spiritual and technical training before being entrusted with the job. Only those with the purest hearts and the highest moral standards could become master swordsmiths. The making of each sword was analogous to a spiritual journey and the sword-maker would undergo ritual purification and fasting before he began to make a sword. While at the anvil he wore white robes and adopted the lifestyle of a monk.

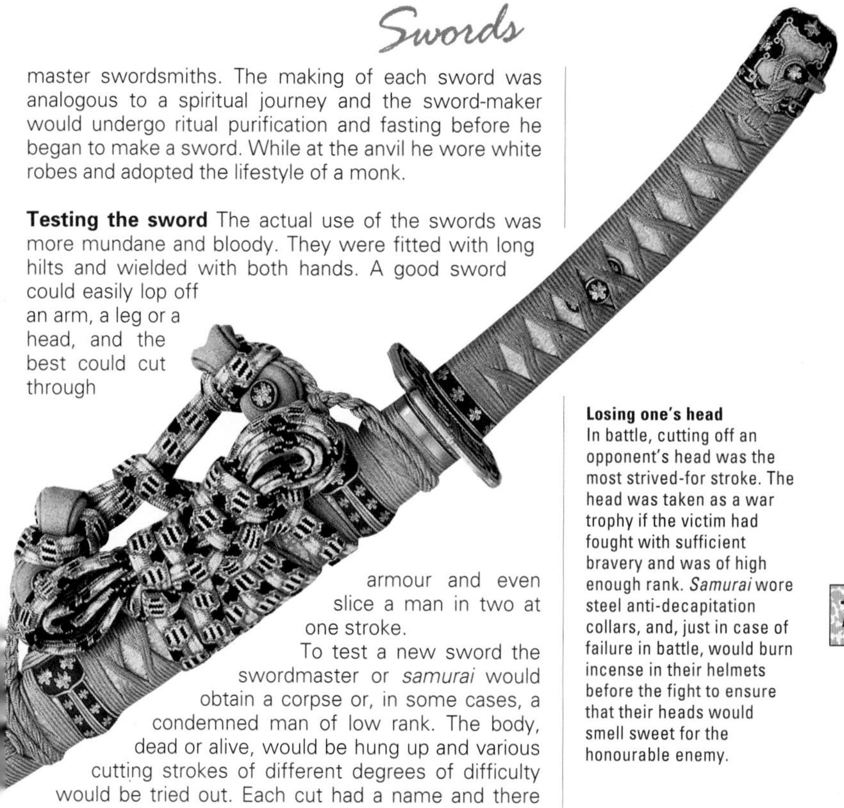

Testing the sword The actual use of the swords was more mundane and bloody. They were fitted with long hilts and wielded with both hands. A good sword could easily lop off an arm, a leg or a head, and the best could cut through armour and even slice a man in two at one stroke.

To test a new sword the swordmaster or *samurai* would obtain a corpse or, in some cases, a condemned man of low rank. The body, dead or alive, would be hung up and various cutting strokes of different degrees of difficulty would be tried out. Each cut had a name and there was even a table listing cuts in ascending order of difficulty of execution. The simplest cut was 'cutting the sleeve' or chopping a hand off at the wrist. The most difficult was a 'pair of wheels' which required the body to be chopped in half by a stroke across the hips.

Losing one's head
In battle, cutting off an opponent's head was the most strived-for stroke. The head was taken as a war trophy if the victim had fought with sufficient bravery and was of high enough rank. *Samurai* wore steel anti-decapitation collars, and, just in case of failure in battle, would burn incense in their helmets before the fight to ensure that their heads would smell sweet for the honourable enemy.

A 19th-century print by Kuniyoshi showing swordsmen in combat

Accommodation

The New Otani Hotel and garden, Tokyo

In general there is no shortage of accommodation for the traveller in Japan. In the cities and in Tokyo, especially, there is a wide variety of options, ranging from hotels that rank with the best in the world to *minshuku*, a Japanese version of bed and breakfast.

Major hotels Tokyo itself has hotel accommodation available throughout the city, but those establishments near a central location are obviously the most convenient. The best locations and the areas with most major hotels are Akasaka, Ginza, Shinbashi and around Tokyo station. Book in advance for luxury class hotels, and for all hotels during major festivals and the month of February, when students arrive in Tokyo to take their university entrance exams. The service in the major hotels is invariably first class and expensive. They offer a wide range of extras, which may include a health club and massage service (for which there is an extra charge), an executive business centre with secretarial services, a guest relations officer to help with any problems, a travel agency, a shopping arcade, cocktail lounges with live music, and Japanese- and Western-style restaurants. Rooms have their own private bathrooms with a tub and shower combination, colour television, clocks and usually radios, hot-water thermos flasks with tea bags, and minibars. Because they are accustomed to foreigners, most hotels in this category employ some English-speaking staff. Services provided include room service, laundry and dry-cleaning and often a complimentary English-language newspaper, such as the *Japan Times*, delivered to guest rooms. Hotels with

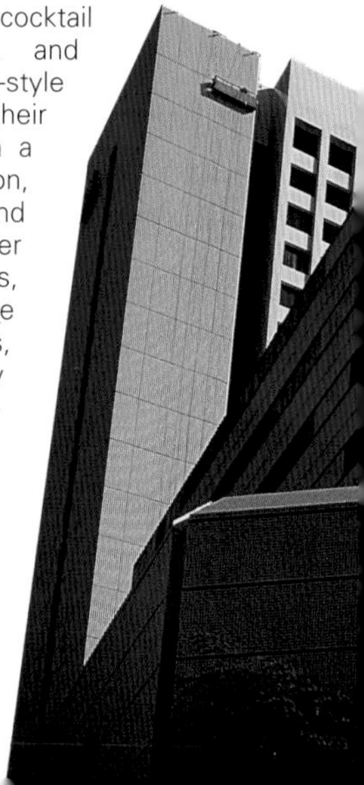

particular character or other merits are listed in the **Hotels and Restaurants** section, on pages 266–8. Whichever class of hotel you choose, standards of hygiene and service are normally excellent.

Other types of accommodation *Ryokan*, traditional Japanese inns, provide the very best of traditional Japanese taste, culture and food. They are usually sited in beautiful areas and/or overlook elegant gardens. The service is restrained and flawless in its maintenance of correct behaviour. *Ryokan* are very expensive but worth at least one night's stay for the experience (see pages 220–1).

Minshuku are family homes that take guests; these give a real insight into Japanese life. They provide a room, bed, breakfast and evening meal (see pages 80–1).

Business hotels offer straightforward, no-frills accommodation and are clean and efficiently run. Rooms are small but well equipped and the hotels provide facilities such as fax and photocopying machines. Food and room service are not always available. The cost is less than a major hotel but more than a Japanese inn. Business hotels are usually located for ease of access to railway and subway stations.

The Japanese inn is a cheap version of a *ryokan* and recommended if you are on a budget and wish to experience traditional Japanese customs and lifestyle. The rooms are *tatami* (straw-matted), divided by paper screens and sparsely but tastefully decorated. Meals are an optional extra. Japanese inns are normally good value and provide an excellent introduction to Japanese home cooking.

The very cheapest places to stay are youth hostels. There are quite a number in Tokyo and their rules and regulations are similar to those in the West. Youth hostels are convenient for one-night stays, but at busy holiday times they are popular and heavily used and need to be booked ahead. Membership and further information are available at the Japan Youth Hostel Association, Hoken Kaikan, 1-1 Ichigaya-Sadohara-cho, Shinjuku-ku, Tokyo (tel: 03 3269 5831). The National Tourist Office (see page 264) has a free pamphlet listing all youth hostels in Japan, with their locations on a map.

Love hotels
Because most Japanese live in very small houses or apartments with their families, it is very hard for young unmarried or even married couples to find somewhere to make love privately and out of earshot of other people. The problem also arises for people carrying on affairs which they want to keep secret from family and neighbours. Society's solution is short-stay hotels, called love hotels or *avec* hotels. Such establishments are quite common and their advertisements giving the details of facilities offered are to be seen in most large cities. The adverts are garish but the hotels themselves are run very discreetly. They are normally surrounded by a high wall and the entrances and exits are separate, to limit the chance of embarrassing encounters. The anonymity of guests is closely guarded, and the management tries to offer all the facilities needed to allow clients to indulge in their wildest fantasies. After 10pm the room rates are often lower than those of regular hotels, so if exotic surroundings do not put you off sleeping, they make a cheap alternative for a single night's stay.

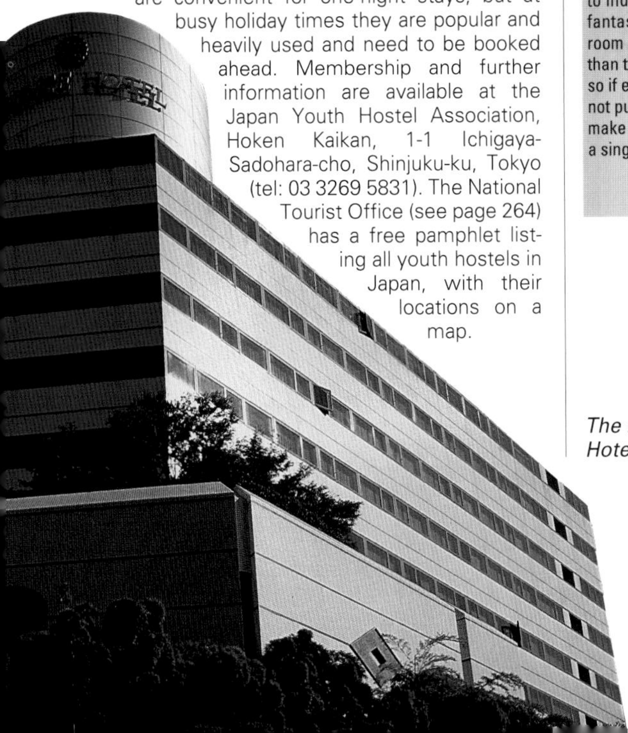

The modern Prince Hotel in Tokyo

■ *Minshuku*, family homes that take in guests, are excellent places to stay for independent visitors to Japan who are on a budget and who want to gain an insight into Japanese life. Foreign guests are treated with real hospitality and warmth by their hosts, once they have established that their visitors respect and understand their customs......■

Enjoying a meal at a minshuku

***Miso* soup**
Japanese meals of the type served at *minshuku* are normally accompanied by *miso* soup and are always served with rice. *Miso* is a very popular soup, which is also served for breakfast. Its base is a fish stock, made from the bonito, which is sold in dried flakes in every food shop in Japan. This stock is then flavoured with *miso* paste. Floating in the soup are small squares of *tofu* and strands of seaweed or finely chopped vegetables. In the Japanese manner the soup is slurped with gusto from the bowl while the solid bits are held back with one's chopsticks. Rice is eaten with every meal, including breakfast.

The most important things to remember are to leave your shoes at the door and not to soap yourself in the hot tub. You can learn other customs as you go along by being careful and observant.

Shoes In Japanese homes, *minshuku* and other places such as temples, small hotels and some restaurants, there are rituals attached to the wearing of shoes that need to be observed. On entering a home, leave your shoes in the hall (this is at a lower level than the house itself), then step up into the house and into a pair of slippers that has been placed out for the family and visitors. Wear these slippers unless you are invited to enter a room laid out with *tatami* mats (closely woven straw flooring). At the entrance to such a room leave your slippers at the door and enter in your stockinged feet. At the entrance to the toilet change your slippers for another pair (these are sometimes marked WC on the toe). Change back into the house slippers when you leave the toilet. Never go into a toilet barefoot.

Bathing For bathing you will be given a small towel and a cotton dressing gown (*yukata*). Undress in the space provided outside the bathroom. Take the small towel into the bathroom with you. Squat on the low stool placed outside the hot tub and scoop water from the tub over yourself with the small bowl provided; alternatively, use the shower that is set into the wall at knee height. Soap up the towel and use it to wash yourself, then shampoo, shave and so on. Finally, shower or scoop water from the tub to rinse off all the soap and rinse out the towel. Now sit in the tub, soak and relax. Once out of the tub, wring out the towel and dry yourself with it, before dressing in your underclothes and the *yukata*. Use of the bath tub is generally restricted to particular times in the evening.

Other customs In a *minshuku* you are expected to set out your own futon and bedding, which will be found in a cupboard in your room. Breakfast and supper are provided, and are served either in your room or in a communal dining area. It is normal for a mixed party of young people to share a room together: this is quite innocent and you will almost certainly be invited to join them for a beer and a chat. The house door is usually locked quite early (at around 11pm).

Finding a *minshuku* Addresses and reservations for *minshuku* can be obtained from the information counters found at most reasonably sized railway stations. It is notoriously easy to get lost in Japanese cities, so ask the information clerk to write the address in Japanese on a piece of paper, take a cab and give this to the driver. As an extra precaution, ask the clerk to mark the location of the *minshuku* on a city map. A detailed list of addresses and *minshuku* customs can be obtained from the Japan Minshuku Association, 1-19-5 Takadanobaba, Shinjuku-ku, Tokyo (tel: 03 3232-6561) or from JNTO.

Japanese toilets
Minshuku sometimes have only Japanese toilets, rather than the Western variety. They are squat, with a hood at one end (this is the end which is faced). The cistern for flushing is filled through a tap which issues water into a sink set over the cistern; wash your hands under this tap. This ingenious flushing method saves both water and space.

A futon bed laid out on tatami *mats*

Food and drink

For Tokyoites, eating out is an integral part of everyday life and many people eat more often in restaurants than they do at home. As a result there is an enormous variety of eating establishments in Tokyo and something to suit every taste and pocket.

This high density of eating places, coupled with the size of Tokyo, usually means that for tourists the most convenient way to eat out is to explore the area in the vicinity of their accommodation. Two notes of caution: first, avoid the places that provide only Western-style fast food, which tend to be expensive; secondly, the Japanese love to eat out and appreciate good food, but they are also happy to pay high prices for an ambience and location that a visitor may not enjoy. Before ordering a meal, always make sure that the price range of a restaurant suits you.

The menu In the restaurant, deciphering a menu and ordering what you want when you cannot read Japanese is greatly simplified by the common practice of displaying very realistic wax models in showcases outside the entrance. The type of bowl or plate containing the model indicates the national origin of the meal: large bowls with patterns round the rim are Chinese; plain or delicately patterned bowls or lacquered boxes are Japanese; and flat plates hold European or American dishes.

Customs Once seated in the restaurant you will be given *oshibori*, *o-hashi* and *o-cha*. *Oshibori* are small, napkin-sized damp cloths, heated in cold weather and cold in hot weather. Use them to wipe your hands and face, and then as napkins during the meal. *O-hashi* are chopsticks. *O-cha* or green tea is as much a part of Japanese life as black tea is for the British. It is the common offering in restaurants, given to customers when they arrive and at the end of the meal, and is always free.

Ready to tuck in at a noodle stall

Economy
If you are travelling on a budget the following tips may help. Western-style foods such as bread, cheese and cakes are more expensive than traditional Japanese foods. Never order a meal before knowing the cost – only the most expensive restaurants do not display prices. Alcohol is expensive, sometimes exorbitantly so, in Japanese bars and clubs. If you are on a budget and would like a drink, it is best to buy it from a supermarket or slot machine and drink it in your hotel room. For snacking or self-catering, buy the made-up lunchboxes of rice, pickles, fishcake and so on sold in grocery shops. Finally, one or other of the many chains of hamburger bars in Japan is always involved in a trade war with a competitor, so look out for special cheap offers.

Fast food in Shibuya

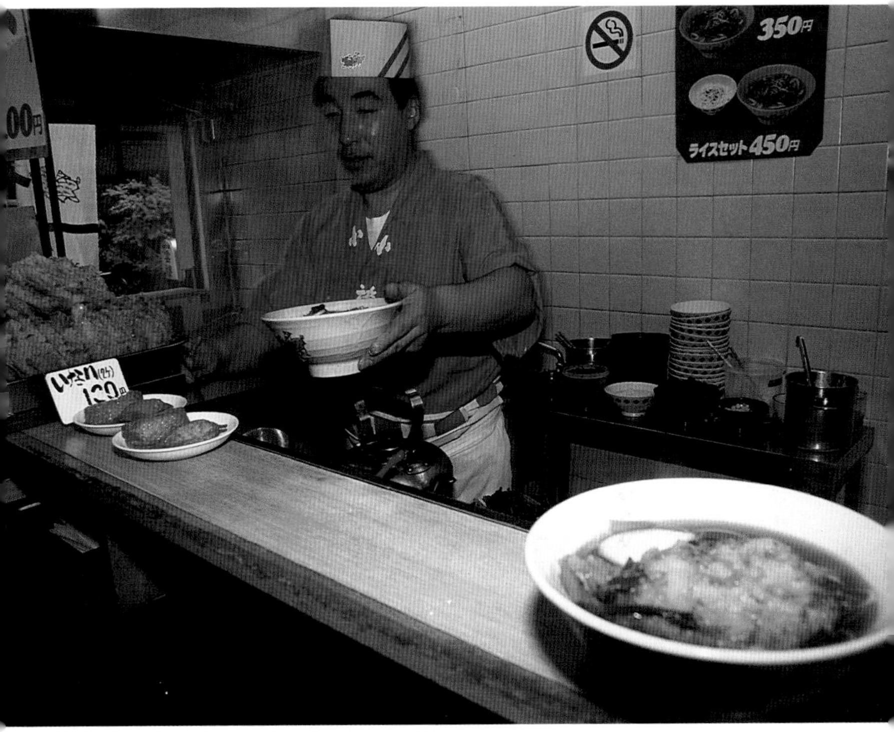

Noodle shop

Places to eat The following are brief descriptions of the various types of Japanese eating establishments.

Sushi-ya, moderately priced *sushi* bars, are the most atmospheric and distinctive of all small Japanese restaurants. They sell rice delicately seasoned with vinegar, sugar and salt, shaped into rolls, patties, balls and so on, and topped and filled with slices of raw, boiled or marinated fish, omelette, vegetables and seaweed. They also sell *sashimi* (raw fish) on its own.

Soba-ya are noodle shops, one of the most common types of restaurant in Japan and one of the cheapest (see pages 84–5).

Nomi-ya are small, basic, local bars and can be recognised by the large red lantern hanging outside. Mainly for drinking *sake* and beer, they also serve snacks, and are relaxing places in which to sit and take time over a drink.

Koryori-ya serve a small menu of popular Japanese dishes such as seasonal fresh fish and vegetables. They are usually small, and each one has a couple of semi-private rooms with *tatami* mats, perfect for a small, intimate, inexpensive dinner.

Chuka Ryori-ya are simple Chinese restaurants, often visited by Japanese families for a cheap meal. They sell Japanese versions of regular Chinese dishes.

Shokudo are small and inexpensive, and sell a selection of the most popular Japanese, Western and Chinese dishes. They always display the complete menu of wax models outside and their relaxed and friendly atmosphere makes them suitable for people travelling alone and particularly popular with students.

***Sushi* chefs**
One of the most entertaining aspects of a visit to a *sushi* bar is watching the chef prepare the *sushi* in front of the customers as it is ordered. Chefs are incredibly deft and quick, and must remember the cost of each person's assortment of orders while preparing and serving the food. The comparative skills of neighbouring *sushi* chefs is a popular topic of debate among connoisseurs.

Noodles

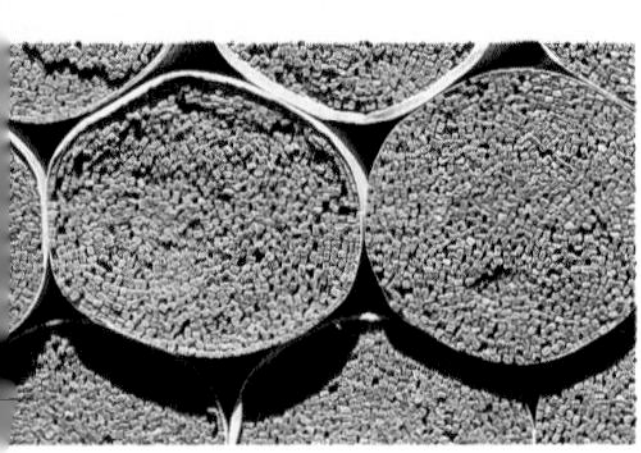

■ Noodles, cheap, fast and tasty, are the original Japanese fast food. Quick service noodle shops are found even in the smallest Japanese town. Many are just stalls or small cafés, while others are more sophisticated establishments with jealously guarded reputations for the quality of their fresh noodles......■

Specialist noodles
Somen, a very fine wheat noodle used in soups, is the only noodle included in traditional Shojin cookery, the vegetarian cuisine of Zen monasteries. In her book *Good Food from a Japanese Temple*, Soei Yoneda mentions that *somen*, in particular, is suited to 'the cooking of nunneries having an Imperial Princess as abbess'. Yellow *somen*, enriched with egg yolk, is called *tamago-somen*; green *somen*, flavoured with green tea and called *cha-somen*, is also available in specialist noodle restaurants.

Above: soba *noodles on sale*
Below: a tempting noodle display

The basic noodle shop menu offers four or five different kinds of noodle, each served in a steaming hot soup with garnishing on top. This is also the way noodles are cooked and served at home. The garnishings could be selected from thin slices of pork, finely chopped leek, *tofu*, *nori* seaweed, *kamaboko* (fishcake), *tempura* (fish or vegetables in batter) or other traditional toppings, but connoisseurs tend to prefer good quality fresh noodles served in a broth, with a little finely chopped spring onion sprinkled over the top – or on their own, with a dipping sauce.

Noodle types Noodles are not differentiated by their shape, as is pasta, but by their ingredients. There are, in fact, only two distinct types: those made with buckwheat flour and those made from wheatflour. The former, called *soba* noodles, are most popular in Tokyo and northern Japan, where the colder climate suits the cultivation of the hardy buckwheat; they are light to dark grey in colour, firm and thin in shape. The most common wheatflour noodle is *udon*, which is soft in texture, flat and round. Other types are the very fine *somen*, the slightly thicker *hiyamugi* and the wide, long and flat *kishimen*. Wheat noodles are white in colour and are favoured in Japan's wheat-growing areas, which stretch south from Osaka. One other popular type, though not traditional, is *ramen*, a Chinese egg noodle. (Incidentally, the Japanese find it difficult to say 'r'; when ordering *ramen* one needs to ask for '*lamen*'.)

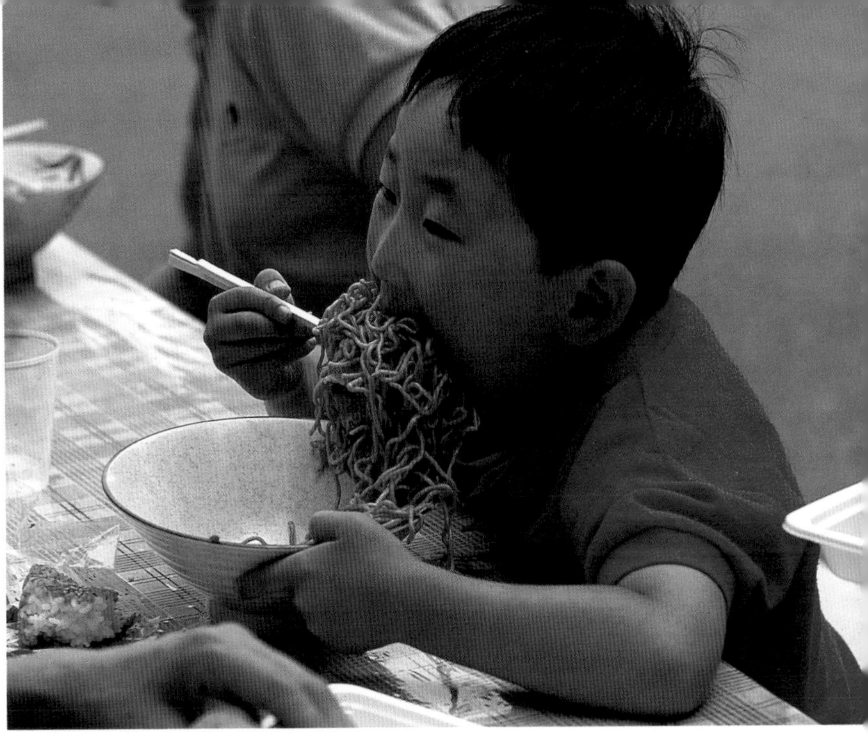

A big helping of noodles for a small mouth

Soba noodles *Soba* is the earliest known variety of Japanese noodle, popular with the noodle *cognoscenti*. Buckwheat was originally made into a gruel, but in 17th-century Edo (Tokyo) a monk called Ganchin discovered that if he mixed wheat and buckwheat flours he was able to make a dough that could be cut into noodles that held their shape. *Soba* noodles became the fashion and there are many references to them in the literature of the time. The best *soba* was (and still is) *ni-hachi* or 'two-eight', meaning two parts wheatflour to eight parts buckwheat. Nowadays, *soba* is served as a hot broth or on its own, boiled, either hot or cold, as a separate course. In this case the cooked noodles are served in individual bamboo lattice baskets, set in a square wooden frame. *Cha-soba*, or green tea *soba*, is made by mixing powdered tea with the buckwheat dough; recognisable by its distinctive green colour, it is often served in this manner. *Udon*, wheatflour noodles, are served in the same way as *soba* and the two are interchangeable in practically all dishes.

The art of slurping Eating noodles in the Japanese fashion requires a lack of inhibition. They should be eaten piping hot, straight out of the broth, and this involves sucking them fast into the mouth while simultaneously drawing in a cooling intake of breath. The result, if done properly, is a loud slurping noise. Once the noodles are finished, the remaining soup is sucked straight from the bowl with equal noise and gusto. For a Westerner, trained to eat quietly, this requires shedding a lifetime's conditioning. For practice without embarrassment, go to any noodle shop in Japan at lunchtime, where you can consume a bowl of steaming noodles among the crowd of customers, with accompanying slurping noises, and not be noticed.

Popular noodle orders
Kake-soba: noodles in broth with chopped leek garnishing, basic and cheap.
Zaru-soba: plain noodles served as *cha-soba*.
Kitsune-soba or *udon*: noodles in broth with fried *tofu* and leek garnish.
Tempura-soba or *udon*: noodles in broth with *tempura* and leek garnish.
Nabe-yake udon: vegetables, *tempura*, egg and noodles cooked in an earthenware pot.
Ramen: Chinese noodles in pork broth with sliced pork topping and leek or spinach garnish.

Shopping

A temple tourist shop

Presents
Choosing from an immense range of options is the biggest problem when buying gifts. Popular items include kitchen knives, paper goods, Japanese pottery, chinaware, chopsticks, fabrics, lacquerware, dolls or cloisonné (fine wire patterned onto a metal base, with a fired glass finish filling the spaces). The following stores sell traditional folk arts and crafts: **Bingoya**, 10-6 Wakamatsucho, open Tuesday–Sunday 10–7 (the nearest subway station is Akebonobashi, a 15-minute walk away); and **Oriental Bazaar**, 5-9-13 Jingumae, open Friday–Wednesday 9:30–6:30 (the nearest subway stations are Harajuku or Meiji-Jingumae, each a few minutes' walk away).

Tokyo is every shopper's dream, not only for the amazing range of goods available but also for the quality of the service. White-gloved, kimono-clad ladies welcome you into the better shops and department stores. Inside, the assistants are polite and helpful, and will wrap even the smallest purchase as though it were a precious stone.

Department stores For presents or souvenirs it is best to go to a department store (*depato*). This will save you a lot of walking about, and the vast range of merchandise offers plenty of ideas. Each store is a self-contained world, in which all human needs, from baby clothes to funeral arrangements, are politely and enthusiastically looked after; and each one has a particular style and price range. If you are on a budget, choose the medium to cheap stores: the service and the goods will still be of an excellent standard.

Some of the best-known department stores include: **Mitsukoshi**, 1-7-4 Nihonbashi Muromachi, Chuo-ku, which has its own subway station; **Seibu**, 21-1 Udagawacho, Shibuya-ku, one of the most innovative and modern stores (visit the separate hardware section called Loft and the basement food hall); **Wako**, 4-5-11 Ginza, Chuo-ku, an exclusive and expensive shop with an amazing range of watches, known for its pre-war clocktower, a favourite meeting place for couples; and **Takashimaya**, 2-4-1 Nihonbashi, Chuo-ku, the flagship of Tokyo's department stores, with opulent décor to match the vast array of famous fashion-named goods. Most of these stores are in the Ginza district, within walking distance of one another.

Fashion and electronics Fashion buildings provide several floors of fashion boutiques, restaurants, bars and other facilities. The best known are **Axis**, 5-17-1 Roppongi, Minato-ku, **Parco**, 15-1 Udagawa-cho, Shibuya-ku and **La Foret** (for everything a teenager may wish to buy), 1-11-6 Jingumae, Shibuya-ku. **Tokyo Hands**, 12-18 Udagawa-cho, Shibuya-ku, is the most amazing DIY shop in the world, said to have over 3 million different items for sale. **Wave**, 6-2-21 Roppongi, Minato-ku, is a 'concept retailing outlet', with several floors of audio and visual software, such as video tapes and discs, compact discs, music cassettes, records, sheet music and books.

Japan is a world leader in electronic goods, but they are often more expensive in Tokyo than elsewhere. There is, however, an incredible variety of goods on offer and the latest models and innovative equipment are often for sale in the showrooms several months earlier than anywhere else in the world. Go to Akihabara subway station and simply choose one of the nearby shops (remember to ask for an export model, as Japanese voltage is 100V).

Tax-free Foreign visitors to Japan can generally buy tax-free goods in any stores that display a 'Tax-free' sign. Most major department stores, hotel arcades and specialist shops in tourist areas offer this facility. Savings range between 5 and 40 per cent. Take your passport with you to the shop; export forms detailing the goods you have bought will be attached to it. Customs officers may wish to see the goods when you leave Japan. Electrical goods, cameras, watches and precious stones are the types of items normally on offer. In large cities like Tokyo, similar goods may also be bought in discount stores at reduced or even lower prices.

Pots and pans for the shoppers

Opening hours and sales
Department stores, and most other retailers, open at 10am, and normally close at 7pm (old-fashioned and family-run shops vary widely). Department stores are closed one day a week (the day varies with each store), and for the New Year (1–2 January). Discounts of 30–50 per cent are common during the summer (mid-July to end August) and New Year (3 January to mid-February) main sales.

A modern shopping mall in Shibuya

Arts and crafts

Japan's long tradition of arts and crafts has come to define its culture not only within the nation itself but worldwide. Among the better known of the fine arts are *ukiyo-e* (the woodblock prints of the Edo period), calligraphy and *ikebana*, the highly skilled art of flower-arranging. The performing arts are defined by *noh* theatre, *kabuki* and *bunraku*, while pottery, ceramics, sword-making and lacquerware are the best known of the Japanese crafts......

The essence of craft
In Japanese arts and crafts the artist or craftsman struggles to extract the essence, or true personality, of the form or material used. The motive is not to dominate the medium but to work with its nature. Realism, rather than romanticism, is usually the watchword.

Under the banner of *mingeihan*, crafts of the people, many less well-known Japanese craft skills are practised. In dance and music traditional forms are still maintained and performed, while in the arts of *chanoyu* (the tea ceremony), bonsai and garden design the Japanese exemplify their love of artifice, nature and ritual. The source of this rich heritage is that idiosyncratic Japanese mix of Zen simplicity and Shinto nature worship, together with a class system that ensured the continuity of the master and apprentice relationship through many generations.

Woodblock printing *Ukiyo-e* ('images of a floating, transient world') was a school of painters in the 18th and 19th centuries who gave new life to the art of woodblock printing. Renowned for their realism, bold designs and striking colours, they were led by four great masters: Utamaro, Sharaku, Hokusai and Hiroshige, 'discovered' by Europeans in the late 19th century (see panel, page 60).

Theatre *Noh* is a stylised dance drama performed to the accompaniment of music and singing. On a stark stage, actors wear masks and gorgeous, elaborate costumes. Movement is slow and the storyline conveyed by a symbolism sometimes difficult for foreigners to understand. However, it is worth a visit for an insight into the contemplative nature of Japanese arts.

Kabuki (see pages 58–9) features only male actors, who play both male and female roles. They wear traditional costume and the plays depict either the lives of ordinary people, or those of the noble classes, in a Japan of earlier times. The dialogue and gestures used to convey the stories are formalised but there is an energy, colour and accessibility in *kabuki* missing from *noh* theatre.

In *bunraku* (puppet theatre), the main character puppets are manipulated by as many as three puppeteers and are very lifelike. The stories told are similar to *kabuki* tales: the scripts are traditional and usually well known by the audience. Osaka is considered the birthplace and capital of *bunraku* theatre (see page 119), although first-class performances are also given in theatres in Tokyo and Kyoto.

The tea ceremony In the authentic setting of a tea garden, the tea ceremony combines the spirit of a religious

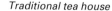

Traditional tea house

Japanese dancers

service with the style of a performing art, and perhaps it best encapsulates all the strands of the Japanese artistic sensibility. At its deepest level 'the way of tea' aspires to create such an atmosphere of harmony and tranquillity that the participants will experience the same qualities in their own hearts and minds. Tea ceremonies are held in Tokyo and Kyoto for foreigners. They are necessarily rather perfunctory affairs but nevertheless interesting, and the green tea gives an unexpected buzz!

The ritual of tea-making
Before the arrival of guests to a tea ceremony, a room or tea house overlooking a garden is set aside and thoroughly cleaned. Utensils are polished, flowers arranged and the garden is swept. When the guests arrive, conversation is quiet and contemplative. At the right moment the host spoons the green powdered tea and hot water into each guest's cup and then whisks it into a foam. As each guest sips tea comment may be passed on the beauty of the tea cups and other utensils as they are handed around for appreciation. Guests may also express their gratitude to the host and mention the delights of the garden or other natural phenomena such as the sky or moon (see also pages 126–7).

Kabuki *theatre*

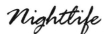

Nightlife

Discos
Entry fees are high for discos, but the price often includes drinks and simple food. Dress is normally smart and the better discos do not welcome unaccompanied males. Roppongi district is the disco heaven, as well as being the centre for live music dance clubs.

Tokyo's nightlife is limitless, and many members of the working population go straight from the office to a bar or club for a drink and a chat before either going home or continuing an evening's carousing. The night starts early, at about 6pm, and, for most, ends before midnight.

After midnight, night owls and young people about town head for Roppongi, where the clubs and discos stay open until the early hours of the morning. For respectable entertainment the Ginza, Asakusa and Akasaka districts provide everything from neon-lit dazzle to the traditional singing, dancing and *samisen-* (guitar-) playing of kimono-clad *geisha*. For a more *risqué* night out, Shinjuku, especially its Kabuki-cho area, and the smaller Dogenzaka in Shibuya provide massage parlours, sleazy bars and strip joints. These places are expensive and not aesthetically pleasing, but even here you do not need to worry unduly about physical safety or theft. For cinema, theatre and other cultural events the monthly *Tokyo Journal*, available in hotels, at the city TIC (Tourist Information Centre) offices or English-language bookshops, gives comprehensive listings and details of performances, as well as restaurant reviews and up-to-the-minute information on events of interest to English-speaking foreigners.

Music Jazz, introduced into Japan during the 1930s and reintroduced after the war by GIs, remains very popular. Tokyo contains a number of jazz clubs, featuring live jazz ranging from Dixieland to *avant garde*. Japanese jazz fans are knowing and dedicated. Japanese and Western pop and rock is widely catered for in clubs and at concert venues. Classical concerts are available most nights of the week, with performances from visiting orchestras or one of the many Tokyo symphony orchestras. Details for all musical events are given in the *Tokyo Journal*. (See also pages 26–7 and 88–9).

A Tokyo night club

Even taxi rides can be slow in Tokyo

Before going to Japan, contact the nearest Japanese National Tourist Organisation office in your country (see page 264) and ask for tourist maps of Japan and Tokyo. If you do not book accommodation in Tokyo in advance, ensure that you arrive in the city in time to visit a Travel Information Centre (TIC) office before 5pm – there is one at Narita airport and one in the city centre – where you will be given help in finding a suitable place to stay.

Information As soon as you arrive in Tokyo obtain, either from the TIC office or from any large railway station, an English-language subway map. This is essential. Before deciding what to do in the city get a free copy of *Tour Companion*, a weekly English-language newspaper for tourists, and buy a copy of the monthly *Tokyo Journal*. Both these publications contain details of current events, and both are available at TIC offices and large hotels. For taped information (in English) on current events phone 3503-2911. The Tokyo English Life Line, on 5721-4347, helps with personal problems. For practical advice and information on hotels, restaurants and sightseeing, contact the TIC office.

Getting about Driving a car in Tokyo is no fun. Traffic is dense and parking expensive and difficult. Buses are slow because of the heavy traffic and destination signs are shown only in Japanese. Fortunately the rail and subway networks are fast, efficient, clean and comprehensive, in terms of the places tourists may wish to visit. Services operate from the very early morning to around midnight. After this time you can rely on a good taxi service; between 11pm and 5am a 20 per cent taxi fare surcharge is payable. See pages 92–3 and 252–4 for more tips on public transport.

Subway signs

Main line stations

■ Shinjuku, Ueno and Tokyo stations are the three busiest stations in Tokyo. Between them they handle over 3 million passengers a day commuting within the city and travelling to destinations throughout Japan......■

The Tokaido Sanyo line
The Tokaido Sanyo Shinkansen rail service opened in 1964, just before the Tokyo Olympics. At that time it linked Tokyo and Osaka, a distance of 552km, and followed for most of its length the route of the old Tokaido highway between Edo (old Tokyo) and Kyoto. Nowadays the line reaches Fukuoka (Hakata station), on the southern island of Kyushu. Trains leave Tokyo station three or four times an hour for the 1,069km, six-hour journey.

Shinjuku station This is said to be the world's biggest and busiest station. It serves nine railroad and subway lines, as well as accommodating huge complexes of shops and restaurants, both above and under the ground. Shinjuku station is the equivalent of a small city; any visitor who masters it will be able to use the city's other stations with ease.

Shinjuku has two wings, divided by two long parallel passageways, off which run a maze of underground shopping parades. Subway and surface lines run into the station for both private lines and Japanese Railways (JR, itself now privatised). If it is necessary to change from a private line to a JR line, you must pass out through a ticket barrier, find your next line and purchase a new ticket (this is not needed if you change lines within the same company's network). To buy a ticket, find your correct rail or subway line, then use the ticket machine nearest the line entrance. If you make a mistake (and it is quite easy to do so, as the signs and instructions are sometimes only in *kanji*), there is a refund office – but it is not easy to find. If you do not know how much your ticket will be, buy the cheapest and pay the excess at your destination. This is a common practice.

If you get lost, take your time to wander around until you pick up a signpost in English to help get your bearings. The ticket collectors at the barrier gates are also very

Bullet trains – coming to rest...

helpful and used to dealing with bewildered travellers.

Avoid Shinjuku if you have a busy timetable. Otherwise, you can happily enjoy it as a place of interest in its own right. On a rainy day Shinjuku is an especially good place for window shopping and people-watching.

Tokyo station Housed in an old red brick building, Tokyo station was designed by Kingo Tatsuno, one of Japan's first modern architects. It was completed in 1914, damaged by wartime bombing and restored in 1954. A new east extension containing the Daimaru department store was added two years later, and there are current plans to renovate and remodel the original building. The bus stop for the Tokyo City Air Terminal (TCAT), where luggage for international flights may be booked in before taking a coach to Narita airport, is located outside the south exit of the station. Buses leave from this exit for Narita airport.

Marunouchi, the district to the west side of Tokyo station, is a major business centre. Its name means 'within the castle compound'; this area was once within the walls of the Shogun's castle. From Marunouchi central exit an avenue leads to the Imperial Palace grounds.

JR Ueno station The JR station at Ueno in northern Tokyo was the gateway to Japan's first public park, museum and zoo, and remains the exit and arrival point for travellers to and from Japan's northern provinces. It was completed in 1883 and became a focal point for people migrating to Tokyo from villages in Tohoku to the north. Ueno-Hirokoji, the main thoroughfare of Ueno, runs from the Shinobazu exit (south side) of JR Ueno station. It is lined with restaurants, stores and discount shops, and the back alleys are teeming with small places to eat and drink.

...and on the move

Travel by Shinkansen
Shinkansen (bullet) train platforms at Tokyo and JR Ueno stations are divided into carriage-length spaces, and above the exact place that each carriage door will be there hangs a numbered plate. This relates to the passenger's ticket, and you should wait in the appropriate place, as the Shinkansen pulls into and out of the station within the space of five minutes.

Leaving Tokyo
JR trains to the Japan Alps (Matsumoto) use Shinjuku station, while the JR Shinkansen and JR express trains on the Tokaido line (to Nagoya, Kyoto, Kobe, Osaka, Hiroshima and the island of Kyushu) use Tokyo station. The JR Shinkansen and express trains on the Tohuku line (to Sendai and Morioka) use Ueno station, as do the JR Shinkansen and express trains on the Joetsu line (to Niigata).

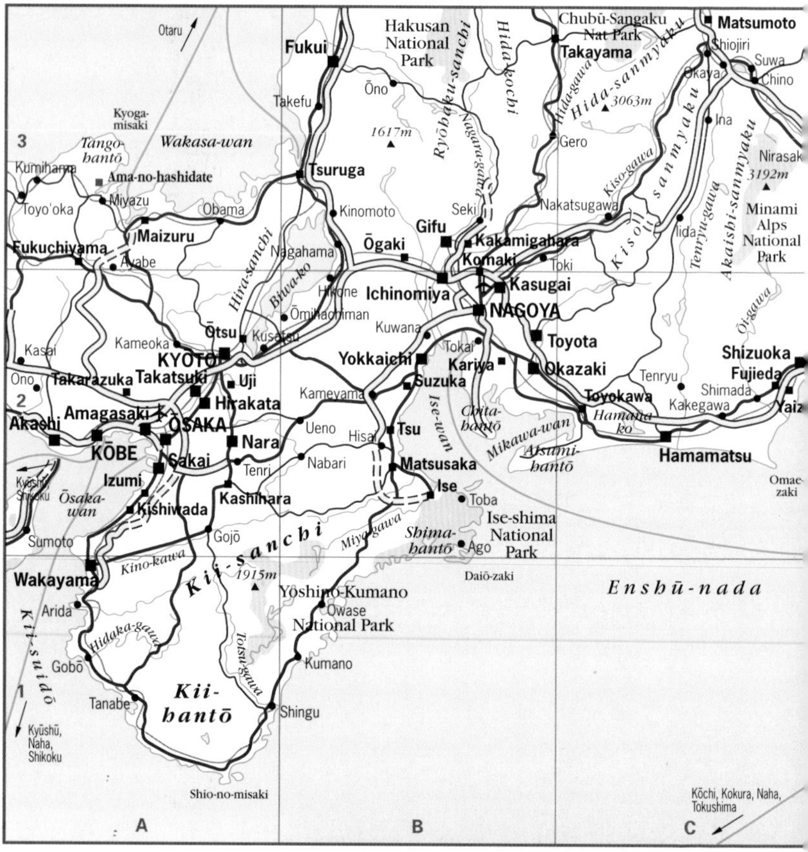

94

Grandeur reflected: Mount Fuji

CENTRAL HONSHU

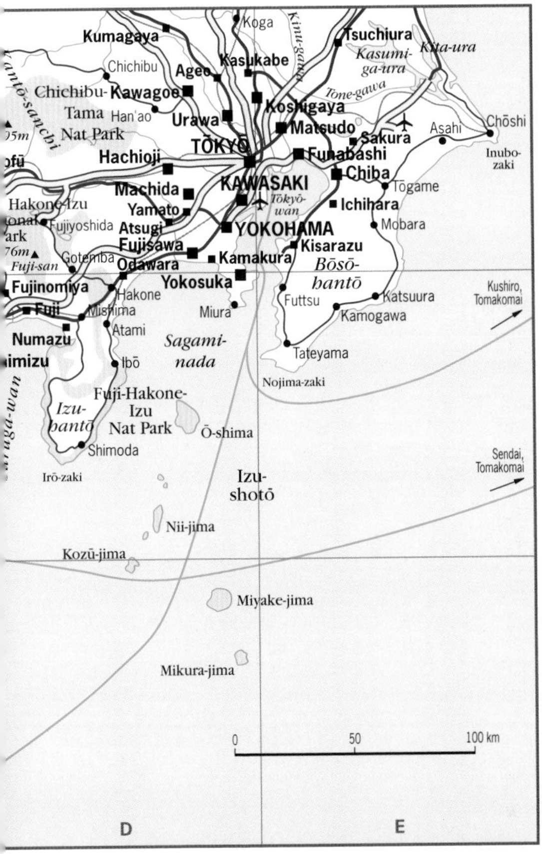

A deity guards the entrance (above) of Horyuji Temple in Nara (detail, below)

Central Honshu With its heavy concentration of business, educational and cultural activities, Central Honshu is second only to Tokyo in economic importance and density of population. Historically, it constitutes the geographical, cultural and spiritual heart of Japan, containing within its boundaries the two ancient capital cities of Kyoto and Nara and the sacred mountain of Fuji-san. This chapter concentrates on the Fuji-Hakone-Izu and the Ise Shima National Parks and the cities of Osaka, Kobe, Nara and Nagoya; for convenience of use and clarity, a separate chapter is devoted to Kyoto.

Fuji-Hakone-Izu National Park Located 96km south-west of Tokyo, this is possibly the most popular excursion destination for residents of the capital, and is busy with visitors throughout the spring and summer months. The park actually includes several distinct areas: Mount Fuji, the Fuji Five Lakes, the Izu Peninsula and Hakone, a hot spring resort area that lies within a 40km-diameter volcanic crater at the base of Mount Fuji.

Osaka Japan's major port and centre of commerce once had a reputation for being grimy, chaotic and cramped. Some of that description still holds true, but Osaka is a city of immense energy and the city fathers, with an eye to the economic and sociological importance of ecological issues, are spending considerable sums of money in an attempt to improve the city environment. Osaka is not a tourist town, nor are there many places of scenic or historic interest to visit, but for a keyhole view of real Japanese city life, and the closest there is to a working-class Japan, it should not be missed.

Kobe Osaka's main port, Kobe, built on a hillside overlooking Osaka Bay, is a major industrial city, rivalling Yokohama as Japan's busiest port. Kobe has a long history as a harbour city, but real growth began in the late 19th century, when the port's docks were opened to foreign shipping. Western-style merchants' houses may still be found in the city, which continues to be occupied by a substantial number of foreign residents. Despite the 1995 earthquake (see page 112) Kobe remains a modern, cosmopolitan and sophisticated city, good for shopping, nightlife and international cuisine.

Nara From AD710 to 794 Nara was the first political and cultural centre of a united Japan. However, the capital moved to Kyoto towards the end of the 8th century and Nara slowly lapsed into relative obscurity. This was a blessing in disguise, as the city escaped much of the war damage suffered by other cities in Japan's long civil wars. As a result, Nara and the monastery estates around it contain some of the best examples of traditional Japanese architecture and art that can be seen today. The sights may be approximately divided into two areas: those in and around Nara Park, a large but not very attractive park well known for its sacred tame deer; and the southwest district of the city, where several major temples are situated. Modern Nara is a large city with a population of 300,000.

Ise Shima National Park Located on the Shima Peninsula, which juts out into the Pacific Ocean, this park is the site of the Ise Shrine, the most venerated Shinto shrine in the whole of Japan. This is the symbolic home of Amaterasu, the sun goddess and ancestral divine spirit of the Japanese imperial line. The park itself stretches to the east from Ise to Toba, centre of the pearl industry, then to the south to Kashikojima, famous for its coastline and pine-clad islands.

Nagoya Japan's third largest city was flattened during World War II by Allied bombs and rebuilt according to the best city planning theories of the time. As a result, Nagoya is architecturally sterile and uninteresting – an agreeable place to live in, but not necessarily to visit. It is, however, a central location for excursions to other towns and areas, especially Gifu for the cormorant fishing.

Kansai and Kanto
For practical purposes, Central Honshu is a sensible description of the area covered in this chapter. However, in terms of the way the Japanese divide their country, it straddles two regions: Kansai and Kanto. Kansai, or 'west of the barrier', refers to the region containing the cities of Osaka, Kobe and Kyoto. Kanto, `east of the barrier', refers to the region around Tokyo. The 'barrier' is an arbitrary division between Kansai and Kanto, made by the government in the 10th century and marked by three barrier stations along its length.

Getting to Osaka
Osaka is connected to Tokyo by more than 100 express trains a day, and international flight connections between the cities are normally free. Prices are a little lower and hotel accommodation is easier to get here than in Kyoto or Tokyo, so it can be a convenient base for exploring Kyoto, Nara and Kobe.

Getting to Nara
Nara tends to be a place that tourists visit on day trips, as there is not much accommodation. The JR Nara line connects Kyoto to Nara (68 minutes); trains run twice an hour. The JR Kansai line connects Osaka to Nara (30 minutes); trains run three times an hour. A city map and walk route is available from the tourist office in Kintetsu-Nara station (first floor). Kintetsu (a private railway) services are quicker and more frequent than those of JR.

Osaka Castle

Mount Fuji and Lake Ashi

Back to Tokyo
As an alternative to returning to Tokyo all the way by bus you may take a bus from Kawaguchiko to Mishima on the Shinkansen JR line for Tokyo. The scenic bus journey, which circles Mount Fuji, takes two hours. From Mishima it is just over one hour by bullet train to Tokyo.

Fuji-Hakone-Izu National Park

This area of crater lakes, volcanic mountain ranges, hot springs and beaches, 100km southwest of Tokyo, is the most heavily visited national park in Japan. The original wildness of the habitat has been sacrificed to some extent to the needs of tourists, but this is still a beautiful area. Indeed, the Japanese believe that the symmetrical reflection of Mount Fuji (Fuji-san) in the calm surface of Lake Ashi-no is *the* most beautiful sight in the world. The park may be divided into four distinct areas. Although a grand tour of them at one time is possible many visitors prefer to make separate excursions from Tokyo. On pages 101, 102–3 and 108–9 three of the areas – Mount Fuji, Hakone and the Izu Peninsula – are described individually; the fourth, the Fuji Five lakes, is described below. Throughout spring and summer the whole park is busy with visitors, but at other times, partly as a result of the colder weather, it is relatively quiet. See map on page 100.

►► Fuji Five Lakes (Fuji-Goko) *100A6*

Kawaguchiko (Kawaguchi-ko)►►, on the southeastern shore of Lake Kawaguchiko, is the area's transportation centre, served by train and bus services from Tokyo and from other regions of the national park. Buses also go from Kawaguchiko station to the other four lakes. The town itself is a busy resort with a mix of *ryokan*, hotels, restaurants, bars and souvenir shops. A 10-minute walk from the station leads to the shore of Lake Kawaguchiko, and fine views of the lake and Mount Fuji can be had from the observation tower at the top of Mount Tenjo, reached by a ropeway (cable-car) operating from the lakeside near the station. From the nearby pier, cruise boats offer 30-minute tours of the lake. Other attractions are the Fuji Museum on the north shore (an odd mix of geology and history exhibits and a display of erotica), open 8:30–4, and the Fuji-kyu Highland Amusement Park, one train stop from Kawaguchiko station. Kawaguchiko is the most developed and visited of the five lakes.

Lake Shoji (Shoji-ko)▶▶▶ opens on its southeast side towards a glorious view of Mount Fuji, while the other three sides are secluded and enclosed by wooded mountains. The smallest of the lakes, and considered by many to be the prettiest, this is the starting point for the Shoji Trail, which leads through Jukai, 'the Sea of Trees' (see panel) all the way to the summit of Mount Fuji. Lake Shoji is 50 minutes by bus from Kawaguchiko station. Ice-skating and fishing (through holes in the ice) are popular winter activities for visitors.

Asahigaoka, a commercial district on the southern shore of **Lake Yamanaka (Yamanaka-ko)▶**, the largest of the lakes, is 35 minutes by bus from Kawaguchiko. Favoured by affluent young Tokyoites, the lake shore is heavily developed with fashionable restaurants, expensive hotels, college and company clubhouses and villas. Cruise boats from Asahigaoka offer short tours of the lake.

Lake Saiko (Sai-ko)▶, the third largest lake, lies to the west of Kawaguchiko and may be reached from there in 25 minutes by bus. The lakeside is only moderately developed and apart from hiking there is little to do.

The westernmost and deepest of the five lakes is **Lake Motosu (Motosu-ko)▶**. It never freezes over and is renowned for its beautiful blue waters and fine trout. The bus stop on the eastern shore is 50 minutes from Kawaguchiko. Apart from the souvenir shops in the immediate vicinity of the bus stop, the lake shore and surroundings are quiet.

Sea of Trees
Called the Jukai in Japanese, this area is a part of the Aokigahara Forest, between lakes Saiko and Shoji. The trees survive on a thin layer of volcanic soil covering a field of lava, which is magnetic and distorts compasses, making it easy to get lost. Fortunately, a marked nature trail can be picked up at the Fugaku Fuketsu (lava caves) near the Fuketsu bus stop, 40 minutes from Kawaguchiko bus station (platform 6).

Getting to Hakone or Izu Peninsula
To go to Hakone from Kawaguchiko take the bus to Gotemba. Change at Sengoku for Hakone-Yumoto or Togendai in the Hakone region. The Izu Peninsula is reached by bus from Mishima (see **Back to Tokyo** panel, opposite page).

Map overleaf: Fuji-Hakone-Izu National Park

Lake Yamanaka

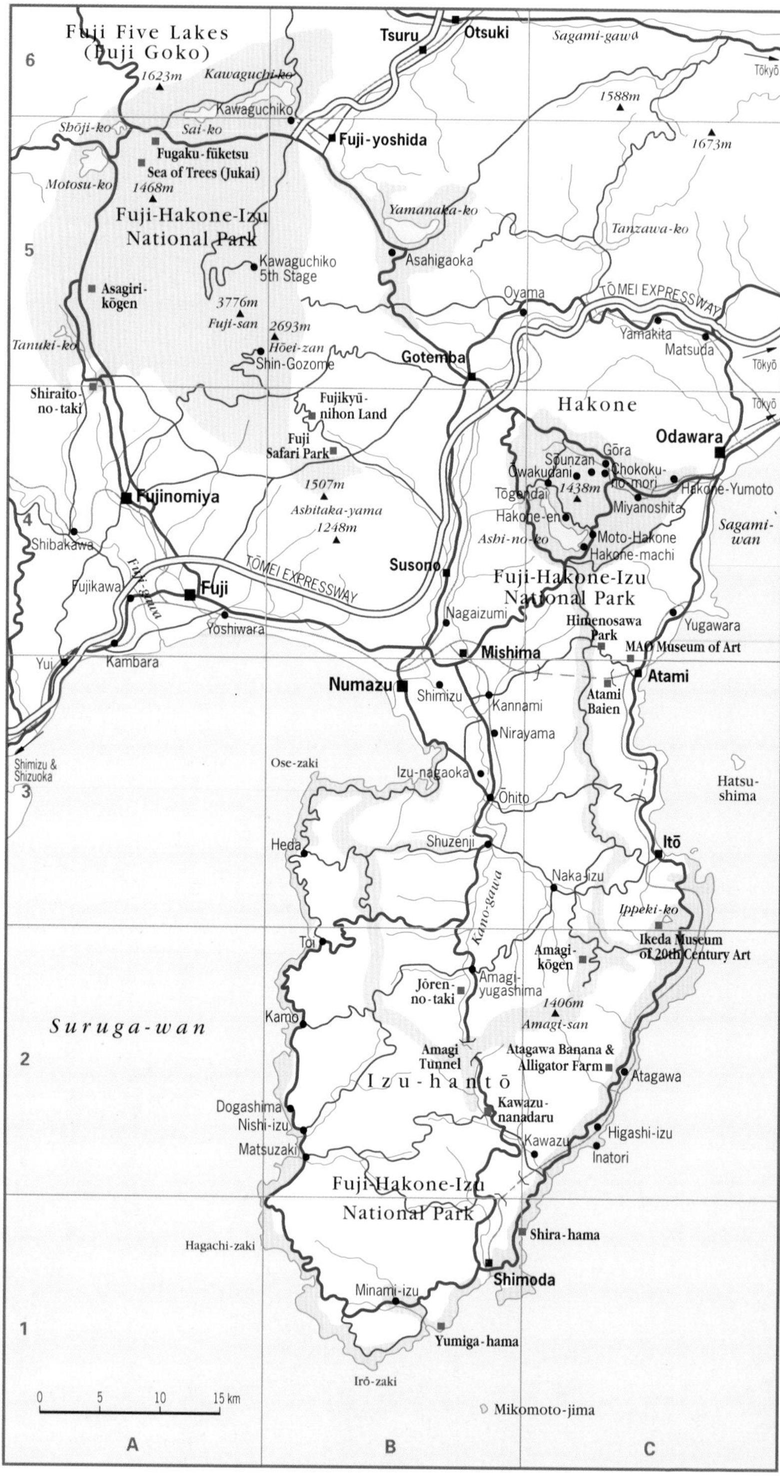
Fuji Five Lakes (Fuji Goko)
1623m
Kawaguchi-ko
Kawaguchiko
Tsuru
Otsuki
Sagami-gawa
Tōkyō
1588m
1673m
Shōji-ko
Sai-ko
Fuji-yoshida
Fugaku-fūketsu
Sea of Trees (Jukai)
Motosu-ko
1468m
Fuji-Hakone-Izu National Park
Yamanaka-ko
Tanzawa-ko
Kawaguchiko 5th Stage
Asahigaoka
Asagiri-kōgen
3776m
Fuji-san
2693m
Hōei-zan
Oyama
TŌMEI EXPRESSWAY
Yamakita
Matsuda
Tanuki-ko
Shin-Gozome
Gotemba
Tōkyō
Tōkyō
Shiraito-no-taki
Fujikyū-nihon Land
Hakone
Odawara
Fuji Safari Park
Gōra
Sōunzan
Chokoku-no-mori
Ōwakudani
1438m
Hakone-Yumoto
1507m
Tōgendai
Miyanoshita
Fujinomiya
Ashitaka-yama
Hakone-en
Sagami-wan
1248m
Ashi-no-ko
Moto-Hakone
Hakone-machi
Shibakawa
Susono
Fuji-gawa
TŌMEI EXPRESSWAY
Fuji-Hakone-Izu National Park
Fujikawa
Fuji
Nagaizumi
Himenosawa Park
Yugawara
Yoshiwara
MAO Museum of Art
Yui
Kambara
Mishima
Atami
Numazu
Shimizu
Kannami
Atami Baien
Nirayama
Shimizu & Shizuoka
Ose-zaki
Izu-nagaoka
Hatsu-shima
Ōhito
Heda
Shuzenji
Itō
Naka-izu
Kano-gawa
Ippeki-ko
Toi
Ikeda Museum of 20th Century Art
Amagi-kōgen
Amagi-yugashima
Jōren-no-taki
1406m
Amagi-san
Suruga-wan
Kamo
Amagi Tunnel
Atagawa Banana & Alligator Farm
Izu-hantō
Atagawa
Dogashima
Kawazu-nanadaru
Nishi-izu
Higashi-izu
Kawazu
Matsuzaki
Inatori
Fuji-Hakone-Izu National Park
Shira-hama
Hagachi-zaki
Shimoda
Minami-izu
Yumiga-hama
Irō-zaki
0 5 10 15 km
Mikomoto-jima
A
B
C
1
2
3
4
5
6

Mount Fuji

Mount Fuji (Fuji-san) is a perfectly shaped volcanic cone, rising to a 3,776m peak. It is the highest and most popular mountain in Japan, praised by Japanese poets through the ages and portrayed in numerous paintings and prints. The summit is frequently covered with clouds but on a clear day it can be seen from as far as 160km away......

Hokusai (1760–1849), the famous artist, immortalised the mountain in two series of woodblock prints featuring Fuji-san in all its moods: *Thirty-Six Views of Mount Fuji* and *One Hundred Views of Mount Fuji*.

The ascent Most people climb Mount Fuji in the hope of witnessing a sunrise from the top. This means either climbing overnight or climbing during the day and staying on the summit overnight in a mountain hut. It is an arduous climb and, once past the treeline, the mountain at close quarters is not beautiful. The rock is black and volcanic and there is no vegetation. Only the view (if there is no cloud) lifts the spirits. The Japanese say that to climb Fuji-san once is wise but to climb it twice is foolish.

Mount Fuji is open to the public for climbing from 1 July to 31 August and every year up to 400,000 people make the ascent along one of the five trails marked off at 10 stations (levels). Kawaguchiko Fifth Station, which is halfway up, is the most popular starting level, and may be reached by bus. From Kawaguchiko the climb to the summit at a moderate pace is about seven hours; the descent takes half this time.

During the winter months Fuji is snow-covered from base to peak, and even in summer the summit is never clear of snow.

Hakone Komagatake Ropeway, with Mount Fuji in the distance

Sacred mountain
A Shinto shrine to Konohana Sakuya Hime, a divine princess who is the spirit of the cherry blossom, is maintained on the summit of Mount Fuji. The mountain itself is considered sacred by Shintoists, and especially revered by a religious sect known as Fujiko. Pilgrims making the ascent dressed in traditional white tunics and gaiters are a regular sight. Women were not allowed on Mount Fuji or other sacred mountains until the Meiji Restoration (1868).

Getting there
The easiest way to reach Kawaguchiko Fifth Stage is by direct bus from either Hamamatsucho or Shinjuku bus terminal, in operation several times daily from 9 July to 31 August. Less frequent bus services are also available from about the end of April to July and again during September and October. Journey times are two and a half hours from Shinjuku and three hours from Hamamatsucho.

Contemplating the view at Lake Ashino

Hakone Shrine
The Hakone Shrine was founded in 757 in Moto-Hakone, one of the busiest tourist towns in the Hakone area. A red *torii* gate out in the lake provides an obvious landmark and a huge Japanese cedar tree (*cryptomeria*), encircled by a sacred rope, sits in the forecourt. Known as *Yatate no sugi* ('standing arrow cedar'), the tree marks the spot where generals fighting battles in the area offered arrows to the gods. The shrine is also famous as the site of an act of filial piety by the two Soga brothers, medieval warriors who earned fame for their military exploits. In the past *samurai* would come here to venerate the spirits of these men of honour.

►►► Hakone *100C4*

Lying between Mount Fuji and the ocean in Fuji-Hakone-Izu National Park, Hakone is an area of high mountains (most over 1,220m), with Lake Ashi nestling in the centre and Mount Fuji nearly always in view to the northwest. This is a very popular day-trip destination from Tokyo, and during the summer months trains, cable cars, buses and accommodation in the region are heavily used. However, Hakone's beautiful scenery, its closeness to Tokyo and its network of public transportation make it an attractive and convenient place to explore.

Travelling to Hakone The cheapest way to travel to and around Hakone is to purchase the Hakone Free Pass. This will allow you to follow the route described below without extra cost. From Shinjuku station in Tokyo take the Odakyu private railway to Odawara (one hour, 25 minutes; buy your pass from the Odakyu ticket office in Shinjuku). If you travel in the more expensive 'Romance Car', with its comfortable seating and viewing windows, go one stop further to Hakone-Yumoto. Hakone-Yumoto is the oldest of Hakone's spa towns, with a famous *sennin-buro* ('thousand-people baths') in the town centre. From here or Odawara, take the Hakone Tozan Tetsudo line for Gora.

The train travels slowly up steep mountainsides; with each switchback the views increase in grandeur. One of the earlier stops is **Miyanoshita►**, a more sophisticated and smaller resort than

Shrine detail, Hakone

Hakone-Yumoto. Further along the line is **Chokoku-no-mori▶▶** and the Hakone Open-Air Museum (open daily 9–4:30), with Western and Japanese sculpture in an open, cliffside setting. The train terminus is at **Gora▶**, a small town popular with hikers and climbers. Transfer to the cable-car up to Sounzan. Here transfer to the Hakone Ropeway, the longest gondola ride in Japan (33 minutes). Some way out of Sounzan the ropeway crests a ridge and suddenly you are suspended over the **Owakundani Gorge (Great Boiling Valley)▶▶▶**, hundreds of metres below. From the gorge floor sulphurous steam spurts out of cracks in the earth and clouds of reeking fumes hover in the air. If you ask the conductor, you can get off at **Owakundi▶▶**, the next stop and the ropeway's highest point, for a hike along a nature trail and a visit to the Natural Science Museum (open daily 9–5).

The ropeway finally descends to Togendai on the shores of **Lake Ashi▶▶▶**. From here cruise boats travel to Hakone-machi. Look out for reflections of the surrounding mountains, particularly Mount Fuji, in the lake surface. The mountains bloom with cherry blossoms in April, azaleas in May and June and red maple leaves in autumn.

Historical route The old Tokaido Road between Kyoto and Edo (old Tokyo) ran through Hakone, and one of the most important barrier gates was in **Hakone-machi▶▶** (see pages 104–5). The Barrier Guardhouse (Hakone Sekisho) has been reconstructed and some of the cobbled and narrow Tokaido Road is preserved. A short walk from where the boat docks, the guardhouse and exhibition hall display mannequins of guards and travellers, *samurai* armour and weapons and macabre early photographs of crucified and beheaded criminals.

For solitude and a feeling of old Japan, walk down the nearby tree-lined stretch of the old Tokaido Road. A bus service operates from Hakone-machi to Hakone-Yumoto (50 minutes) and onwards to Odawara (one hour). From here take the Odakyu line back to Tokyo.

Volcanoes
The Japanese islands lie in the volcanic zone that surrounds the Pacific Ocean and volcanic eruptions have always affected the lives of Japanese people. Physically, many Japanese volcanoes are shaped like a cone with a wide base (Fuji-san is the best-known example). They are formed by a build-up of layers of lava issuing from an erupting crater. The death and life brought by volcanoes and their imposing presence on the landscape have always given them an elevated place in the Shinto pantheon of divine spirits (*kami*). Many traditions and festivals designed to appease them are still maintained.

Mount Fuji provides a dramatic backdrop to Lake Ashino

Alternate attendance

■ The second Tokugawa *shogun*, Iemitsu, inherited his title in 1616. An even more ruthless soldier and cunning politician than his predecessor, Ieyasu, he understood how to maintain and widen his power. With the introduction of his political control system, *sankin kotai* or 'alternate attendance', he ensured that the Tokugawa clan would stay in power in Japan for over 200 years......■

Signposting
As the remaining short stretch of the original Tokaido Road shows, the Tokaido was not very wide and, because no carts used it, was unmetalled. Distances were carefully marked, as this quote from a 17th-century Portuguese traveller illustrates: 'There is no need to enquire about distances because all the leagues are measured out, with a mound and two trees to mark the end of each one. Should it happen that a league ends in the middle of a street, they will do no man a favour by making the measurement either longer or shorter, but pull down the houses there in order to set up the sign.'

Sankin kotai required each of the feudal lords, or *daimyo*, of Japan's noble families to build a substantial home in Edo (old Tokyo) and to spend alternate years in residence there while in attendance at the *shogun*'s court. The year in between was to be spent on the noble's own estates. Close family members of the *daimyo* were restricted at all times to their homes in Edo and the surrounding district. At one stroke, the *shogun* ensured that at any one time half his feudal lords were under his eye at court and for the rest of the time he could, if need be, hold their families hostage. He also required that on his journey from his estate to Edo each *daimyo* should have with him a stipulated entourage of soldiers, ladies-in-waiting, servants and craftsmen. The size of the entourage was directly proportional to the size of the *daimyo*'s estate, and the outlay required to pay for it was designed to ensure the *daimyo* never had enough money to finance a rebellion.

The Tokaido Road This law also meant that *daimyo* had to travel between their estates and Edo once a year. There were five main routes radiating from Edo, and the Tokaido, which followed the eastern seaboard to Kyoto, was the most travelled. It was used not only by nobles from the western provinces but also by normal traffic journeying between the seat of government and Kyoto, the home of the emperor and the religious capital of the land.

The Tokaido followed the coast from Edo to Yokkaichi before striking inland to Kyoto via Kameyama, Otsu and the southern end of Lake Biwa. The scenery along the way was both picturesque and rugged: open sea, land-locked bays, distant mountains (including Mount Fuji), high cliffs, paddy fields and many towns and villages all came in and out of view along the route. These changing

The changing seasons upon the Tokaido Road

landscapes and colours and the human traffic on the road were the inspiration for Hiroshige, the great woodblock print artist, in his *Views from the Fifty-Three Stations of the Tokaido*.

Noble progress The journey of a great lord along the Tokaido was an impressive sight. Nobles were carried in beautifully lacquered palanquins. Attendants bore aloft colourful banners and the marching men and *samurai* on horseback wore full uniform. The whole effect was designed to illustrate the power and authority of the lord.

A noble procession was heralded well in advance so that post stations and inns could prepare beforehand for the extra provisions, horses and accommodation that would be required. Other travellers who knew of it would also stay clear of the road, both for their own safety and in order not to hinder the progress of the lordly personage. The procession was preceded by horsemen, who would shout 'Down! down!' and people of inferior rank were required to prostrate themselves on the ground as the *daimyo* passed. Anyone foolish enough to show disrespect and refuse to pay homage in this way was literally chopped down by one of the *samurai* escorting the lord.

Barrier gates Barriers such as the Hakone barrier gate ensured that none of the *daimyo* could move any of their families out of Edo without permission. This applied especially to womenfolk and any woman travelling with a procession was subjected to the closest scrutiny. As well as discouraging travel, the system also gave rise to many Japanese stories of intrigue, adventure and thwarted love.

Aristocratic traffic
Carriages drawn by oxen were the sole privilege of the imperial court and would normally only be seen in and around Kyoto. If a *daimyo*'s procession leaving the Tokaido crossed the path of the carriage of an aristocrat from the Imperial Palace, the *daimyo* himself would have to get out of his palanquin and prostrate himself on the ground. To avoid this embarrassing situation the *daimyo* would send a guard ahead to offer gifts of money to travelling aristocrats with the suggestion that it was a good time to stop for refreshments.

▶▶▶ Ise Shima National Park *94B2*

Set on Shima Peninsula, which juts out into the Pacific Ocean in east central Honshu, Ise Shima National Park covers a total area of over 550 sq km. Its fame derives from the Ise Jingu Shrines, also called the Grand Shrines of Ise, which enshrine the Sun Goddess Amaterasu o Mikami, the ancestral divine spirit of the Japanese imperial line. Apart from its beautiful coastline and mountainous interior, Ise Shima's other attractions are the cultured pearl farms at Toba, the 'wedded rocks' of Futamigaura, and Ago Bay, at the southern tip of Shima Peninsula, with its host of tiny islands and abundant marine life. The simplest way to tour Ise Shima is to start in the small town of Ise, the northern gateway to the park and location of the Grand Shrines, then move south down the peninsula to Toba and on to Kashikojima town (on Ago Bay's largest island, connected by bridge to the mainland) for a boat trip around Ago Bay.

Ise is one hour, 25 minutes from Nagoya on the private Kintetsu Ise Shima line and two hours from Kyoto or Osaka on the Kintetsu Yamada line. Trains and buses connect Ise to Toba and Kashikojima. Tour buses travel from the Inner Shrine to Toba along the Ise Shima Skyline Highway, crossing over Mount Asama, the roof of the peninsula.

The **Ise Jingu Shrines▶▶▶** are the most important of Shinto shrines, consisting of the Outer Shrine, the Inner Shrine and over 100 minor shrines. The Outer Shrine (Geku), first erected in the 5th century AD, is dedicated to the goddess of food, clothing and housing and is surrounded by a tranquil forest of old Japanese cedars. Each morning offerings of food, attended by a white stallion from the emperor's stables, are made at the shrine. The main building, like that of the Inner Shrine, is made of unpainted cypress wood joined without nails. Both shrines stand on wooden piles and are roofed with thatch in the style of ancient Japanese houses. Only members of the imperial family and high-ranking priests are allowed into these buildings, which are surrounded by wooden palisades and are out of sight of the ordinary tourist. This does not deter the thousands of Japanese who visit the shrines every year. For them Ise Shrine is a magical place, embodying the very heart of old Japan. The Outer Shrine, 10 minutes' walk from Ujiyamada, Ise town's main

Futamigaura
Futamigaura, connected to Ise and Toba by bus or train, is the site of the 'wedded rocks', which represent man and wife. Large straw ropes, used in the Shinto religion to mark sacred spaces and to symbolise marriage, connect the two rocks. On the larger, 'husband' rock is a *torii* gate, which is also used to denote a sacred space. The Japanese tend to visit at dawn, to see the sun rising between the two rocks.

The Three Sacred Treasures
Ise Shrine houses the sacred mirror (*Kagami*), one of the three imperial regalia symbolising imperial power. According to legend, the sun goddess sent her grandson to Japan so that he and his descendants could rule over the country. Before he left she gave him three insignia: a mirror, a sword and a set of jewels. As she handed him the mirror, she is said to have remarked, 'When you look upon this mirror, let it be as if you look upon me'. The sword is kept in Atsuta Shrine in Nagoya and the jewels are in the Imperial Palace in Tokyo.

Shopping in traditional dress at Ise

station, is approached through a large wooden *torii* gate and down a long avenue lined with various pavilions. Visitors are stopped at the third of the four gates that lead to the shrine.

The Inner Shrine (Naiku), founded in AD260, is about 6km from the Outer Shrine; the two are connected by a regular bus service. By far the most important of the two, it closely resembles Geku Shrine in its structure, general layout and practical arrangements. Enshrined in the deepest recesses of Naiku is the Sacred Mirror, one of the Three Sacred Treasures of the Shinto religion (see panel). Through the first *torii* gate and after the second small bridge approaching the shrine, pilgrims and visitors wash and purify their hands and mouths with water from the Isuzu River, whose source lies within the Inner Shrine.

Toba▶ is a prosperous port town, whose main point of interest is Mikimoto Pearl Island, a five-minute walk from Toba station, connected to the mainland by Pearl Bridge. The Pearl Museum and Mikimoto Memorial Hall, on the island, trace the fascinating story of the cultivation of pearls. *Ama* (women divers) in traditional white outfits demonstrate how the women of Shima Peninsula used to dive for oyster pearls as well as abalone, seaweed and other sea foods (open 8:30–5; 9–4:30 20 November to 28 February). Toba Aquarium, five minutes from Toba station, has an impressive collection of sea creatures including otters and the dugong, a small whale.

Crossing the bridge to the Inner Shrine

Reconstructed shrines
The Inner and Outer Shrines are torn down and rebuilt every 20 years in a ritual known as *shikinen sengu*. The present buildings are the 60th in succession. Financial difficulties recently resulted in an embarrassing delay of the tradition, due to have been repeated in 1993. For each shrine there are two sites, one occupied and one vacant. The old wood from a demolished shrine is cut into pieces and given to the pilgrims at the ceremony.

Loose tea ready for sale at the Grand Shrines of Ise

►► Izu Peninsula *100C3*

The Izu Peninsula, which juts out from the mainland into the Pacific Ocean in Fuji-Hakone-Izu National Park, has a mountainous interior, a dramatic coastline, fine beaches and many hot springs. Only about an hour from Tokyo station by Shinkansen bullet train to Atami, at the northern

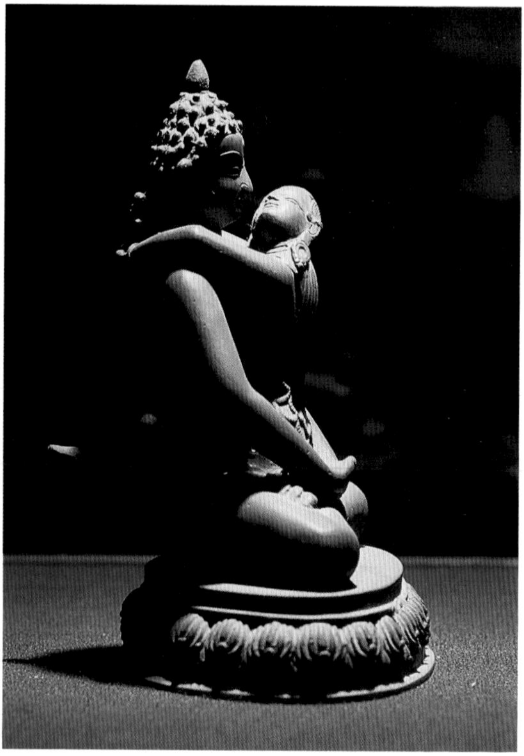

Erotic art at Ryosenji Temple, Shimoda

end of the peninsula, Izu is a popular resort with the residents of Tokyo. During mid-July to the end of August the region is very crowded and to be avoided (at the least, make sure your accommodation is reserved in advance). Regular train and bus services operate along the scenic east coast from Atami to Ito, a spa resort and Shimoda, location of the First American Consulate. From Shimoda there are bus services around the southern tip of the coast to Dogashima, a small fishing village, on the less developed west side of the peninsula, or through the mountainous interior to Shuzenji, a traditional and rather prestigious spa town. From Shuzenji there are trains back to Atami or Mishima and on to Tokyo. Alternatively, for a complete peninsula round trip, there is a bus service from Dogashima to Shuzenji. The Izu Peninsula has numerous hotels, *ryokan* and *onsen minshuku*, a sort of hot-spring bed and breakfast where your room is in a large family-style house fitted with a public bath fed by underground hot springs.

Atami►, one of the largest and best-known hot spring resorts in Japan, is a collection of hotels, souvenir shops, red-light districts, bars and restaurants. Many of the

Will Adams
William Adams was born in Kent in 1564. At the age of 12 he was apprenticed to a shipyard, where he studied astronomy and navigation as well as shipbuilding. In 1598 he set out from Holland as chief pilot of a fleet heading for the Orient. After a long voyage his ship was caught in a gale and washed ashore off the coast of Kyushu. He was taken to Osaka castle and interrogated by Tokugawa Ieyasu himself. The *shogun* was so impressed by Adams and his knowledge of ships that he appointed him adviser on foreign affairs. In 1604, on the *shogun*'s orders, Adams built an 80-ton Western-style sailing ship on the estuary of the Matsa-Kawa River in Ito. Pleased with the result, Ieyasu ordered Adams to build an ocean-going vessel, which the *shogun* lent to a Spanish diplomat, who sailed the ship to Acapulco and never returned it to Japan. Adams was rewarded for his services with a large estate and the status of a *samurai* and adopted the Japanese name Miura Anjin. He died in Japan of natural causes aged 56.

town's visitors are businessmen or workers on company-sponsored vacations and they can get rather noisy and rowdy in the evenings. Unless you wish to visit the MoA (Museum of Art) it is best to treat Atami as a transit point. The museum, located on a hill above the station, was opened in 1982 by a religious organisation founded by Mokichi Okada (1882–1955). It has an excellent collection of Japanese, Chinese and European art, as well as a garden, tea-ceremony room and theatre for *noh* drama (open 9:30am–4:30; closed Thursday).

In 1605 Will Adams, the English ship's pilot who inspired the novel *Shogun*, built a ship at the old established spa town of **Ito▶** for Tokugawa Ieyasu (see panel). Near the harbourmaster's office a shabby memorial stone records his exploits in Japanese and English. Thirty minutes by bus from Ito station is the Ikeda Art Museum, which houses a collection of 20th-century Japanese and Western art in an impressive stainless steel building (open 10–4:30pm; July–August 10–5:30).

Shimoda▶▶ holds an important place in Japanese history, since it was here, in 1854, that the first important trade treaty between America and Japan was signed. All the major sites in Shimoda are connected in one way or another with its American associations (see panel). Shimoda Tourist Office, in front of the station, has an easy itinerary in English.

About one hour by bus from Shimoda, **Dogashima▶▶** is a quiet fishing village in an area of unusual rock formations jutting out from the coast into the sea. A sightseeing boat leaves from the village pier. Dogashima is a place for gentle exploration and relaxation, where you can swim and sunbathe in season.

Shuzenji▶ is a rather expensive inland spa town. The trip there through the mountainous interior from Shimoda is of rather more interest than the town itself (see panel). From Shuzenji, you can travel back to Atami or catch the private railway line to Mishima and change for the Shinkansen to Tokyo.

The road to Shuzenji
From Shimoda, the road to Shuzenji zigzags up Mount Amagi to Nonadani Bridge near the summit, where the mountain is too steep to continue the road. Four massive steel legs standing on a ledge halfway down the mountain support a double spiral structure that carries the road and juts out over the valley thousands of feet below.

Tojin Okichi
In 1857 the first US Consul to Japan, Townsend Harris, moved to a village near Shimoda with his Japanese consort, Tojin Okichi. According to the Japanese, she was forced to leave her lover for Harris and, as soon as he left, committed suicide. She has since become a folk heroine. Harris's version was very different: he claimed that he was offered the girl but refused her, and that after his departure she attempted a reconciliation with her lover which failed. She then opened a restaurant, which was not a success, and finally took to drink.

Fishing boats on the Izu Peninsula

FOCUS ON *Earthquakes*

■ **Earthquakes (*jishin*) are a common phenomenon in Japan. The country sits over the junctions of four tectonic plates, huge sections of the earth's crust which slip against each other, sometimes gently, occasionally violently. Within the plates are fault lines where slippage is rarer but can be catastrophic. Scarcely a day passes without a tremor in some part of the archipelago. Fortunately, almost all are mild, hardly noticed by the inhabitants......■**

Top: the Great Kanto Earthquake of 1923. Above: an earthquake cartoon

Being prepared
Every year on 1 September, the anniversary of the 1923 Tokyo earthquake which left a death toll of over 140,000, Japan observes Disaster Prevention Day. Evacuation procedures are tested and children run through smoke-filled corridors with wet handkerchiefs over their noses and mouths. The Self Defence Force practises helicopter rescues and fire departments rehearse their routines. Simulators the size of a small house put people through the experience of a violent tremor while they try to remember the survival drill.

Unpredictably, every ten or twenty years, a more powerful shock hits a populated area and causes fatalities. At even longer intervals, disaster strikes on the scale of the Great Kanto Earthquake of 1923, which is estimated to have reached 8.2 on the Richter Scale. Its midday timing meant that countless *hibachi*, charcoal grills ready for cooking lunch, ignited the wooden houses of Tokyo and Yokohama as they collapsed. Far more people died in the resulting firestorms than in the quake itself.

Kobe At 5.46am on 17 January 1995, the Great Hanshin Earthquake shook a wide area of southern Honshu with a force measuring 7.2 on the Richter Scale. Its epicentre was somewhere under Awaji island offshore from Kobe, Japan's second largest port with a population of 1,500,000. Worst hit were the residential areas of the city, built in the 1950s and '60s. Thousands of wooden houses collapsed, their heavy tile roofs falling on their inhabitants as they slept, causing many of the 5,000 fatalities. Domestic gas heaters running during the cold winter night ignited fatal fires when main pipes fractured.

The attitude of the survivors was remarkable – a resigned acceptance of their misfortune. In the world's most technologically advanced country, 310,000 people were left with nothing. Their legendary grit was displayed as many walked to work that same morning. If the Japanese reputation for stoicism was reinforced, that for efficiency was undermined. Fire and rescue services were woefully slow to react, and local authorities had to make a written request for help from the Self Defence Force.

Lessons The media savaged the government and bureaucracy for their inadequate response. There was great alarm, too, that buildings, expressways and the tracks of the fabled Shinkansen had not stood up to the shock as well as predicted. What was wrong with the calculations? When cooler assessments were made, it turned out that post-1980 structures, including high-rise buildings, had survived well. More worrying is the evidence that reclaimed land can shake like a jelly, or even behave like a liquid, causing severe damage to Kobe's port installations.

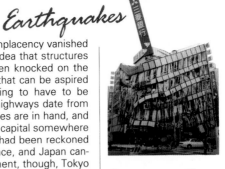

Tokyo In the capital, 20 years of complacency vanished overnight in a shudder of fear. The idea that structures could be 'earthquake proof' had been knocked on the head. 'Earthquake resistance' is all that can be aspired to now, and levels of that are going to have to be stepped up. Some of the elevated highways date from the 1960s. Strengthening programmes are in hand, and there has been talk of relocating the capital somewhere safer, but where? Until 1995, Kobe had been reckoned safe. Seismology is an inexact science, and Japan cannot change its geology. For the moment, though, Tokyo watches and waits for the next inevitable, but unpredictable, earthquake.

Damage caused by the Kobe Earthquake

Painted screen, Kobe City Museum

Cormorant (*ukai*) fishing
Trained cormorants on leashes are used to fish for *ayu* (small trout). To prevent them swallowing the fish the birds are fitted with small rings around their necks. The boats that carry the birds work at night and a bright wood brazier is suspended from the bow to attract the fish.

▶▶ Kobe

94A2

Japan's sixth largest city prospered as a gateway for trade with China in the 15th and 16th centuries. When Japan's isolation ended in 1868, Kobe was among the first ports to open to Western ships. Many foreign traders settled here and it became a cosmopolitan centre, with one of the world's busiest harbours. The narrow strip of land between the mountains and the sea was soon outgrown: residential quarters climbed the slopes, and the port facilities occupied reclaimed land and artificial islands.

Before dawn on 17 January 1995, a devastating earthquake shook the city. Thousands of older houses and small apartment blocks collapsed. More than 5,000 people died and 310,000 were made homeless. Part of the elevated Hanshin Expressway fell over and rail links, including Shinkansen lines, were severed (fortunately the early hour meant that the bullet trains themselves were not running). Buildings put up since 1980, to higher standards of earthquake resistance, survived with little or no damage. Communications were restored, although parts of the port will take years to rebuild.

Many restaurants and shops and most hotels are within walking distance of the two central stations, Sannomiya and Motomachi. The lively entertainment quarter, Ikuta, lies west of Sannomiya and Japan's biggest 'Chinatown' is just south of Motomachi. Main street names are given in English as well as Japanese.

Shinkansen trains connecting Kobe and Osaka (15 minutes), Kyoto (33 minutes) and Tokyo (3 hours 30 minutes) use Shin-Kobe station, a short subway ride from Sannomiya station. Both have good information desks.

Kobe City Museum▶▶, 24 Kyomachi, Chuo-ku, is a 10-minute walk south of Sannomiya station. It specialises in the history of Kobe, the influence of Western taste and techniques on Japanese design, and the way the Japanese viewed Westerners, shown in amusing scrolls and screens. The building and some exhibits suffered damage in the 1995 earthquake and the museum closed for repair. (Normal hours 10–5, closed Mondays. Ask hotels or information centres whether it has reopened.)

Kitano▶▶ is a hilly district of narrow streets, a 15-minute walk north of Sannomiya, where Western traders and other foreign residents have lived since the 19th century. Some of the houses are open to the public.

The Atsuta Sword
Prince Yamatotakeru was a legendary war hero of the 3rd century. The sword which saved his life during a military campaign is that held (but not displayed) in Atsuta Shrine, Nagoya. It is called Grass-Cutting Sword, because the prince used it to cut the grass down around him when it was set alight by attacking bandits. The Yamato originated the rule of the Japanese emperors, and the shrine housing the sword was later given the highest rank of a Shinto shrine.

▶ Nagoya *94B2*

Razed to the ground by Allied bombing during World War II, Nagoya has since been rebuilt and is now the fourth largest city in Japan. There are few historical attractions for the visitor except its two national treasures; Nagoyajo Castle and the Atsuta Jingu Shrine. This is, however, a convenient base for the Grand Shrines of Ise (see pages 106–7), Nara (see pages 114–15) and Gifu (see below). Shinkansen bullet train services connect Nagoya with Kyoto (43 minutes), Osaka (one hour) and Tokyo (two hours, 30 minutes).

Nagoyajo Castle▶▶▶ was built in 1612 as a residence and military base for the Tokugawa clan. The five-storey donjon castle was destroyed in World War II, and a copy, built in 1959, houses treasures such as screen paintings and sliding doors. Two bronze dolphins covered with gold scales, reconstructed atop the castle roof, are believed to protect it from fire. Ninomaru garden and Ninomaru Tea House are next door (open 9:30–4:30).

Atsuta Jingu Shrine▶▶▶, 1-1-1 Jingu, Atsuta-ku (subway: Jingunishi), houses the sacred sword that is one of Japan's most treasured objects (see panel; open sunrise to sunset).

Gifu▶▶ is 30 minutes by JR train from Nagoya. The main reason to visit is to view the cormorant fishing on the Nagara-gawa river (see panel). This event takes place every evening between 11 May and 15 October. Before and after the fishing, the Japanese gather on the banks of the river to drink, eat and make merry. The tourist office at the station will give you details of how to get to the river and book accommodation.

Atsuta Jingu Shrine

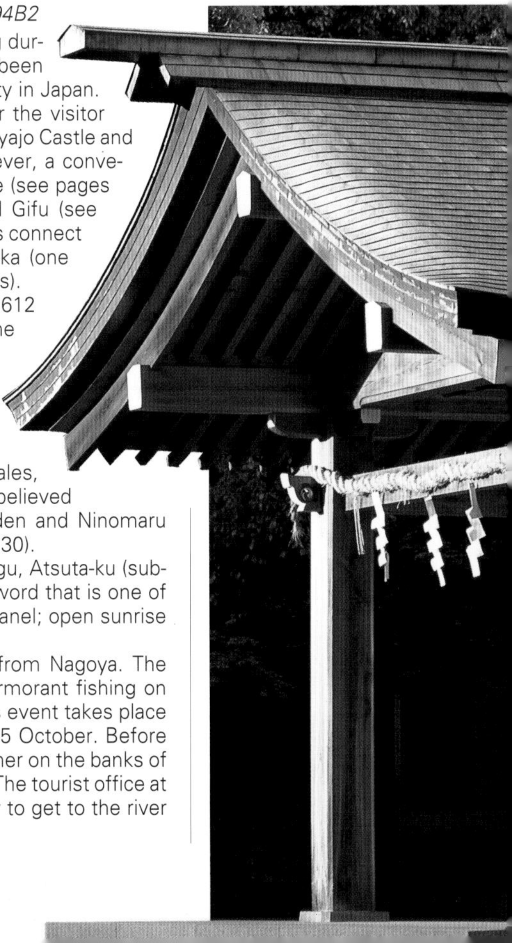

Horyuji Temple

The Great Bronze Buddha
Daibutsuden, the bronze buddha in Todaiji Temple, is 16.2m tall, weighs 750,000kg and took five years to cast. Its completion in AD749 was marked by a spectacular ceremony of consecration in 752, attended by the imperial family. The cost of building Todaiji itself crippled the economy and led to a peasants' revolt.

►►► Nara *94A2*

In order to preserve Shinto ritual purity, the imperial court of ancient Japan moved to a different location on the succession of each new emperor. However, by the 8th century, the size of the state and the administrative arrangements needed to run it finally made this tradition too impractical to maintain. In AD710 Nara was chosen as the first permanent political and cultural centre of a newly united Japan. There followed a great flowering of every field from art to religion, influenced by the imported culture of the Tang Dynasty in China and Buddhism, which was promoted by the Japanese imperial court as a way of unifying the country. During this period many remarkable temples and monuments were built, some of which have survived in Nara and are described below. (For details of how to get to Nara see panel page 97).

To the southwest of Nara, **Horyuji Temple►►►** is a little off the beaten track but well worth a visit. It is the oldest intact temple complex in Japan and houses the world's oldest wooden buildings. Horyuji was founded in 607 by Prince Shotoku, a great patron of Buddhist religion and culture, who made his court into a renowned centre of learning. The complex is divided into the West Temple, containing the Kondo main hall and pagoda, and the East Temple, mainly comprising the Yumedono pavilion and Chuguji Nunnery. Horyuji owns a magnificent collection of Buddhist art (open 8–5; till 4:20pm 20 November–10 March; bus from Kintetsu-Nara station, 40 minutes).

Kofukuji Temple►► is famous for its five-storey pagoda (built in 1426 as an exact replica of the 8th-century original). It is Nara's best-known landmark, and its name, meaning 'Happiness-Producing Temple', dates back to AD710, when it was constructed as a teaching temple for children of the Fujiwara family. Nanendo Hall, which contains a fine gilded statue of Kannon carved in 1188, is a sacred pilgrimage site and is often very crowded. The Kokuhokan Treasure House contains the best of the temple's works of Buddhist art (open 9–5; access from Sanjo-dori Street, running east from Nara JR station).

Founded in 745, **Todaiji Temple►►►**, in Nara Park, was built to be the headquarters of all temples in Japan. For the Japanese it remains the most important sight in Nara. Todaiji's main hall, the Daibutsuden, is claimed to be the largest wooden building in the world. It houses the Great Buddha of Nara, the largest bronze Buddha ever cast, completed in 752 after many years of

Detail, Horyuji Temple

failed attempts (see panel). Entrance to the temple is through the massive Nandaimon gate; look out for the giant wooden statues on either side (open October–February 8–4:30, March 8–5, April–September 7:30–5:30; walk or take number 2 bus from JR or Kintetsu stations: alight at Daibutsuden stop). Todaiji took several thousand carpenters, metal-workers and labourers five years to complete. Its cost crippled the economy and led to a peasants' revolt. Nearly all the original buildings were destroyed in 1180 by the Taira clan, to punish the armed monks of Todaiji for their support of the rival Minamoto clan.

Toshodaiji Temple▶▶, near Nishinokyo station on the Kintetsu Kashiwara line, is one of the loveliest of Nara's temples. It was founded in 759 by the Chinese priest Ganjin, who had been invited to Japan by the Emperor to spread Buddhism and faced many trials on his journey to Japan, including the loss of his sight. At the age of 66 he supervised the construction of this fine temple. The main hall and lecture hall are national treasures. The eight pillars at the front of Kondo Hall show the influence of Greek architecture, which reached Japan via the 'Silk Road' even at this early time (open 8:30–4:30).

Todaiji Temple

Priestly power
The great Buddhist temples of Nara owned large, tax-free estates and with growing prosperity they became increasingly powerful and avaricious. The priest Dokyo, an 8th-century Rasputin figure, became mentor and love of the Empress Koken (718–70). Alarmed by the power of the very temples they had helped to foster, the Fujiwara ruling clan moved the court to Heiankyo (Kyoto) and severed the government's strong Buddhist connections.

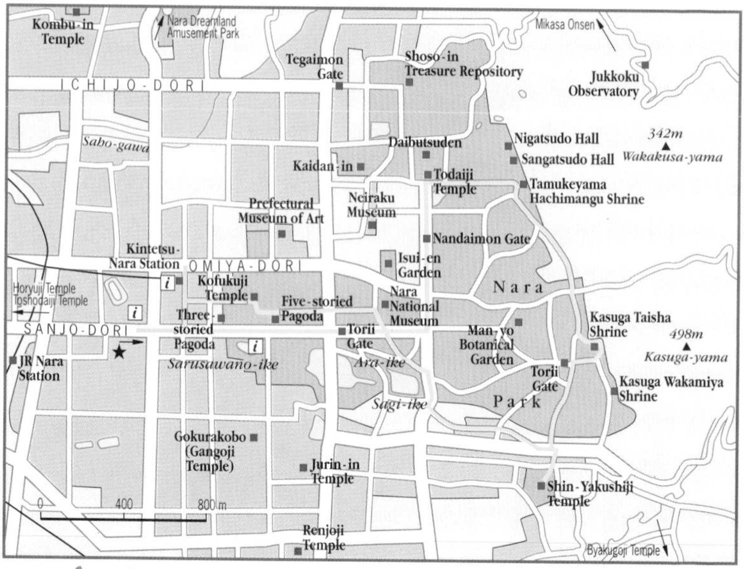

Walk Nara

Distance: 3km; time: two and a half to three hours.

The major historical sites of Nara are laid out in a huge deer park, with the green slopes of the Wakakusayama Hill as a backdrop. Despite crowds of sightseers, Nara is imbued with a sense of peace, a tonic for jarred nerves.

Start from the **Nara City Tourist Centre**, between JR Nara and Kintetsu-Nara stations. Walk two

Main hall, Shin-Yakushiji Temple

Figure at Kofukuji Temple

blocks to the east to discover the three-storey pagoda of **Kofukuji Temple►**, founded in 710 and once comprising over 1,300 buildings. Of the remaining structures, the three-storey pagoda dates from the 12th century, the five-storey pagoda and eastern main hall from the 14th century. The view of the five-storey pagoda from across the neighbouring Sarusawa-no-ike Pond is one of the most famous in Nara. From Kofukuji, continue east, passing through the *torii* gate into the park area, then turn left for the approach to **Todaiji Temple►►**. The temple's main building, the world's largest wooden structure, houses a 16m bronze statue of Buddha, completed in 749.

Over 1,000 tame deer roam the park in Nara. From Todaiji, walk southeast through the park to the **Kasuga Taisha Shrine►►►**, one of the most famous Shinto shrines, with vermilion lacquered buildings set against the deep green woodlands. Thousands of stone lanterns line the approach to the shrine, and many hundreds of bronze lanterns hang from the eaves of the shrine buildings. The grassy slopes of the 342m-high Wakakusayama Hill, north of the shrine, are ritually burned each year on 15 January. South of Kasuga Taisha Shrine, outside the park, is **Shin-Yakushiji Temple►**, another 8th-century monument. Picturesque old houses line the street which leads west from Shin-Yakushiji along the edge of the park. Return to the park, and go back towards the *torii* gate, passing three ponds to the left. This leads to the **Nara National Museum►►**, housing a collection of works of ancient art, including masterpieces of early Buddhist art.

From the National Museum, walk back past Kofukuji to either station.

Bunraku
One of the three classical forms of theatre in Japan, *bunraku* or puppetry has been popular since the 17th century. A typical play could deal with a story of tragic love, a well-known historical event or a comic story of urban life. The puppets, usually dressed in elaborate period costume, are about two-thirds human size, each one made up of interchangeable parts. Each of the major characters is handled by three puppeteers dressed in black. The chief puppeteer (it takes 30 years to become an expert) manipulates the puppet's head, eyes, mouth and right arm and hand.

Nightlife
The busiest nightlife area is around the narrow Dotonburi Street, near Namba station. Here there is a hive of bars, coffee lounges, discos and nightclubs, lit up after dark by gaudy neon signs and a huge, open-air video screen. Singles and *avecs* (couples) throng the streets. For low life, the seamy but fascinating place to go is Shin-Sekai, west of Tennoji Park. This is an area of massage parlours, cheap restaurants and strip joints. The Yakuza (Japanese Mafia) control most of the business and occasionally you can see members cruising by in their extravagantly large, chrome-laden Ford Cadillacs.

▶▶▶ Osaka *94A2*

Osaka is Japan's third largest city. Like Tokyo, it is an important industrial, financial and commercial centre but it has an energy and pride of its own, and its styles and fashions are very different from those of the capital. Osakans describe themselves as *shiminteki*, people with no time for pretensions, and consider Tokyoites to be effete. It is a crowded, busy city with no obvious town planning, where cherry orchards, Buddhist temples, choked traffic, grimy commercial buildings and chrome and glass high-technology skyscrapers all exist side by side.

Getting there and around Osaka is connected to Tokyo by frequent domestic flights and a Shinkansen train service (two and a half to three hours). All trains arrive at Shin-Osaka station. Change here and travel a few stops south on the loop line to Osaka station in the centre of town. Osaka also has a futuristic new airport, the Kansai International Airport (see pages 16–17). The Osaka tourist information office is found at the east exit of Osaka station; staff speak English and the office is open 8–7. The Osaka street system and subway are complicated and it is easy to get lost. Do not explore without a map and a copy of your accommodation address in Japanese.

Osaka is a place to wander, shop and eat. Of the tourist sights the two priorities are Osaka Castle and the National *Bunraku* Theatre. To find out what is going on in Osaka, pick up a copy of *Kansai Time Out*, a monthly magazine with information on sightseeing, festivals, restaurants and other items of interest, available at bookshops, restaurants and other places frequented by English-speaking tourists.

Osaka façades

Downtown restaurant

Osaka is famous for its food and its citizens are known to the rest of Japan as *kuidaores*, or those who will eat to physical and financial ruin. There are restaurants of every type and price throughout the city and choice is limitless. Compared with Tokyo, prices are low.

Shopping For shopping the Umeda area, around Umeda and Osaka station, is the hub of department stores and high fashion shops. It extends beneath the ground, where there is a maze of streets and arcades. Three of the local department stores have their underground basements descending into this subterranean complex. If you get lost, take a lift to the ground floor of one of the stores and head for an open-air exit.

Sightseeing Osaka is considered the capital of *bunraku* (see panel), and if you are in the city you should take the opportunity to see a performance in the **National *Bunraku* Theatre▶▶**, 1-12-10 Nipponbashi, Chuo-ku. Performances are scheduled for six periods each year, with each production running for two to three weeks. Information is available at the Osaka tourist information office. The theatre is two minutes' walk from Nipponbashi station on the Kintetsu line (exit 7).

Toyotomi Hideyoshi, the warlord who unified Japan, built **Osaka Castle▶▶** (Osaka-jo) in 1583 on a strategic hilltop in the city's northern district and used it as his headquarters. After he died, armies of the Tokugawa shogunate (1603–1867) took Osaka Castle in 1615. The castle was also damaged in the fighting that led to the Meiji Restoration of 1868. Its main gate and several towers have survived, however, and the eight-storey donjon, the main stronghold, was rebuilt in 1931. Illuminated at night, it is one of the city's best-known landmarks. Inside the castle is a museum with displays and exhibits relating to old Osaka and the Toyotomi family, but the main reasons to visit are the view from the top of the donjon and the castle's majestic exterior. The park which surrounds the castle is also one of the best places in the city for people-watching (open 9–5). To get to the castle take the JR loop line from Osaka station to Osaka-jo Koen-mae station and walk up the hill.

Food
Favourite local specialities are the street food, *takoyaki*, a wheatflour dumpling stuffed with octopus meat and baked over charcoal; *udon*, a fat, white wheat noodle; and Osaka *sushi*, squares of sticky sweet rice and raw fish. *Chanko-nabe* restaurants, also very popular, are named after the unpretentious stew that is the mainstay of a *sumo* wrestler's diet. The stew is not fattening – the huge amounts of rice wrestlers eat performs that function – but it is tasty and nutritious. Retired *sumo* wrestlers often open their own *chanko-nabe* restaurants and jealously guard their favourite recipes.

Detail, Osaka Castle

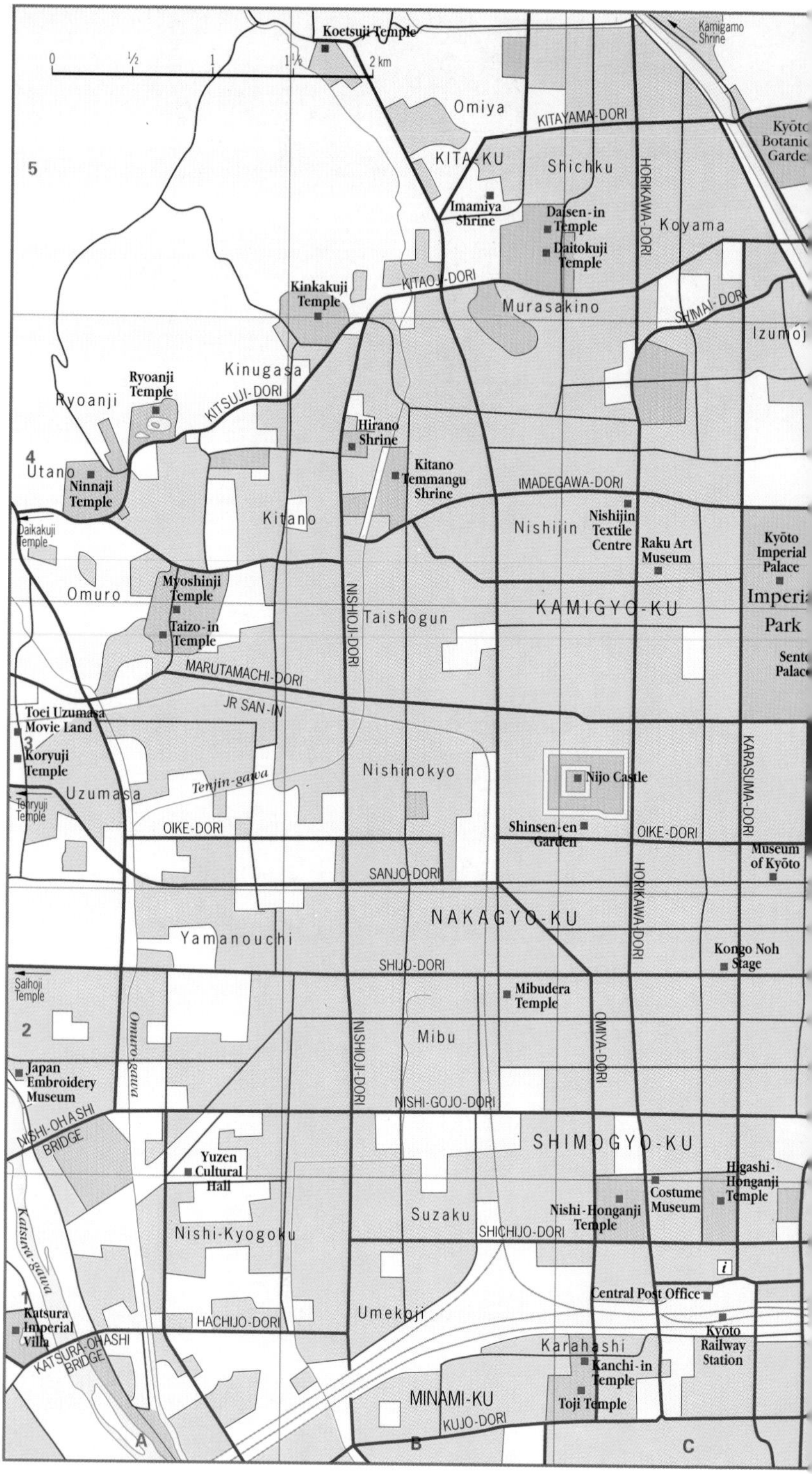
Koetsuji Temple
Kamigamo Shrine
0 ½ 1 1½ 2 km
Omiya
KITAYAMA-DORI
Kyōto Botanic Garde
5
KITA-KU
Shichku
HORIKAWA-DORI
Koyama
Imamiya Shrine
Daisen-in Temple
Daitokuji Temple
KITAOJI-DORI
Kinkakuji Temple
Murasakino
SHIMAI-DORI
Izumoj
Kinugasa
Ryoanji Temple
Ryoanji
KITSUJI-DORI
Hirano Shrine
4
Utano
Ninnaji Temple
Kitano Temmangu Shrine
IMADEGAWA-DORI
Nishijin
Nishijin Textile Centre
Raku Art Museum
Kyōto Imperial Palace
Daikakuji Temple
Kitano
Omuro
Myoshinji Temple
Taizo-in Temple
NISHIOJI-DORI
Taishogun
KAMIGYO-KU
Imperia Park
Sento Palace
MARUTAMACHI-DORI
JR SAN-IN
Toei Uzumasa Movie Land
3
Koryuji Temple
Nishinokyo
KARASUMA-DORI
Nijo Castle
Tenjin-gawa
Uzumasa
Tenryuji Temple
OIKE-DORI
Shinsen-en Garden
OIKE-DORI
Museum of Kyōto
SANJO-DORI
NAKAGYO-KU
HORIKAWA-DORI
Yamanouchi
Kongo Noh Stage
SHIJO-DORI
Saihoji Temple
Mibudera Temple
2
Omuro-gawa
NISHIOJI-DORI
Mibu
OMIYA-DORI
Japan Embroidery Museum
NISHI-GOJO-DORI
NISHI-OHASHI BRIDGE
SHIMOGYO-KU
Yuzen Cultural Hall
Higashi-Honganji Temple
Costume Museum
Nishi-Honganji Temple
Katsura-gawa
Suzaku
SHICHIJO-DORI
Nishi-Kyogoku
i
Central Post Office
1
Katsura Imperial Villa
HACHIJO-DORI
Umekoji
Kyoto Railway Station
KATSURA-OHASHI BRIDGE
Karahashi
Kanchi-in Temple
MINAMI-KU
Toji Temple
KUJO-DORI
A
B
C

KYOTO

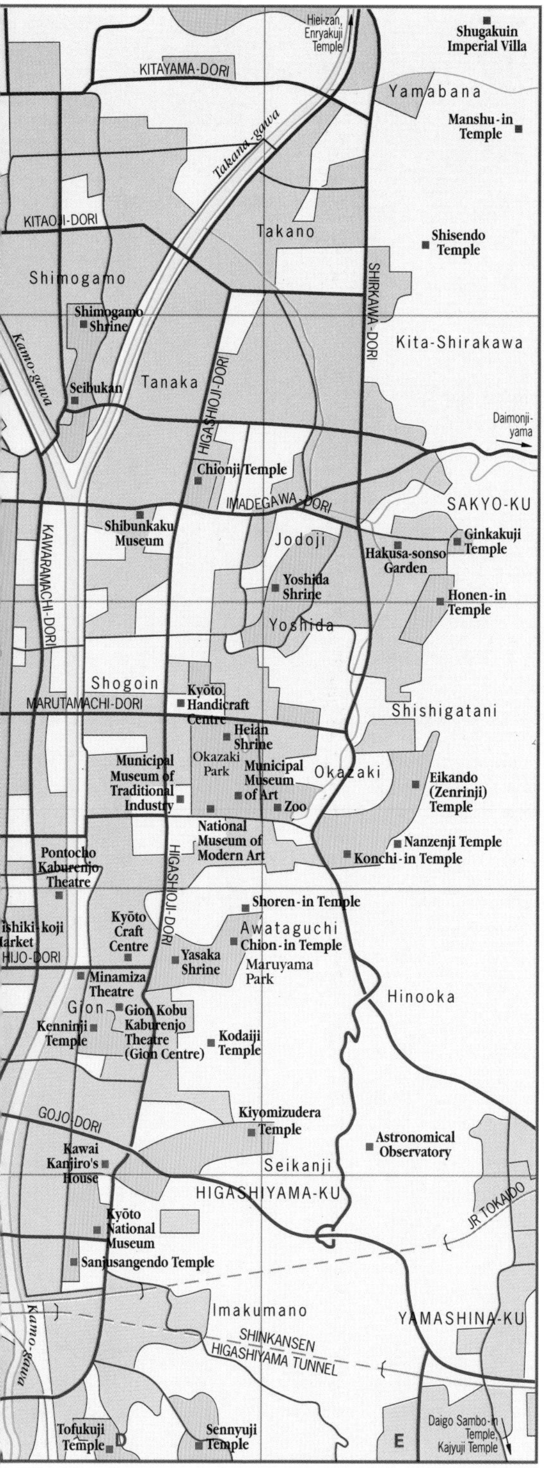

Hiei-zan, Enryakuji Temple
Shugakuin Imperial Villa
KITAYAMA-DORI
Yamabana
Manshu-in Temple
Takano-gawa
KITAOJI-DORI
Takano
Shisendo Temple
Shimogamo
SHIRKAWA-DORI
Shimogamo Shrine
Kita-Shirakawa
Kamo-gawa
Seibukan
Tanaka
HIGASHIOJI-DORI
Daimonji-yama
Chionji Temple
IMADEGAWA-DORI
SAKYO-KU
Shibunkaku Museum
Jodoji
Ginkakuji Temple
Hakusa-sonso Garden
KAWARAMACHI-DORI
Yoshida Shrine
Honen-in Temple
Yoshida
Shogoin
Kyōto Handicraft Centre
MARUTAMACHI-DORI
Shishigatani
Heian Shrine
Municipal Museum of Traditional Industry
Okazaki Park
Municipal Museum of Art
Okazaki
Eikando (Zenrinji) Temple
Zoo
National Museum of Modern Art
Pontocho Kaburenjo Theatre
Nanzenji Temple
Konchi-in Temple
HIGASHIOJI-DORI
Shoren-in Temple
Kyōto Craft Centre
Awataguchi
Chion-in Temple
Yasaka Shrine
Maruyama Park
HIJO-DORI
Minamiza Theatre
Hinooka
Gion
Gion Kobu Kaburenjo Theatre (Gion Centre)
Kenninji Temple
Kodaiji Temple
GOJO-DORI
Kiyomizudera Temple
Astronomical Observatory
Kawai Kanjiro's House
Seikanji
HIGASHIYAMA-KU
JR TOKAIDO
Kyōto National Museum
Sanjusangendo Temple
Imakumano
YAMASHINA-KU
Kamo-gawa
SHINKANSEN
HIGASHIYAMA TUNNEL
Tofukuji Temple
D
Sennyuji Temple
E
Daigo Sambo-in Temple, Kajyuji Temple

Kyoto cherry blossom

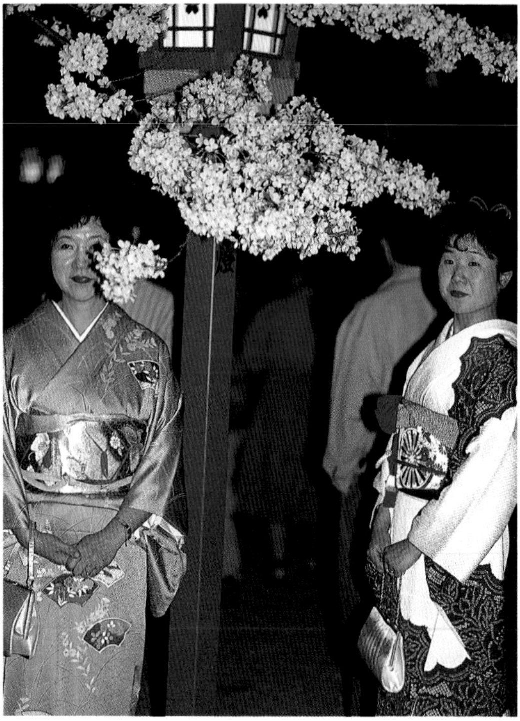

Geisha girls
In the Gion quarter of Kyoto, young *geisha* girls called *maiko* can be glimpsed. These apprentice *geishas*, aged between 17 and 25, will graduate to full *geishas*, when they will probably acquire a rich patron. There is no age limit for *geishas*, who are hired, often in pairs, to entertain parties of men after dinner, at a restaurant or tea house.

Mount Hiei
In the eighth century the Emperor Kammu decided to build a new capital city, to be called Heian-Kyo, on the site of present-day Kyoto. Before the work started he ordered a Buddhist monk, Saicho, of the Tendai sect, to establish a temple on Mount Hiei to protect the new city from evil spirits. The temple became the centre of a monastery complex that grew in size and importance as rapidly as Heian-Kyo below. By the 11th century Enryaku-ji contained over 3,000 temple buildings and had become the headquarters of the Tendai sect. The monks had their own army and, far from protecting Heian-Kyo, they warred with any political or religious faction that opposed their control of the city and even with the incumbent emperor. In 1571 General Nobunaga invaded the mountain, burned every temple to the ground and executed every monk. Although the monastery was re-established in the 17th century, it never regained its former power.

Kyoto Established in AD794, Kyoto remained the centre of civilisation in Japan for over a thousand years. Even today, although the capital has now moved to Tokyo, Kyoto retains its unique position as the country's historical and cultural centre, birthplace of much of the spirit and technology of traditional Japan. The Japanese describe the city as *Nihon no Furusato* – 'The Heart of Japan'.

The Allies spared Kyoto from bombing during World War II, and it remains a living museum of Japan's great artistic heritage, the setting for historical and religious sites and a vast wealth of traditional art, crafts, architecture, dance and drama.

The original layout of the city was modelled on Changan (modern Xian), the ancient capital of Tang Dynasty China. Its grid plan makes it easy to get around and the mountains that ring Kyoto on three sides help in keeping your bearings. On the approaches to these mountains, modern Kyoto gently reverts to its older self, with Buddhist temples and Shinto shrines, villas, gardens, craft shops, Japanese inns and narrow streets of old houses that lead back into the countryside. The most famous mountain, Mount Hiei, rising above the city to the northeast, is the site of the Enryakuji Temple complex, at one time the most influential Buddhist monastery in Japan.

Sightseeing More than 30 million tourists a year visit Kyoto but there is so much to do (nearly 2,000 temples and shrines alone) that crowds tend to form only at the most popular places. Avoid the city on public holidays and the best-known sites at weekends if you dislike crowds.

The major attractions are the Kyoto Imperial Palace, Nijo Castle and gardens, Daitokuji Temple, with its many sub-temples, Ginkakuji (Temple of the Silver Pavilion), Kinkakuji (Temple of the Golden Pavilion), the sand and rock Zen garden at Ryoan-ji Temple, the Heian Shrine and Kiyomizudera Temple, built on a steep hillside with wonderful views over the city. Kyoto also has several museums and a botanical and zoological garden.

Festivals and crafts There are also many popular annual festivals held in Kyoto, normally associated with the changing of the seasons or with religious occasions. For the three best known, the Gion (16–17 July), Jidai (22 October) and Aoi (15 May) Festivals, hotel bookings should be made well in advance.

Kyoto is renowned for traditional Japanese crafts, especially pottery, lacquer ware, woodblock prints, fans, Yuzen silk-dyeing and Nishijin silk-weaving. Major schools of the tea ceremony, flower arranging, classical dance and Noh drama have their headquarters in Kyoto.

Contrasts Apart from its temples, shrines and gardens Kyoto is also a city of fashionable shops and restaurants. The gods of spirit and mammon live happily here cheek by jowl. The atmosphere of the city is perhaps best captured in the Gion district. Here, a famous centre where the classical Japanese arts are performed is next door to a very busy betting shop, itself adjacent to the entrance of Kennin-ji Temple. In the spring, cherry blossom might be blowing down streets busy with traffic, *geisha* girls, monks and tourists, while peace and tranquillity are found inside the grounds of Kennin-ji. Kyoto, like much of Japan, is a place of contradictions.

Festivals

22 October: Kurama-No-Hi-Matsuri. The Fire Festival of Kurama takes place in Sakao-ku in Kyoto. The main event is a procession of people carrying lighted torches to the gate of Yuki Shrine, passing between rows of bonfires.

15 May: Aoi Matsuri. The *aoi*, or hollyhock, is thought to prevent hurricanes and earthquakes. This festival is said to date back to the 6th century. People in traditional court costume walk from the old imperial palace to two Shinto shrines.

16 August: Daimonji Gozan Okuribi. Huge bonfires form Chinese characters on five of the mountains that surround Kyoto.

See also pages 30–1.

Kyoto worshippers burning incense

Ikkyu Sojun
Ikkyu Sojun (1394–1481) entered Daitokuji at the age of 20 to study Zen and, according to tradition, achieved enlightenment when he heard crows cawing, while he was sitting in a boat meditating. He constantly criticised the Zen priesthood as corrupt, and scandalised the Buddhist establishment by frequenting the pleasure quarters of Kyoto. As an old man he became involved with a young blind singer named Mori, dedicating poems to her in his *Kyounshu* (Crazy Cloud Collection). Ikkyu described himself as:
'Hating incense,
Distrusting Satori,
Disbelieving talk of Zen,
Thoroughly despising priestly piety,
Wrinkling my nose with disgust here in the dimness of the Buddha Hall'.

▶▶▶ Daitokuji Temple *120B5*

Daitokuji-cho, Murasakino, Kita-ku

Bus: 1, 12, 61, 204, 205, 206 to Daitokuji-mae.

The Daitokuji (Temple of Great Virtue) is composed of the main temple plus 23 sub-temples (*tatchu*) belonging to the Rinzai sect of Zen Buddhism. Founded in 1319 by Daito Kokushi (1282–1337), the original buildings were damaged by fire in 1453 and 1468 during the Onin Wars. In 1474 the Zen monk Ikkyu Sojun (1394–1481) became head priest of Daitokuji. Although he once said that 'brothels are more suitable settings for meditation than temples' he solicited funds from rich merchants and rebuilt the temple. The great warlord Toyotomi Hideyoshi (1537–98) also contributed to the restoration of the complex; one of the sub-temples, Soken-in, was built by Hideyoshi in memory of his predecessor, Oda Nobunaga (1534–82). Both Nobunaga and Hideyoshi were devotees of the tea ceremony (*chanoyu*), and its greatest master, Sen no Rikyu (1521–91), built tea houses and gardens in the grounds of the Daitokuji (see panel, opposite page).

From north to south the temple buildings are: the Chokushi-mon, the Sanmon Gate, Butsuden (Buddha Hall), Hatto (Lecture Hall) and the Hojo (Abbot's Quarters), which are entered through the Karamon (Chinese Gate). The Hojo is open to the public only on 10 October, when its famous collection of paintings is put on display. The Chokushi-mon (Gate of the Imperial Messengers) was originally the south gate of the Imperial Palace in Kyoto. Built in 1590 with curved gables, typical of the style of the Momoyama period, it was given to the Daitokuji by the Empress Meisho in 1640.

Daisen-in▶▶ is a sub-temple of the Daitokuji, famous for its eastern Zen garden, created by the founder Kogaku Zenshi with some help from his friend, the artist Soami. The arrangement of rocks (representing mountains), sand (representing a stream of water, the flow of life) and sparse vegetation is symbolic of an individual's journey through life. A rock symbolising Mount Horai, the home of immortal sages in the Eastern Sea, stands in the north-eastern corner. A stream of imaginary water flows rapidly from the rock, representing youth. Then various obstacles present themselves, with the 'tigerhead stone' repre-

The Zen Garden at Daitokuji Temple

Stone Buddhas...

Tea master
Sen no Rikyu (1521–91) was the greatest master of the tea ceremony. The son of a rich merchant, he became one of Hideyoshi's most trusted advisers, until he was forced to commit suicide by Hideyoshi in 1591. Why this happened is unclear, but it is said that Hideyoshi objected strongly to walking under a statue of Rikyu which the artist had placed on the upper floor of the outer gate (*sanmon*) of the Daitoku-ji, thus placing himself 'above' the warlord.

senting tragedy. The flow of the water is checked and slowed by the stones and a rocky wall, representing doubt and contradiction, and the water eddies and swirls as if lost and confused. Once the stream moves past this point it becomes faster and wider, having learned from hard experience. In the middle of this section of the stream a turtle is observed trying to swim against the flow, demonstrating the pointlessness of trying to return to the past. The southern end of the garden is apparently empty, composed only of white sand, which symbolises the mind freed from thoughts and emotions.
Open: 9–4:30 (only eight of the sub-temples are usually open to the public).

...and a monk at Daitokuji Temple

▶▶▶ Ginkakuji Temple *121E4*

Ginkakuji-machi, Sakyo-ku
Bus: 5, 17, 203.
Ginkakuji (The Temple of the Silver Pavilion) is one of Kyoto's most popular sights. Built originally as a retirement villa for the *shogun* Ashikaga Yoshimasa (1453–90), it was originally to be covered in silver foil, in imitation of his grandfather Yoshimitsu's building the Kinkakuji or Gold Pavilion. The silver was never applied, but the name survived. Yoshimasa surrounded himself with a circle of artists and aesthetes and devoted his time to the appreciation of women, the tea ceremony, moon-gazing, incense-sniffing and other refinements. The arts that flourished under Yoshimasa's patronage are known as the *Higashiyama Bunka* (Culture of the Eastern Mountains), taking their name from the Higashiyama mountains faced by the villa.

In 1485 Yoshimasa became a Zen Buddhist monk, and after his death the villa became a Buddhist temple, known as the Joshoji. The gardens are attributed to the artist Soami and are famous for two piles of white sand which sparkle in the moonlight.
Open: 8:30–5 (last entry 4:30pm).

Koto-in gardens

■ One of the most beautiful Zen gardens in Kyoto, and possibly one of the least visited, is that of the Koto-in Zen Temple, a small sub-temple of Daitokuji with only three buildings. The garden is a masterpiece of elegant simplicity, renowned for the beauty of its maple trees in autumn......■

Ceremonial excesses
During the 14th century, the *chanoyu* or tea ceremony became a social ceremony, a luxurious court ritual. In their splendid apartments, richly decorated and adorned with precious objects, amid odours of incense, great lords reclining on couches would receive their guests and offer them exotic dishes, and tea, whose origin they were supposed to guess to be rewarded with a prize.

Above: Zen garden, Ginkakuji Temple
Below: Daitokuji graves

Early morning reverie The best time to arrive at Koto-in is at around 9am, just as the doors are being opened. Only the door-keeper is likely to be there. The altar room in the main temple is dark and you will only just be able to distinguish the Buddhas and other images surrounding the altar itself. The temple rooms are divided by *shoji*, paper screens, which can be opened or closed to make rooms of different sizes, or taken away altogether to make one large room. There is a tangible atmosphere of peace and calm as you pass over the *tatami* floors onto the veranda overlooking the gardens. Outside the light strikes the bamboo fences, *shoji*, roof eaves and unpolished wooden beams of the monks' quarters. At this time of the day, if you listen carefully, you may also catch the sound of Zen clappers somewhere in the grounds of Daitokuji, calling the monks to meditation, prayer or morning tea.

Lord Hosokawa Koto-in was established in 1601 at the behest of a famous military leader, Hosokawa Tadaoki. Hosokawa was a great warrior of his time and one of the

Views of the tea ceremony Toyotomi Hideyoshi and other warriors were great lovers of the tea ceremony. Hideyoshi's interpreter, the Portuguese Jesuit Juan Rodriguez, observed that in all aspects the tea ceremony 'is as rustic, rough, completely unrefined and simple as nature made it, after the style of a solitary and rustic hermitage'. It is intended to 'produce courtesy, politeness, modesty, exterior moderation, calmness, peace of body and soul without any pride or arrogance, fleeing from all ostentation, pomp, external grandeur and magnificence'.

The stone lantern grave of Lord Hosokawa and Lady Gratia, Koto-in Zen garden, Daitokuji

few to survive the bloody civil war which culminated in the establishment of the Tokugawa shogunate. In addition to his martial skills he was a man of considerable intellectual achievement and an accomplished diplomat. His wife, Lady Gratia, was a devout believer in the then outlawed Catholic faith and her father was the disgraced leader of an unsuccessful revolt against the then *shogun*. Hosokawa overcame this potentially fatal association and became a prominent figure in the early Tokugawa regime. He was rewarded with vast domains of land but later in life devoted himself to the study of Zen under the famous Daitokuji abbot Seigan (1588–1661). He was also noted as one of the most distinguished disciples of the great tea master Sen no Rikyu. Lord Hosokawa and Lady Gratia are buried in the garden of Koto-in; their grave is marked by a stone lantern.

The tea pavilion Shoko-ken, one of the main buildings in Koto-in, is a tea house built by Hosokawa but inspired by the teachings of Sen no Rikyu. During the 15th and 16th centuries the rituals surrounding the tea ceremony became ever more elaborate and luxurious, finally provoking a return to simplicity and austerity. The reaction was initiated and led by Sen no Rikyu, who devised a set of rules governing the tea ceremony (*chanoyu*) that still applies today. Shoko-ken, reached by a stone flagged path across a small landscaped garden, has a tiny kitchen for washing the vessels used in the ceremony and a *tokonoma* (alcove) decorated with an elegant *kakemono* (hanging scroll) and a simple vase with simple flowers, and complies perfectly with Sen no Rikyu's rules for the tea pavilion (open 9–4:30).

Heian Shrine

Heian Shrine festivals
Emperor Komei is honoured at a festival on 30 January and the Emperor Kammu on 3 April. Perhaps the most interesting festival is the Jidai Matsuri (Festival of the Ages), on 22 October, when men and women wear costumes dating from the end of the Tokugawa period to the Heian period, when Kyoto was founded. Their procession starts at the Imperial Palace at 10am and ends at the Heian Shrine at 3:30pm.

Kinkakuji architecture
One unusual feature of the Kinkakuji is its architecture. The first floor is built in the Shinden style of the Heian palaces, while the second floor resembles a temple hall and enshrines a statue of Kannon Bosatsu. The third floor is as sparse as a Zen hall, yet contains a statue of a Jodo-style Amida, the Buddha of the Western Paradise, or Pure Land.

▶▶▶ Heian Shrine *121D3*

Okazaki Park
Bus: 2, 3, 5.
The Shrine of Peace and Tranquillity is a Shinto shrine, built in 1895 to celebrate the 1,100th anniversary of the founding of Kyoto and dedicated to the spirits of Emperor Kammu (781–806), who established Kyoto, and Emperor Komei (1831–66), the father of Emperor Meiji.

Built as a two-thirds scale replica of the original Imperial Palace (erected in 794 and destroyed by fire in 1227), the Heian Shrine is decorated with vermilion paint and roofed with glazed green tiles and features an enormous ferro-concrete *torii* gate. Behind the main buildings may be found a modern version of Heian period gardens, which centre on a large pond spanned by a Chinese-style bridge. Unlike many of the Zen gardens found in the Kyoto area, the gardens of the Heian Shrine make extensive use of flowers, and are famous for their display of cherry blossom in spring, lotus flowers in summer and maple trees in autumn.
Open (garden): 15 March–31 August 8:30–5:30pm, September–October and 1–14 March 8:30–5, November–February 8:30–4:30.

▶▶▶ Kinkakuji Temple *120B5*

Kinkakuji-cho, Kita-ku
Bus: 59 to Kinkakuji-mae, 204 or 205 to Kinkakuji-michi.
The Temple of the Golden Pavilion was built by the *shogun* Ashikaga Yoshimitsu (1358–1409) for his retirement in 1394. Built with three storeys, topped with a bronze statue of a phoenix, the pavilion is covered in gold leaf and extends over a pond which reflects the building. The Golden Pavilion was built according to descriptions of the Western Paradise of the Buddha Amida and is intended to illustrate the harmony between Heaven and Earth.

Like other buildings erected by powerful warriors and politicians, the Kinkakuji symbolises the mandate to rule granted by Heaven to the Ashikaga shogunate.

On Yoshimitsu's death his son, obeying his father's wishes, turned the building into a temple known as the Rokuonji. In 1950 one of the temple priests set fire to the building, but an exact replica was built in 1955. The writer Yukio Mishima based his novel *The Temple of the Golden Pavilion* (1956) on the destruction of the Kinkakuji. The temple was further restored in 1990 and houses many treasures of Buddhist art. The grounds include a beautiful landscaped garden and a large pond.
Open: October–March 9–5, April–September 9–4:30.

▶▶▶ Kiyomizudera Temple *121D2*

Kiyomizu 1-Chome, Higashiyama-ku
Bus: 16, 202, 206, 207 to Kiyomizu-michi or Gojo-zaka (10-minute walk up Kiyomizu-michi or Gojo-zaka).
The Clear Water Temple was established in 780 by a Buddhist priest from Nara named Enchin, who was commanded in a vision to seek the pure source of the Kizu river. In 798 the main hall was rebuilt by General Sakanoue no Tamuramaro, using materials taken from the abandoned Imperial Palace at Nagaoka. Damaged in the power struggles between the monks of Mount Hiei and Nara, most of the present buildings were erected in 1633 by Tokugawa Iemitsu. Originally the Kiyomizudera was affiliated to the Kofukuji temple in Nara, but it now belongs to the Shingon-Hosso sect, dedicated to the worship of Kannon, the personification of divine mercy. The main attraction for visitors is the *butai* (dancing stage), a large platform in front of the *hondo* (main hall). Wooden scaffolding 12m high supports the *butai* above a gorge, giving a panoramic view of Kyoto.

Stone steps lead down from the main hall to the Otowa-no-taki (Sound of Feathers Waterfall), the source of the pure water found by Enchin. Where pilgrims often drink the water, said to be efficacious for all illnesses.
Open 6am–sunset.

The streets around Kiyomizudera Temple

Kiyomizudera proverb
Kiyomizudera is the source for a Japanese saying – 'to leap from Kiyomizu's *butai*' – which means to take an important decision, or do something which demands great courage.

Kiyomizudera Temple

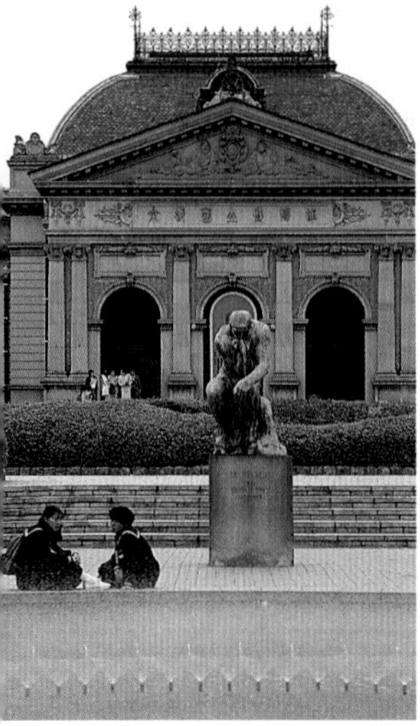

Kyoto National Museum

Nanzenji 'cathedral'
Following the Chinese tradition, Zen temples are grouped into fives. Nanzenji Temple was the head of the Gozan (Five Monasteries) of Kyoto and when Ashikaga Yoshimitsu wanted to include the Shokokuji among the group, the Nanzenji was promoted above all others. In effect Nanzenji acted as a kind of Zen 'cathedral'; whoever was the abbot held the highest Buddhist office in Japan.

Boiled alive
The Sanmon Gate was the hiding place of Ishikawa Goemon, a kind of Japanese Robin Hood. When he and his young son were captured in 1632 they were sentenced to be boiled alive in a big iron tub, but Goemon held the boy above the boiling water until he himself died. His courage is remembered in the *kabuki* play *Sanmon Gosan no Kiri* and Goemon was the subject of a woodblock print by the artist Kunisada. Goemon's name was also used for the old-fashioned iron baths known as *Goemon-furo*.

►► Kokuritsu Hakubutsukan (Kyoto National Museum) 121D1

Yamato-oji-dori, Higashiyama-ku
Bus: 206.
Established in the second half of the last century, the National Museum is a repository for works of art gathered from private collections and temples. Housed in two buildings, its extensive collection is shown in continuously changing displays. Neolithic relics from the Jomon and Yayoi periods may be found in the archaeology section, along with clay figurines (*haniwa*) associated with the burial mounds (*misasagi*) of the early rulers of Japan.

The museum is noted for its collection of Japanese pictorial art, which is displayed chronologically. The sculpture section is dominated by Heian period statues. There are also examples of metalwork, ceramics, calligraphy, and lacquerware from many periods of Japanese history.
Open: Tuesday–Sunday 9–4:30 (last entry 4pm).

►►► Kyoto Gosho (Kyoto Imperial Palace) 120C4

Imperial Park
Subway: Marutamachi, Imadegawa.
The Imperial Palace was originally built in 794 but has been destroyed by fire on many occasions. The present building, smaller than the original and on a different site, was built in 1855. The imperial household moved to Tokyo after the Meiji Restoration, but the Kyoto Gosho is still used for the ceremonies which must be performed when a new emperor ascends the throne.

Foreign visitors are given preferential treatment when it comes to access. Admission is organised by the Imperial Household Agency (Kunaicho), located in Kyoto Imperial Park near the Imadegawa subway station (tel: 075 211 1215). Visitors must complete an application form and show their passport.
Open: 30-minute tours of the grounds start at 10am; arrive by 9:40am (except Sunday and the second and fourth Saturday of every month). An English-language tour is available Monday to Friday at 2pm; arrive by 1:40pm.

►►► Nanzenji Temple 121E3

Fukuchi-cho, Sakyo-ku
Bus: 5 to Eikan-do-mae, then a five-minute walk.
Nanzenji (Southern Zen) Temple was built as a retirement villa for the Emperor Kameyama (1249–1305) at the base of the hills in the east of Kyoto. The building was given to the Rinzai sect of Zen Buddhism in 1291 at the Emperor's command, and is now the headquarters of Rinzai Zen. During the Onin Wars the temple was badly damaged but was restored in the late 16th and early 17th centuries; the Sanmon (Triple Gate) was built in 1628 and offers a famous view of Kyoto and the Higashiyama mountains from the second floor. The Hojo Hall contains screens painted by Eitoku Kano (1543–90).

Next to the Hojo Hall is a Zen rock garden known as the Leaping Tiger Garden, the name deriving from the shape of some of the rocks used by Enshu Kobori (1579–1647) when he set it out.
Open: 6 March–16 November 8:30–4:30, 16 November–5 March 8:30–5.

Kyoto Gosho

Squeaking floors
While Nijo castle may not have been built primarily as a fortress it does contain surprises for any potential spy or assassin. Every building contains hidden rooms, where the *shogun*'s *samurai* could observe visitors for signs of treachery, and many of the corridors were constructed with 'nightingale floors' (*uguisu-bari*), which squeak when walked upon to warn of anyone approaching.

Path of philosophy
Nanzenji Temple and Ginkakuji Temple are linked by a canal-side path about 2km long, known as Philosopher's Walk (see page 136). It was named after Nishida Kitaro (1870–1945), a noted philosopher whose speciality was the comparison of Western and Zen philosophies, and who enjoyed walking along this route. The walk is now lined with cherry trees, interesting shops and coffee bars and is busy with tourists, as well as academics.

▶▶▶ Nijo Castle and Gardens *120C3*

Horikawa Nijo, Nijojo-cho, Nakagyo-ku
Subway: Oike, then a 10-minute walk; bus: 9, 12, 50, 52, 61, 67.
Built in 1603 by Tokugawa Ieyasu, Nijo Castle has thick outer walls and a moat to defend it. Within the walls, the main buildings are beautifully decorated with paintings by Kano Tanyu (1602–74) and his pupils. The gardens to the southwest of the Great Hall were laid out by Enshu Kobori shortly before the Emperor Gomizno-o's visit in 1626; no trees were used, as falling leaves are suggestive of the transience of life, and the *Shogun* wanted to impress the Emperor with his power. The central island in the lake is flanked by two smaller islands in the shape of a crane and a tortoise, symbols of strength and longevity.

Entrance is through the East gate, then via the Karamon (Chinese Gate) to a diagonal row of five buildings. The Ohiroma Hall contains a reconstruction of the occasion when Keiki Tokugawa returned power to the Imperial line. Open: Tuesday–Sunday 8:45–4. Closed: 26 December–4 January.

Nanzenji Temple

►► Nishiki-Koji Market *121D2*

Situated in the heart of town on Nishiki-Koji-dori Street, this fresh produce and fish market is the main food-buying centre for the city's restaurants and hotels, as well as for the general public. Open stalls, selling everything from seaweed to beans, line the market lanes.
Open: daily early morning–7pm. Some stalls close on Sunday, others on Wednesday.

Nishiki-Koji Market

Ryoanji tea house
In the small garden behind Ryoanji there is a teahouse, the Zoroku, whose stone wash basin (the *tsukubai*) has a unique inscription arranged as a rebus around the rim, which can be translated as 'I learn only to be content-ed'. In Zen he who achieves contentment is considered to be spiritually rich. The *tsukubai* is said to have been given to the temple by the *daimyo* Tokugawa Mitsukuni (1628–1700), remembered as the compiler of the great history of Japan, the *Dai Nippon Shi*. Copies of the inscription may be pur-chased as souvenirs.

►►► Ryoanji Temple *120A4*

13 Goryoshita-machi, Ryoanji, Ukkyu-ku
Bus: 59 to Ryoanji-mae.
The Temple of the Peaceful Dragon was founded in 1473. Originally the estate of Katsumoto Hosokawa (1430–73), it became a Zen temple of the Rinzai sect on his death. For the visitor, the main attraction is the famous rock garden. Attributed to the famous artist Soami, it was created in the 16th century in a space of 30m by 10m. Following the *karesansui* (waterless stream) style, the garden is composed of fifteen rocks set into raked white gravel. Simply sit and enjoy the view, but arrive early to avoid the crowds and try to ignore the intrusive 'explanations' which are broadcast over the loudspeakers, destroying the mood (see also pages 134–5).
Open: 8–5, December–February 8:30–4:30.

►►► Sanjusangendo *121D1*

657 Sanjusangendo, Mawari-cho, Higashiyama-ku
Bus: 206, 208 to Sanjusangendo-mae, or 15 minutes' walk east of Kyoto station.
Sanjusangendo, the Hall of the 33 Bays, is also known as the Rengeo-in Temple; its popular name derives from the 33 spaces between the 35 pillars found in the hall, which is 118m long by 18m wide. Thirty-three is also the number of the manifestations of Kannon, the Buddhist 'goddess' of mercy to whom this Tendai sect temple is dedicated. A gilded statue of the 1,000-armed Kannon, carved by Tankei (1173–1256) in 1254, is enshrined in the middle of the hall surrounded by 1,000 smaller gilded statues of Kannon, the work of 70 sculptors supervised by

Tankai and his father Unkei. A tradition has developed among visitors to the Sanjusangendo of trying to find the features of a relative or friend among the faces portrayed on the statues.

The Sanjusangendo was originally built by the Emperor Goshirakawa (1126–91) in 1164. It was burned down and rebuilt in 1266, when the statues of Kannon were installed in the middle of the hall and the statues of the 28 guardians of Buddhism were erected in the corridor behind the main hall. Many of the guardians are derived from the Hindu pantheon, such as the bird-man playing the flute, Karurao (Garuda), and the emaciated holy man, Basusennin.

Open: 16 March–October 8–5, November–15 March 8–4.

▶▶ Zenrinji Temple *121E3*

Shishigatani-dori Avenue, Higashiyama (north of Nanzenji Temple)

Bus: 5 to Eikan-do mae, then a 15-minute walk.

Located at the end of the Philosopher's Walk (see panel, page 131), Zenrinji Temple is also known as Eikando. Established in 836 by the priest Shinsho, the buildings were destroyed during the Onin Wars (1467–77) and rebuilt in the 16th century. The temple enshrines a statue of the Amida Buddha with his face turned to the side as if he is looking over his shoulder. According to legend this came about when the statue came to life and joined a group of worshippers who were dancing to honour the Amida Buddha. The dancers were led by the priest Eikan, who stood still in surprise. The statue looked backwards to encourage Eikan to keep dancing, and when he climbed back on his pedestal he retained the twist in his neck.

Those with the energy to climb the stairs to the top of the pagoda will be rewarded with a superb view of Kyoto. The excellent gardens include many maple trees best seen in the autumn as the leaves begin to change

Open: 9–4:30.

Archery contest

Sanjusangendo is the site of an archery contest first held in 1606. On 15 January and 2 May archers gather at the temple to see who can fire the greatest number of arrows at a target placed at the end of the hall's outer veranda. The record of 8,133 bull's eyes established in 1686 has yet to be beaten, but the upright wooden posts bear the scars of many misdirected shots.

Temple food

Two restaurants which serve vegetarian and *tofu* dishes typical of the meals served in Buddhist temples may be found on the road leading to Eikando Temple to the north of Nanzenji Temple. The Okutan Restaurant is the most famous and most expensive. Cheaper and nearby is the Koan restaurant, which also serves good vegetarian meals and *tofu*.

Sanjusangendo

There are three basic types of Japanese garden: the tea garden, usually designed by tea masters as a site for the tea ceremony; the hill garden, designed for private estates as a small park with miniature artificial hills; and the flat garden. The Zen garden at Ryoanji Temple is a famous version of the flat garden......

Garden tours in Kyoto
A convenient way to see a variety of gardens in Kyoto is to take a guided bus tour. The commentaries are in Japanese but this leaves you more time to enjoy the gardens in your own company. All buses leave from the front of Kyoto station (Keihan Bus Company tel: 075 672 2100). Ask at the TIC opposite the station for further details.

Above: taking tea in Daitokuji Temple's Zen Garden
Below: Ryoanji

Ryoanji Zen Garden In the flat garden style few shrubs are used and the most common elements are stones, sand and gravel. They are designed, like a painting, for contemplation. Several of the best Zen gardeners were also well-known painters in ink, and in this medium they intended, with just a few strokes of black ink on white paper, to evoke an atmospheric natural scene. Their gardens were three-dimensional evocations of the same idea using sand or gravel instead of silk, and shrubs, trees or stones instead of brush strokes. The stones they chose were also charged with different meanings according to their shapes, their textures and the angles at which they were placed.

The garden at Ryoanji was said to have been created by Soami (although this is by no means certain), a famous ink-line artist. It consists of raked gravel and 15 stones in five groupings, and certainly obeys the injunction of an anonymous 16th-century painter and gardener: 'Caution should be taken not to be too anxious to overcrowd the scenery to make it more interesting. Such an effect often results in a loss of dignity and a feeling of vulgarity.' The temple authorities publish a small pamphlet describing the garden as symbolising 'a group of mountainous

Daisen-in Zen Garden

Tour itineraries
F: Kyoto Station–Tenryuji Temple–Ryoanji Temple–Daitokuji Temple–Daisen-in Temple–Myoshinji-Taizoin Temple–Kyoto station (9:30am; five hours, 30 minutes, including a Japanese-style lunch).
J: Kyoto Station–Hakusasonso–Konchi-in Temple–Nanzenji Temple–Shoren-in Temple–Daigo Sambo-in Temple–Kajyuji Temple–Kyoto station (10am; six hours, including a Japanese-style lunch).
R: Kyoto Station–Tenryuji Temple–Ryoanji Temple–Zuihoin Temple–Kyoto station (2pm; three hours, 30 minutes).

islands in a great ocean, or mountain tops rising above a sea of clouds. We can see it as a picture framed by the ancient mid wall, now in itself regarded as a national treasure, or we can forget the frame as we sense the truth of this sea [the grave] stretching out boundlessly.'

Daisen-in Zen Garden Soami was an official painter in the court of Yoshimasa, the eighth Ashikaga *shogun*. In 1480 he designed and built one of the earliest and, to this day, most famous Zen flat gardens for the abbot's residence at Daisen-in, a sub temple of Daitokuji Temple (see pages 124–5). At the time Soami was influenced by Chinese Song period paintings which, by their portrayals of dramatic and awe-inspiring mountain landscapes, highlight human vulnerability. His garden at Daisen-in, designed to be viewed from the veranda of the abbot's quarters, rather than to be walked around, is constructed of rocks and sand. Unlike the abstract garden of Ryoanji Temple, it is a three-dimensional representation of a Song-style painting featuring a mountain (Mount Horai, the mythical home of enlightened beings), a river and a boat with a cargo of treasure. It has been suggested that the garden may be seen as a representation of the bridge between being and non-being. As such it rewards quiet contemplation, and it is a good idea to visit Daisen-in early in the day and to avoid weekends and public holidays.

Like other Zen gardens, Ryoanji and Daisen-in *kare sansui* ('waterless stream gardens') were designed to promote the meditative practice of Zen monks. Rock and sand gardens, unaffected by the changes of the seasons, gave the monks a sense of the calm of eternity.

The perfect precision of Ryoanji

Walk Along the old canal

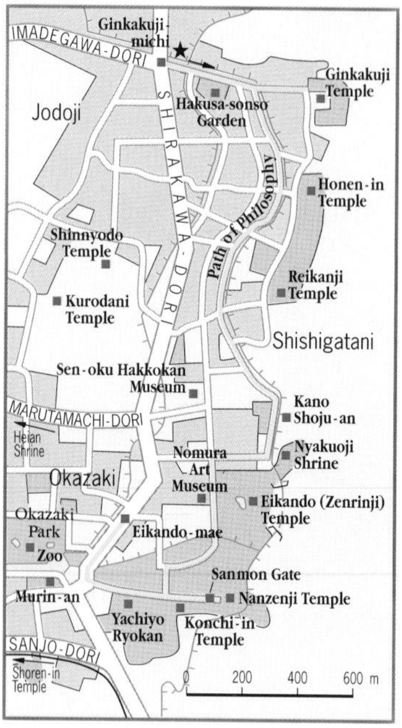

Distance: 2km; time (excluding temple visits): 50 minutes.
This pleasant canal-side stroll follows the Philosopher's Walk, from Ginkakuji, the Silver Pavilion, to Nanzenji Temple.

Begin at bus stop A-1, Ginkaku-michi (City Bus 5), and walk towards the entrance of Ginkakuji Temple. On the right-hand side, before the coach parking lot, is the pleasant and modest **Hakusa-Sonso Garden▶**, once the home of the early 20th-century painter, Hashimoto Kansetsu. Ahead are the immaculate hedges that form the entrance to the **Ginkakuji Temple** (see page 125). From Ginkakuji, walk back to join the path that runs south along the little canal. This is the beginning of the Philosopher's Walk (see panel, page 131). The canal passes through a quiet, residential district (with the occasional smart coffee shop along the way). After passing the Kano Shoju-an Japanese cake shop, with its elegant tearoom, the canal goes underground by the entrance to the Nyakuoji Shrine. Turn right, then left, to pass the gate to **Zenrinji Temple** (see page 133). To the right is the **Nomura Art Museum▶▶**, which has a collection of tea-ceremony artefacts. The lane bends to the right and then left before reaching the entrance to **Nanzenji Temple** (see page 130), where the massive Sanmon Gate, Konchi-in Temple and the Abbot's quarters are worth a visit: the latter two have exquisite Zen gardens. The restaurants at the entrance to the temple specialise in *yu-dofu*, a Buddhist vegetarian dish.

From Nanzenji, walk away from the entrance, past Yachiyo *ryokan*'s elegant forecourt on the left, then turn right and walk for three minutes to the Eikando-mae bus stop to catch City Bus 5 back to Kyoto station.

*As evening descends, paper lanterns (*chochin*) are lit to decorate a canal-side restaurant*

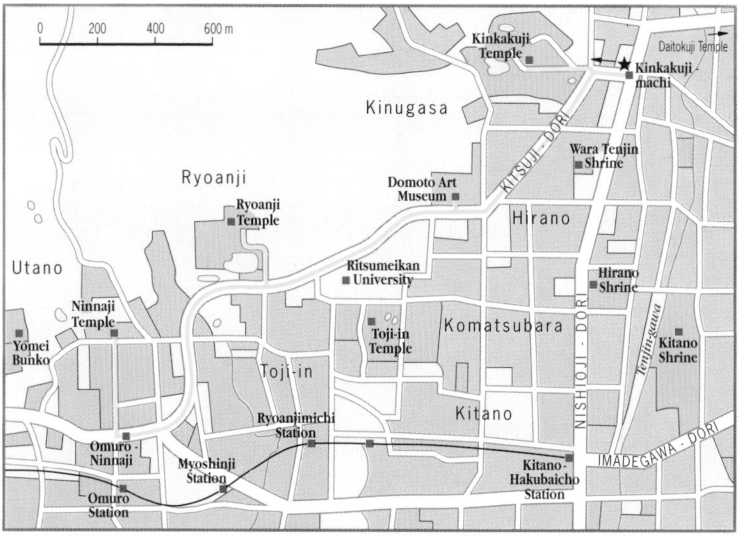

Walk Kinkakuji and Ryoanji Temples

Distance: 2km; time: about one hour, including visits to both temples. This walk in the western foothills links two of Kyoto's most celebrated monuments: the dazzling Golden Pavilion and the minimalist Ryoanji rock garden.

Start from Kinkakuji-michi bus stop, B-3 (City Bus 59 or 205). A driveway lined with low, clipped pine trees and hedges leads to the temple entrance, to the left of an enormous coach park. Bamboo groves and tile-capped walls striped in ochre and white line the approach path to **Kinkakuji** (see pages 128–9), built as a villa retreat at the end of the 14th century by the third Ashikaga *shogun*. Once through the gate, the path turns sharply right. A high bamboo fence obscures the view until suddenly the Golden Pavilion appears, floating above its reflection in the lake. Covered in thick gold leaf, the pavilion glows even under rainy skies. The path skirts around the lake, with the main temple buildings to the right, past the pavilion, then winds up and around the garden, past a lotus pond and a tiny thatched tea house, before leading to a flight of steps back to the entrance. In the gardens of the temple, visible from the path, is a large pine tree in the shape of a boat. The gift shop by the coach park has a surprisingly good selection of high-quality souvenirs.

Leaving the temple, walk back to the main road and turn right. Follow the road, which curves along the hillside, past the **Domoto Art Museum▶** and on to **Ryoanji Temple** (see page 132).

From Ryoanji, the walk can be extended, turning right again along the main road to visit **Ninnaji Temple▶▶**, first built in the 9th century and famous for its late-blooming cherry trees. From Ninnaji, take City Bus 26 back into the city centre.

Kinkakuji Temple

Self-discipline
The monks of Mount Hiei still discipline themselves by undergoing austere practices involving chanting, meditation and fasting. One of the most severe disciplines is conducted by the famous 'Marathon Monks' who, for 1,000 days, complete a daily 30km marathon. During a specially intensive period of 100 days they are expected to cover 85km a day. Jodo-in is the temple for the practice of Sweeping Hell. Here the monks rise very early and spend half the day brushing the temple grounds and the other half in prayer. At the Mudo-Ji-Dani (the Valley of the Still Temple), in the eastern precinct, they rise at 2am and set out to walk to each temple in the monastery complex, praying at each one on the way – no easy task, with 125 temples in the complex.

▶▶▶ Mount Hiei

Sakamoto Honmachi, Ohtsu, Shiga Prefecture

Bus: 16, 17, 18 to Yase-Yuenchi stop. Entrance to Keifuku cable-car on the left; departs every 30 minutes. Transfer at Hiei to the Hieizan Ropeway to the observatory on the summit; from there follow the path down to Enryakuji.

Standing to the northeast of Kyoto, Mount Hiei is, at 850m, the second highest mountain in the vicinity of the city. Its location is significant: the northeast was feared as the 'Devil's Gate' (*Kimon*), through which all malevolent forces entered the city. Even today buildings in Kyoto may be seen with the northeast corners cut off to ward off evil.

The Emperor Kammu (737–806), concerned for the city's safety, ordered the priest Saicho (767–822) to build a temple on Mount Hiei to protect the city from malign influences. Saicho built a small meditation hut on Mount Hiei in 785, which he enlarged three years later into a small temple. When the temple was inaugurated in 794 the Emperor climbed Mount Hiei to attend the ceremony. In 797 Saicho was appointed one of a group of 10 'imperial monks' and Kammu ordered that his temple be supported by funds gathered from Saicho's home province of Omi. The temple was renamed Enryakuji in 823 after Saicho's death, and Saicho was given the posthumous title of *Dengyo Daishi* or 'Great Teaching Master'.

Saicho was the founder of a new sect of Japanese Buddhism known as Tendai. He believed that the world was coming to an end and was convinced that the only way to avert this catastrophe was to unify all the sects of Buddhism. He went to China in 804 and studied Buddhism at Mount T'ien-t'ai. In the summer of 805 he

The view of Kyoto from the Mount Hiei cable-car

Buddha of Healing
The Kompon-chodo of the Enryakuji Temple enshrines an image of the *Yakushi Nyorai* (Buddha of Healing), carved by Saicho from the trunk of a sandalwood tree. It is faced by three lanterns glowing with the 'eternal light of the Dharma', said to have been lit by Saicho himself, and kept burning through the centuries.

returned to Japan with over 460 works on Buddhism, Taoism and various schools of Chinese philosophy. Within a very short time Tendai was acknowledged as an independent sect by the court, and the temple on Mount Hiei became the recipient of a great deal of patronage by the court and aristocracy.

Within two centuries or so the complex of temples on Mount Hiei had become very wealthy. To protect their wealth the monks established their own army of *sohei*, fierce warrior-monks willing and able to fight and destroy anyone who offered any kind of threat to their power and authority. The Emperor Shirakawa (1053–1129) once said that there were three things he could not control: the fall of dice when gambling, the floodwaters of the Kamo river and the monks of Mount Hiei.

Eventually the arrogance of the monks proved their undoing. They challenged the might of Oda Nobunaga (1534–82), who ordered his forces to destroy the monastic complex of over 3,000 buildings and slaughter the monks. In response to protests from some of his advisers he said 'I am not the destroyer of this monastery. The destroyer of the monastery is the monastery itself.'

Set among towering cedar trees, Enryakuji was later rebuilt on a smaller scale: most of the buildings seen today date from the 17th century. From the train station the path leads to the Daidoko (Great Lecture Hall), rebuilt after a fire in 1956. Climb the hill to the Kaiden-in, built in 1604 as the ordination hall for Tendai priests. Following the path through the trees, turn left at the Sanno-in (the Temple of the Mountain King) and down the stairs to the Jodo-in (Pure Land Temple), founded by Saicho and rebuilt in the 17th century. His tomb may be found behind the main hall. Go down the steps to the Kompon-chudo (Fundamental Central Hall), erected in 1642, which contains paintings of flowers on the ceiling 'donated' by all the *daimyo* (great landowners) at the command of the Tokugawa shogunate.

Open: March–November 8:30–4:30, December–February 9–4.

Enryakuji Temple

Miscreant monks

The monks of Mount Hiei influenced Japanese political and religious life until the 16th century and the arrival of General Oda Nobunaga. He is quoted as saying: 'If I do not take them away now, this great trouble will be everlasting. Moreover, these priests violate their vows: they eat fish and stinking vegetables, keep concubines, and never unroll the sacred books. How can they be vigilant against evil, or maintain the right? Surround their dens and burn them, and suffer none within them to live.' Nobunaga invaded the mountain, burned every temple to the ground and executed every monk.

Sandals at Enryakuji

Pavilion in Katsura Imperial Villa garden

Three conditions
It is said that when Kobori Enshu was commissioned by Hideyoshi to build the Katsura Villa he imposed three conditions on his employer: no limit on expense, no limit on time, and no interference until the building was completed. Hideyoshi died before the work was complete and he never saw the building that he paid for.

Borrowed scenery
In contrast to Katsura Imperial Villa, Shugakuin is reputed more for its gardens than for its architecture. They make particularly good use of the style of landscaping known as *shak kei*, or borrowed scenery, in which views of distant hills and, in this case, of Kyoto itself, are incorporated into the design.

▶▶▶ Katsura Imperial Villa *120A1*

Katsura Shimizu-cho, Ikyo-ku
Train: Katsura station on the Hankyu Arashiyama line (10-minute walk from station), Kyoto station (5km cab ride); bus: 33 from Kyoto station to Katsura Rikyu-mae.
Katsura Imperial Villa, in western Kyoto, was originally built at the beginning of the 17th century by Prince Toshihito, the brother of the Emperor Goyozei. Set on the banks of the Katsuragawa River, it is constructed from carefully selected materials so that the buildings and gardens harmonise elegantly with their natural surroundings, within sight of the Arashiyama and Kameyama Hills.

The Katsura garden is judged to be the masterpiece of Kobori Enshu, Japan's greatest landscape gardener. Each turn of the path which meanders through the garden brings a new view. Stone lanterns, carefully cultivated trees, bridges gracefully arching over water and a number of rustic tea houses are all cleverly arranged to provide the visitor with an aesthetic experience reminiscent of the tea ceremony. The garden is built around a central pond with tea houses designed to reflect each of the four seasons. Katsura has been described as the epitome of Japanese culture and aestheticism, and many 20th-century Western architects have been drawn to it and influenced by its elegant simplicity, its use of natural materials and the harmony of interior and exterior design. For example, the ground running away from the building is laid in strips of bare earth, pebbles, stepping stones and then moss with the intention of gradually leading one away from the human order of the house to the naturalness of the garden or vice versa.
Open: tours on weekdays at 10am and 2pm, Saturdays at 10am. Closed Saturday afternoon, Sunday, national holidays and 25 December 25 January. Special permission to visit the villa must be obtained from the Imperial Household Agency, Kamigyo-ku, Kyoto (tel: 075 211 1211). Visitors must be aged at least 20 and must take their passports when collecting permits. Tours are in Japanese, but information is available on an English-language video tape which is played in the waiting room before the tour begins. Apply for a permit as many days in advance as possible.

▶▶▶ Shugakuin Imperial Villa *121E5*

Shugakuin Muromachi, Sakyo-ku
Train: Eizan Railway from Yase Yuen station to Shugakuin-mae station, then a 30-minute walk; bus: 5 from Kyoto station to Shugakuin Rikyu Michi bus stop, then a 15-minute walk.

This villa in northeast Kyoto was built in 1659 on a foothill of Mount Hiei by the Tokugawa shogunate, as a retirement home for the Emperor Go Mizuno-o. The grounds are divided into three large gardens, each with its own tea house. The upper garden, which is the largest, is centred around a lake with islands, bridges, waterfalls and a long winding path through the gardens which gives fine views over Kyoto to the surrounding hills.

The Rakushiken pavilion, in the middle garden, was built for the emperor's daughter, Princess Ake. When she became a nun, the building was converted into a temple for her use. Jugetsukan pavilion in the lower garden contains only four rooms. They are laid out in an 'L' shape and surrounded by a veranda. The three raised and framed mats in the 15-*tatami* mat room were the emperor's sitting place. From the back gate of the lower garden you step on to a patio area that gives unimpeded views of far-off mountain ranges.

Open: tours in Japanese at 9am, 10am and 11am. On Saturday extra tours are held at 1pm and 3pm. Closed: Sunday, national holidays, 25 December–5 January. Permission must be obtained from the Imperial Household Agency (see above).

Imperial patrons of the arts
Emperor Go Mizuno-o and his Empress Tofukuman-in designed Shugakuin themselves and continued to visit their 'rustic' retreat after their retirement from office and into old age. Both were keen patrons of the arts, especially the tea ceremony and flower-arranging, and were also the driving force behind the 17th-century rebuilding of Kyoto after the ravages of many centuries of war.

Looking across the lake from Shugakuin Imperial Villa

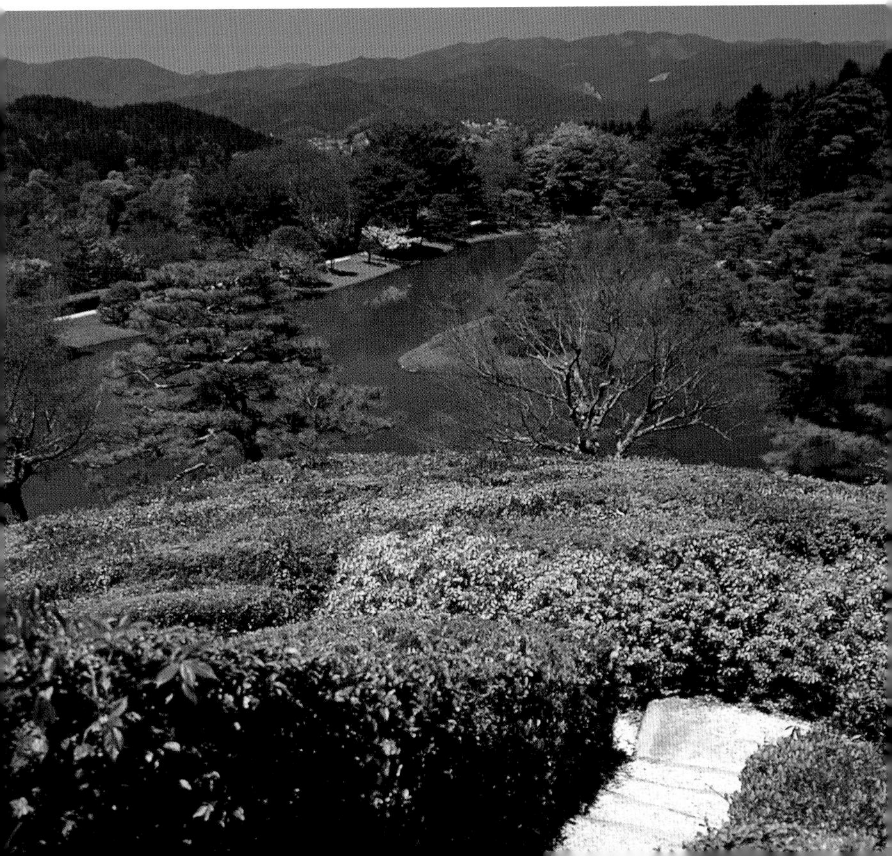

Accommodation

Ana Hotel, Kyoto

Temple lodging
Temple accommodation is a speciality of Kyoto. Rooms are small, in the traditional *tatami* mat style, and the lodgings are usually located in temple grounds, often in a quiet garden setting. Facilities may or may not include a bath or shower but one or the other will be available nearby. Breakfast is provided if required and in some places an evening meal may be ordered. Prices for lodging and food are usually very reasonable (see **Hotels and Restaurants**, page 270).

Gion Hotel, Kyoto

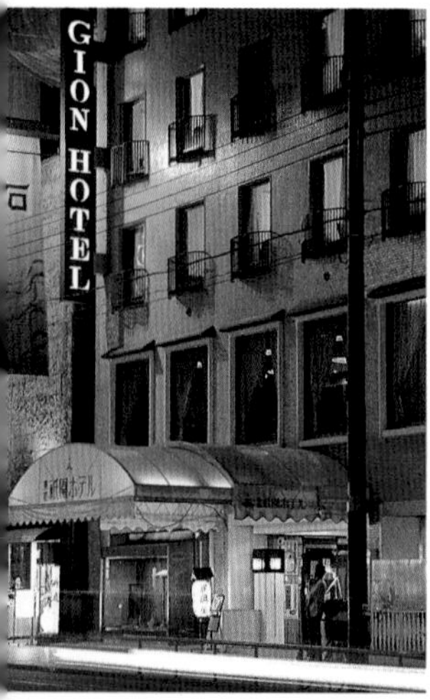

The hotels and *ryokan* of Kyoto are renowned for their impeccable service and hospitality. However, Kyoto is essentially a tourist town and space is at a premium. Rooms are not large and during the peaks of the spring and autumn seasons and over public holidays the best places need to be booked ahead.

Fortunately, Kyoto is also rich in a variety of accommodation and those who wish to travel on a flexible timetable will find, except at exceptionally busy festival times, somewhere to rest their heads, even if it is only a dormitory-style lodging (see pages 80–1). *Ryokan*, traditional Japanese inns, are found in an unusually wide range of price categories in Kyoto; if you particularly wish to stay in one, Kyoto is the ideal city (see pages 220–1).

Budget accommodation The Japanese Inn Group has a number of member inns in the Kyoto area, providing cheap and simple *tatami* mat rooms and communal dining areas in youth hostel-style environments. These are a good choice for those travelling on a budget, who may also wish to meet fellow foreign travellers. Other tips for the economy-conscious: book a room without a bathroom; in more expensive hotels ask for a small or inconveniently placed room, so that you can enjoy the facilities without paying the full price; do not use the hotel telephones, bars or restaurants. Much *ryokan* and hotel accommodation is focused around the Kyoto station area, but as Kyoto is not a large city, and is served by an excellent bus network, it is not essential to stay in the heart of the city, and accommodation is sometimes cheaper further out.

The best First-class hotels in Kyoto are excellent and the services they provide are of an international standard. English-language television, English-speaking staff, well-stocked information desks, a plethora of computer equipment and communications systems for businessmen, rapid room service and guest relations officers are all standard, even in the less than top notch establishments. Tea bags, instant coffee sachets and thermos flasks of hot water are provided in the rooms of every category of hotel. A 3 per cent government tax is added to all Japanese hotel bills and, for hotels in Kyoto, a further 3 per cent city tax is added to bills over a certain amount. The highest class establishments also add a 10 to 15 per cent service charge. Tipping is not expected.

Where to stay The Kyoto bus network operates on a grid pattern and is easy to follow (maps of the bus routes are available from the Tourist Information Centre). If, however, you have only a few days in Kyoto and wish to explore on foot it would be best to choose one area and to stay in that vicinity. For most visitors the eastern district, Higashiyama, provides the best cross-section of attractions, including Gion, an area with many traditional shops and a *geisha* entertainment quarter plus some of the most famous sights in Kyoto, such as Ginkakuji Temple (the Silver Pavilion) and the Heian Jingu Shrine. Central Kyoto has a similar mix of shopping, evening entertainment and major sights, while western and northern Kyoto are areas to stay for those wanting a quieter experience of Kyoto.

Hotel-vetting
If you are visiting Japan as part of an arranged trip or for business reasons, your travel agent will book you into a vetted hotel. Some offer Japanese as well as Western-type rooms; if you want a room with a *tatami* mat floor and sunken bath tub, request a reservation in a Japanese-style room.

Kyoto Tower

Food and drink

O-bento and _eki-ben_
O-bento are everyday lunchboxes prepared at home or bought in local shops. *Eki-ben* are train journey lunchboxes. They are sold on train platforms, in and around stations and on express trains. The boxes themselves are made from thin, unpainted wood or, for the deluxe version, lacquered wood. Inside they divide into neat compartments and contain such foods as *sushi* rice, grilled chicken, mushrooms, smoked fish, pickled plums, fresh and cooked vegetables. They are sold neatly wrapped in decorative paper and tied with string. Each area of Japan has its own variety of *o-bento* and *eki-ben*, containing a particular selection of food and one or two local specialities.

Kyoto's cuisine is derived from that of the imperial court and the vegetarian food of Buddhist temples. *Kyo-ryori* or Kyoto cooking is the most refined of all styles of Japanese cooking, the *haute cuisine* of culinary traditions.

Kyoto's specialities may be divided into two categories: *shojin-ryori*, Zen-style vegetarian dishes developed to serve the needs of monks and pilgrims; and *kaiseki-ryori*, food originally prepared for the tea ceremony but eventually transforming into an elegant full-course meal, popular with the nobility. A restaurant advertising *kyo-ryori* will usually offer a selection of each of these styles of cooking. Many of Kyoto's traditional Japanese restaurants are located in the heart of the city. *Yusoku-ryori*, cooking inspired by the dishes of the imperial court, is not now generally available and only one restaurant, the Mankamero (see **Hotels and Restaurants**, from page 266), specialises in this style of cuisine. The Kyoto Tourist Information Centre publishes a *Kyoto Gourmet Guide* which is worth picking up.

Zen food The *shojin* cook emphasises the importance of simple meals prepared from locally available foods. These include rice, fresh vegetables, pickled vegetables, sea vegetables (seaweed) and soya-bean products such as *miso*, *tofu* (beancurd) and *shoyu* (soy sauce). The cook strives to create a harmonious balance of five flavours – *shoyu*, sugar, vinegar, salt and spices (ginger root, sesame seeds and *wasabi*, a Japanese mustard) – with the other ingredients to make a vegetarian meal that is appropriate to the season as well as delicious, good to look at and nutritious. Local *shojin-ryori* specialities are *yudofu*, a pot of *tofu* simmered at your table, and other *tofu* dishes (see pages 146–7), *fu*, a glutinous wheat cake and *yuba*, dried soya-bean milk skin.

Kyoto noodle restaurant

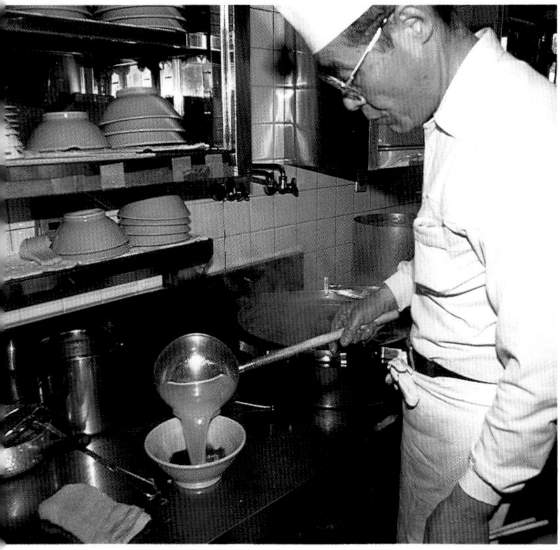

Noodle soup: preparation...

Tea ceremony food *Kaiseki-ryori* is often quite expensive but is an essential experience for visitors to Kyoto. The meal consists of a procession of tiny courses, each presented in carefully selected porcelain dishes or lacquered bowls, chosen to match in shape and size their portions of vegetable, fish or other foods. The ingredients of the dishes are valued for their scent, texture, flavour and seasonal freshness. Ideally, a *kaiseki-ryori* meal should be presented in a traditional *tatami* mat room decorated with a hanging scroll and flower arrangement, within earshot of running water.

For those on a budget, a commonly available version of *kaiseki-ryori* is the *kyo-bento*, or boxed lunch (see panel). These are very popular in Kyoto and are available in the basement food shops of most of the city's department stores. Exquisite versions of *kyo-bento* are also offered by many *ryotei*, the top restaurants that serve *kaiseki-ryori.*

Tradition and convenience Many of the restaurants in Kyoto have been in business for generations and old practices die hard. Several still do not accept credit cards so check ahead if you plan to use one. The better places expect you to dress reasonably formally and tend to serve dinner early (7–8pm). If you wish to try a variety of Japanese cooking styles visit the inexpensive restaurant complexes in the Hankyu department store (see page 149) or the Kintetsu Mall, under the tracks on the west side of Kyoto station. In eastern Kyoto there is a variety of informal restaurants selling temple-style *shojin-ryori* food in and around the Kiyomizu Temple.

Kyoto is also well provided (perhaps too well) with American fast-food chains.

Daily special The *teishoku* is a daily, fixed-price menu offered by many Japanese restaurants at lunchtime. The menus of expensive restaurants offering *kaiseki-ryori* meals are also often much better value at lunchtime than in the evening.

Healthy cooking
Shojin cookery is also sometimes referred to as *yukuseki* or 'medicine'. Food selection and preparation are seen to be inseparable from the treatment of disease and the cultivation of good health. The traditional Chinese medical view is the same: 'If one falls ill one should first examine one's diet, then choose well, chew carefully and give thanks. In this way the curative powers of nature, with which mankind is blessed, are given full rein to act and nearly all diseases are conquered.'

...and presentation

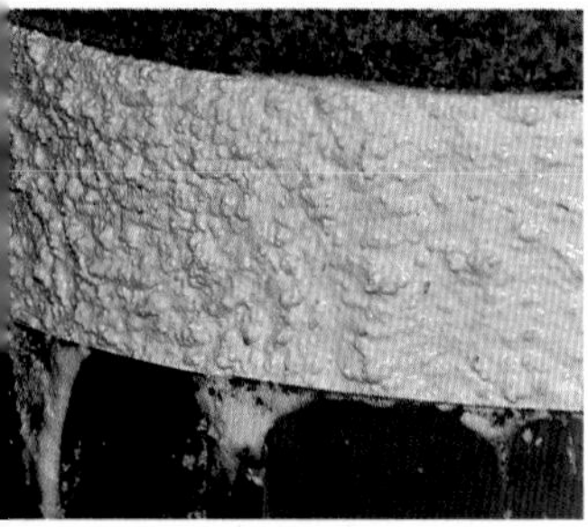

■ *Tofu* (beancurd) is rich in protein, vitamins and minerals and is fat-free. This wonderfully versatile food can be used fresh or deep fried, grilled (broiled), simmered or baked, and is one of the world's richest sources of vegetable protein. Once all Japanese towns and villages had their own *tofu*-maker. This is less common now, but in Kyoto, where the *tofu* has the reputation of being the finest in Japan, the tradition is still alive and thriving......■

***Tofu*-making contests**
In the past, each year throughout Japan, *tofu*-making contests were held among master craftsmen. First on the city, then on the provincial, and finally on the national level, master craftsmen met for a period of several days and were judged by retired masters on the speed and accuracy of their cutting, and, above all, on their ability to make *tofu* with fine flavour, texture, bouquet and appearance.

Types of *tofu* and dishes
Momengoshi-dofu: regular cotton-strained *tofu*.
Kinugoshi-dofu: delicate silky *tofu*.
Aburage: thin sheets of deep fried tofu.
Nameage: thick blocks of deep-fried *tofu* with soft centres.
Ganmodoki: deep-fried balls of *tofu* and vegetables.
Goma-dofu: sesame-flavoured *tofu*.
Yudofa: *tofu* heated in seaweed-flavoured water and served with soya sauce, grated ginger, *bonito* (dried fish) shavings and chopped spring onions.
Hiyayakko: chilled *tofu*, served as *yudofa*.
Agedashi-dofu: *tofu* dipped in potato flour and deep fried, served with soya sauce and grated *daikon* (a type of white radish).

Tofu is made by soaking and grinding soya beans, extracting the milky liquid from the resulting mixture and curdling it. The set product is pressed into slabs to produce soft-textured, delicately flavoured, pale cream *tofu*, which is sold the day it is prepared.

The *tofu* shop At the Morika *tofu* shop on the outskirts of Kyoto, the family tradition of *tofu*-makers has been maintained and the shop is owned and run by brothers whose father was a *tofu* master. Work starts at 5am and by 6:30am the shop is a hive of controlled activity. The stone floor of the work area is awash with water from the rinsing of beans, buckets and wooden storage boxes. Deep tanks of water hold huge slabs of *tofu*, ready to be cut into standard 400g blocks. Large drums hold soaking soya beans which will later be crushed between stone rollers and boiled, before filtering through a cotton cloth into a steel mould. The hot soya milk collected in the mould will be set with *nigari* (magnesium chloride), an almost tasteless salt that serves the same function as rennet in cheese-making, before being pressed under weighted wooden boards.

Fresh *tofu* made in this way and seasoned with a little good-quality soya sauce is delicious and creamy and as

The raw materials: soya beans

Making tofu*, the traditional way*

different from day-old *tofu* as newly baked French bread is from a stale baguette.

The *tofu*-maker's wife Traditionally, the *tofu* craftsman's wife has complete responsibility for all deep-frying work and at Morika the mother of the family is still in charge of this task. Apart from their reputation for the highest standards of cleanliness, *tofu* shops are known for their lack of waste and the mother at Morika is also responsible for collecting *tofu* left from the previous day and that day's offcuts. She crumbles and mixes it with slivers of vegetables, forms the mixture into small balls and deep fries them golden brown to make *ganmodoki*, a popular *tofu* snack and lunch-box food.

***Tofu* seasons** For the *tofu*-maker, the year has a rhythm. January and February, when the air and water are cold, are the best months for making regular *tofu* (*momengoshi tofu*) and keeping it fresh. With the arrival of spring, the demand starts for *kinugoshi*, a silky smooth, more watery *tofu* supplied throughout the summer months. During the hot months the *tofu*-maker begins work even earlier to take advantage of the cool pre-dawn air. During the autumn months production of *kinugoshi* is replaced with that of grilled *tofu* (*yakidofu*), which is a firmer ingredient for winter vegetable stews. In November the new crop of soya beans arrives and the *tofu* has an added sweetness and aroma. Towards the last day of the year demand for *yakidofu* peaks, as it is a traditional New Year food. From New Year's Eve the *tofu* shops all over Japan are closed and the *tofu*-maker and his family take a holiday.

Origins of *tofu*
Tofu is said to have been discovered in about 200BC in China by Lord Liu of Huai-nan, a Chinese scholar, philosopher and ruler. He was a Taoist and undertook experiments to make *tofu* in order to introduce variety and nutrition into a meatless diet. In the craft tradition of old Japan the daily work of the craftsman was regarded as part of a spiritual path that had as its goal self-realisation and liberation. The paths of the swordsmith, the potter, the calligrapher and the *tofu*-maker were united by this same underlying principle.

Shopping

Gift shop sign, Kyoto

Kyoto was the nation's capital for over 1,000 years and during this time a collection of the best craftsmen of each generation lived in the city and catered for the demanding needs of the imperial court. Even today, Kyoto is a centre of artistry and refinement and the place to shop for all traditional goods as well as contemporary craftware.

Speciality shops The largest concentration of small speciality shops is in the Gion district, along both sides of Shijo-dori Street, which runs east–west, and Kawaramachi-dori Street running north–south. In the square formed by these two avenues and Sanjo-dori Street and Teramachi-dori Street are shops selling everything from lacquerware to combs to swords. The square also encloses Shin-Kyogoku, a shopping arcade with many souvenir shops. For the latest in modern shopping malls, try the huge underground arcade called Porta at Kyoto station. The shopping avenues radiate, like subterranean catacombs, outwards from the Karasuma (north) side of the station. There are over 200 boutique-style shops and restaurants. For pottery shops, food shops and tea houses the establishments that line the steep roads leading up to Kiyomizudera Temple in Higashiyama-ku district are the places to explore.

Shuensu
The *shuensu* is a brocade-covered booklet of blank, heavy paper sheets, available at any stationery store and many temples. Used as a passport to collect ink stamps from places visited, the *shuensu* is very popular with the Japanese; most sights and places of interest provide stamps and ink stamp pads.

Art and antiques Head towards Shinmonzen-dori Street, also in the Gion district, for art and antiques. This small, unprepossessing street of two-storey wooden houses runs parallel and to the north of Shijo-dori Street. The shopkeepers here have an excellent reputation for selling authentic goods at the correct price. Together they publish a free booklet called *Shinmonzen Street Shopping Guide*. Copies are available at the TIC and from some hotel reception desks. *Netsuke* (see panel, opposite), woodblock prints, scrolls, paintings and antiques are some of the specialities of the Shinmonzen traders.

Antiques on sale in Kyoto

Netsuke
Netsuke are carved, ornamental ivory toggles by means of which purses, pouches or medicine boxes were suspended from waist bands. During the Tokugawa regime they were popular with merchants, who wore them to vie with the ornamental sword guards of the *samurai*. Later *netsuke* carving developed into a specialised art form. The international trade ban on ivory has reduced the number of contemporary practitioners of *netsuke* carving.

Nishijin Textile Centre

Department stores Kyoto department stores are not as large or glamorous as their Tokyo counterparts but they are the places to visit for modern goods, clothing and accessories. The basement floors are always given over to a cornucopia of food counters. Many offer free samples of their particular foodstuffs, and are good places to wander, to taste and to put names to the strange and wonderful array of foods that are often uniquely Japanese. **Takashimaya** department store (closed Wednesday), right in the centre of Kyoto, is one of the oldest such stores in Japan, and has a good selection of traditional and modern goods, a money exchange facility and an information counter with English-speaking staff. **Hankyo** department store, right opposite Takashimaya, has two floors devoted to a variety of restaurants, each with window displays showing the types of dishes available and their prices, which are usually very reasonable.

Silk Kyoto is celebrated for its silk and in the Nishijin silk-weaving district, to the west of Horikawa-dori Street and north of Ichijo-dori Street, the sound of looms fills the air. The **Nishijin Textile Centre** in central Kyoto, (Horikawa-dori, Imadegawa-minamiiru, Kamigyo-ku, admission free, open 9–5) is a museum established in 1915, where a large display of Nishijin products is exhibited and kimonos are on sale. Note that new silk kimonos are *very* expensive. **Aizan Kobo** (Omiya Nishi-iru, Nakasuji-dori, Kamigyo-ku, open 9–5) is the home of a traditional weaving family, who show and sell a variety of hand-woven and dyed silk goods and garments.

Flea markets
On the 21st day of each month a famous flea market is held at the Toji Temple, 15 minutes' walk southwest of Kyoto station. Renowned throughout Japan, it is said to be part of a tradition going back several hundred years. The market opens from dawn to dusk and is the place to buy old kimonos at a fraction of the cost of new ones (the Japanese are not keen on second-hand goods and old bric-à-brac is very cheap). There is another good flea market held on the 25th day of each month at the Kitano Temmangu Shrine.

■ **Gifts are an important part of Japanese life and ritual. Meeting for dinner at a friend's house, saying goodbye, meeting someone important for the first time, thanking someone for their help or a service provided are all occasions marked by giving or receiving a gift, and as a place to buy appropriate Japanese presents, Kyoto is second to none......■**

Gift-wrapping
In Japan the wrapping of a present is an art form in itself. Whether you buy from an expensive department store or a street vendor your goods will be deftly, swiftly and beautifully wrapped. When receiving a gift, unwrap it with care and respect.

Souvenir shops
One of the regular features of Japanese life is the many small souvenir and gift shops found near temples and railway stations and in holiday resorts. They provide for the tiny numerous presents bought to take home to relatives and friends after a day out or a weekend away from home. For the Japanese one of the joys of travelling is the purchase of such gifts.

The art of giving Before leaving home, it is useful to buy a number of small, lightweight gifts with some characteristic of your home country. Always wrap your gifts and do not press the recipient to open it while you are there. As with much else in Japanese life there are many subtleties to present-giving that you will not understand, but the one golden rule to remember in this situation and others is that neither party should be embarrassed or lose face.

Kyoto craftware The boundary between art and craft is not clearly defined within the tradition of Japanese craftwork and nowhere is this more evident than in Kyoto, where craftsmen serving the imperial court left a legacy of artistry and refinement maintained to this day. Locally made specialist craftwork is prefixed with *kyo* – for example, *kyo-yaki* are ceramics made in local kilns. Such items are relatively expensive but renowned throughout Japan for their craftsmanship.

Traditional gifts Dolls are generally regarded as works of art to be appreciated for their beauty rather than playthings. Expensive dolls are often encased in glass cases and displayed in Japanese homes. *Kyo-ningyo* are display dolls, produced in Kyoto since the 9th century, made of wood coated with a white paste and dressed in traditional costumes of the finest materials.

Souvenir ideas: china...

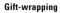

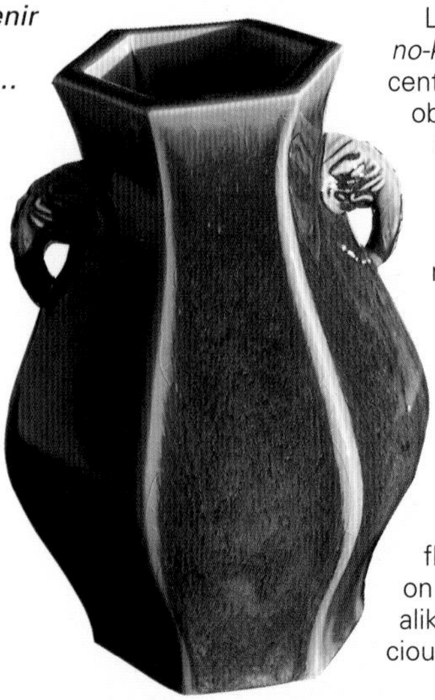

Lacquer, the sap of the lacquer tree (*urushi-no-ki*), has been used in Japan since the 6th century to coat both precious and well-used objects to give them a beautiful appearance and to protect them from the elements. Lacquerwork is commonly decorated with designs created by sprinkling gold and silver powders onto damp lacquer; mother of pearl, ivory and metals are also used. While decorative and often precious, lacquerware is intended for daily use. *Kyo-shikki*, Kyoto lacquerware products, include cabinets, writing boxes, bowls, serving trays and spoons.

The two most common types of Japanese fan are the folding fan and the flat fan. The former, called *sensu*, are used on ceremonial occasions by men and women alike. They are given as presents on auspicious occasions and used as accessories in the *noh* play and classical Japanese dance and as props in story-telling. *Kyo-sensu* are decorated folding fans made by Kyoto craftsmen.

The craft and art of making pottery and ceramic objects has attained an exceptional degree of refinement in Japan. Skills flourished particularly in the 16th century with the popularity of the tea ceremony. In the Kyoto region especially, numerous kilns produced tea bowls, serving dishes, tea storage jars and so on. Feudal lords competed with one another to have the finest wares, and their demands inspired technical and artistic enterprise. The most popular *kyo-yaki* products are perhaps the hand-painted red, green and blue on white tableware, made in the Kiyomizu district. The area around Kiyomizudera Temple is also a good place to look for shops specialising in *kyo-yaki*.

Kimonos Nowadays most Japanese wear Western clothing and only put on their kimonos for special occasions such as the New Year Festival or a wedding. New kimonos are extremely expensive, but second-hand kimonos can be a tenth of the price and are frequently in perfect condition.

... or wind-chimes

Money and tipping
If you receive a present and plan to give one back it should be of approximately the same value. If you plan to give money to a Japanese, be it to a child or for exceptional services rendered, always present it in an envelope. Remember, however, that tipping is not a custom in Japan and tips will not be expected or in some cases accepted.

Good-luck doll
The *papier-mâché daruma* doll is a popular good-luck figure and present, named after the legendary monk Bodidharma. A *daruma* doll is always painted red, with a fierce, bearded face. It is weighted at the base and if pushed over will right itself.

... or Japanese parasols

Nightlife

Kyoto after dark

Geisha girls
Gei means culture and *sha* person; a *geisha* is therefore a person practised in the arts. The profession of *geisha* is traditionally respected in Japan and the young ladies who follow it are highly esteemed. Most *geisha* never marry, although some may form a liaison with a regular client and prominent Japanese men may sometimes maintain a *geisha* as a sort of social secretary. Nowadays it is said that a few *geisha* do in fact accept sexual assignations outside their professional activities – yet a *geisha* is never obliged by the terms of her contract, and *makura* ('*geisha* cushions') can be summoned as stand-ins, if necessary, after dinner. Seasonal dances (Miyako Odori and Kamogawa Odori) performed by *geisha* and their apprentices to celebrate spring and autumn are held in Kyoto in April, May and October. These ravishing spectacles are held at the Gion Kaburenjo Theatre, Gion Hanamikoji, Higashiyama-ku and the Pontocho Kaburenjo Theatre, Pontocho Sanjo-sagaru, Nakagyo-ku.

A geisha *in Gion*

Kyoto is not noted for its nightlife, nor does it aspire to be, but for those who wish it there are enough bars, restaurants, *geisha* houses and hostess bars for several nights' exploration. For a more cultural experience the Gion quarter after dark gives one a real taste of old Japan, as well as the opportunity to see performances of traditional theatrical arts. Strolling the streets of Kyoto or the banks of the Kamo River on a fine evening is an excellent way of finding free entertainment. For a whole range of night-time entertainment, from pool to disco to karaoke, go to the eight-storey entertainment building, **Imagium**, Shijo-dori, Kobashi-nishi-iru.

Culture Gion, a small district of Kyoto, is the *geisha* entertainment quarter of the city. Here especially in the evening one can see *geishas* and their *maiko* (apprentices), dressed in gorgeous kimonos with beautiful hair and make-up, on their way to work. Gion Corner, a theatre in the heart of Gion, presents one-hour shows that give a brief taste of a variety of Kyoto's performing arts. Dancing, puppet theatre, court music, demonstrations of the tea ceremony, flower arrangement and *noh* comic routines are all included. The show is very good value. Tickets are available at most hotels, travel agents and Gion Corner. Two performances are given nightly at 7:40pm and 8:40pm, 1 March–29 November (no performances are offered on 16 August or from December to February).

Bars and clubs Kawaramachi-dori Street and the area around it, including Kiyamachi-dori Street to the east, is a district of small, inexpensive drinking clubs, bars and restaurants. Those with red lanterns outside are the most reasonable. If you are unsure of the cost, order a drink and then ask for the bill. In hostess bars you will quickly be offered tiny titbits to eat. Avoid these places unless you are rich or on an expense account.

Tourist Information Centre, Kyoto

Avoid Kyoto on public holidays and avoid the best-known temples at weekends. Otherwise it is very easy to get around on foot, by bus, subway or hired bike or, if you are in a hurry, by taxi. There are probably more guidebooks on Kyoto than on any other city in the world.

What's on If you arrive by train do not be put off by first impressions. The area around the main railway station is faceless and modern and not representative of much of the city. Almost opposite the main entrance of the station, across a wide, busy road, is the Tourist Information Centre (TIC) office, at the base of Kyoto Tower (an eyesore visible from most places in town). At the TIC you can obtain free brochures, street and subway/railway maps of Kyoto and you can book accommodation. They have the latest information on what is going on and also stock *Kyoto Visitors Guide*, a monthly publication in English for tourists. Kyoto also has two English-language telephone information services: call 361 2911 for a recording of the week's events, including sporting and arts events and festivals (24 hours); or 371 5649 for general information and an English-speaking guide (9–5).

Walking and cycling It is best to see the city in sections and to catch its flavour at a meditative pace, rather than rushing from place to place. A fun way to get around and to feel more 'local' is to go by bicycle. Several places hire cycles by the day, including **Nippon Rent a Car** (tel: 672 3045), opposite the Hachijo exit of Kyoto station; **Rent a Cycle Heian** (tel: 431 4522), on the west side of the Imperial Palace and **Cycle Yasumoto** (tel: 751 0595), near Keihan Sanjo station.

Getting to Kyoto
Journeys to Kyoto take about two hours, 40 minutes (514km) from Tokyo station, 45 minutes (148km) from Nagoya and three hours, 20 minutes (663km) from Fukuoka (Hakata), by the 'Hikari' on the JR Shinkansen. A long-distance night bus leaves from Tokyo station, arriving in eight hours, and a bus from Nagoya takes two hours, 40 minutes.

Taxis
Taxis in Kyoto come in three different sizes, increasing in price from the smallest to the largest category. Taxis are readily available from taxi stands and hotels, or they can be flagged down.

City traffic

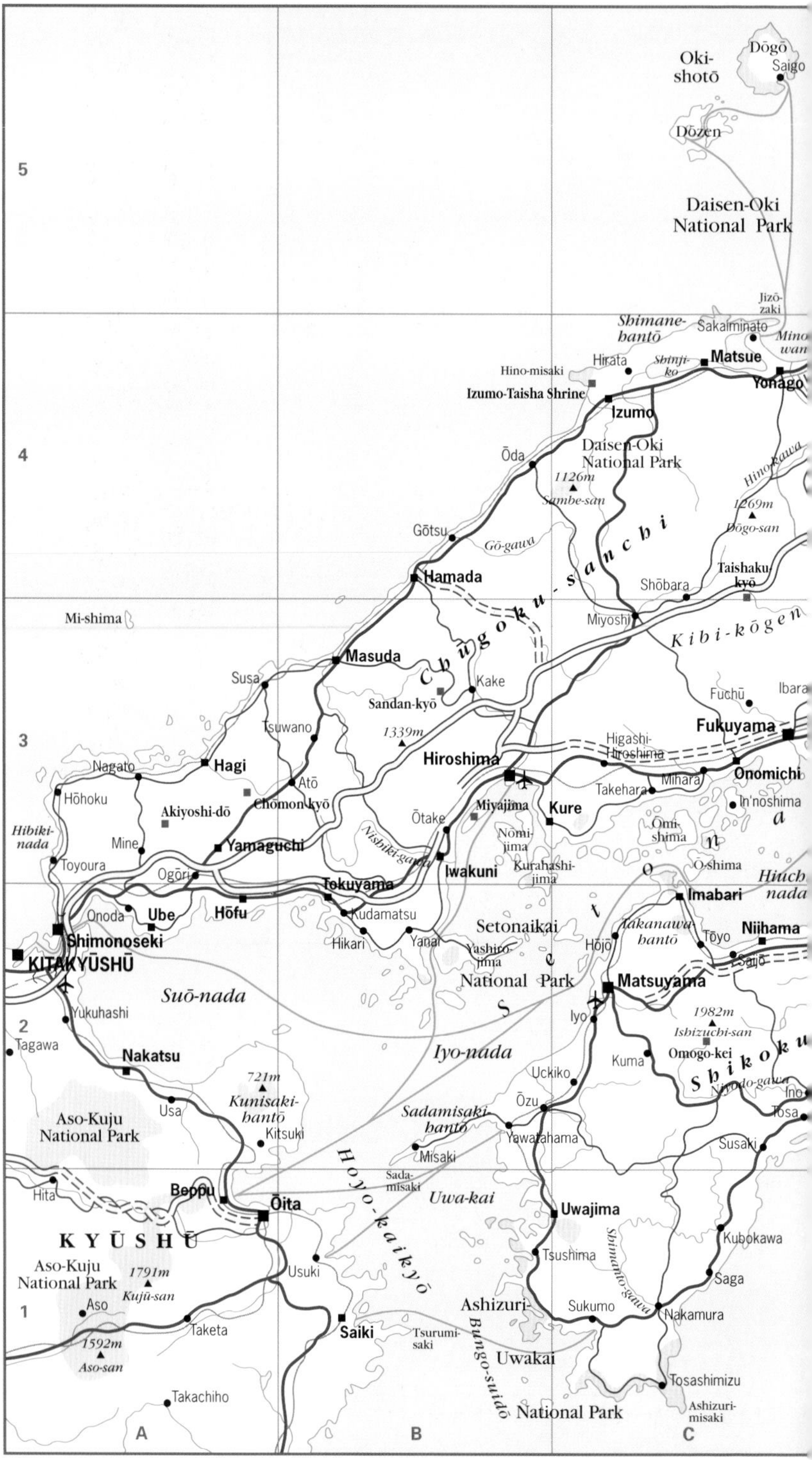
Oki-shotō
Dōgo
Saigo
Dōzen
Daisen-Oki National Park
Jizō-zaki
Shimane-hantō
Sakaiminato
Hino-misaki
Hirata
Shinji-ko
Matsue
Yonago
Izumo-Taisha Shrine
Izumo
Daisen-Oki National Park
Ōda
1126m
Sambe-san
Hino-kawa
1269m
Dōgo-san
Gōtsu
Gō-gawa
Chūgoku-sanchi
Hamada
Shōbara
Taishaku-kyō
Mi-shima
Miyoshi
Kibi-kōgen
Masuda
Susa
Kake
Sandan-kyō
Fuchū
Ibara
Tsuwano
1339m
Higashi-Hiroshima
Fukuyama
Nagato
Hagi
Hiroshima
Onomichi
Hōhoku
Atō
Mihara
Takehara
In'noshima
Akiyoshi-dō
Chōmon-kyō
Ōtake
Miyajima
Kure
Hibiki-nada
Mine
Yamaguchi
Nishiki-gawa
Nōmi-jima
Ōmi-shima
Toyoura
Ogōri
Iwakuni
Kurahashi-jima
Ō-shima
Tokuyama
Imabari
Hiuchi-nada
Onoda
Ube
Hōfu
Kudamatsu
Setonaikai National Park
Takanawa-hantō
Tōyo
Niihama
Shimonoseki
Hikari
Yanai
Yashiro-jima
Hōjō
Saijō
KITAKYŪSHŪ
Matsuyama
Suō-nada
Iyo
1982m
Ishizuchi-san
Yukuhashi
Tagawa
Iyo-nada
Omogo-kei
Nakatsu
Kuma
Shikoku
721m
Uchiko
Niyodo-gawa
Ino
Kunisaki-hantō
Ōzu
Tosa
Usa
Aso-Kuju National Park
Sadamisaki-hantō
Kitsuki
Yawatahama
Susaki
Misaki
Hoyo-kaikyō
Sada-misaki
Hita
Beppu
Uwa-kai
Ōita
Uwajima
KYŪSHŪ
Shimanto-gawa
Kubokawa
Tsushima
Usuki
Aso-Kuju National Park
1791m
Kujū-san
Saga
Aso
Ashizuri-Uwakai National Park
Sukumo
Nakamura
Bungo-suidō
Taketa
Saiki
Tsurumi-saki
1592m
Aso-san
Tosashimizu
Takachiho
Ashizuri-misaki
A
B
C
1
2
3
4
5

WESTERN HONSHU AND SHIKOKU

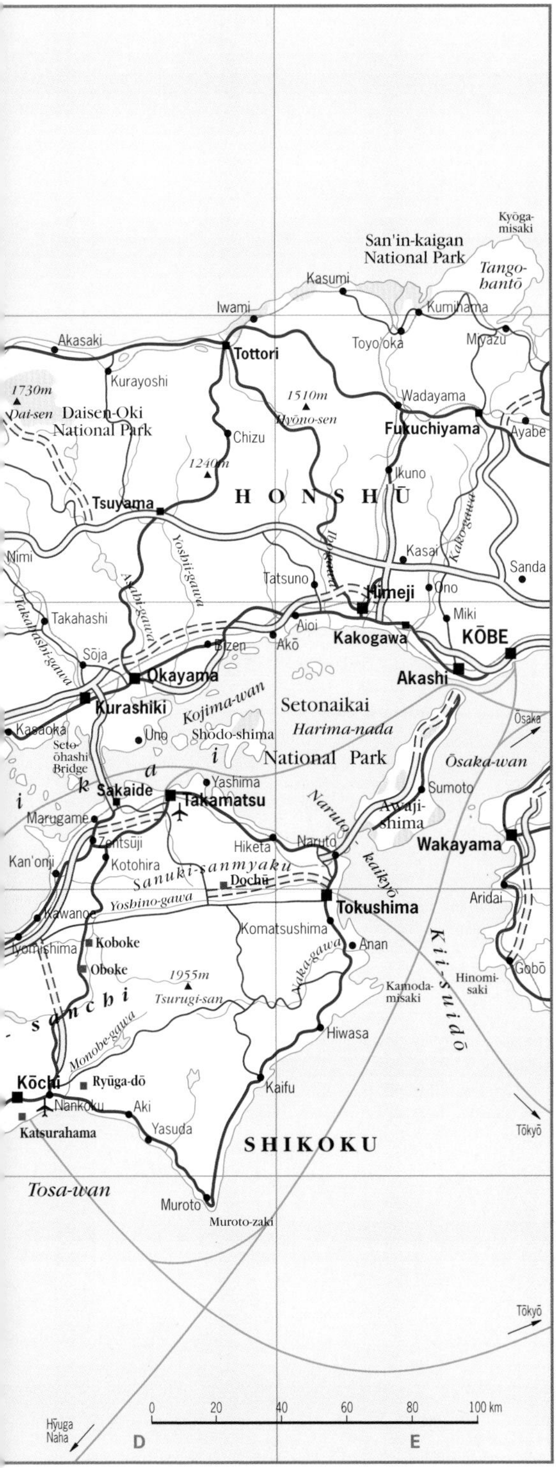

Tourist tips
Before visiting more remote areas, buy a Japanese phrase book and learn a few useful phrases. Pronunciation is not difficult and once you try a few words the Japanese lose their shyness and try out their English. If asking somebody for directions or other help, choose a young to middle-aged man or woman or a teenage boy. Old people tend to be shy of foreigners and teenage girls are often self-conscious and tongue-tied. Do not haggle or tip; neither would be either expected or understood.

Western Honshu This region is divided down the middle by a chain of mountains running from east to west. The San-yo region on the southern coast, facing the Seto Inland Sea, is a corridor of heavy residential development and industry. The San-in region, which stretches along the northern coast and faces the Sea of Japan, is, by contrast, a less developed area where tourists are few and agriculture and fishing remain the major economic activities.

San-yo coast The JR Shinkansen express Tokaido train line, from Tokyo to Kyushu, runs along the San-yo coast. Three of the main stops, Hiroshima, Okayama and Himeji, are also the cities of most interest to the tourist.

For the Japanese, Hiroshima has been an important town since the early 16th century; to the rest of the world it is known and visited as the target of the first nuclear weapon attack in history. For the tourist, apart from a trip of homage to the bomb victims, one of the reasons to visit Hiroshima is to take an excursion from there to Miyajima, a picturesque small island in the Inland Sea. Miyajima is traditionally regarded as one of the 'Big Three Scenic Attractions' in Japan.

Okayama is of interest chiefly for its Korakuen Gardens, which were laid out on the banks of the Ashigawa River 300 years ago, and are one of the three most famous gardens in Japan (Kenrokeun, in Kanazawa and Kairakuen, in

Miyajima

One section of the vast Seto-Ohashi Bridge

Kanazawa and Kairakuen, in Mito being the other two). Kurashiki, reached in 15 minutes from Okayama JR station, is an oasis of traditional Japan amid the industrial development of the San-yo coastal plain. After a visit to Korakuen Gardens in Okayama, Kurashiki is a good place to spend the rest of the day and the following morning.

Himeji is the site of perhaps the finest surviving castle in Japan and the second largest after Osaka Castle. Set on a hill overlooking the city, the castle goes by the name of Shirasagi, the White Egret (or Heron). The train services to Himeji are excellent and it is possible to arrive, visit the castle, and to leave within a morning or afternoon.

San-in coast There is much to see of ordinary Japanese rural life along the San-in coast: the main reason to go there is to enjoy a quiet part of Japan not often visited by foreign tourists nor catering for them. There are three towns and a famous shrine worth special visits: Matsue, a pleasant, busy town best known for being the home of Lafcadio Hearn, the 19th-century writer, and for its hot springs; Tsuwano, a small, well-preserved castle town; Hagi, a castle town and port, and Izumo-Taisha Shrine near Matsue, a famous Shinto shrine. Many Japanese travel there to pray for good fortune in marriage.

The Inland Sea Separating western Honshu from Shikoku island (see pages 168–77), the Inland Sea (*Seto-Naikai*) is about 500km long and ranges in width from 64km to just 6km. Mountainous coastlines and over a thousand small, pine-covered islands, scattered throughout its length, add to the beauty of this area, which has been designated a national park. Nevertheless, the once abundant marine life has been decimated by pollution and over-fishing. Increased environmental awareness and the growth of fish-farming offer the way to a brighter future. In the past the Inland Sea was the major route for the distribution of goods and the spread of culture between Kyushu and the old capitals of Nara and Kyoto in Honshu. Sightseeing cruises are available from Hiroshima and Takamatsu, on Shikoku.

The Seto-Ohashi Bridge
Seto-Ohashi, the longest bridge in the world, is actually composed of six bridges that connect a series of small islands in the Seto Inland Sea, using them as stepping stones from western Honshu to Shikoku. Claimed to be virtually earthquake-proof, the bridge was built using cables that could wrap around the earth several times. The authorities proudly advertise that construction costs measured in Y10,000 notes would create a stack three times as high as Mount Fuji. Train and bus services from Okayama to Takamatsu, on Shikoku, cross the bridge.

San-In Region

▶▶▶ Hagi *154A3*

In 1601 the Mori family built their castle at Hagi. Suspicious of the Tokugawa shogunate, they selected a defensive site bounded by the Hashimotogawa and Matsumotogawa rivers on two sides and the Sea of Japan on the third. For tourist information contact the Hagi Ryokan Association (tel: 0832 27 599). Their office is to the left of the Higashi-Hagi station, near the entrance of the Rainbow Plaza shopping arcade. Hagi downtown area is a 30-minute walk from the station or a short cab ride. Tamachi Mall is the busiest shopping street, with shops offering everything from French ballgowns to local crafts products, particularly pottery (Hagi is best known for a pinkish-beige tea ceremony stoneware).

Toko-ji Zen Temple

Lafcadio Hearn
The son of an Irish father and a Greek mother Lafcadio Hearn (1850–1904) spent his childhood years in Greece and later travelled to Britain and the US. Having arrived in Japan in 1890 and taken a teaching post in Matsue, he met and married a Japanese woman who had nursed him during a bout of illness. Hearn took Japanese citizenship and the name Koizumi Yakumo, and started to write about Japan. His accounts, including *Glimpses of an Unfamiliar Japan* (1894) and *A Japanese Miscellany* (1901), enthralled Westerners and the Japanese, who were fascinated to see themselves through the eyes of a foreigner. Hearn's books are still in print in Japan.

Hagi is equally accessible by bus and train. Express buses run from Ogori (one hour, 15 minutes); from Tsuwano (one hour, 50 minutes) and from Akiyoshi-do (one hour, 10 minutes). By train there is a JR San-in line express from Masuda (one hour, 10 minutes) and from Shimonoseki (two hours).

The castle of **Hagi-jo Ato▶▶** was built in 1604 and dismantled in 1874; only the massive outer walls and moat now remain, and the grounds have been turned into the Shizuki-koen Park. From the castle walls there are wonderful views of Hagi, the Sea of Japan and the mountains that surround the city on three sides.

Horiuchi▶▶▶ is an old *samurai* quarter southeast of the castle ruins, between the castle moat and the town centre. Once the domain of high-ranking *samurai* of the Mori Lords, this area is a maze of the earthen walls that surround each residence. There are three imposing *samurai* mansion gates still standing.

Toko-ji▶▶▶ is a simple but impressive Zen temple of the Obaku sect. The austere but grand tombs of five of the Mori Lords stand at the end of a pathway lined with 500 stone lanterns donated by the Lords' retainers. Each year, on 15 August, all the lanterns are lit in a guard of honour. Toko-ji is east of the Matsumotogawa River along the road which crosses Matsumotobashi Bridge.

▶▶ **Matsue** *154C4*

Situated on the Ohashi River, the town of Matsue is best known as the home of Lafcadio Hearn, a Western-born writer who took Japanese nationality in the 1890s (see panel). Somewhat off the beaten track for Western tourists, this relatively small town is a popular resort destination for many Japanese who spend their summer vacations here.

The simplest way to visit Matsue is by train. From Tsuwano, east on the San-in line, it takes three hours, 30 minutes. From Okayama the trip takes three hours, and the single daily express from Hiroshima takes one hour. On arrival at Matsue station visit the tourist information office in the station (open 9:30–5:30), where English-language brochures and maps of the city are available. Most of the sights are within walking distance of each other and the station and there is a good bus network.

Lafcadio Hearn's residence, **Koizumi Yakumo Kyukyo**▶▶, is a former *samurai* dwelling, opposite the northern moat of the castle. The house has been preserved as Hearn left it in 1891, and next door is a memorial hall where items of memorabilia concerned with his life and work are collected (open 9–12:30, 1:30–4.30; closed Wednesday).

Matsue-jo Castle▶▶ was built in 1611 and partially restored in 1642. Never taken or damaged, the castle's five-storey façade actually contains six levels. There is a collection of *samurai* arms and armour on the lower floors, and the view from the top floor makes the climb worthwhile. Take the bus to Kencho-mae from stop 1 or 2 outside the JR station, then walk to the castle in Jozenkoen Park. The Western-style building within the grounds is a fascinating museum of local history. There are displays of items from everyday life and photographs covering the period 1808 to the present day (castle and museum open 8:30–5).

Boats at Matsue

Castle auction
Matsue Castle is one of the few original Japanese castles to have survived without major reconstruction or rebuilding. In 1875 it was sold at auction for $90 to an individual who planned to demolish it. Fortunately it was saved for posterity by a group of interested local people, who pooled their money to buy it off the successful bidder.

Matsue-jo tea house

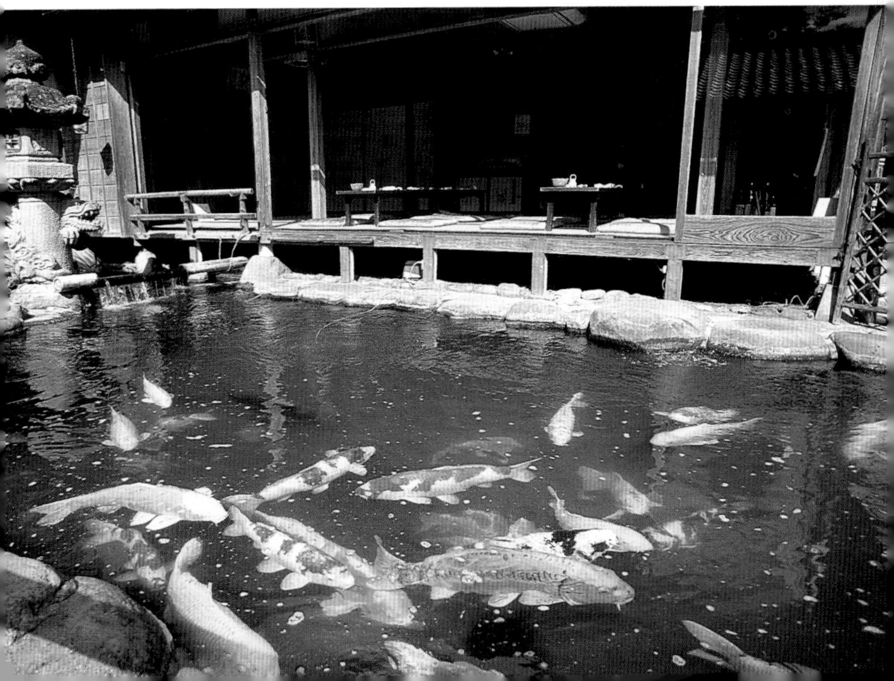

Izumo Taisha Shrine

■ The Izumo Taisha Shrine is the oldest and largest Shinto shrine in Japan and the second most important, after the imperial shrines at Ise. The original buildings collapsed in 1031 and were later rebuilt on a smaller scale, the main shrine being built in 1744 and other important buildings dating from 1874......■

Daikoku
To the northwest, behind the main shrine buildings, the former Treasure House (Shokokan) houses a large collection of images of Okuninushi-no-mikoto in the form of Daikoku, a happy, chubby character standing on a number of rice bales, holding a sack over his shoulder with one hand and a mallet in the other. He is normally accompanied by his son Ebisu, who stands beside him with a fish under his arm.

Getting there
The Izumo Taisha Shrine is several kilometres northwest of Izumo, and is served by two railway stations – the Ichihata Izumo Taisha station and the JR Izumo Taisha station – and a bus terminal. A more or less straight road leads up to the shrine and the visitor can find a range of accommodation and restaurants in the shrine area. A tourist information office can be found on the main street close to the shrine entrance.

Happy marriage Set in pleasantly wooded grounds against a backdrop of the Yakumo Hill, the Izumo Taisha Shrine is dedicated to the worship of Okuninushi-no-mikoto (Master of the Great Land), the *kami* or spirit god of fishing, silk production and marriage. According to legend, Okuninushi-no-mikoto was a descendant of Susa-no-o, a *kami* of the Yamato line who married an Izumo Princess. In time Okuninushi-no-mikoto married a Yamato princess and agreed to serve the Yamato line, as long as he was worshipped at a great shrine. Scholars believe that this tale reflects the struggle for dominance between rival clans during the earliest period of Japanese history, and that Okuninushi-no-mikoto's acceptance of Yamato authority reflected the emerging political and military dominance of the Yamato clan. The legend has led to the belief that a visit to the shrine is extremely beneficial to those who are contemplating marriage or to promoting harmony for any union. Visitors to the shrine clap four times instead of the normal two to attract the deity's attention; twice for themselves and twice for their intended partner or partners.

Taisha architecture The shrine buildings are constructed according to the Taisha style, an ancient form of architecture thought to be purely Japanese. The Haiden (Hall of Worship), with extremely heavy, tapering *shimenawa* (sacred twisted straw ropes) hanging over the entrance, is the first building to be seen inside the entrance *torii* gate. The Honden (Main Hall) is not open to the public. Along the sides of the shrine compound are to be found *juku-sha*, special buildings or shelters erected to house the 8 million *kami* which are said to assemble at Izumo every year. To the southeast is the Shinko-den, or Treasure House (open 8–4:30), which contains a collection of shrine artefacts.

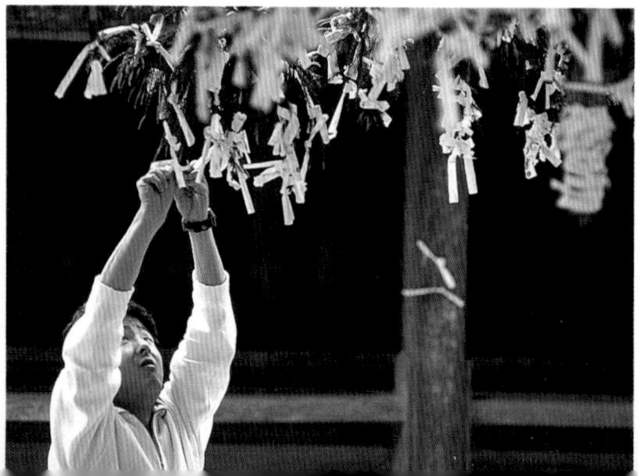

Hanging good luck notes at the shrine

▶▶▶ Tsuwano *154B3*

This small town in a narrow valley, high in the mountains, is nicknamed 'Little Kyoto' and preserves many features of the past, including large numbers of carp, originally bred as food in case of siege. They now live in the water channels flowing through the old *samurai* quarter of Tonomachi. There are good mountain walks, well maintained temples and castle ruins above the town. The tourist office has maps and details of cycle hire shops.

Tsuwano is just over one hour by train on the JR from Ogori, which is on the Shinkansen line, 40 minutes west of Hiroshima. From 29 April to 5 May and 20 July to 31 August, and on Sundays and National Holidays in May, September, October and November, the trip from Ogori may be made by the last steam locomotive in Japan.

Maria Sei-do▶▶ is a tiny chapel on a hill east of the station, built in 1948 by a German Catholic priest in memory of Japanese Catholics who were exiled to Tsuwano.

High on a hillside above Tsuwano, the vermilion red **Taikodani-Inari Shrine▶▶▶** is reached by stone steps and through a long tunnel of over a thousand small red *torii* gates. The steps, which are quite steep, start behind the Yasaka Shrine, on the river bank.

Tsuwanojo Castle▶▶ was originally built over a period of 30 years and completed in 1325, but was dismantled during the Meiji Restoration. The grounds, high above the town, offer spectacular views, and are reached by a steep walk or by chairlift, followed by a 10-minute walk.

Detail of the tunnel of torii *gates at Taiko dani-Inari Shrine*

The Ogai Mori connection

Yomei-ji, a Soto Zen temple to the east of Tsuwano station, has a charming garden and a handsome thatched roof main hall, but is best known as the tomb of Ogai Mori (1862–1922). One of the leading literary figures of the Meiji Restoration, Ogai Mori spent his childhood in Tsuwano. On Tonomachi Street, lined with the whitewashed walls that used to surround *samurai* residences, the Yorokan Museum was once Ogai Mori's house and the local *samurai* school. It now houses exhibitions of folk craft in what was once the fencing *dojo* or training hall (open 8:30–5:30).

Taiko dani-Inari Shrine

Well whispers
Himeji Castle is rich in myths and stories. One of them concerns a well known as Okiku no Iso, found within the castle precincts. According to legend a maid, Okiku, was found guilty of breaking a valuable plate and thrown down the well as punishment. Her voice can still be heard at night as she mournfully counts her lord's remaining crockery.

Lessons in culture
Himeji Shinmen Kaikan, at 112 Sosha Nonmachi, Himeji (tel: 84 2800), offers free lessons in the arts of flower-arranging, tea ceremony and the proper way to wear a kimono, on an alternating basis from Monday to Friday. A free English-language leaflet giving more details is available at the tourist information office at the station.

San-Yo Region

►► Himeji *155E3*

Himeji was severely bombed during World War II and has little to interest the foreign visitor except its magnificent castle, which has survived almost intact. Bullet trains run here on the JR Shinkansen line from the following major cities: Tokyo (four hours), Kyoto (one hour), Okayama (30 minutes) and Shin-Osaka (40 minutes). The private Hankyu line also operates a service between Kobe and Himeji. A tourist information office is located to the right of the north exit of Himeji station.

Himeji-jo Castle►►► is also known as Shirasagi-jo, or 'The Castle of the White Crane', because of its white plastered walls and silhouette from a distance. One of the few original medieval castles remaining in Japan, and one of the most beautiful, its first fortifications were erected in the 14th century and extended by Hideyoshi in 1581. The main tower is supported by three smaller towers and three rings of defensive compounds, which feature loopholes for firing guns or arrows at the enemy as well as *ishiotoshi*, openings through which rocks or boiling oil could be dropped on to attackers. Altogether the castle presented the best defensive system of its day in Japan. From the central, north exit of Himeji station, the castle is a 15-minute walk (open 9–5; closed Monday).

Housed in a fine building in the northeast corner of the Himeji-jo grounds, the **Hyogo-kenritsu Rekishi Hakubutsukan (Hyogo Prefectural Museum of History)►** contains material from prehistoric times to the present, including displays of Himeji Castle and other castles from around the world. There is also a splendid exhibition of puppet heads, used in *ningyo joruri* (puppet

Himeji-jo Castle

Hiroshima's peace bell

drama), from Awajishima, an island in the Inland Sea, where the art originated (open 10–5; closed Monday).

Founded in the 12th century, the large complex of temples making up the **Shoshazan Enkyoji▶▶** includes the oldest surviving Kamakura period (14th-century) structure, the Yakushido, and the Kongo Satta Buddha, carved in 1395. To get there take a number 6 or 8 bus from the front of Himeji station to the Shosha bus stop. Walk to the temple grounds or transfer to the ropeway, by the bus stop, which takes you to the temple. Alternatively, take one of the horse-drawn carriages usually waiting at the stop. They are as cheap as the ropeway.

▶▶▶ Hiroshima *154B3*

The city of Hiroshima is known worldwide as the target of the first atomic bomb used in a war. The bomb exploded on 6 August 1945 at 8:15am, killing half the population of 400,000 people (about 80,000 people died immediately) and almost totally destroying the heart of the city. Hiroshima has been rebuilt, but the charred and twisted skeleton of the Industrial Promotion Hall, renamed the A-Bomb Dome, has been allowed to remain as a reminder of the destruction.

A new airport was opened in Hiroshima in 1993, connected by flights to Tokyo (Haneda Airport), Kagoshima (Kyushu) and Sapporo (Hokkaido). Bullet trains on the JR Shinkansen line run from the following major cities: Tokyo (4 hours, 30 minutes), Kyoto (2 hours), Fukuoka/Hakata (1 hour, 20 minutes).

Two tourist information offices in Hiroshima station provide maps and English brochures.

A visit to the **Peace Memorial Park▶▶▶** is a solemn and sobering experience. Set in the centre of the city, it contains a number of monuments, including the Peace Memorial Museum and the Peace Memorial Hall, all concerned with recording and describing the story of the A-bomb which devastated the city. A Peace Flame burns in front of the Memorial Cenotaph, never to be extinguished until all nuclear weapons are abolished.

Korean victims
As well as the Japanese killed by the A-bomb there were 20,000 Koreans who had been brought to Japan as slave labour during World War II. Koreans and their descendants still suffer discrimination in Japan, and their fate was ignored by the authorities until 1970, when a Cenotaph for Korean Victims was erected outside the Park.

A-bomb children
The Statue of the A-Bomb Children in the Peace Memorial Park was inspired by Sadako, a girl dying from radiation poisoning who believed that if she folded 1,000 paper cranes she would recover. She died after folding 664 cranes. Children now fold paper cranes in her memory and the statue is surrounded by millions of paper cranes.

Paper cranes in the Peace Memorial Park

Kurashiki Toy Museum

Sacred Miyajima
Miyajima is considered so sacred that there are no cemeteries on the island. The heavily pregnant and those approaching death are not allowed to stay there; they are taken to the mainland instead.

Feeding deer on Miyajima island

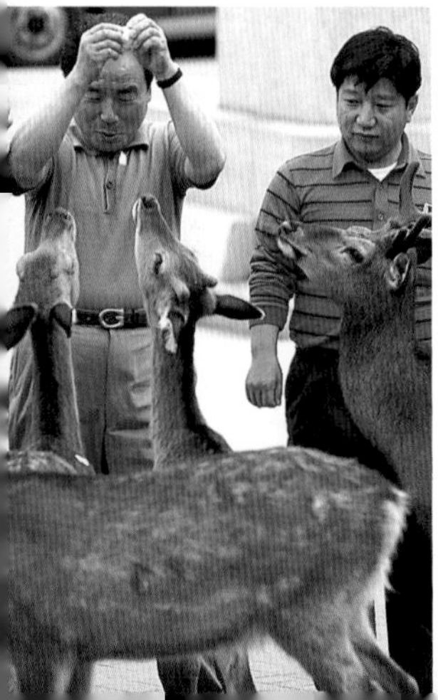

▶▶▶ Kurashiki 155D3

'Warehouse Village' was originally an important centre of the rice trade. Surprisingly, it escaped war damage and many of the large rice granaries still exist in the old part of the town known as the Bikan Historical Area. They and many other Edo-period buildings have been turned into museums, shops, *ryokan* and restaurants. Kurashiki is famous for its museums and art collections; it is also a picturesque and charming town, and its tourist appeal now sustains the Kurashiki town coffers.

Bullet trains run on the JR Shinkansen line from Kyoto (two hours) or Tokyo (four hours, 30 minutes) to Shin-Kurashiki station. Here you change for the local train to Kurashiki station (departure every 15 minutes). There is also a frequent commuter train service from Okayama JR station to Kurashiki station, journey time about 15 minutes. The tourist information office, on the second floor of Kurashiki station, has maps and information available in English.

Kurashiki Folkcraft Museum▶▶▶ is well worth a visit. It houses a collection of Japanese and foreign items to tie in with its slogan, 'Usability Equals Beauty' (open December–February 9–4:30, March–November 9–5; closed Monday).

The **Nihon Kyudo Gangukan (Japan Rural Toy Museum)**▶▶▶ contains a fine collection of over 2,000 toys from all over Japan and other countries, and sells Japanese rural toys (open 8–5).

▶▶▶ Miyajima 154B3

'Shrine Island' is considered to be one of the three most beautiful islands in Japan. The entire island has been consecrated as a shrine, and is also the site of the famous Itsukushima Shinto Shrine, noted for its huge *torii* gate, set in the sea.

The easiest way to visit the island is to take the JR Sanyo line from Hiroshima station to Miyajima-guchi station (25 minutes); from there it is a short walk to the pier and the ferry to the island (22 minutes). A tourist information office is located in the JR ferry terminal on arrival in Miyajima.

The island is 30km in circumference, with Mount Misen at its centre rising to 530m. Although its beauty has been tainted by tourist attractions, this is still a lovely place and worth a day's visit or an overnight stop.

To the west of the ferry pier, **Itsuku Shrine▶▶▶** is approached through Miyajima Village (a tourist trap) and then a park where many tame deer roam. Originally built in AD593 and last rebuilt in the 16th century, the shrine is dedicated to the three daughters of Susano-o-no-Mikoto, the Shinto god of the moon and oceans. Most of the shrine is private, but the five-storey pagoda and Senjokaku Hall, situated on a small hill above the shrine, are open to the public.

▶▶ Okayama *155D3*

This major city lies on the Inland Sea and is famous for its Korakuen Gardens. Okayama is on the JR Shinkansen line, four hours from Tokyo and just under one hour from Hiroshima. The tourist information office is located near the central exit of the east side of Okayama station.

Okayama is a busy commercial city, not a tourist destination, but it is worth visiting Korakuen Gardens▶▶▶, constructed between 1687 and 1700 and considered to be one of the three most beautiful landscape gardens in Japan. The 11 hectares feature streams, a pond, bamboo groves, pine, plum and cherry trees, as well as 'borrowed views' of the surrounding hills and Okayama castle (open April–September 7:30–6, October–March 8–5).

Okayama-jo▶▶, or 'Crow Castle', was destroyed in World War II and rebuilt in 1966. Painted black to contrast with Himeji's famous castle, Okayama-jo houses a collection of *samurai* arms and armour, palanquins etc. There is also an elevator to the top of the donjon (open 9–5).

Itsukushima *torii* gate
The Itsukushima gate is the subject of countless photographs and paintings, always taken or painted when the tide is in and the *torii* shimmers above the water. In fact it stands most of the time in mud flats. From inside the Itsukushima Shrine grounds there is a good view of the brilliant vermilion gate. Offerings are often made by individuals or companies to have the lanterns in the shrine galleries lit at night, producing a spectacular sight if viewed on a dark night at high tide.

The striking torii *gate at Itsukushima Shrine*

Landscape gardens

■ The Japanese approach to landscape gardening has traditionally veered away from military precision and geometric perfection. Forcing mechanical order on nature is unattractive to the Japanese spirit, and it is also felt to be wasteful in terms of time and energy. Japanese landscape gardeners thus aspire to work with nature, extending and enhancing natural beauty......■

Garden poems
Japanese poets have always been inspired by a love of nature. The garden, reflecting nature, has served as inspiration for a number of poets. In the following poem the Emperor Meiji (1852–1912) uses the image of the garden as a symbol of Japan:
'In my garden
Side by side
Native plants, foreign plants,
Growing together.'

Artificially natural Japanese landscape gardeners design their work as microcosms of the real world, aiming to show nature on a small scale. For example, when Muso Soseki laid out the gardens of the Saihoji Temple (the 'Moss Temple' of Kyoto), he did not first level the ground to form a flat surface. Instead he allowed the moss to follow the natural undulations of the ground, and to display a wide range of different shades of green, complementing and contrasting with one another. Trees and stones were then placed subtly among the moss, so that they would seem quite natural; the art of the landscape gardener is unseen.

As well as moss, Japanese gardens feature extensive use of trees such as pine and maple, bamboo groves, small streams and ponds, rocks, stones and sand. The materials are arranged so as to represent mountains, rivers, lakes and waterfalls, and are planted with flowering trees such as cherry, peach and plum. Other features are flowering shrubs such as azaleas, wisteria, camellias, and rhododendron and evergreen plants and ferns, normally planted alongside streams and ponds. From these components three basic types of garden evolved: the *tsukiyama* (hill style), the *kare sansui* ('waterless stream gardens', see pages 134–5) and the *chaniwa* (tea garden).

Hill gardens The *tsukiyama* style of garden typically features streams with stepping stones and a bridge leading to a small island set in a pond. A twisting path leads the visitor from one feature to another, so that various changing scenes can be viewed. Some gardens feature miniaturised versions of actual beauty spots famous in Japanese art or literature. One variation of the *tsukiyama* style of garden is known as the *kaiyu* or 'many pleasure' style. Popular with the *daimyo* (feudal lords) of the Tokugawa shogunate, the *kaiyu* style features several gardens built around a central pond. Often one or more of them incorporates views which lie outside the garden itself, a technique known as 'borrowed views' (*shakkei*) or 'capturing alive' (*ikedori*). This feature is often seen in gardens in the Kyoto area, where the spectacular mountains that surround the city are seen framed by gateposts and trees.

Tea gardens The *chaniwa* garden is designed to enhance the peaceful, spiritual nature of the tea ceremony, hence its description as the 'fourth wall' of the tea house. The traditional *chaniwa* always features ferns, moss, ever-

A gardener tackles the water feature

Rikugien Garden in Tokyo

A Western view
In his book *Around the World Through Japan*, written at the turn of the century, Walter Del Mar described the requirements of a Japanese landscape garden as: 'a cart-load of rocks, a pail of water, a modicum of ingenuity, and unlimited imagination – all concentrated on a space the size of a mat.' A more elaborate garden would need a dwarf pine, tortured out of its natural shape with permanent bandages and bits of wood and string, or some which 'the patient gardeners have bent, interlaced, tied, weighed down, and propped up the limbs and twigs.' Multiplied by 10, these would provide 'a leafy, lake-centred paradise, and a marvel of artistic arrangement'.

green trees and shrubs, set against bamboo fences and stone lanterns. The visitor moves through the *chaniwa* and towards the tea house along stepping stones placed asymmetrically on the ground. He or she then encounters a waiting room (*machiai*), separated from the inner garden around the tea house by a small gate (*chumon*). Within the inner garden there is a stone water basin, used to wash hands and rinse the mouth before entering the tea house. The tea gardens of the Kinkakuji Temple and the Katsura Imperial Villa, both in Kyoto, are among the most famous in Japan (see pages 128–9 and 140).

Kenrokuen Garden, Kanazawa

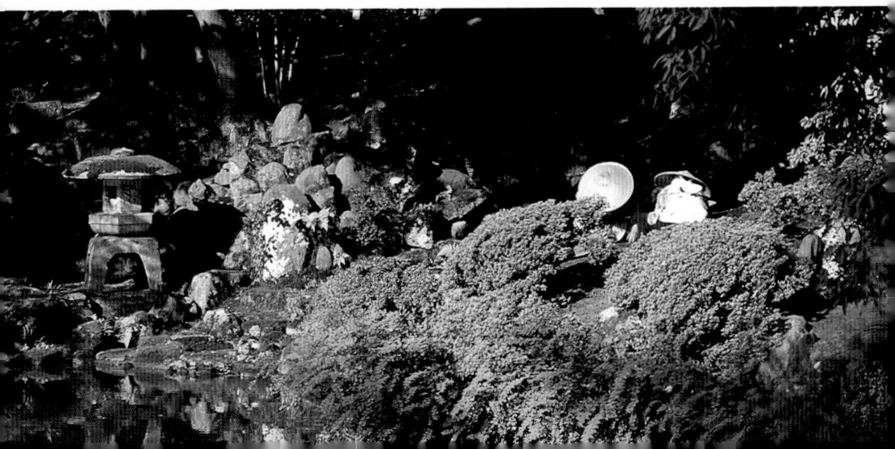

Shikoku

Climate
Shikoku has two climatic regions, separated by the mountain ranges that run east to west across the island. The Pacific Coast area, to the south, is subtropical, with hot summers and mild, wet winters. The Inland Sea region, to the north, is less rainy and most days are bright and sunny.

Shikoku The smallest of the four main islands of Japan lies across the Seto Inland Sea from the San-yo coast of Honshu. It is a mountainous, wooded island, lacking in natural resources, limited in industrial development and restricted in inter-island communications. Except for its major sights, Shikoku is still relatively unexplored by foreign and Japanese tourists. However, in 1988, after 10 years of construction, the Seto-Ohashi Bridge connecting Shikoku with Honshu by road and rail was opened and tourism is already increasing.

Geography The hinterland of the northern coast has attracted most of the island's industry and is the location of its two largest cities, Takamatsu and Matsuyama. Here also, rice, wheat, mandarin oranges and tobacco flourish on terraced mountain slopes and any flat land not taken by housing or industry. The interior of the island, to which access is difficult, is a place of clean rivers, Buddhist temples, small villages and remote hiking trails. The southern half of the island, except for the Kochi plain, is steeply mountainous and outside of the few towns sustains a small population of rice farmers and fishermen.

Paper crafts
Shikoku, and especially the Kochi area, is famous for its paper products. The raw material is pulp from Japanese mulberry trees, cultivated on the mountain slopes of Shikoku's interior. High-quality paper is used to make many goods, including *shoji* screens, lanterns, paper wallets, *daruma* dolls and masks. Small, flat paper items make excellent, lightweight presents to take home.

Kobo Daishi To the Japanese, Shikoku is best known as the centre of Shingon Buddhism. Every year thousands of followers make a pilgrimage by walking tour (or, more recently, bus tour) of the island's 88 temples in memory of Kobo Daishi, founder of the sect (see pages 184–5 and 178). Many temples offer overnight accommodation.

Main towns Takamatsu is a medium-sized town and a pleasant, convenient centre for exploring the rest of Shikoku. Ritsurin Park is the town's main tourist destination. After dark, Takamatsu has a busy nightlife and the 'entertainment area' is a maze of neon-lit, pedestrian-only arcades lined with bars, restaurants and late-night shops.

Matsuyama is Shikoku's largest city, but with more of a country town atmosphere than Takamatsu, and is famous for its Dogo Onsen, one of the best-known hot-spring public baths in Japan. A unique cultural aspect of Matsuyama is the local love of *haiku* poetry.

Aspects of Shikoku: a floating restaurant...

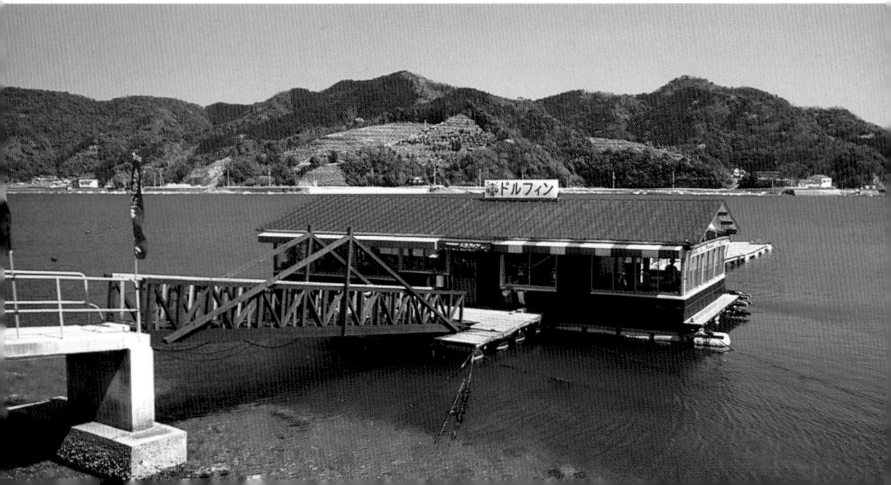

...dramatic mountain scenery...

Kotohira, also in the north of the island, is a small town nestling beneath the nationally revered Kotohiragu Shrine, to Omononushi-no-mikoto, the Shinto protector of travellers and sailors, whose popular name is Kompira-san. For tired pilgrims there is a *kago* service (a chair suspended from poles and carried by porters) up the hundreds of stairs to the shrine summit. Kotohira also has one of the oldest *kabuki* theatres in Japan.

Uwajima is the last stop on the railway line west from Takamatsu – a five-and-a-half-hour journey. Trains leave Takamatsu about five times daily for this small country town, well known locally for its bullring (two bulls, like four-legged *sumo* wrestlers, try to push each other out of a small ring). Outside Uwajima railway station is a small tourist office. Taga Jinja is the local Shinto shrine, where the priest is an avid collector of sexual memorabilia.

Kochi, in the south of the island, is a friendly market town. For the tourist the major attraction is Kochijo Castle, which is in almost pristine condition.

Getting there A direct train to Takamatsu leaves Tokyo station every night at 9:05, arriving at 7:35 the following morning. There are regular services to Takamatsu from Okayama station on the Shinkansen line (one hour). JR ferry and hovercraft services connect Uno on Honshu to Takamatsu. Uno is connected to Okayama by a frequent train service, and Takamatsu is connected by an air service to Osaka and Tokyo. Shikoku's three main railway lines begin at Takamatsu: the JR Yosan line to Matsuyama; the JR Dosan line to Kochi; and the JR Kotoku line to Tokushima.

Haiku poetry

Haiku is a highly stylised and refined form of Japanese poetry, in which the poet aspires to express deep and spontaneous insights about nature and human life. The *haiku* always consists of 17 syllables, arranged in three lines, the first of 5 syllables, the second of 7 and the last of 5. It is traditional to use the name of a flower, animal, custom or event which invokes the feeling of a particular season. Basho (1644–94) is considered the father and greatest exponent of *haiku* in its present form. Here are two examples of his poetry:

The sea dark
The call of the teal
Dimly white

Soon it will die
Yet no trace of this
In the cicada's screech.

...and hay stacks in the rural centre

Bargaining at Kochi's Sunday market

Dog-fighting
Dog fights are popular in particular areas of Japan. Among *aficionados*, top dogs and their owners achieve the same status as star *sumo* wrestlers. A *sumo* ranking system is used and winning dogs are even paraded around the ring in miniature *sumo*-style aprons. Fights take place on a caged circular stage, surrounded by tiers of seats. The dogs, which unexpectedly do not bark, weigh in at around 150kg; they jockey for a grip on one another's shoulders and then try to throw the other dog down. The fight is over when one dog stays down. A judge sits in a high chair within the caged stage, punishing illegal moves such as nose- or testicle-biting by spraying the nose of the offender with a stinging liquid or, in severe cases, placing a lit piece of paper under the penis of the attacker!

►► Kochi *155D2*

This castle town is located on the central southern coast of Shikoku, two and a half hours by train from Kotohira. The local microclimate is subtropical and farming and agriculture are the main industries in the surrounding countryside, which is lush and fertile..

Almost every day of the week there is a street market in Kochi; the biggest is on Sunday morning, on palm-lined Otesumi-dori Avenue, near the centre of town. *Onagadori* show birds (see panel) may also be on display.

Kochi-jo Castle►►, in the middle of Kochi Park in the west of the city, dates from 1603. The top of the intact five-storey keep (donjon) provides a panoramic view of the city. There is a museum in the grounds with much information about Lord Sakamoto Ryoma (1835–67), a local swashbuckling hero who helped topple the shogunate. The Lord's Residence, Kaitokukan, is open on the first floor of the donjon; kept in its original condition, it gives an insight into how the *daimyo* lived (open 9–4:30).

Katsurahama beach►►, a white, coarse, sand beach, 35 minutes by bus from Kochi station, is popular with locals in the summer, particularly for the swimming, and in the autumn for moon-viewing. Kochi is famous for breeding the Tosa fighting dog (see panel), and the Tosa Fighting Dog Centre is based here.

►►► Kotohira *155D3*

Kotohira, 45 minutes by JR Dosan line express from Takamatsu, is best known for its Kotohiragu Shrine, one of the oldest, grandest and most popular Shinto shrines in Japan, and for the Kyu Kompira Oshibai, the only complete Edo-period *kabuki* playhouse left in Japan.

Known as Kompira-san, **Kotohiragu Shrine►►►** was originally founded in the 11th century. It is dedicated to Omononushi-no-Mikoto (nicknamed Kompira), the guardian of seafarers, who would visit the shrine to pray for safe journeys at sea. Part of the shrine complex houses models and photographs of boats left there by fishermen soliciting protection. Nowadays his aid is sought by all travellers, and by those seeking better fortunes.

The shrine is built on the slopes of Mount Zozu and the main complex is at the top of 785 stone steps. Turn left out of Kotohira station, under a *torii* gate, and then turn right down a narrow shopping street and you will quickly come to the start of the steps. The climb will take 30–40 minutes and is quite daunting if you are not fit. Litter-bearers will carry you up in a *kago* for a reasonable sum, given the arduousness of the task. The steps are lined with souvenir shops, inns and refreshment stalls, but once through the main gate the atmosphere becomes more refined. At the top there are wonderful panoramic views of the surrounding Sanuki Plain, the Inland Sea to the north and the Shikoku mountain ranges to the south.

Near the first flight of steps leading to Kotohiragu Shrine is the ***kabuki*** **playhouse**►►►, built in 1835 in traditional style, with paper lanterns, *tatami* mats and sliding *shoji* screens to adjust the light. The revolving stage, which has two trap doors, is turned by eight men in the basement. The entrance to the building is small, to keep out gate-crashers. Plays are staged once a year in April but the theatre is open daily for viewing (open 9–4; closed Tuesday).

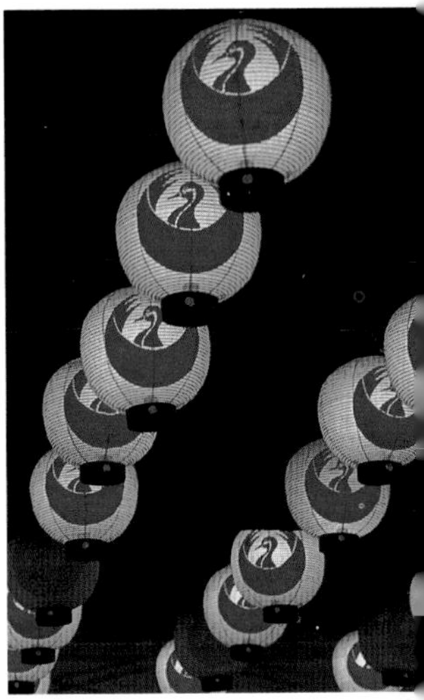

Kotohira's kabuki *play-house lit by lanterns*

Long-tailed roosters
An unusual feature of Kochi is the rearing of long-tailed roosters. The tradition began with the wish to provide decorative features for the processional standards of local *daimyo*. Three centuries later, selective breeding has produced roosters with tails as long as 10m. Specimens strut in the grounds of local shrines. *Onagadori*, as they are called, may be seen at the Nagaodori Centre, a 15-minute cab ride from the centre of Kochi (open 9–5; closed Monday).

Kotohiragu shrine
The inner shrine complex includes the Treasure House, which contains scrolls, sculpture and Noh masks; Shoin, the original reception hall, housing paintings by Maruyama Okyo, an 18th-century artist; Asahi-no Yashiro, a carved hall, dedicated to Amaterasu, the sun goddess; and Ema-do, a pavilion containing ship models and old photographs, offered by pilgrims.

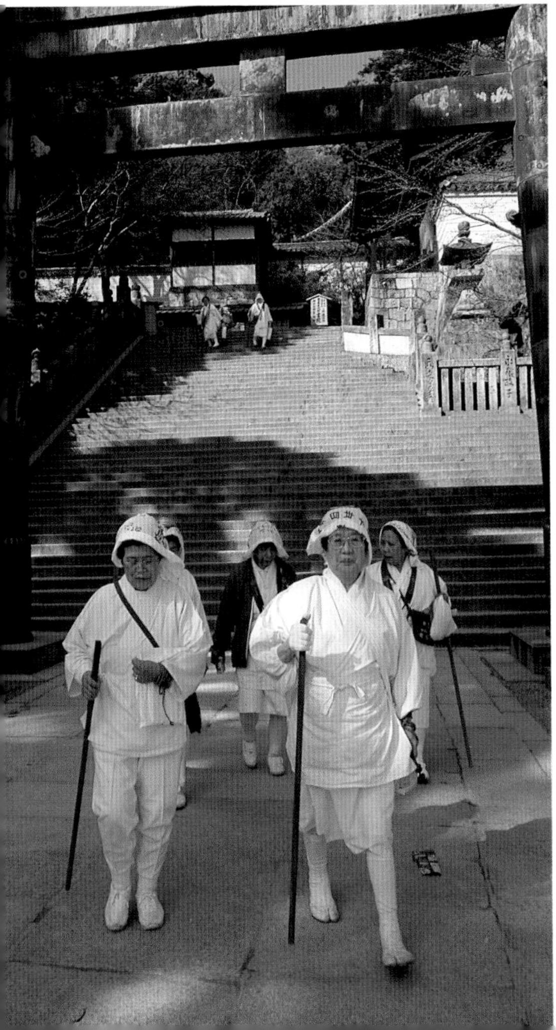

Pilgrims at Kotohiragu Shrine

Swords and armour
Omishima Island is one hour by hydrofoil boat from Imabari Port, 40 minutes on the JR Yosan line from Matsuyama. The boat docks at Miyaura and from here it is a short cab ride (1km) to Oyamazumi Shrine. There, most unexpectedly, housed in the shrine treasure hall, is the best collection of swords and armour in Japan. For many centuries Oyamazumi was a popular place of worship for emperors and *shogun* and it became a tradition for them to donate swords and armour to the shrine. Today 80 per cent of the nation's most treasured items of this type are to be found here, including armour worn by Minamoto Yoritomo, first *shogun* of the Kamakura period (1192–1333).

►►► Matsuyama *154C2*

Matsuyama, on the northwest coast of Shikoku, is the island's largest city, renowned in the past as a centre of art and literature. The most convenient way to get there is by train from Okayama, Honshu (2 hours, 40 minutes) or Takamatsu, Shikoku (2 hours, 50 minutes). The city tourist information office is located just inside the JR station. The main sights in town are Matsuyama Castle, one of the finest surviving feudal castles in Japan, and Dogo Onsen, a celebrated public bath. Matsuyama has an excellent network of street cars and finding one's way around is quite easy. (World War II bombing devastated Matsuyama and post-war city planners favoured practicality, hence the characterless network of straight avenues and boulevards, given colour only by the street cars.)

Matsuyama's local crafts include *iyo-kasuri*, an indigo-dyed cotton once used to make working clothes for farming women; *tobe-yaki*, a thick porcelain decorated with brushed cobalt-blue designs on a white ground; and oval-shaped dolls designed in honour of Empress Jingu, who visited Dogo Onsen when she was pregnant. For these and other items from the Ehime Prefecture visit the Ehime no Bussan store, Ichibancho 4-chome (Kencho-mae street car stop; open 8:30–5, Monday–Friday).

Matsuyama Castle►►► was constructed in 1603 by the head of the Matsudaira clan and later destroyed by fire. The stone walls, turret and keep, all in good condition, dominate a hill in the centre of the city and command fine views of the Inland Sea and the central mountain ranges of Shikoku. A castle museum exhibits the armour and swords of the Matsudaira family, and the surrounding park is worth exploring. Street car (tram) 5, from the square in front of the station, takes you to the entrance to the castle grounds; from here you can take the steep walk or a cable car to the castle summit (open 9–4:30).

Dogo Onsen►►► is one of the best-known hot spring public baths in Japan. (A street car line runs here from the railway station.) Part of the baths, still preserved and open

Looking out over Matsuyama from the castle

Ishiteji Temple, near Dogo Onsen, is the 51st on the Shikoku pilgrimage route

Haiku masters
Matsuyama was the birthplace of many famous *haiku* poets, including Masaoka Shiki (1867–1902) and Takahama Kyoshi (1874–1959) and the people of Matsuyama have a very special affection for *haiku* poetry (see panel, page 169). Throughout the city one can see stone monuments inscribed with the finest poems of the great *haiku* masters. The city office even organises *haiku* contests with special '*haiku* postboxes' for residents to post their entries.

for viewing, was originally set aside for the exclusive use of visiting royalty from Kyoto. This area is ornate, but the section open for public bathing is simply designed in the best tradition of functional Japanese architecture. At the entrance one pays a small fee, collects soap and a miniature towel. This is used for washing, then wrung out for drying, and also to wear while in the baths. Inside the baths, the natural mineral water is just cool enough to sit in and the salts it contains soften and vitalise the skin. For an extra fee you can gain access to a communal *tatami* mat room on the second floor; a more expensive private room with tea and access to the imperial bath is also available.

Ishiteji Temple►►, a short walk east of Dogo Onsen station, is the most interesting of eight temples in Matsuyama that are part of the Shikoku pilgrimage. Built in 1318 it is a fine example of Kamakura architecture, with a three-storey pagoda, main gate, hall and bell tower. The deity has a reputation for relieving aching legs and hanging from the main gate are the straw sandals of many elderly Japanese hoping for a cure for their failing legs.

Slippers from the weary feet of worshippers

Onsen and Sento

■ Japan sits on a geological region of intense volcanic activity. This gives rise to many hot springs (*onsen*). Baths, fed by these natural sources of mineral-rich hot water, are popular with the Japanese for their curative, health-giving and relaxing properties. Public washing baths, *sento*, were invented as a public service when most houses had no bathrooms. They provide hot running water for washing and a large bath full of extremely hot water for soaking in. Many also have mineral baths, whirlpools, electric baths and cold plunges......■

***Rotemburo* etiquette**
Young women do not generally bathe in outdoor pools during the day, but in the evening mixed groups gather in the pools. After dinner *saké*, floated from person to person in tiny wooden tubs, is drunk, inhibitions drop away, singing may start up and formal conversation gives way to gossipy chatter and heart-to-heart revelations.

Onsen Built near or directly above a hot spring source, *onsen* are Japanese inns where guests hope to benefit from the water's health-promoting qualities as well as enjoying the regional food that is often a speciality. Some of the larger *onsen* are built like modern hotels, catering for large family groups and parties of company workers; others are set deep in the mountains, in beautiful, isolated areas. The latter are usually composed of three or four thatched wooden buildings around a series of *rotemburo* (outdoor pools). For the *cognoscenti*, exploring such places in search of the ultimate bath can be akin to a spiritual journey. Most are open all year round and in the smaller country establishments one may sit in the winter in a steaming outdoor pool surrounded by snow-covered rocks and trees.

***Onsen* cities** The Japanese love to do things together, not only as a way of socialising but, particularly with company and sports parties, to engender group solidarity. For this reason many of the best-known *onsen* have become resort areas with hotels, busy nightlife districts and huge bathing halls with an exotic variety of baths. The Arita Kanko Hotel in Kinki district, Honshu, offers hot baths inside a cable car that rises high above a dramatic

Dogo Onsen, where the Emperor had his own baths built

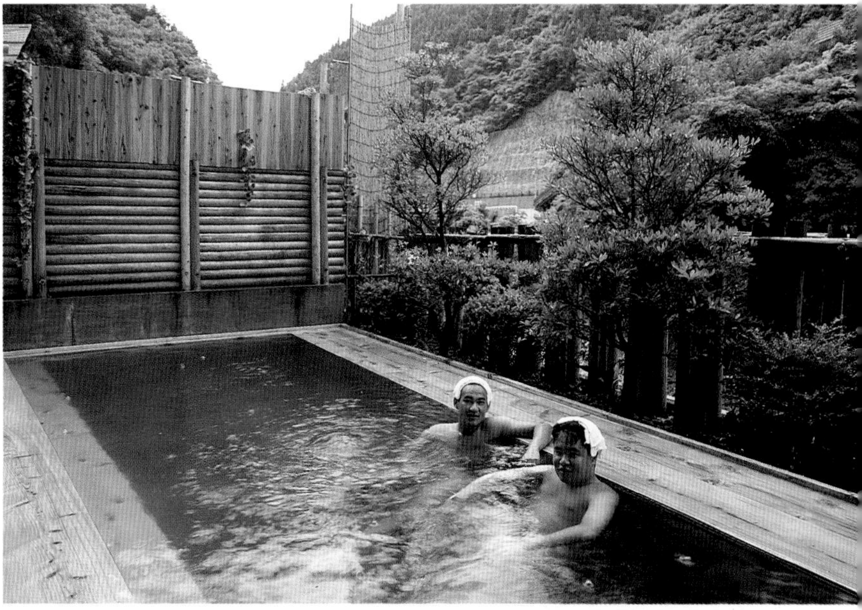

coastline. Famous resorts such as Beppu in Kyushu, Noboribetsu in Hokkaido and Atami in Honshu are often vulgar, gaudy and kitsch, but they have their own charm, and offer the chance to join in with ordinary Japanese letting their communal hair down.

Sento For independent tourists travelling on a budget, *sento* are excellent places in which to relax and to experience something quintessentially Japanese. They can be identified by their tall, narrow, metal chimneys and the distinctive flame logo painted over the entrance. In the last few years they have become fashionable with young people, and, like old cinemas, are being renovated in their original style.

Nowadays *sento* are not mixed, and the men's and women's baths are usually looked after by an old woman, or *obasan*, who sits on a platform inside the entrance to the baths astride the wall that divides the two sides. Men enter on the right and women on the left. The *obasan* takes entrance fees and sells shampoo, soap and razors. Towels can be hired but most Japanese make do with a small piece of cotton towelling called a *tenugui*, used initially as a flannel and then as a towel.

Bathers put their clothes in a locker and lock it with a numbered wooden key, which is kept on the wrist. Inside the bath area, plumbed into the walls, is a series of pairs of hot and cold taps. Visitors sit at these on low plastic stools and pour water over themselves with one of the small bowls scattered about the bath floor, before rubbing soap into the *tenugui* and soaping themselves all over. They then rinse the soap off thoroughly and sit in the hot tub, adding cold water if the heat is unbearable. The same facilities and washing procedure are used at *onsen* establishments before and after entering one of the communal hot-spring pools.

Hot spas outdoors...

Massage chairs
Many *sento* provide a massage armchair in the changing rooms to relieve backs stiff from too much walking. To use one, put the correct coins into the slot in the arm of the chair and adjust yourself against the moving rollers. They can be moved up and down your back with a control lever near your right hand.

...and indoors

▶▶ Takamatsu 155D3

The second largest town in Shikoku, Takamatsu is the most convenient arrival point and centre for exploring Shikoku. It was bombed flat in the war but rebuilt, exceptionally, on a human scale, and fortunately Ritsurin Park in the north of the city, famous even outside Shikoku, escaped damage. The main railway station, the ferry port, the downtown and nightlife area and the park are all within walking distance. For travel directions to Takamatsu from the main island of Honshu see page 169.

Ritsurin Park▶▶▶ is part of the former estate of the Matsudaira clan, originally designed as a summer retreat. An unusually wide variety of species of trees and flowers grows in the park, including Neagari Kashi oak trees, with exposed, leg-like roots, and Hako Matsu pine trees, characterised by their surreal branch configurations. Plum trees bloom in February, followed by camellias and yulan in March, cherry blossoms in April, wisteria and azalea in May, irises and water lilies in June and lotus flowers in August. Work was begun on the park in the early 17th century and was not completed on the formal gardens until over 100 years later. Two distinct areas make up the park: the south garden is of classical design featuring the landscaping, rock arrangements, ponds and artificial hills of the kind popular in the early and middle part of the Edo period. Winding paths and bridges lead the visitor past striking, stark trees with sculpted branches, over ponds stocked with carp and through flower beds of seasonal flowers. Be sure to stop at the Scoop The Moon Tea house (*Kikugetsu-tei*) for some whisked green tea and bean-jam cake. The north garden is landscaped in a more

Crossing the bridge at Takamatsu

Ritsurin Park

open, European style. It was originally designed for wild duck hunting parties led by the *daimyo* of Takamatsu. Nowadays the open spaces are used for picnics, park games and, in season, for Cherry Blossom Viewing festivities. The park is open daily from sunrise to sunset.

Very near the entrance to Ritsurin Park is **Sanuki Mingeikan▶▶**, a folk art museum which exhibits handicraft products from Sanuki (the old name for the Kagawa Prefecture of which Takamatsu is the capital) and sells a range of locally made pottery (open 8:45–4).

Zentsuji Temple▶▶, 1km west of Zentsuji station, 40 minutes south of Takamatsu on the JR Dosan line, is the birthplace of Kobo Daishi, who founded the temple in AD813, and the 75th station of the 88 temples (see pages 184–5). An imposing statue of the saint holding a walking-stick guards the entrance to the main temple. Within the complex is a five-storey pagoda and a treasure house exhibiting various 'Important Cultural Properties', including Buddhist artefacts brought back from China by Kobo Daishi. The two large camphor trees growing in the grounds are said to have been planted at the time of the temple's foundation. Near the main entrance are two wooden cut-outs of traditionally dressed pilgrims with holes where their faces should be, offering a photo opportunity for those dressed in civilian clothes. If offered a little money, one of the temple monks may agree to lead you through a 'secret' tunnel that runs beneath the main temple building. A pitch black passage, its walls worn smooth by countless searching hands, finally leads to the back of the main altar. According to a temple leaflet the tunnel darkness allows one to reflect on the human condition while the tunnel itself represents life before and after the light of spiritual enlightenment.

Ritsurin Park and Mount Shiun
The original design of the park incorporated the green backdrop provided by the adjacent Mount Shiun and took into account the way it would influence views from particular vantage points in the garden. To appreciate this aspect of the design, walk anti-clockwise around the garden.

The Imperial emblem at Zentsuji Temple

Kobo Daishi

Kobo Daishi is the posthumous name of a Buddhist monk known as Kukai (AD774–835), born in Zentsuji in Shikoku and famous as the founder of the Shingon (True Word) sect of Buddhism. Kobo Daishi, or 'Dharma-Spreading Great Master', is the name by which he is best known. It was given to him in AD921, nearly a century after his death......

Mount Koya monastery Kobo Daishi petitioned Emperor Saga to give him Mount Koya, claiming that: 'According to the meditation sutras, meditation should be practised preferably on a flat area deep in the mountains. When young, I ... often walked though mountainous areas and crossed many rivers. There is a quiet, open place called Koya, located two days' walk to the west from a point that is one day's walk south from Yoshino. High peaks surround Koya in all four directions; no human tracks, still less trails are to be seen there. I should like to clear the wilderness in order to build a monastery there for the practice of meditation, for the benefit of the nation and of those who desire to discipline themselves...'.

At 19 Kukai abandoned his study of Confucianism and Taoism and a potential career in the government bureaucracy to become a pupil of the Buddhist priest Gonso. In April 795 he was ordained as a monk at the Todaiji (Great Eastern Temple), taking the name Kukai ('Sea of Void').

In 804 Kukai joined the retinue of the Japanese imperial ambassador to the Tang Court and travelled with him to China, where he studied esoteric Buddhism under Hui-kuo, the seventh patriarch of a line of teachers which had originated in India. Kukai was an exceptional student. He collected many scrolls of esoteric lore and ritual and studied tantric Buddhist traditions from Central Asia. When Hui-kuo died in 804 Kukai was chosen to be the eighth patriarch of the sect and entrusted with the task of introducing its teachings into Japan.

Return home Kukai returned to Japan in August 806. He settled in the Kanzeonji Temple in Kyushu and sent a list of the Buddhist sutras and other works to the Japanese court. As a result, Kukai's esoteric teaching earned the support of the court and in 823 the Emperor Saga gave Kukai a new temple: Toji (Eastern Temple), in Kyoto, which became the headquarters of the Shingon sect.

Death and reincarnation Kukai died on 20 April 835, at the age of 61. His followers claim that he did not actually die, but went into the meditative state known as the 'Diamond Meditation', from which he will return as the Buddha Maitreya. His remains were entombed on Mount Koya, where his grave is now a shrine for the faithful.

A statue of Kobo Daishi at Takamatsu Temple

Togyo bullfights at Uwajima

▶▶ Uwajima *154C1*

This charming, small country town is the last stop on the JR Yosan line west of Takamatsu (five hours) and Matsuyama (two hours), worth visiting for its castle, bullfights and the outrageously explicit sex museum at Taga Jinja, a local Shinto shrine.

Although it is one of the few surviving feudal strongholds in Japan, **Uwajimajo Castle▶** was never a great castle. For defence, it depended on its excellent position on a promontory once surrounded by interlocking sea moats. The castle is a short walk from the centre of town.

Uwajima is famous for **Togyu Bullfights▶▶▶**, in which two bulls test their strength by locking horns and trying to push one another out of the ring. Tournaments are held six times a year, usually on 2 January, the first Sunday in March, April and November, the third Sunday in May and 14 August. The bull ring, or Togyuju, is at the base of Mount Tenman, a cab ride or a 30-minute walk from the middle of town. Dozens of bouts take place, and the atmosphere is usually less than sober.

Taga Jinja▶▶▶, a Shinto shrine 10 minutes' walk from the station (directions from the tourist office), is said to be something of an embarrassment to local people, for the priest in charge is an avid collector of sexual memorabilia. Next to the shrine he has built a three-storey museum to house his collection, which includes perhaps the only catalogued display of pubic hair in the world. At the entrance, there is a statue of a masturbating Buddha and this sets the tone for what follows. Cabinets display sexual gadgets, sexually explicit statues and representations of penises and vaginas of all sizes and shapes, and every inch of the walls and ceilings is covered with soft and hard porn. Taga has become a fertility shrine and nowadays infertile couples and newly weds make up the shrine's and the museum's usual customers (open 8–5).

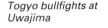

Dutch bulls
Bull-fighting started here in the 19th century with a gift of bulls from a Dutch sea captain, saved from a typhoon by Uwajima fishermen. Bulls were new to the Japanese, and were set to fight each other because they were so fierce.

Festival
Uwajima's biggest festival, Warei Jinja Matsuri, is held on 23/4 July at Warei Jinja Shrine. The main features are a parade of decorated fishing boats, bullfights and an appearance by *ushi-oni* or ox demons.

FOCUS ON *Sex in Japan*

In Japan, sex is not something to be shy about or to be separated from the spiritual life. The traditional belief is that we have two souls: one that is timeless and sublime and another that is earthbound and pleasure-seeking; and both parts of our being need nourishment. Within this context, romantic love and male and female sexuality have been equally celebrated in Japanese cultural and religious life......

Erotic art
Remains of erotic pictures of sexual activity have been preserved in Japan from as early as the 8th century. Of the two earliest complete *shunga* (a general term for erotic art painted or printed on to scrolls to be viewed horizontally), one, *The Phallic Contest*, depicts a test of male sexual powers by ladies of the imperial court, while the other, *The Catamites*, portrays the homosexual activities of Buddhist monks.

Sex Comic

In the past the sexual emphasis has always been on male gratification; the woman's role was to fulfil a man's needs. Until recently this was the view accepted and approved by society. Lack of inhibition and a confidence in his role gave the Japanese male a reputation for coarseness in his bold approach to sex, while the female became known for her demureness and willingness to please. There is still much truth in these notions, but the reality is more complicated and paradoxical.

Sex comics and prudery One of the shocks to a Westerner visiting Japan is to flick through the popular sex comic books sold at all newspaper outlets and available to read in many coffee shops. Glossy nude female pinups are followed by cartoons and a centre-page picture story in which the woman heroine undergoes all sorts of sexual humiliations at the hands of an evil monster or pervert. Neither Japanese men nor women (nor children, who do read them) seem embarrassed or surprised at these comics; neither do they take them seriously. In contrast, real-life sexual violence towards women is rare in Japan. Assaults are virtually unknown and women are generally safe to move around at any time of the day or night without fear of violence or theft.

Another paradox, given their ribald history and the explicit nature of their comics (and some Shinto shrines), is the prudery of the Japanese authorities towards pubic hair and the genitals. As a result, cartoonists and film-makers are experts at being as explicit and as titillating as possible without actually showing the offending organs.

Personal relations It is more common for Western men to date Japanese women than vice versa, but either practice is socially acceptable. However, public displays of affection are embarrassing for the Japanese: holding hands is about as far as you

The neon signs of soapland

should go. It would be sensible for visiting males or females to take condoms. Contraceptive pills are not generally available, and Japanese condoms are said to be too small for *gaijin*. (They are packed in boxes, chocolate style, and called 'skinless skins' in English or *boshi* ['hats'] in slang.)

Gay sex Homosexuality is neither discouraged nor flaunted in Japanese society. In the past some Buddhist sects taught that homosexuality was natural and even virtuous compared with sex with women. These teachings were mainly from sects forbidding sexual relations with women, but they did for a time influence the upper-class *samurai* of the time, who developed a school of thought that homosexual love was purer than the heterosexual variety.

The Floating World
Ukiyo, 'The Floating World', was a description of the areas licensed by the Tokugawa shogunate (1603–1868) for sex and entertainment. The name carried the sentiment that life is short and that one might as well enjoy its pleasures while one can. Teahouses, theatres and bath houses were the venues and money and sex the catchwords. Woodblock print (*ukiyo-e*) artists of the era are well known for their portraits of the women and kabuki actors of the pleasure quarters. 'Water trade' was the phrase used to describe the night-time world of bars, adult entertainment and sex found in 'soapland' districts of Japanese cities.

Taga-jinja Shrine, Uwajima

A fisherman's house, Shodo-shima Island

Touring Shodo-shima
If you have the time Shodo-shima Island may be explored on foot or bicycle. All details can be obtained from the island tourist office, in the Town Hall at Tonosho, or from the Kagawa Prefecture tourist information office, 1-10-4-chome, Bancho, Takamatsu.

Yashima plateau
The highest point of the Yashima plateau is reached by a short cable-car ride, which operates from a terminal close to Yashima station, or by a 30-minute walk, north along a tree-lined path. From the top (300m) there is a magnificent view which takes in the Inland Sea, Shodo Island, Takamatsu and Mount Goken.

►► Shodo-shima Island *155D3*

Lying 20km off the coast to the northeast of Takamatsu, Shodo-shima is the second largest island in the Inland Sea (there are almost 1,000 in all). There is a frequent ferry service from Takamatsu Pier to Tonosho port, on the western side of the island, which takes approximately one hour (or 35 minutes on the high-speed ferry). The island has a warm, dry, almost Mediterranean climate and it was here that olives were first cultivated in Japan. Shodo-shima is best known for its scenic beauty.

The main attraction is **Kankakei Gorge►►►** ('Cold and Misty Valley'), found in the central mountainous region of the island. Imprisoned by mountainous rock faces, eroded into surreal shapes by the weather, the gorge is brightened by wild cherry and azaleas in the spring and pine and maple trees in the autumn. A one-hour bus journey from Tonosho takes you to a nerve-wracking aerial ropeway ride up and over the gorge to the summit of a precipice. There is a bus back to Tonoshu from the top via Kusakabe.

A shorter bus ride from Tonosho (25 minutes), *en route* to Kankakei, takes you to **Choshikei Gorge►►**, which lies on the upper reaches of Denpo River and is known for its spectacular waterfall and profusion of spring and autumn colours. Near by is the Monkey Park (*Osaru-no-Kuni*), a reserve where wild Japanese monkeys roam freely and show off for the visiting humans.

An extensive public network of buses and sightseeing buses operates from Tonosho for all the island sights and along the coast to the east. Buses on the coastal route depart for Sakate every 30 minutes, passing Futagoura Beach, just outside Tonosho.

▶▶ Yashima and Shikoku Mura Village *155D3*

Yashima station is 20 minutes by train on the JR line east of Takamatsu station. On the hill outside the station is **Shikoku Mura▶▶▶**, an exceptionally good open-air museum, exhibiting a collection of reconstructed Shikoku architecture brought from all over the island. Included in the display are thatched-roof farms and fishermen's houses dating from the Edo period; an open-air *kabuki* theatre; a sugar mill; a tea house; a paper-maker's hut and a suspension bridge made of vines, a feature once common across the many rivers, valleys and gorges of Shikoku (open April–October 8:30–5, November–March 8:30–4:30). Near the entrance to the 'village' are two restaurants, one of which is designed as a traditional farmhouse and sells good *udon* noodle dishes.

Yashima was formerly an island but is now a headland connected to the Shikoku mainland. Its summit plateau is the site of the 12th-century battle in which the rival Taira and Minamoto clans fought for the supremacy of all Japan. The Minamoto family won and went on to establish the country's first shogunate in Kamakura. **Yashimaji Temple▶▶**, the 84th of Shikoku's 88 temples, on the southern ridge of the plateau, close to the cable car, houses a collection of relics of the land and naval battles fought by the two opposing clans. It was originally constructed in 754.

Yashima and Minamoto
In 1182 Taira Munemori, third son of the then head of the Taira clan, was pursued out of Kyoto by warriors of the Minamoto clan. Among his party was the Emperor Antoku, son of Munemori's sister. They fled to Yashima and there enlisted the aid of clan chiefs from Shikoku. With new forces they transferred their headquarters back to Kobe on the Honshu mainland, but were defeated again by Minamoto forces and fled back to Yashima. It was here, in 1185, that the Taira clan was finally destroyed by its old foes, easing the way for Minamoto Yoritomo to unite Japan under his command and become the country's first *shogun*.

Cleaning the nets, Shodo-shima

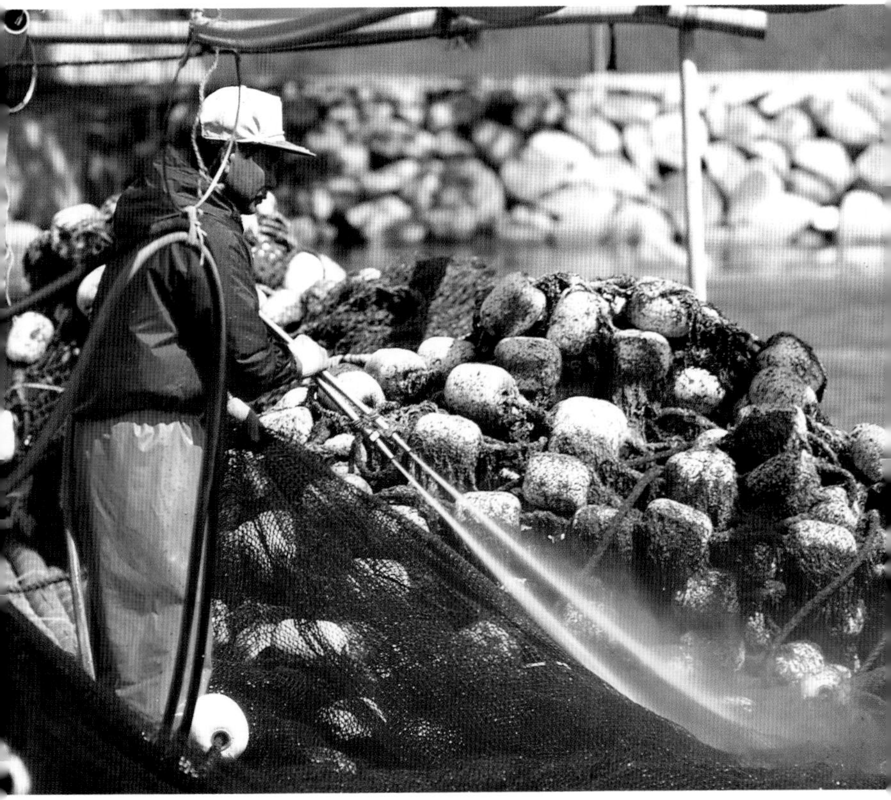

■ The pilgrimage around the 88 temples of Shikoku is the most famous of the Japanese Buddhist temple pilgrimages. It is part of a tradition of religious discipline that has a long history in Japanese Buddhism. The whole journey is undertaken on foot and pilgrims dress in white breeches and jackets, straw sandals and straw hats. They carry no money and depend on charity for all their needs......■

Naked Festival
Every year, on the Saturday closest to 20 January, the *Hadaka Matsuri*, or 'Naked Festival' is held at Zentsuji Temple, the 75th temple on the route and the site of Kobo Daishi's birthplace. In the bitter cold, hundreds of young men dressed only in white loin cloths (nakedness symbolising innocence and white cloth purity), fight over two 'good luck sticks' blessed and tossed into the crowd by the abbot of the temple. The winners, known as the 'fortunate men', carry good luck with them throughout the following year. Zentsuji Temple is 20 minutes' walk from JR Zentsuji station, which is 40 minutes from Takamatsu on the JR Dosan line.

Most pilgrimages are connected with Kannon, the Goddess of Mercy, who is regarded as the deity of the common people but the Shikoku route is inspired by the Shingon patriarch, Kobo Daishi (see page 178). The journey does, however, attract Buddhists of all sects.

The pilgrims' route The 88 temples are visited along a 1,450km route, taking between 40 and 60 days on foot. Nowadays most people travel by bus or taxi and wear everyday clothes with perhaps just a white scarf to indicate their purpose. This is not surprising, since the walk is long and arduous and Shikoku is an island of high mountains, deep valleys and a rugged coastline. For foreigners who wish to follow some or all of the route, problems increase, since maps and instructions are essential and all those available are published only in Japanese. Traditionally there are two pilgrim seasons: spring and autumn. At the respective equinoxes pilgrims are presented with gifts and goods by people living near the temple where they are spending the night. Generally accommodation is available in and around all the temples.

Best foot forward on the pilgrims' route

Zentsuji Temple, the 75th temple on the pilgrimage route

Origin of the pilgrimage
In the spring of 835, Kobo Daishi (*Daishi*, or 'Great Saint', is a title bestowed by the imperial court on the most accomplished Buddhist priests) announced that he would die on 22 April of that year. He bade farewell to the ruling emperor and the two retired emperors, appointed successors to maintain his spiritual legacy, made a will and then retired to a monastery on Mount Koya in Wakayama prefecture, where his tomb had been prepared. He died on the predicted day, and soon after his death many disciples began the pilgrimage to places on Shikoku associated with his name, as a mark of their commitment to the spiritual path which he had established.

A four-temple alternative To give some idea of the variety of style and location of the 88 temples, it is possible to reach four temples by bus from Kochi. The same bus connects all four – or you may walk between them.

Hotsumisakiji temple (24), Murotomisaki-cho, Muroto City, takes two hours by bus from Kochi City and 40 minutes on foot from the bus stop. Located at the cliff top, Cape Muroto, it is often called the Mecca of the pilgrims. The temple's local name is Higashi Dera, 'East Temple'.

Shinshoji Temple (25), Murozusakai, Muroto City, is one hour and 50 minutes by bus from Kochi City and then 10 minutes on foot. Called Tsuji by locals, Shinshoji is known for its image of Jizo, guardian deity of children. It is also a popular temple with those making a living from the sea.

Kongochoji (26), Moto, Muroto City, takes one hour and 40 minutes by bus from Kochi City. Found at the top of Cape Gyodo, its local name is Nishi Dera ('West Temple'). The treasure house contains important Shingon artefacts, and there is a whale museum in the temple grounds.

Konomineji (27), Tonohama, Yasuda-cho, is one hour and 20 minutes by bus from the JR Gomen station, 15 minutes from Kochi station on the JR Dosan line. Considered to be one of the five temples most difficult to reach, it is now accessible by road. The temple's principal deity is the 11-faced image of Kanzeon.

For further information visit Kochi tourist information office, just outside Kochi station exit. All buses for these temples travel in the Muroto direction.

Feeding the birds at Zentsuji Temple

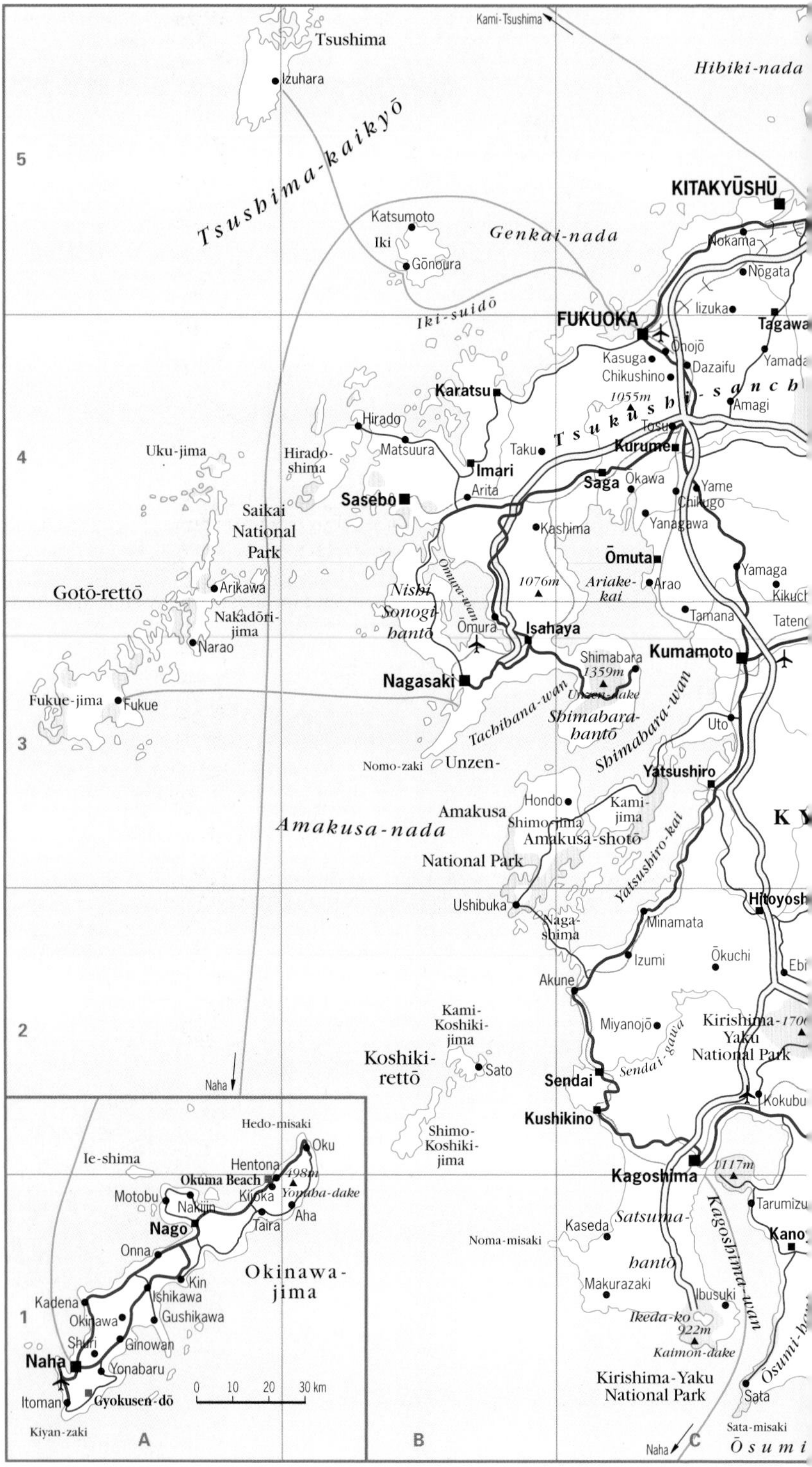
Kami-Tsushima
Tsushima
Izuhara
Hibiki-nada
Tsushima-kaikyō
KITAKYŪSHŪ
Katsumoto
Iki
Gōnoura
Genkai-nada
Nokama
Nōgata
Iki-suidō
FUKUOKA
Iizuka
Tagawa
Ōnojō
Kasuga
Dazaifu
Yamada
Chikushino
Karatsu
1055m
Tsukushi-sanchi
Amagi
Hirado
Tosu
Uku-jima
Hirado-shima
Matsuura
Taku
Kurume
Imari
Saga
Ōkawa
Yame
Arita
Chikugo
Sasebo
Saikai National Park
Kashima
Yanagawa
Ōmuta
Yamaga
Ōmura-wan
1076m
Ariake-kai
Arao
Gotō-rettō
Arikawa
Nishi Sonogi-hantō
Kikuchi
Nakadōri-jima
Tamana
Tateno
Ōmura
Isahaya
Narao
Shimabara
Kumamoto
Nagasaki
1359m
Unzen-dake
Fukue-jima
Fukue
Tachibana-wan
Shimabara-hantō
Shimabara-wan
Uto
Nomo-zaki
Unzen-
Yatsushiro
Hondo
Kami-jima
Amakusa
Shimo-jima
Amakusa-shotō
Amakusa-nada
National Park
Yatsushiro-kai
Hitoyoshi
Ushibuka
Naga-shima
Minamata
Izumi
Ōkuchi
Akune
Ebino
Kami-Koshiki-jima
Miyanojō
Kirishima-Yaku National Park
1700
Koshiki-rettō
Sato
Sendai
Sendai-gawa
Naha
Kokubu
Kushikino
Shimo-Koshiki-jima
Hedo-misaki
Oku
Ie-shima
Hentona
Okuma Beach
498m
Yonaha-dake
Motobu
Nakijin
Kijoka
Kagoshima
1117m
Tarumizu
Nago
Taira
Aha
Satsuma-hantō
Kaseda
Kagoshima-wan
Noma-misaki
Kanoya
Onna
Okinawa-jima
Kin
Makurazaki
Kadena
Ishikawa
Ibusuki
Okinawa
Gushikawa
Ikeda-ko
922m
Shuri
Ginowan
Kaimon-dake
Naha
Yonabaru
Kirishima-Yaku National Park
Ōsumi-hantō
Itoman
Gyokusen-dō
0 10 20 30 km
Sata
Kiyan-zaki
Sata-misaki
Naha
Ōsumi
A
B
C
1
2
3
4
5

KYUSHU AND OKINAWA

The bomb
Kumamoto is said to have been the original target of the atomic bomb later dropped by the American airforce on Hiroshima. On the day of the flight Kumamoto was covered in cloud and the bombers passed it by. A peace pagoda, donated by the Indian government, has been erected in memory of the event on a hill overlooking the city.

Kyushu and Okinawa The most southerly and third largest of the four main islands of Japan is separated from the main island, Honshu, by the 2km-wide Kammon Strait. Rail and car tunnels connect the two islands. Four great volcanic ranges cross the island from north to south.

Okinawa is the largest and most developed island of the Ryukyu archipelago, a group of subtropical islands stretching south from Kyushu through the Pacific and East China Sea, almost to the tip of Taiwan.

Foreign influences Because of its geographical position, Kyushu became a staging post for the transmission to Japan of Korean and Chinese cultural ideas, influences which significantly shaped the development of early Japanese civilisation. The first European explorers, traders and missionaries to Japan also arrived via this island, and its people are traditionally less xenophobic and easier to know than their northern cousins.

Kyushu is mountainous and volcanic. The mountain ranges contain many peaks over 1,525m and the caldera in Aso-Kuju National Park, with the active volcano, Mount Nakadake, at its centre, is the largest in the world. There are hot-spring resorts scattered around the island, and the spas of Kyushu are popular with Japanese tourists.

Fukuoka A modern, commercial city, Fukuoka is the gateway to Kyushu and a good base from which to explore the island. The rewards of the economic success of Japan have been put to unusually good use in this city. Stylish modern architectural developments and a state-of-the-art subway system have been happily married to older dockland, residential and parkland areas. There is also a thriving night and street life.

Kumamoto Kyushu's third-largest city is at the heart of the island geographically and administratively and was

Kagoshima port, on Kyushu Island

once the southwestern headquarters of the Tokugawa shogunate. For the tourist it is an alternative to Fukuoka as a base, lying at one end of the scenic Yamanami Highway, which splits Kyushu in two. Kumamoto is between the two volcanic areas of Aso-Kuju National Park, to the east, and the Amakusa and Unzen National Parks, to the west.

Dragons and lions adorn the ancient city in Naha, Okinawa

Nagasaki This lovely harbour town with a cosmopolitan atmosphere, was the first Japanese port to establish trading contacts with foreign countries, and during the 220 years of Japanese seclusion from the rest of the world one tiny island in Nagasaki Bay was allowed to continue as a trading post. Ironically, given its history of communication with the West, Nagasaki was the second target after Hiroshima for atomic bombing.

Okinawa The climate of the Ryukyu archipelago group of Japanese islands is subtropical and luxurious plants and fruits thrive all year round. Many of the islands are surrounded by coral reefs and fringed by sandy beaches. Okinawa, in Okinawa prefecture, is the largest and by far the most heavily developed island of the group and the one most popular with mainland Japanese tourists, who go not only for the sun, sea and nightlife, but for Okinawan arts, crafts and customs, all of which are markedly different from their own. Okinawa is also the focal point for a network of inter-island ferries that make even remote and barely inhabited islands accessible. US forces occupied the island until 1972, when it was handed back to the Japanese. It is still the site of several US military bases.

Okinawan traditions
Okinawan culture has survived the influence of mainland Japan, especially on the more remote of the surrounding islands and in small towns and villages. Festivals of folk-dancing and music, contests such as tug-of-war and boat races and various craft exhibitions are popular forms of local entertainment, often based on ancient Shinto ceremonies and providing a happy mix of noisy religious ritual and other, more earthy pursuits.

The Eight Hells

The Eight Hells
Beppu's most popular attractions are eight hot springs known as Jigoku (Hell Pools), in which the waters reach boiling point. Each pool has a particular characteristic: for example, Chino-ike Jigoku (Blood Pond Hell) runs blood red as a result of dissolved clay. The Eight Hells are a year-round attraction and almost always crowded. Regular sightseeing bus tours taking in the pools and other major sights run from Kitahama bus station, just east of Beppu JR station. The Beppu city information office, in Beppu JR station, has maps and leaflets in English.

Old and fantastical baths
One of the oldest baths in Beppu is the Takegawa bath house, built in 1879, with an interior reminiscent of an old, well-used boxing gym. Takegawa is best known for its sand baths, where attendants bury customers in hot, black sand up to the neck and leave them to sweat for 10 minutes. Afterwards there is plenty of hot water to wash it all off. The most fantastical baths are in Suginoi Palace, adjoining the Suginoi Hotel. Two aircraft-hangar-sized baths provide every variety of hot-spring and other bathing experience (including a coffee bath for improving the complexion). One bath is for men, the other for women, and as each one is different, the facilities are alternated daily.

▶▶▶ Aso-Kuju National Park *187D4*

Aso-Kuju National Park lies in the centre of Kyushu between Beppu and Kumamoto, and a trip there is best planned in conjunction with a visit to one or both of these towns. Mount Aso is, in fact, a joint name for five volcanic peaks, all sitting in the world's largest crater basin (technically a caldera). The most central peak, Mount Nakadake, is a very active volcano. There is a cable-car service to the rim of its crater, where you can catch glimpses, through the rising vapour, of the green lake at its bottom, smell the lake's sulphurous fumes and sometimes even hear the mountain's portentous volcanic rumblings. On a clear day the outer rim of the Aso caldera (128km in circumference) is also visible. The floor of the caldera (125m deep at its lowest point) is undulating grassy meadow land, a most unusual landscape feature in Japan. Cows and horses grazing there bear *kanji* ideogram brand marks – an unusual sight to Westerners.

From Kumamoto there is a regular service on the JR Hohi line to Aso town (one hour). Aso itself is not a place of great interest, but from just outside the JR station there is a frequent bus service to the Aso-zan Nishi ropeway (cable-car) station (40 minutes). From Kumamoto there is also a direct bus service to the Nishi ropeway station (one and a half hours). If the volcano is too active the cable-car does not operate, and the road and rail links may even be closed. This is unusual, but you may wish to check with your hotel or local tourist office before leaving for Aso.

The journey to Mount Aso from Kumamoto is itself interesting, passing through areas of traditional farmland neatly planted with crops of rice, tobacco, wheat and bamboo. Within the park the designated sights have not been sensitively developed (the power of Nakadake overwhelms most human interference) and are usually crowded but outside these areas, particularly in the south-west around Takamori, there are delightful old-fashioned, rustic hot-spring *minshuku*, inns and hotels. Takamori is 30 minutes by train, or 40 minutes by bus from Tateno (which is between Aso and Kumamoto). Takamori is connected to Takachiko, another small *onsen* (hot-spring town), by a very scenic bus route along back roads (one and a half hours).

▶▶ Beppu *187D4*

Set on the east coast of Kyushu, Beppu is Japan's most popular hot-spring holiday centre. With more than 3,000 hot springs Beppu can accommodate the 12 million or so tourists who visit the resort each year to relax in the waters of the public bath houses or in the private baths of their hotel, inns or *ryokan*. Baths in mineral-rich waters, mud and sand as well as steam rooms, outdoor pools, saunas and virtually any other form you can imagine are all available in Beppu. Many of the hot springs are said to have healing qualities, and the University of Kyoto runs an institute there to study the therapeutic benefits of mineral baths. In contrast the town itself is an unattractive place of souvenir shops, garish signs, *pachinko* (pinball) parlours, neon lights and amusement arcades. The only way to enjoy Beppu is to enter into the unsophisticated spirit of it; the town may be tawdry, but its position on Beppu Bay, with the sea on one side and mountains behind it, is glorious.

Beppu is connected to Kumamoto by the JR Hohi line (three hours) and to Hakata station in Fukuoka by the Nichirin limited express train (two and half hours). Bus services also operate between Beppu and Kumamoto (via Aso on some journeys) along the Trans-Kyushu Highway (three hours, 55 minutes).

Mount Nakadake trail

Yufuin sea town
Yufuin is a quiet, rural and elegant spa town, one hour by bus from Beppu. It is situated on a highland plateau and contains delightful, traditional Japanese inns and *minshuku*, as well as a thatched-roof public bath house.

Mount Nakadake trail route
From the cable-car terminus on the rim of Mount Nakadake there is a path up to the highest point of the mountain. From here, a trail leads to Mount Takadake, then on to Sensui-kyo, a volcanic gorge, and finally to Miyaji JR station, one stop down the line from Aso station. The route takes from five to six hours and covers some rough ground. Few people follow it, but the views are exhilarating.

Beppu, on the coast

Shopping in Fukuoka
Fukuoka's best-known local products are silk textiles (*Hakata-ori*), Hakata dolls and kimono sashes (*Hakata-obi*). Hakata silk is not as smooth as most Japanese silk but it is this slight roughness in texture for which it is valued. *Hakata-obi* are woven from local silk and Hakata dolls are made from fired clay and then hand-painted. Their trade marks are bright colours, characteristic expressions and depiction of *geisha*, women and young girls. The Iwataya department store, in the centre of the Tenjin district, stocks a wide selection of local products.

▶▶▶ Fukuoka *186C4*

The largest city on Kyushu Island, Fukuoka is also Kyushu's gateway to the rest of Japan. Fukuoka and the port of Hakata, now connected, were once separate cities, hence the confusion between the two names that sometimes arises in train timetables and maps.

This is a modern, commercial city and a good starting point and base for exploring the island. The people here (and in Kyushu generally) are said to be straightforward and warm-hearted; they certainly retain a friendliness towards foreigners perhaps lost in the more cosmopolitan cities of Tokyo and Osaka.

The Shinkansen bullet train terminates at Hakata (Fukuoka) station. Journey times from Tokyo and Osaka are six hours, 10 minutes and three hours, 20 minutes respectively. By air to Fukuoka Airport, the only international airport in Kyushu, travel times are reduced to one hour, 40 minutes and one hour, five minutes respectively. If you have the time, the train journey is an interesting way of seeing the area. All the main cities in Kyushu are connected to Fukuoka by train and bus.

There are two subway lines in the city. Line 1 links Hakata station to Tenjin, a major dining, shopping and nightlife area, and to Ohori-koen Park, the attractive city park surrounding Fukuoka Castle. Buses and tour buses leave from the Kotsu bus centre opposite Hakata station and the Tenjin bus centre near the subway stop. There is a tourist information office in Hakata station, where English is spoken and good maps of the city and surrounding area are provided.

Fukuoka is well known for its tented **food carts▶▶** that illuminate and line the pavements at night. Under canvas, customers squash onto a bench seat in front of a low counter, while the cook prepares local specialities on a mobile gas range and serves beer and *saké* (hot in the winter months). Shunko-bashi Street, at the southern end of Nakasu-kawa-bata (subway line 1) is the best known location for outdoor eating carts.

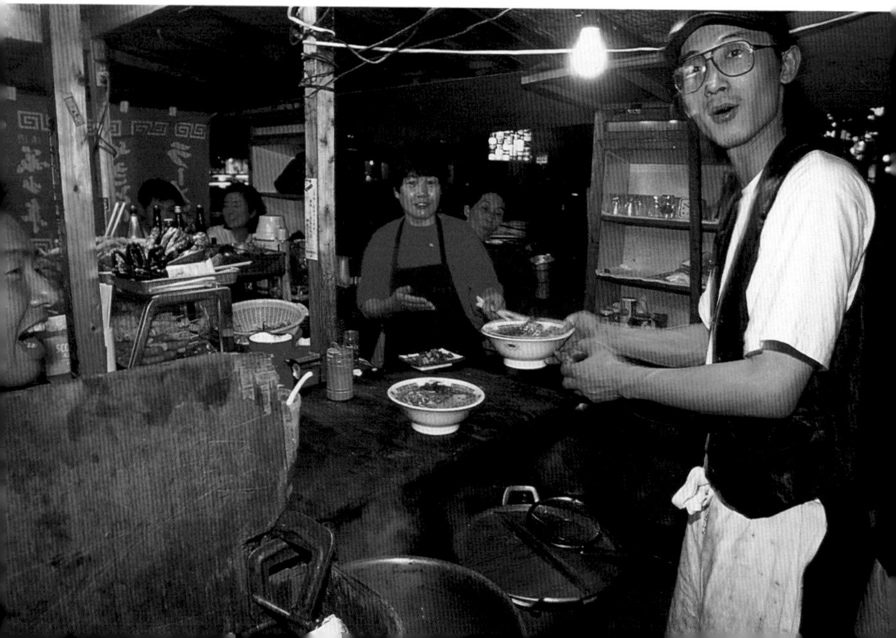

A tented food cart dishes out the goods in Fukuoka

Shofukuji Temple

Sengai, Shofukuji abbot
Sengai Gibon (1750–1837), one of Japan's most famous ink painters and calligraphers, was a Zen monk, having become a novice at the age of 11. His final formal position as a monk was as abbot of Shofukuji Temple in Fukuoka. Sengai retired in 1811, aged 61, and devoted the rest of his life to his work, which is renowned for its spontaneity and humour. A large collection of his art is on display in the Idemitsu Art Museum, Tokyo (see page 55).

Fukuoka Castle and Ohori-koen Park▶▶, 20 minutes by subway from Hakata station, provide an oasis of greenery for city residents. Only a few gates and a simple turret remain of the castle, but it is sited on a high hill that commands a view of Fukuoka in every direction. The park was originally part of the castle's outer defences and some of it has been planted over the site of the old moat. In the centre is a large pond surrounded by willow and azalea trees. Over 2,500 cherry trees grow here and in early April the park is a favourite place for raucous cherry blossom-viewing parties. Facing the lake to the southeast of the park is the Fukuoka City Art Museum, containing a collection of modern and Buddhist Japanese art and tea-ceremony utensils (open 9:30–5:30; closed Monday).

Shofukuji Temple▶▶ is believed to be the oldest Zen temple in Japan. It was founded in 1195 by the priest Eisai, who went on to establish many other important Rinzai sect Zen temples in Kyoto and Kamakura. Eisai spent four years in China and returned not only with Zen Buddhism (known as Chan in China), but with the seeds of the country's first tea plants. The temple itself now seems rather neglected, although the bronze bell in the belfry is designated an important cultural property. However, to anyone interested in Zen it is an important shrine. Shofukuji is 15 minutes' walk from Hakata station and easy to find with a city map.

Examination shrine
Temmangu Shrine in Dazaifu, the ancient capital of Kyushu and within easy reach of Fukuoka, is dedicated to the god of scholarship. Secondary-school students sitting the tough university entrance examinations come here in droves to pray for help, and local restaurants sell good-luck noodle dishes. The grounds of the shrine, planted with many cedar trees, are spacious and worthy of a long stroll. Dazaifu is 30 minutes by train from Nishitetsu Fukuoka station in Tenjin.

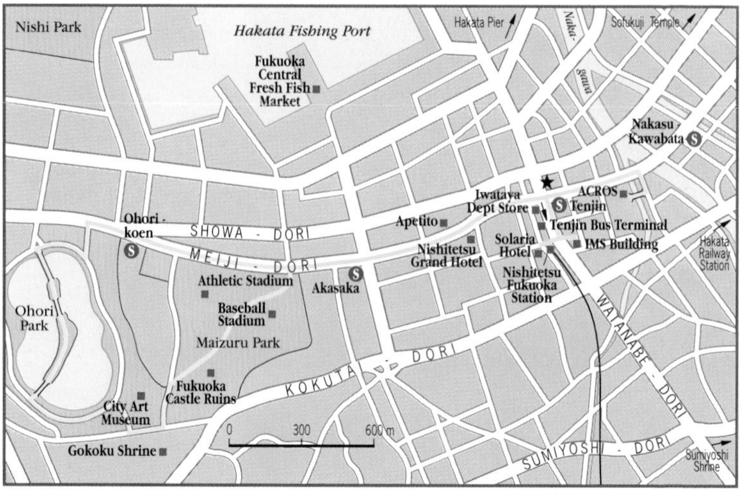

Walk Fukuoka

Distance: 3km; time: about one and a half hours.
This walk leads through Fukuoka's busy downtown shopping area, then follows the route of the old castle moat to Ohori-koen Park and the castle remains.

The Intermedia Station: outside...

Start at the **Tenjin Iwataya department store▶▶**, located above the Tenjin subway station. There is an especially good food hall in the basement and there are occasionally cultural exhibitions on higher floors. From here walk south past the bus terminal, with the **Solaria Hotel Building▶** on your right, a recently constructed modern hotel built around a central well, with glass-walled elevators. There is a sports centre and swimming-pool open to non-residents, as well as boutiques, restaurants, three cinemas, an exhibition space and an arena with fountains. On the opposite side of the road is the **Intermedia Station (IMS)▶▶**, a new, open-plan example of modern Japanese architecture. IMS contains many shops, restaurants, galleries, a car and motorcycle showroom with latest models, a music store and, on the eighth floor (the Rainbow Plaza), a free library with newspapers, videos and an information desk (English is spoken). From here walk north to **ACROS (Asian Crossroads Over The Sea)▶▶**, a vast building with four basement floors and 14 floors above ground devoted to all things Asian, including cultural events,

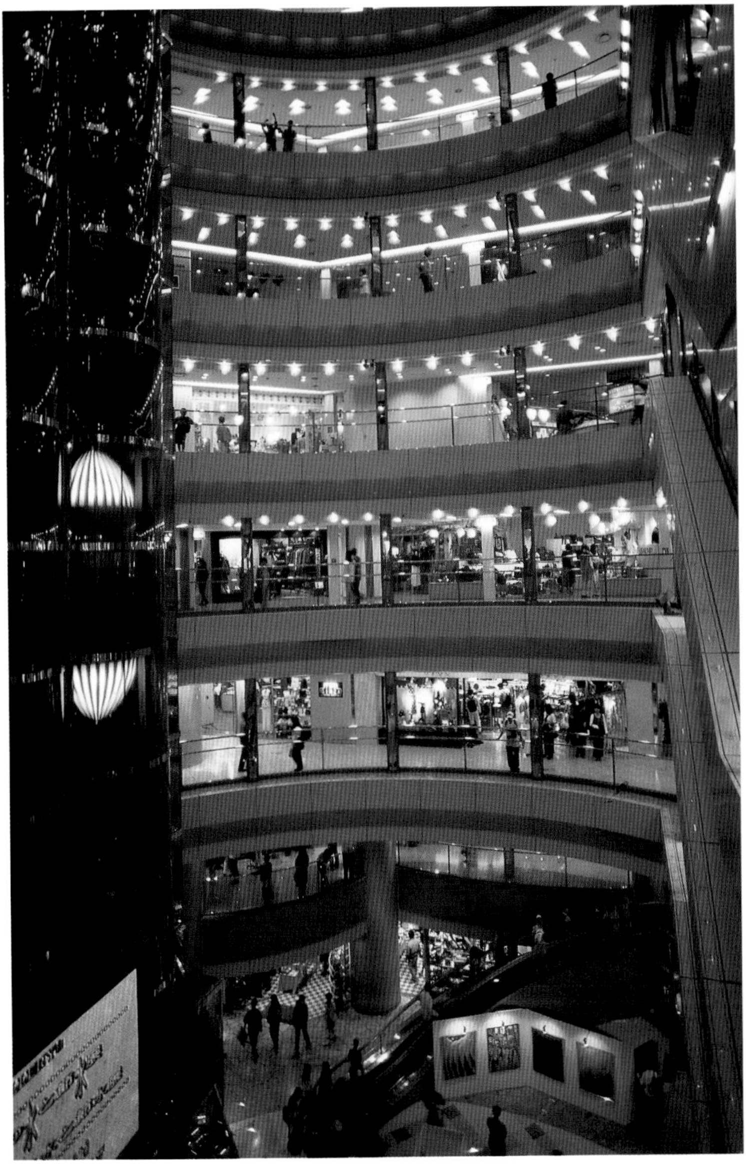

...and inside, with its dazzling galleries, shops and showrooms

conventions, company offices, restaurants and films. Walking west towards the castle you will pass the **Nishitetsu Grand Hotel▶** on your left, where there is a reasonably priced piano bar with views over city, and the **Apetito▶▶**, a Western-style bread and cake shop and restaurant, on your right. Continue following the main road to Ohori-koen Park, passing the moat of the old castle. Inside the park there is a **coffee shop▶▶** with a terrace overlooking the lake and distant mountains. After a rest, visit the remains of **Fukuoka Castle** (see page 193), which has good views over the city from the highest point.

Pottery prison
Okawachi-yama village, a short bus or cab ride from Imari, was both home and prison for the many Korean potters brought there by the Nabeshima *daimyo*. A reconstruction of a porcelain factory here illustrates the conditions in which they worked out their lives. Okawachi-yama is still a functioning pottery village with 20 kilns are in operation, and its narrow streets are crammed with shops and studios. Maps and information are available from the community showroom (*tenjikan*).

▶▶ The Saga pottery towns *186B4*

Saga prefecture, in northwest Kyushu, is one of Japan's most important areas for the production of traditional porcelain and pottery. The two best-known kiln sites are Karatsu and Arita, each of which has given its name to a particular ceramic style. Imari, the port town from which all Saga ceramics have been shipped to the rest of Japan, has benefited by association and Imari-yaki is also a famous name in Japanese porcelain.

Until the 17th century the Japanese imported porcelain from China and Korea. Saga, which lies only 250km from the Korean Peninsula, was a staging post for Japanese invasions of Korea and many potters from that country were brought back there as captives and obliged to teach their techniques to the Japanese. One of their number, Ri Sanpei, discovered kaolin, the raw material of porcelain production, near present-day Arita in 1616. The Nabeshima family, the local ruling clan, ensured that the Saga district retained a monopoly on porcelain by keeping their Korean artisans under close guard.

Nearby, Karatsu also benefited from Korean know-how and the town's elegant stone pottery, much influenced by Korean Yi dynasty ware, is highly valued, especially by devotees of the tea ceremony.

The suggested itinerary for this excursion is Fukuoka–Karatsu–Arita–Fukuoka. To visit all three places in one day you will need to use cabs to travel from Imari to Okawachi-yama (see panel), from there to Arita and for travel around Arita itself. Each of the towns has a tourist office in or near the station.

Karatsu Depart from Hakata station, Fukuoka, initially by subway line 1 to Mei Hama, and then on the JR Chikuhi line (one hour, 20 minutes in all). Karatsu, in northwest Saga, was for many centuries an important centre of

Hard at work in the Kyushu Ceramics Museum

Ranks of ceramics: the finished products on display

trade and commerce with China and Korea. It remains a relatively busy fishing port but is best known as a summer beach resort. For pottery enthusiasts two local kilns are particularly worth visiting. **Naka Zato Taroemon kiln▶▶**, a 10-minute walk or a short cab ride from Karatsu station, has been with the same family for 13 generations. When the immediate past master, Nakazato Muan, was still alive he was designated a 'Living National Treasure' for his artistry. There is a gallery exhibiting work for sale by the present master, Muan's son, and apprentices, and an area where visitors may watch potters at the wheel and in the various other stages of pot production (open 8:30–5:30).

Ryuta-gama kiln▶▶, a 15-minute cab ride from Karatsu station, is run by Nakazato Takashi, one of the younger sons of Nakazato Muan. The Ryuta-gama kiln incorporates a gallery, workshop and potter's house. While demonstrating the best of traditional techniques, the work produced here also shows freedom of spirit (open 8:30–5:30). Imari is one hour by JR Chikuhi line or by bus from Karatsu.

Arita Reached by train (20 minutes) or bus (40 minutes) from Imari or by cab (20 minutes) from Okawachi-yama (see panel), Arita is the birthplace of Japanese porcelain. Over 150 kilns still operate in and around the town. The **Kyushu Ceramic Museum▶▶**, a short walk (10 minutes) from Arita station, gives a good, clear introduction to the development and various characteristics of particular Arita kilns, as well as to the ceramic art of Kyushu as a whole (open: 9–4:30; closed: Monday). The **Ceramic Art Museum▶**, 15 minutes' walk from Kami-Arita station (three minutes by train from Arita station), exhibits a collection of Arita porcelain dating from the 17th century to the present day. The nearby **Izumiyama Jisekiba▶▶**, the quarry discovered by Ri Sanpei, is still open, with a working kiln museum alongside.

Arita porcelain
The first porcelain products made in Arita were influenced by Korean, and later Chinese designs, but in the 1640s the Japanese potter Sakaida Kakiemon (1596–1666) introduced Japanese motifs and a technique of overglaze decoration. His own trademark colour was persimmon red but as his methods inspired his contemporaries, Arita ware came to be associated with colourful pieces decorated in patterns and influenced by Japanese textiles, especially those incorporating birds and flowers. The fine clay and translucent glazes that typify Arita ware came to the notice of the West and, following its acclaim at the Philadelphia Exhibition in 1876, became much valued by collectors.

Tatsuda Shizen Park
This natural park (as opposed to a formal landscaped park, such as Suizenji-koen) in Kumamoto contains the burial temple of the Hosokawa family, who took control of the district from the Kato clan, as well as the grave of Hosokawa Gracia (1563–1600), one of Japan's most famous female converts to Catholicism. Gracia was killed by order of her husband to ensure her freedom from capture by his enemies. Mariko, the heroine in James Clavell's book *Shogun*, was modelled on her. The park is a 15-minute cab ride from the city centre

► Kagoshima 186C2

This small, modern but relaxed city at the southern tip of Kyushu is a terminal point for railways and national highways, and a main port for boats to Okinawa and other islands of the Ryukyu group. Mount Sakurajima, across the Kinko Bay from Kagoshima, is an active volcano that occasionally showers the city with black ash. Its last big eruption in 1914 generated enough lava flow to form the land bridge that now connects Sakurajima to the mainland. Kagoshima boasts no particular tourist attractions but it is off the beaten track and has a distinguished, cosmopolitan history. The three-hour rail trip from Kumamoto passes through picturesque mountain and coastal terrain. JR Nishi Kagoshima station is a short walk from the city centre; the local tourist office is next to it.

►►► Kumamoto 186C3

Kumamoto was badly damaged during the war but the modern city, with its many tree-lined avenues and open spaces and a convenient streetcar network, has developed its own character. This was once a nationally important political centre and castle town and retains the strong sense of identity and independence such power brings. The city's main attractions are the castle and the landscaped gardens of Suizenji-koen Park, both dating from the early 17th century. During this time the city was chosen as the site of the southwestern headquarters of the Tokugawa shogunate. Despite its loss of national influence Kumamoto remains at the geographical and administrative heart of Kyushu and provides a good alternative to Fukuoka as a touring base for the island. Kumamoto is one hour, 30 minutes from Hakata station, Fukuoka, on the JR Kagoshima line. Within the city there are two streetcar lines that connect all the main centres of interest. The tourist information office is in a kiosk in front of the JR station entrance.

Suizenji-koen Park

Mount Sakurajima

Kagoshima and the Meiji Restoration
For almost 800 years from the late 12th century, Kagoshima was the feudal seat of the Shimazu family. In 1868, the Shimazu, with the *samurai* chief Saigo Takamori at their head, rebelled against the shogunate. Saigo negotiated the surrender of the *shogun*'s army and was treated as a national hero. But he wanted to end all foreign influence and provoked a further revolt, this time against the Meiji government which he had helped to establish. After this uprising was suppressed he committed *seppuku* in a cave on Shiroyama Hill, Kayoshima, in 1877.

Kumamoto specialities
Kumamoto is famous for its *higo zogan* products, in which gold and silver are inlaid on black iron. *Obake no kinta*, a toy ghost with rolling eyes and a tongue that sticks out, is another local product. Goods are sold at the Traditional Crafts Centre, next to the Kumamoto Castle Hotel, 3-35 Chiga-jo, Kumamoto (open 9–5; closed Monday).

Kumamotojo Castle▶▶▶, right in the heart of Kumamoto, was burned down in 1877 after a long siege, but the reconstruction (unlike other examples) has been well managed, and walking around the castle gives a real sense of its former magnificence. The original fortress was built in 1607 by Kiyomasa Kato, feudal lord of the prefecture and a recognised master of castle architecture. It was originally constructed with 49 watch towers (11 survive), 29 castle gates and remarkable concave defensive walls (fitted with overhanging eaves and missile-dropping openings), which rendered conventional siege tactics almost useless. Nowadays, there are two main entrances to the castle, the most impressive being the southwest. From the top of the castle there is a magnificent view of Kumamoto and Mount Nakadake smoking in the distance. A museum within the walls exhibits relics of the castle's military past (open 8:30–5:30, October–March 4:30pm).

Suizenji-koen Park▶▶▶ was constructed in 1632 as part of the villa grounds of the Hosokawa clan. It is designed as a miniature version of the old Tokaido highway, between Kyoto and Edo. Generations of gardeners have created a completely artificial landscape here from a natural habitat. Each pruned tree, hill, patch of water or stone has been designed or chosen to represent a natural feature along the Tokaido. A tea house with *tatami* mats and fine views is located near the pond. To reach Suizenji-koen catch streetcar 2 or 3 from outside the castle to Suizenji-koen Mae stop.

Shrine offerings at Kumamotojo Castle

Japanese castles

■ Much of the history of Japan is a history of warfare. Over the centuries powerful landowners, warriors and clerics fought to control the rich rice-producing regions which would in turn give them political control of the country. The earliest types of castles (*shiro*) were built mainly from wood and earth, and during the *Sengoku Jidai*, the Age of the Country at War (1490–1600), large numbers of castles were built by *daimyo* to protect their domains from enemy attack......■

The wooden warriors
During the 14th century Kusunoki Masashige defended Chihaya Castle against enormous numbers of Hojo *samurai*. He put a number of life-sized dummies dressed in armour behind shields near the castle walls. At dawn the *samurai* saw what they thought was the defenders trying to flee, and attacked. As they drew close, hidden archers opened fire while others dropped rocks from the walls, injuring or killing over 800 of the attackers.

Above: detail, Himeji Castle
Below: Kumamoto

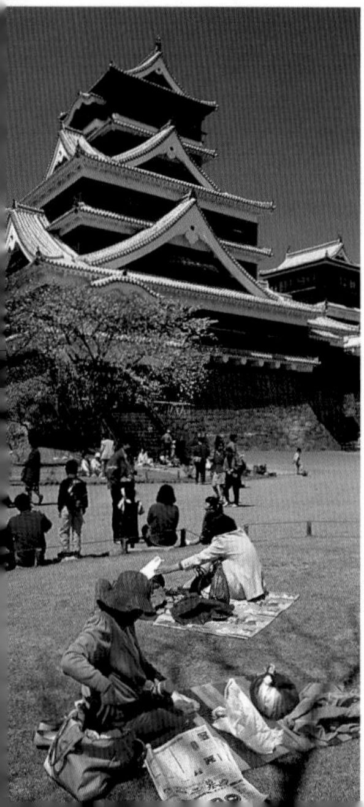

Early construction Building techniques were originally quite simple. Large wooden posts were driven into the earth at intervals of one *ken* (2m). Between the large posts a framework of lighter bamboo poles was inserted, to which bundles of bamboos and reeds were tied. The walls were then coated with a mixture of red clay and stones to give them greater strength. Defensive towers and other buildings were made of wood. Walls built using this kind of wattle-and-daub technique were highly susceptible to weather damage, and a great deal of work was required to maintain the castles ready for battle.

As warfare increased both in intensity and duration during the Sengoku Jidai period, *daimyo* began to build more permanent and more powerful castles. Western techniques of fortification were introduced through the efforts of Portuguese Jesuit missionaries, and *hirajiro* ('castles on the plain') and *hirayamajiro* ('castles on the plateau') made their appearance. Whenever possible, natural features such as rivers, lakes, hills and mountain crags or the sea were incorporated into the defences, which in a typical castle would consist of a moat surrounding a number of concentric courts protected by massive stone walls. At the centre stood a central compound (*honmaru*), within which a large central tower (*tenshu*) was built on a platform of rammed earth faced with huge stones.

Defence techniques Attackers faced a formidable number of defences and obstacles. Openings (*hazama*) were left in the walls as loopholes through which archers and gunners could shoot down into the ranks of the enemy. Special chambers (*ishiotoshi*) were constructed over the walls with openings in the floors through which large stones or boiling water could be dropped on to the enemy. In some castles the inner courtyards and buildings were constructed in such a way as to confuse any attackers who might breach the outer defences: by abrupt changes of direction enemy troops were forced into killing grounds, where they could be attacked by archers and gunners firing from strongpoints built into the defences.

At the heart of the castle stood the main tower, consisting of a number of storeys of decreasing size, with curving roofs and overhanging gables. The *tenshu* was the command post and watch tower from which any defence of the castle would be controlled. When Hideyoshi built his massive castle at Osaka in 1583 as both the seat of his government and as a symbol of his power, the *tenshu* was over 80m high and coloured blue and gold.

Castle-smashing Ironically it was under Hideyoshi, one of the greatest of castle builders, that many castles were destroyed. As Hideyoshi increased his power he sent out 'castle-smashing commissioners' (*shiro wari bugyo*) to destroy the fortifications built by his defeated enemies. This policy was continued by the Tokugawa shogunate after they came to power. They decreed that each *daimyo* could only retain a single castle in his domains; all others had to be demolished. The surviving castles became centres of trade and industry, and 'castle towns' (*joku machi*) grew up around the castles to supply the goods and needs of the *daimyo* and his retainers.

Many of the surviving castles have been almost completely rebuilt, but some remain in their original state. Probably the most famous of all Japanese castles is the Shirasagi-jo Castle (Castle of the White Crane) built at Himeji by Hideyoshi (see page 162).

The last siege
In 1877 Satsuma *samurai* under the leadership of Saigo Takamori rose in rebellion against the imperial government of Emperor Meiji. Imperial troops held Kumamotojo Castle against a rebel force three times larger, who attacked the castle with both traditional and modern weapons. In an echo of the past both attackers and defenders used units equipped only with swords, who fought man to man on the battlements. Eventually the rebels were defeated and the castle relieved.

Matsumoto Castle

Dutch in Nagasaki
During the period of Japanese seclusion between 1639 and 1854 the only Westerners allowed by the Japanese to trade with Japan were the Dutch, who were restricted to a small, man-made island called Dejima in Nagasaki harbour. Only traders and prostitutes were allowed on and off Dejima, which has since been swallowed up in a land reclamation scheme and is marked only by a streetcar stop. There is, however, a reconstruction of the island at the Dejima Historical Museum (streetcar 7 to Dejima; open 9–5, closed Monday). Orandazaka, or Hollander Slope, a cobbled street behind the station, is lined with 19th-century Dutch residents' houses, and Nagasaki Holland Village, an hour by bus from Nagasaki station, is a complete reconstruction of a genuine Dutch village.

►► Miyazaki *187D2*

At Miyazaki, the administrative and economic centre of Miyazaki prefecture in southern Kyushu, the climate is subtropical all the year round. The town's broad avenues are lined with palm trees, lush greenery abounds and flowers are always in bloom. A seaside promenade and a beautiful coastline, designated as the Quasi-National Park, stretch to the south. Miyazaki was once a popular honeymoon destination but nowadays Japanese couples prefer the more exotic shores of Australia and Hawaii or the capital cities of Europe. Nevertheless, Miyazaki remains principally a Japanese tourist destination and very few foreigners visit.

There are direct trains from Hakata station, Fukuoka, (six hours), Beppu (three hours, 45 minutes) and Kagoshima (three hours), and direct flights from Tokyo (one and a half hours). Tourist offices can be found at the JR station and at the airport.

►► Nagasaki *186B3*

The target of the second atomic bomb to be dropped on Japan in World War II is, understandably, not a city of particular sights. However, its history, coastal location, scenery, old city and foreign quarters and the warm climate, tempered with sea breezes, make it a perfect place for relaxed exploration on foot or by streetcar. The city is easy to navigate and many signs are in English.

Nagasaki is two hours by rail from Hakata station on the JR Nagasaki line. The railway station is connected to the city centre by streetcar, part of a system that links all the main sights. Most shopping, dining and cultural activities are located in the south of the city. North of the city is the Peace Park and to the west Inasayama, a mountain-top park offering splendid views. It is also possible to take rickshaw rides around Nagasaki. A tourist information centre is located outside Nagasaki station.

Glover Gardens►► is an open-air museum, featuring Western-style houses built in the 19th-century Meiji period. The main attraction is the oldest Western-style

Glover Mansion

Nagasaki's Chinatown

building in Japan, Glover Mansion, built by a Scotsman, Thomas Glover, in 1863 and still much as it was in his day. The park grounds which overlook the city are well looked after and peaceful but the hillside escalators leading to Glover Mansion rather spoil the atmosphere. Take streetcar 5 to Oura-Tenshudoshita stop to reach the gardens (open November–March 8:30–5, March–November 8–6). Situated in Teramachi, the Nagasaki temple district, **Kofukuji Temple▶▶▶** was an important Obaku-Zen temple in the style of the Chinese Ming dynasty (open 8–5:30). Kofukuji is a 10-minute walk from the Kodai-mae streetcar stop. A 20-minute walk south through the Teramachi district leads to **Sofukuji Temple▶▶▶**, the first Obaku-Zen temple in Japan, founded in 1629 by a Chinese monk. Attractive, grassy gardens with tropical palms surround the temple, whose beautiful, red-painted main hall was constructed by Chinese carpenters (open 8–5).

The bomb that exploded on Nagasaki on 9 August 1945 was three times more powerful than the one that dropped on Hiroshima, but it missed the main city and fell on a village on the outskirts of town. Even so, over three-quarters of the population of Nagasaki died (150,000 people). **Peace Park (Heiwa-koen)▶▶▶** was built on a hill near the site of the explosion. A bronze statue stands as a symbol of hope for peace, and several other sculptures have been given by foreign countries. In the International Culture Hall there is a display of records and relics of the attack (open 9–6). Take streetcar 1 or 3 to Matsuyama-cho stop.

Nagasaki and the Portuguese
Francis Xavier was the first missionary to set foot in Japan. He arrived in 1549 and died in 1551, leaving converts to continue his work. By 1579 Japanese Christians included six *daimyo* among their numbers. One of them, Omura Sumitada, ruled a remote area of northwest Kyushu, where the coastline was blessed with a good natural harbour. Here, with Portuguese help, Omura built the port of Nagasaki, which attracted the majority of Japan-bound Portuguese ships and quickly became a rich melting-pot of Eastern and Western cultures

Detail, Sofukuji Temple

Tojin Yashika Ato
In 1698 the shogunate ordered all Chinese in Nagasaki to live in a walled compound in the Tojin Hashika Ato quarter, in southeast Nagasaki. With its narrow, winding streets and busy market places, the area is evocative of an old Chinatown settlement. Nearby Shinchimachi district is the present-day Chinatown, an excellent place for Chinese food.

Battle of Okinawa
The final land battle in World War II between Japan and the Allies took place on Okinawa. The American flag was raised on 22 June 1945 after 82 days of fierce fighting. The Japanese commander, General Ushijima, committed suicide, as did many soldiers and civilians. Over 250,000 Japanese died; 12,500 Allied soldiers were killed and 37,000 wounded. Despite such losses the Japanese on the mainland did not surrender and the US Command decided to drop atomic bombs on Hiroshima and Nagasaki.

Okinawan *saké*
Okinawan islanders make a variety of very potent *saké*. Two of the strongest are a *saké* matured in jars full of garlic cloves, and a concoction known as 'snake juice', matured in a wide-necked jar containing the coiled body of a small, dead, poisonous snake. After 10 years' maturation the flesh is dissolved and only the bones remain. The drink is said to enhance stamina and sexual power.

▶▶▶ Okinawa *186A1*

Okinawa is the largest island in the Ryukyu archipelago, which stretches south 1,300 km from Kyushu through the Pacific and East China Sea almost to the tip of Taiwan. Like the rest of the Ryuku group, its culture has been influenced in the past as much by China as by Japan.

Okinawa is a tropical island, warm in any season and scorchingly hot in July and August. The south of Okinawa, particularly around the capital, Naha, is heavily developed and ugly. However, in Naha itself the jumble of hotels, temples, McDonald's hamburger bars, ice-cream parlours, Shinto shrines, Japanese tourists, strip joints, karate *dojos* (gyms), old men and women in kimonos, and dense traffic, all fit comfortably together. The city is a great repository of Okinawan culture and the location of the best of Okinawa theatre, dance, music and cuisine.

Much of the north of the island is now also developed, but a few small, traditional fishing and farming villages, surrounded by sugar cane and pineapple fields, and unspoilt beaches (nowadays often annexed by the smart hotels) still exist. Coral-diving and tropical fishing are popular tourist pursuits. Okinawa is also the birthplace of Japanese karate (see pages 206–7). To experience the unique Sino-Japanese lifestyle of this archipelago, one has to travel to other islands in the Okinawan prefecture, such as Kumejima, Taketomi and Irimote; Okinawa is the centre of ferry and air services to these islands.

Getting there There are direct flights and sea ferry services to Okinawa from Tokyo, Osaka and Fukuoka. Flight times from mainland Japan are between one and two and a half hours; the ferry takes over two days from Tokyo and over a day from Fukuoka. Ferries travelling from Okinawa link all the inhabited islands of the Ryukyu group. An air service links the larger islands. Tourist information is available at Naha airport (15 minutes by bus to Naha centre) or Naha bus terminal.

Irimote Island

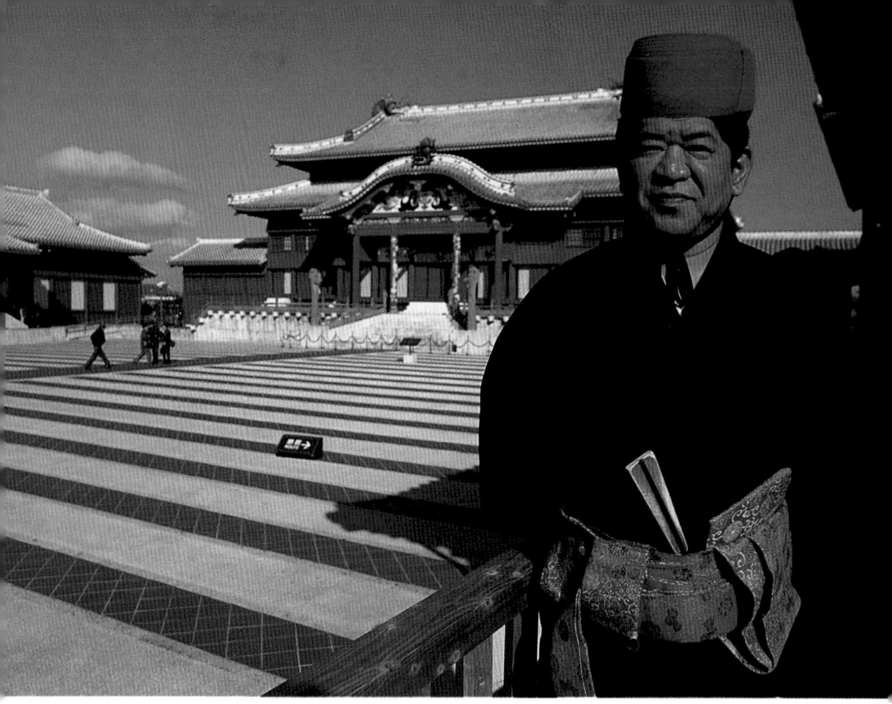

Northern Okinawa The least spoiled part of the island, this is the most satisfying area to explore. Unfortunately, access to the north by public transport is difficult and services are infrequent.

Hedo Misaki▶▶ is the island's northernmost headland, where a clifftop road offers spectacular views of blue sea and outlying islands. The road rounds the headland and passes through the tiny village of Oku, worth visiting for its traditional Okinawan houses. To reach Hedo Misaki take bus 20, 21 or 77 from Naha to Nago (two hours, 20 minutes), bus 67 Nago to Okuma Beach (two hours, 50 minutes) and bus 69 from Okuma to Hedo Misaki-iriguchi. From here it is a 15-minute walk to the cliff.

Kijoka▶▶, a traditional village in northern Okinawa, is famous for *bashofu*, a textile similar to linen but made from banana fibre. Take bus 73 or 74 from Nago to Kijoka (one hour).

Southern Okinawa The island's principal craft, fashion shopping and dining thoroughfare is Kokusai-dori, the long main street of **Naha**▶▶. Along its east side is Heiwa-dori Street, the central branch of a network of covered alleys and passageways that make up the market district. With stalls selling everything from obscure Okinawan vegetables to baseball caps, this area is the heart of the city.

Shuri, now a district of Naha, was the capital of the Ryukyu dynasty (1429–1879). The once royal city was used by Japanese high command as their headquarters and destroyed by American Forces in 1945 in the Battle of Okinawa. Parts of the castle – some exterior walls and two castle gates – have been restored. *Shureimon*, the Gate of Courtesy, a typical example of Okinawan architecture, was restored in 1958 and represents a symbol of the islanders' culture and independence.

Above and below: traditional costume in Shuri

Festivals
The Okinawan calendar is busy with events. *Jiriuma* (20 January) is a parade of women dressed in colourful *bingata* kimono; *Hari* (3 and 4 May) has dragon-boat races, and in *Naha Otsunahiki* (10 October), two 250m-long fat ropes, one 'male' and one 'female', are intertwined, and a tug of war ensues between thousands of people.

■ Japanese martial arts are now practised worldwide as methods of self-defence, self-discipline and sport. While the classical systems of swordsmanship and related methods attract a devoted following, the systems of judo, kendo, aikido and especially karate-do are the most popular, and highly skilled non-Japanese teachers and practitioners can be found in countries throughout the world......■

Uechi-Ryu karate
One of Okinawa's most popular karate styles, Uechi-Ryu, was developed by Kanbun Uechi (1877–1945). He studied Chinese boxing at the Central Temple in Fukien province, China, where he was a student of Chou Tze-ho. After training with him for 13 years, Kanbun Uechi returned to Japan and became a farmer near Osaka. A young Okinawan persuaded him to start teaching and soon he opened a school. He taught there for 24 years before returning to Okinawa.

Weapons used in Okinawan karate

Okinawan karate origins Karate developed in Okinawa in the 19th century from a fusion of Chinese martial arts, brought by Okinawans from the Fukien province of mainland China, and an indigenous Okinawan system of empty-hand fighting called *te. Te* and simple weapon systems using farming and fishing implements were developed in response to a decree by the Chinese invaders of Okinawa, which forbade the use by the islanders of swords and other orthodox weapons.

In 1921 Crown Prince Hirohito visited Okinawa and for the first time saw a demonstration of karate by some school children. The demonstration was arranged by Funakoshi Gichin, then the chief instructor of a karate school on the island. It was a great success and Funakoshi went to Tokyo in 1922 to demonstrate his skills. This was the start of karate in Japan and around the world.

Modern karate Karate stresses kicking and punching, although some styles also teach throwing techniques, arm and wrist locks and the use of traditional Okinawan weapons, such as the staff (*bo*), jointed flail (*nunchaku*) or knuckle dusters (*tekko*).

Following the example set by the founders of judo, Funakoshi Gichin and other karate-do masters wanted karate to be seen as something more than simply a method of fighting. The development of a strong fighting spirit was important, but this had to be accompanied by an equally strong spiritual and moral element to avoid the misuse of the art.

Funakoshi Gichin wrote a code of 20 precepts, among which he said 'Karate begins and ends with courtesy'; 'There is no first attack in karate'; and 'Karate is an auxiliary of justice'. The teachings and practices of the arts of the sword were applied by him to the art of the empty hand; by so doing he hoped that karate would become a means of preserving and developing the *samurai* spirit.

In the West, karate is most commonly taught as a sport but the older ideals of self-defence and self-discipline still have many followers.

Other martial arts Judo was described by its founder Kano Jigoro (1860–1938) as 'The Way of Gentleness or of first giving way in order ultimately to gain the victory'; judo is practised today as a contest sport, in which the

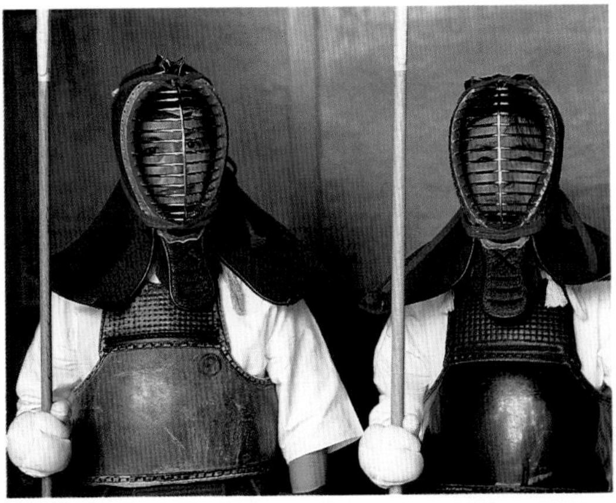

Martial artists

aim is to throw or lock an opponent according to strictly defined rules. The martial element has gradually declined because of this stress on sport, especially since judo became an Olympic event in 1964.

Aikido ('The Way of Harmony') was created by Ueshiba Morihei (1883–1969). As a young man, Ueshiba studied a number of ju-jitsu systems, as well as swordsmanship and spear-fighting. The techniques of aikido feature rapid turning movements, designed to blend with an attacker's movements so as to throw or unbalance him. An aikido master is often compared with the eye of a hurricane: quiet in himself but difficult to approach because of the tremendous forces swirling around him.

Kendo ('The Way of the Sword') is very popular in Japan and has a growing number of followers in the West. Generally, kendo is taught as a system of sporting combat, in which the practitioners wear protective armour and try to score points on designated targets with a bamboo sword (or *shinai*). The practice is derived from the older, classical systems of swordsmanship, and kendo practitioners generally regard the sporting aspect of their art as the least important part of the discipline.

Everyday karate
Karate on Okinawa is an everyday part of many people's lives. Training sessions do not have the obvious intensity and seriousness evident in Western and mainland Japanese schools. This sometimes disappoints Western visitors, who expect tough training schedules and strict discipline. Okinawan *karateka* train steadily, year in, year out, working on form, strength, body conditioning and speed and developing a style which looks deceptively relaxed.

***Samurai* kendo**
It is common for kendo practitioners also to train in *ken-jutsu*, which features training with a real blade in techniques designed to dispatch an enemy as quickly and effectively as possible. The methods taught in the older *ken-jutsu* styles are the same techniques as taught to the *samurai*, and are based on the conditions and circumstances likely to be faced by a *samurai* on the field of battle.

A karate staff swinging into action

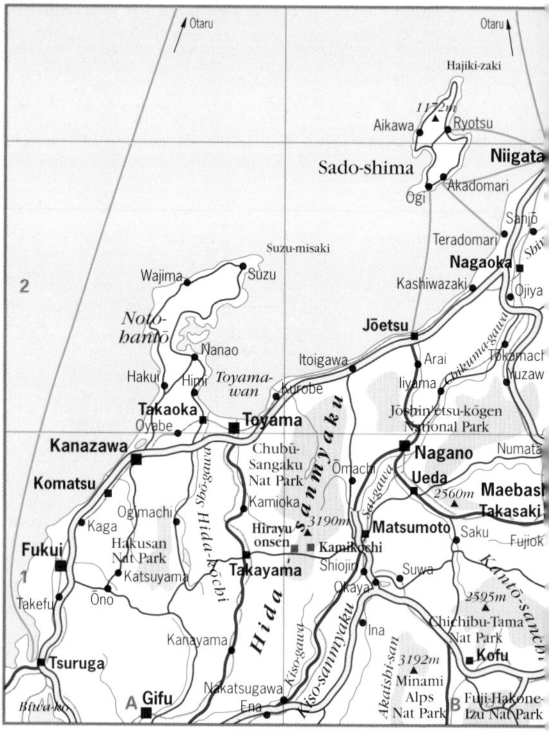
Otaru
Otaru
Hajiki-zaki
1172m
Aikawa
Ryotsu
Sado-shima
Niigata
Akadomari
Ogi
Sanjō
Teradomari
Nagaoka
Suzu-misaki
Wajima
Suzu
2
Kashiwazaki
Ojiya
Noto-
bantō
Jōetsu
Nanao
Itoigawa
Arai
Tokamachi
Hakui
Himi
Toyama-
wan
Kurobe
Iiyama
Chikuma-gawa
Yuzawa
Takaoka
Oyabe
Toyama
Jōshin'etsu-kōgen
National Park
Kanazawa
Chubū-
Sangaku
Nat Park
Nagano
Numata
Komatsu
Ōmachi
Ueda
Maebash
Kamioka
2560m
Takasaki
Ogimachi
Kaga
Hirayu
onsen
3190m
Matsumoto
Saku
Fujiok
Hakusan
Nat Park
Kamikochi
Fukui
Katsuyama
Takayama
Shiojiri
Suwa
1
Okaya
Takefu
Ōno
2595m
Ina
Chichibu-Tama
Nat Park
Kanayama
Hida
3192m
Kofu
Tsuruga
Minami
Alps
Nat Park
Biwa-ko
A
Gifu
Nakatsugawa
Ena
Kiso-gawa
Kiso-sanmyaku
Akaishi-san
B
Fuji-Hakone-
Izu Nat Park

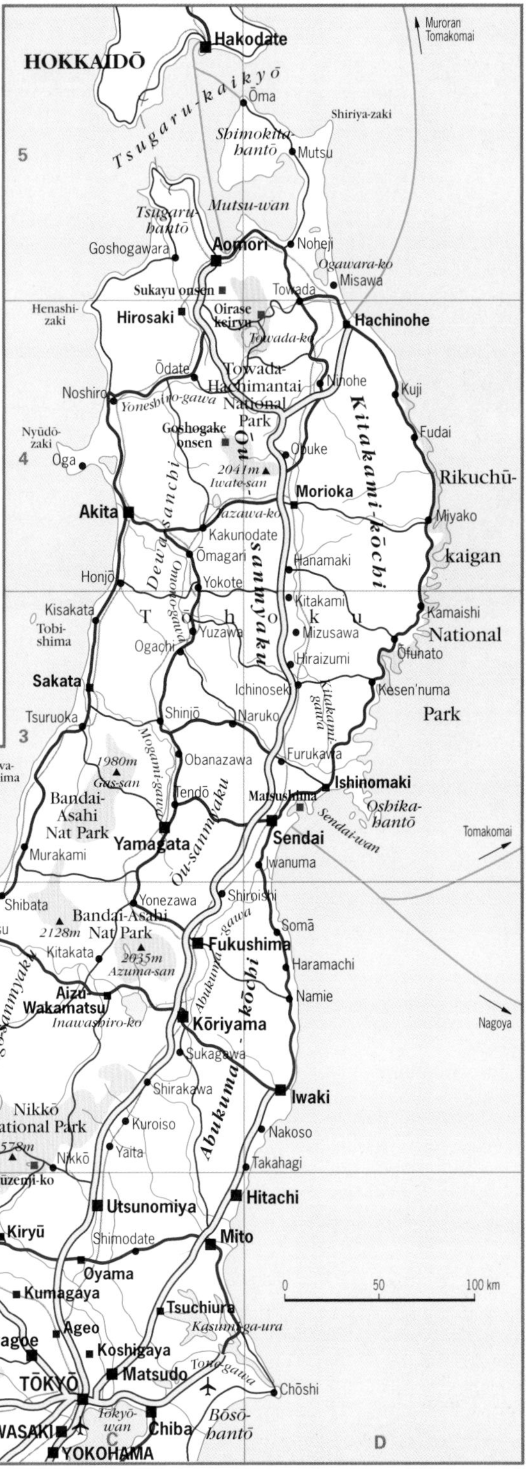

NORTHERN HONSHU

The Northern Honshu town of Takayama *(see pages 214–15)*

Northern Honshu Tohoku Province, in the northernmost region of Honshu, has severe winters and a mountainous terrain, and remains one of the areas of Japan least affected by industrialisation. The Hide, Kiso and Akaishi ranges of mountains, known together as the Japan Alps, rise in a series of high, jagged snow-capped peaks strung across the middle of the southern end of northern Honshu, covering a vast area and providing a wide range of hiking, climbing and skiing challenges. Nagano prefecture, within the Japan Alps, has been selected to host the 1998 Winter Olympics.

Tohoku Until the late 19th century, Tohoku was inhabited mostly by nomadic tribes of people known as Ainu. Gradually, Japanese settlers from the south drove the Ainu north to the island of Hokkaido, but the very cold, snowy winters and the distance from Tokyo continued to restrict Tohoku's settlement and commercial development. Even today the area retains its long-standing traditions of farming and local crafts. It has a relatively rural, untouched air, marred only by some tourist facilities in the most popular national parks and historic towns.

Travel to Tohoku is quick and convenient via the Tohoku Shinkansen bullet train, but once there and off the beaten track, local train journey times are slow and route-planning more complicated.

The main tourist season is the summer, which tends to be mild and dry; the first 10 days of August are particularly busy, with big festivals in Sendai, Akita and Aomori.

Tohoku back-country
Tohoku is the collective name given to the six prefectures of northern Honshu. It was once known by the Japanese as Michinoku or 'the end of the line'. This image still sticks and, as a consequence, the area is avoided by conventional Japanese tourists, despite the many attractions of the region and the remarkable friendliness of the people.

Sendai The largest city in Tohoku, Sendai was flattened in World War II and has since been rebuilt along the lines of most modern Japanese cities, with no exceptional features. It is, however, a reasonably good base from which to explore the rest of Tohoku and especially the neighbouring Yamagata prefecture, a rural district where life is very much in traditional Tohoku style. Sendai is two hours by Tohoku Shinkansen from Tokyo's Ueno station.

Japan Alps Mountains in Japan were once believed to be the sacred dwelling places of divine spirits. Some were climbed, consecrated and made places of religious pilgrimage, but most mountain summits were avoided. However, in 1896 the Reverend Weston, a British missionary and mountaineer, set out to explore the area now known as the Japan Alps, and in the process popularised mountain-climbing in Japan (see panel, page 212). Many Japanese now take their vacations in the Japan Alps, and a festival honouring Weston is held in Kamikochi Village in the northern Hida Range every year on the first Sunday in June. Matsumoto, an old castle town located on a high alpine plateau, is the gateway to the Japan Alps and a good base for exploring central Honshu, to the east.

Kanazawa Although popular with the Japanese, Kanazawa is away from the usual foreign tourist routes, five hours by train from Tokyo across the Japan Alps. Partly an old Japanese castle town, with a thriving reputation as a centre of traditional religions and arts and crafts (especially *noh* theatre), and partly a very modern city with sophisticated shops and nightlife, Kanazawa is of manageable size and is best explored on foot.

Sado Situated in the Sea of Japan, off the coast of Niigata prefecture, Sado Island was once a place of banishment for criminals and those out of political favour. It is a beautiful island with a slow pace of life, even during the summer months (May to September), when there is usually a large influx of tourists.

Alpine tour
Tateyama–Kurobe Alpine Route Tour takes a spectacular journey through the mountains using a variety of means of transport. Tickets for the whole trip may be bought from Shinano-Omachi railway station (one hour from Matsumoto on the JR Oito line), where the tour starts; it ends at Toyama, having proceeded *en route* by bus, cable-car, train and foot. The route is open from the end of April to the end of November, but is expensive and busy during holiday periods.

Vegetable handcart, Sado Island

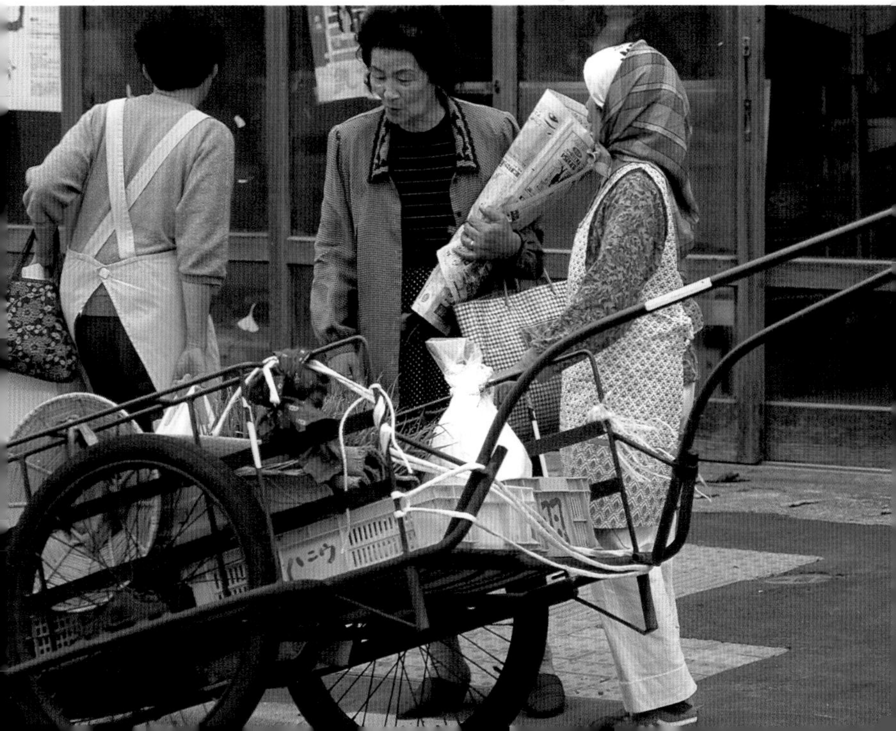

Father of the mountains
The Reverend Walter Weston dubbed the mountains of central Honshu 'the Alps' in his Japan Guide, published in 1881. In 1896 he published another book, *Mountaineering and Exploration in the Japanese Alps*, which sparked much interest in Japan and earned him the title 'Father of Mountaineering'. Until that time the Japanese had shown little interest in the recreational possibilities of their country's mountain peaks, valleys and passes. In recognition of his exploration he was awarded the Order of the Sacred Treasure (Fourth Class) by the Emperor and a memorial was erected in his name in Kamikochi.

The Japan Alps

▶▶ Kamikochi *208B1*

This village, really a collection of inns and lodges, shares its name with the high valley in which it stands. The area provides excellent hiking and climbing and there are trails and mountain routes for every level of expertise.

Kamikochi is reached via Matsumoto by the private Matsumoto Dentetsu line to Shin Shimajima station (30 minutes) and then by bus (one hour, 20 minutes). The bus route takes a narrow and twisting mountain road and the scenery for the last 30 minutes of the journey is stunning. The road is closed by snow during the long winter months and opens only from the end of April to the beginning of November.

Hotel development thankfully has been limited in Kamikochi but it means that during the summer months accommodation is very scarce. Early spring and mid-autumn (early October) are the best times to visit. Camping and hiking equipment are available for hire and maps, route directions and provisions may be collected from local shops. Mountain huts with comfortable accommodation are found along the hiking trails.

▶▶ Matsumoto *208B1*

Once an important castle town, Matsumoto is now a modern city in an alpine setting on a high plateau near many hot-spring resorts. As one of the gateways to the Alps and the centre of an excellent communications network, this is a particularly fine base for exploring both the Alps, to the west and north, and central Japan (Chubu district), to the east.

Matsumoto is two hours, 20 minutes by JR Chuo line limited express from Nagoya and two hours, 50 minutes on the same line but in the opposite direction from Tokyo (Shinjuku station). There is a tourist office at the front of Matsumoto station.

The view from Matsumoto Castle

Hiking country at Kamikochi

Key to paradise
The object for most pilgrims visiting Zenkoji Temple in Nagano is to touch 'the key to paradise', and ensure their salvation. The key is a specific stone set in the wall of a tunnel that runs below the floor of the main hall. Devout pilgrims, most of whom are elderly, wend their way to the key along a pitch-black passageway.

Matsumotojo Castle▶▶▶ is one of the oldest, best preserved and most architecturally beautiful in Japan. Also known as Crow Castle (Karasujo), because the exterior walls are mainly black, it was begun in 1504, while the impressive six-storey donjon was completed in 1597. Climb the donjon's narrow, steep wooden staircase for panoramic views of the city. This castle was built for serious combat and its walls are peppered with battlements from which arrows and guns were fired and stones dropped on the attacking forces. To avoid crowds go out of season or early in the day. The castle is a 20-minute walk through old Matsumoto, north and east of the railway station; a map is available from the tourist office (open 8:30–5).

The private **Matsumoto Folk Art Museum▶▶**, a 15-minute bus ride from the station to Shimoganai Mingeikan Guchi bus stop, exhibits domestic products of wood, bamboo, glass and porcelain from Japan and other Asian countries (open 9–5; closed Monday).

▶ Nagano *208B1*

Nagano prefecture was selected in 1991 to host the 1998 Winter Olympic Games. The resulting construction work includes a new Shinkansen bullet train line from Tokyo to Nagano, but current access is from Tokyo's Ueno station on the JR Shinetsu line (two hours, 50 minutes) or from Matsumoto on the JR Chuo line (55 minutes). Nagano's main attraction, 10 minutes by bus or cab from Nagano station, is the famous **Zenkoji Temple▶▶▶**, founded in the 7th century by Yoshimitsu Honda. One of the most important pilgrimage temples in Japan, it is attached to no particular Buddhist sect and is equally available to women and men. Millions of visitors flock to the temple every year (open 5:30–4:30).

Sacred mountains
The practice of leaving a monetary offering on mountain peaks is common throughout Japan. Many peaks have religious associations, and shrines and objects of veneration may be encountered (along with more worldly items such as vending machines) on some of the highest peaks. The first woman to climb Mount Fuji, in 1867, was Lady Parkes, the wife of the British Ambassador, who ignored the taboo that women were not allowed on sacred peaks (it was believed that the resident god abhorred 'red pollution', or menstrual blood).

Ogimachi village

Praying roofs
The steep roofs of the thatched farmhouses in Shirakawago are designed to prevent a build-up of the snow that blankets the valley throughout the winter. They are described as *gassho-zukuri* – 'hands held in prayer'.

***Saké* breweries**
The many traditional *saké* brewers in Takayama old town work from small home breweries, indicated by balls of woven cedar fronds hung from the roof eaves. The fronds are cut at the beginning of the brewing cycle, and by the time the *saké* is ready to drink have turned from green to brown. Brewers welcome visitors inside to look around, to taste and, if they wish, to buy their *saké*.

Festival carts
Takayama's famous festivals, the spring Sanno Matsuri (14–15 April) and autumn Yahata Matsuri (9–10 October), feature elaborate and gorgeous floats (*yatai*), said to be among the finest in Japan. Four floats designed in the early 19th century are on display at the Takayama Yatai Kaikan, up the street from Yoshijima House (open 8:30–5). The guardian shrine of Takayama, Sakurayama Hachiman-gu, celebrated in the autumn festival, is housed next door.

►►► Ogimachi 208A1

This village is set in the Shirakawago Valley, a two-hour train ride from Takayama (see below). Surrounded by high mountains, the narrow valley is dotted with thatched *gassho-zukuri* farmhouses (see panel), terraced rice paddies, vegetable gardens and flower beds. About 150 thatched dwellings have been built here, many serving as *minshuku*. The farmhouses were constructed to hold extended families: living space was on the ground floor, while the upper floor was used for storage and craft work.

Ogimachi is well off the beaten track and a visit is best planned in conjunction with a trip to Takayama. To reach the village take a bus from Takayama to Makido on the Nohi bus (one hour, 35 minutes) and a bus from Makido to Ogimachi (one hour). Buses are infrequent; plan your trip in advance. There is a tourist office in the village square.

►►► Takayama 208A1

Takayama is a highland city in the heart of the mountainous Hida district of west central Japan. The city has been modernised but retains a compactness and richness of traditional architecture and culture, earning its nickname 'little Kyoto'. The old town, centred around two narrow streets called Sannomachi and Ninomachi, contains many well-preserved old inns, tea houses, shops and merchants houses with the latticed windows and overhanging roofs characteristic of the Edo period.

There is much to see in Takayama but one of the joys of being there is just to wander around on foot or hired bicycle. The city is laid out on a grid pattern and is easy to negotiate. English-language booklets and maps are available from the tourist office at the station and there are several cycle rental shops in the area. The Sannomachi district and most of the best sights are east of the station.

Takayama is two hours, 45 minutes by JR Takayama limited express from Nagoya. By bus from Kamikochi (May to October only) the journey is in two stages: first a bus to Hirayu Onsen (one hour, 15 minutes), then a bus to Takayama (one hour, 10 minutes).

The **Hida Minzoku Mura Folklore Village▶▶▶** is an open-air museum of old thatched Hida farmhouses, which demonstrates how farmers and craft workers would once have lived and worked in this region and gives a vivid account of rural life in medieval Japan. The village is within bus, cycle or walking distance, west of Takayama station (open 8:30–5).

A daily **Morning Market (Asa-ichi)▶▶** (7am–noon) is held along the east bank of the Miyagawa River and in front of Takayama Jinya. Stalls sell local produce, flowers and crafts brought in from the surrounding countryside.

Sanmachi Suji▶▶▶ was the merchant area during feudal times. Yoshijima House, at the north end of Shimo-Ninomachi Street, was built in 1905 as the fine but rustic home and factory of the well-to-do Yoshijima brewing family (open 9–5; closed Tuesday, December–February). Kusakabe merchant's house, next door, is less rustic and more imposing than its neighbour (same opening hours).

Once the residence of the *daimyo* of Hida, **Takayama Jinya▶▶▶**, a group of whitewashed buildings, is perhaps the best example of provincial Edo government offices in Japan. They were in use until 1969 and the audience chambers, the interrogation rooms (which contain instruments of torture), the gardens and the rice stores, where the shogunate's rice tax was stockpiled, are now open to visitors (open 8:45–5, November–March 8:45–4:30).

Making rope sandals at the Hida Minzoku Mura Folklore Village

Shorenji Temple
The Zen Shorenji Temple was transported to Takayama in 1961 from the Shokawa Valley, part of which was flooded to make a reservoir. *Shojin-ryori* (Zen vegetarian food) is served at the temple (open November–March 8:30–5, April–October 8–6).

Takayama's Morning Market (Asa-ichi)

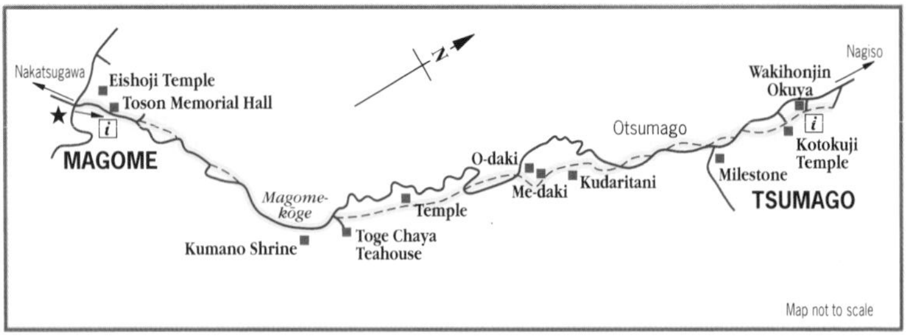

Walk Kiso Valley

Distance: 9.3km; time: three hours (wear hiking boots in winter)

This gentle hike between two post towns in the Kiso Valley follows the Magome Pass, tracing the path of the old Nakasendo Highway, a major route between Edo (Tokyo) and Kyoto during the 18th and early 19th centuries. To get to Magome take the Chuo Honsen line from Nagoya to Nakatsugawa station (one hour, 15 minutes). From there take the bus to Magome (35 minutes). From Tsumago take a bus to Nagiso station on the Chuo Honsen line and then back to Nagoya or Matsumoto.

Leaving Magome, follow the main street away from the bus station past houses which appear ancient, but which are actually faithful copies of those destroyed by fire at the end of the last century. Once clear of the town, walk for 50 minutes along the paved road to the **Magome Pass▶▶▶**. Past the Toge Chaya tea house, a path drops away to the right from the main road. From here, the walk is downhill all the way to Tsumago.

The path leads past a small temple on the left, then, further along, the site of a guardhouse which controlled the movement of timber from the Kiso Valley and meted out severe punishments to anyone smuggling timber.

After about 45 minutes, having twice crossed the paved road, the path comes to two waterfalls, the **Odaki** and **Me-daki▶▶**, one male, one female. Further on is a milestone at a fork in the road, recording the distance in *ri* (79 *ri* or 320km) from the capital, Edo (Tokyo). Take the right fork of the path, and walk for a further 30 minutes to reach **Tsumago▶▶▶**.

The second post town from the south on the Nakasendo Highway, Tsumago retains the atmosphere of an Edo-era post town. Its main street,

which is lined with dark, wooden, shuttered houses, is particularly evocative. Although it is now enjoying new prosperity as a thriving tourist centre, Tsumago was virtually deserted by the mid-1960s, due both to its position – far away from the main transport routes – and to the massive migration to the big towns and cities during the post-war years. All of Tsumago's buildings are now under a strict preservation order.

Above and below: views of Tsumago, which still has the air of an Edo-period post town

Rebellion
Five hundred years ago, rebellious priests and peasants overthrew Kanazawa's feudal lord. They established an independent republic, which survived for 100 years until subdued by the warlord Oda Nobunaga, who awarded the city to his retainer, Maeda Toshiie.

Above and below: the geisha *quarter*

Beyond the Alps

▶▶▶ Kanazawa *208A1*

This important provincial city, bordering the Sea of Japan in north central Honshu, is partly an old castle town and partly a modern city with busy department stores and a thriving nightlife. For those wishing to explore both modern and traditional Japanese cultures and architecture, it is an excellent place to visit. Off the main thoroughfare, which differs little from those of other Japanese cities, there are winding streets, dead-end alleyways and moats designed to confuse would-be attackers of the central castle site, now marked only by its original eastern entrance, the Ishikawamon Gate. Kanazawa is most easily reached by JR limited express from Kyoto (two hours, 30 minutes) or Nagoya (three hours). Alternatively, if you have visited Ogimachi and do not wish to return to Takayama, there is a bus direct to Kanazawa (three hours). There is an information office by the Kanazawa station exit.

The **Eastern Pleasure Quarter▶▶** in the Higashi-yama district was set aside in 1820 by the Maeda government as an entertainment area for high-ranking citizens. The most talented and beautiful of 'free' *geisha* girls provided evenings of music, dancing, conversation and perhaps other more intimate pleasures. The area is distinguished by a neat row of *geisha* tea houses, each with a slatted wooden façade and an oblong paper lampshade over its entrance. Rising costs and a demand for sleazier entertainment have reduced business but some of the old atmosphere can still be experienced along Higashi main street. Shima-ke, the fifth house down the street on the left going east, is an elegant former *geisha* house open for viewing (open 9:30–5; closed Monday).

Situated beneath the castle mound is **Kenrokuen Garden▶▶▶**, Kanazawa's most famous attraction. Once

Kanazawa Market

the private garden of the Maeda lords, who ruled the city for three generations, Kenrokuen is officially categorised as one of Japan's three best gardens, and is said to combine perfectly the six qualities by which a park is judged: size, seclusion, running water, views, artificiality and age. The best time to visit is early morning, before the arrival of parties of Japanese visitors. The moss-covered earth will still be moist with dew and one can sit in solitude in the Moonflower Pavilion tea house, and order bean-jam cakes and green whisked tea. Flowers bloom all year round (open 6:30–6pm, 16 October–15 March 8–4:30).

The ordinary-looking **Myoryuji Temple▶▶** is, in fact, a complex of secret chambers, trap doors, hidden tunnels and staircases and a maze of corridors. It was constructed to confine and hold off invaders while the Maeda *daimyo* made his escape in the event of invasion of the city castle. Myoryuji, also called Temple of the Ninja (Ninjadera), was connected to the castle by a tunnel. To get there, take a cab from the station or a bus to Nomachi Hirokoji stop and a further five-minute walk. Reservations are required: call at the temple or telephone 41 2877 (open 9–4; tours last 30 minutes).

The old **Nagamachi *Samurai* District▶▶▶** is in the area which begins just behind the 109 Korinbo department store in central Kanazawa. Nowadays it consists mainly of one street, lined with traditional, privately owned *samurai* wooden houses, each hidden behind roof-topped mud walls. Fortunately, the Nomura Family House, once the home of a well-to-do *samurai* warrior, has been maintained in its original condition and is open to visitors. The design of the interior is severe but extremely elegant, making extensive use of cypress, ebony and persimmon wood (open 8:30–5:30; closed first and third Wednesday of the month).

Eastern Temple Quarter
Rising behind the Eastern Pleasure Quarter, overlooking Kanazawa, is the Utatsuyama mountain, scattered with 40 Buddhist and Shinto temples and shrines. Some are still in use; others are in decay. An exploration along the spiral roads and wooden paths reveals a history of changing architectural styles and old statues of Japanese heroes. On the flat summit is a park with trees, shrubs and patches of grass on which sitting is allowed – a rare freedom in Japanese parks.

Western Pleasure Quarter
This district was inhabited by enslaved, as opposed to 'free' *geisha* girls, and was guarded by heavy gates. Its narrow streets and the temple quarters of the adjacent Teramachi district border the city on the western bank of the river.

■ ***Ryokan*, traditional Japanese inns, are usually two- or three-storey wooden buildings with the outward appearance of ordinary houses. They are, in fact, an expensive and exquisite way of experiencing Japanese culture and food......■**

Japanese inns
These are cheap versions of *ryokan* and recommended if you are on a budget and wish to experience traditional Japanese customs and lifestyle. The rooms are *tatami* (straw matted), divided by paper screens and sparsely but tastefully decorated. Meals are an optional extra.

New *ryokan*
In recent years some Western-style hotels have begun to offer a '*ryokan*-style experience' for guests staying in *tatami* rooms. There are also a few private *ryokan* situated in modern apartment buildings. The ritual and service are the same as in traditional *ryokan* and often good value, but the ambience is less authentic.

A ryokan *interior...*

Many *ryokan* are sited in naturally beautiful areas, but even those in cities have inner gardens in which rocks, trees and running water are combined to create a feeling of natural scenic beauty. Service is flawless but restrained – as is the expected behaviour of the guests. Room décor, the timetable of meals and general ritual tends to be the same in every inn.

Ryokan are generally costly and some of the more famous establishments in places such as Kyoto and Nara charge more than the best hotels, but they are worth at least one night's stay for the experience. The price includes a *kaiseki ryori* dinner (traditional and classic Japanese cooking) and breakfast in your room, and the services of a personal maid, who serves the 10- or 12-dish meal (which includes beautifully presented local specialities). After dinner the maid converts the living room to a bedroom by pushing back the low, lacquered dining table and putting a futon and cotton-filled quilts on the *tatami* floor.

Furnishings in *ryokan* rooms are simple but elegant. In one corner there is an alcove with a flower arrangement and a hanging scroll of a painting or poem. A lacquer dining table is surrounded with cushions and a television set is discreetly available. Most rooms have a veranda overlooking the garden, with chairs outside for periods of quiet contemplation.

Arrival and procedure On arrival, leave your shoes at the entrance; you will be handed a pair of slippers. On reaching your room, leave the slippers at the doorway and enter in your stockinged feet. The maid makes green tea for you and leaves. A perfectly ironed and starched *yukata* (kimono-style dressing gown) is available to wear after you have bathed in your private hot tub. It is perfectly acceptable and expected for you to wear a *yukata* for dinner, or if you leave your room to explore your surroundings. In cold weather a *tanzen* (padded kimono) is provided as well. The maid arrives later with dinner arranged on a very large tray of assorted lacquer dishes and pottery bowls. She places the tray just inside the door, bows, picks it up again and carries it to the table, then backs away, bows again and leaves. (If you do not want a Japanese breakfast – rice, fish, *miso* soup – the following morning, you can order coffee, toast and orange juice instead.)

Room rates *Ryokan* rooms are designed to accommodate one to four people and charges depend on how many people are staying in the room. They cater only for short stays. Unlike hotels, room rates vary greatly depending on the day and the time of the year.

Weekends, public holidays and peak seasons are the most expensive times. On an off-peak mid-week day you can book a *ryokan* for the price of a good hotel. A service charge of 10 to 15 per cent is added to the room rate and tipping is not necessary.

...and courtyard

Ryokan are divided into three categories: deluxe, superior and standard. The deluxe establishments do not necessarily accept foreign guests, as some managers are concerned that they will not understand the etiquette involved and thus embarrass themselves or other guests.

Exile
For the Japanese, exile was an appalling fate. Their identity was rooted in their place in society, and to be cut adrift from this relationship was akin to death. Depending upon the severity of the crime, banishment could be to a place between 1,100km and 5,000km away. The modern Japanese Penal Code, enacted in 1908, contains no provision for exile.

▶▶ Sado Island 208B2

Exile was once a common Japanese punishment for criminals and politicians, religious leaders or members of the imperial family who had fallen out of favour. Many such deposed statesmen and even emperors were banished to Sado Island, in the Sea of Japan off the coast of Niigata prefecture, western Honshu. When gold was discovered there during the Edo period, homeless people and prisoners were sent to Sado to work as forced labour in the gold mines. Its history has given the island a rather grim image and an air of melancholy; but Sado does offer dramatic scenery, well-preserved villages, traditional farming landscapes, lovely beaches and a culture all of its own.

Although relatively small, Sado is Japan's fifth largest island in size. The population of less than 100,000 is increased tenfold by vacationers during the summer season. Two mountain chains run east to west along the north and south coasts divided by an extensive plain, where the main towns and farmland areas are found. The old gold and silver mines, major tourist attractions, are located in the mountains, and the storm-battered coastline, with its sheer, plunging cliffs and tiny offshore islands, is also worth exploring.

Three main ferry crossings connect Sado Island with Niigata. Each offers a regular ferry and a hydrofoil. The hydrofoil crossings are approximately twice as expensive and take half the time. Niigata to Ryotsu (two hours, 20 minutes by ferry) is the most popular and frequent crossing; other alternatives are Niigata to Akadomare (three hours by ferry) or Naoetsu (just south of Niigata) to Ogi (two hours, 40 minutes by ferry). Ogi is the most attractive port. All crossings are cancelled during rough seas. Towns on the island are connected by regular bus services but the main sights are less accessible; the *Sado Teiki Kanko Josha-ken*, a two-day pass, allows unlimited

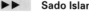

Tarajbune, *the wash-tub-style boats at Ogi*

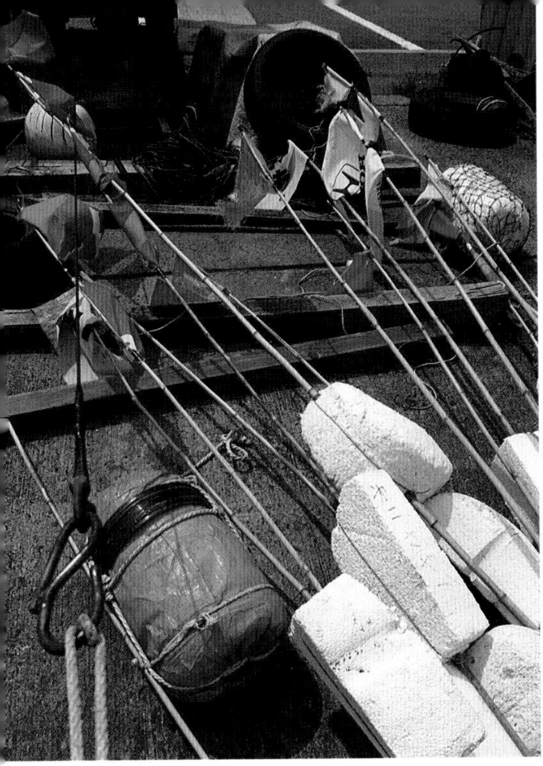

Fishing tackle at Ogi

Drums
Taiko are large, barrel-shaped Japanese drums. Village boundaries were determined by the furthest point at which a *taiko* could be heard. In recent times village drumming rituals have become popular in Japan and many drumming troupes have been established. The most famous is the Kodo (the word means both 'heartbeat' and 'children of the drum') troupe, also known as the 'Ondekoza Demon Drummers'. When not on tour the drummers live communally on Sado Island in spartan conditions.

use of all tour buses, the most convenient means of transport. Comprehensive tours of the island depart from Ogi and Ryotsu (four to eight hours long). Alternatively, car hire is available at each of the main ports.

The original centre of the gold mining industry, **Aikawa▶▶**, one hour, 15 minutes by bus from Ryotsu, is one tenth the size that it was during the boom times. Visitors now come here to tour the Sado Kinzan Mine and other related sights. Some of the extensive underground tunnels are open for viewing. Realistic mechanical figures and sound effects are used to re-create the original working conditions of mine labourers; many men died within a few years of their exile to Sado (open 8–5:30).

Senkaku Bay▶▶▶, to the north of Aikawa, boasts a stunning coastline with surreal rock formations. Excursion boats operate from Tassha, 15 minutes from Aikawa by bus; a clifftop path also starts from here. The west coast of the island, from Senkaku Bay to Cape Hajiki on the northern tip, is called Soto-Kaifu (Outer Coast); the east coast, southward from Cape Hajiki, is known as Uchi-Kaifu (Inner Coast). The former has a dramatic, rugged beauty composed of strange rock formations, reefs and cliffs, and is popular with tour buses. The latter is less exciting and quieter.

Ogi▶ is a working port, once best known for its strange, wooden tub-like boats (*taraibune*), used by local women to collect seaweed and shellfish. They are now available for hire and visitors may paddle themselves around the harbour. The best reason to visit Ogi is to travel on to **Shukunegi▶▶▶**, 15 minutes to the west by bus. This is a delightful fishing village set in a cove with traditional houses and surrounded by trees and rice paddies.

A seashell mountain on Sado Island

Chusonji Temple

Rikuchu-Kaigan National Park
This stretch of rugged, rocky coastline is famous for its high cliffs, fantastic rock formation, small fishing villages and marine life. It was, until very recently, an inaccessible area, but nowadays, with two private railways, it is easier to explore. Buses go from Morioka to Kuji (about three hours) and from here you can take a train on the Kita Rias line to Shimanokoshi on the coast, where buses leave for the coastal zone of the park.

Tohoku Central and East

►► Hiraizumi *209D3*

Today Hiraizumi is a small country town, but during the 11th and 12th centuries the Fujiwara clan paid for the construction of many temples and palaces there with the proceeds of the gold they mined in the area, and Hiraizumi rivalled Kyoto. Few buildings remain from this great age but The Golden Hall (Konjiki-do) of Chusonji Temple has survived and has recently been fully restored as one of Tohoku's major cultural attractions. The farmland areas around Hiraizumi are worth visiting for their wealth of traditional Japanese houses. Hiraizumi is 25 minutes from Ichinoseki, which is two hours, 25 minutes by Tohoku Shinkansen from Ueno station, Tokyo. Alternatively, Hiraizumi is two hours by local train from Sendai. There is a tourist office on the town's main street, to the right of the station.

Chusonji Temple►►►, a short walk (20 minutes) or bus ride from the station, was founded in 850 and restored in the 12th century. Two halls, Konjiki-do and Kyozo, remain from this period: the other buildings in the temple complex date from the later Edo period. Konjiki-do, a small but impressive structure (now housed in a fireproof building) has black, lacquered exterior walls and gold-leaf and mother-of-pearl interior panelling. Kyozo, the original temple library houses a magnificent Monju Bosatsu image riding a lion (open 8–5) .

Once the most important temple complex in Tohoku, **Motsuji Temple►►** is now marked only by the foundations of the 40 original main temples, but the beautiful Jodo-style paradise gardens (Heian period) have, remarkably, survived. The Hiraizumi Museum, housing relics of the Fujiwara clan, is in the garden domain (open 8–5).

►► Morioka *209D4*

Morioka is a castle town, founded by the feudal lord Nambu in the 16th century, and an old-established provincial university town. It is a charming place with many temples, an old merchant quarter, a vigorous cultural life and

Detail, Chusonji Temple

a successful local craft industry. The Tohoku Shinkansen to Morioka from Ueno station in Tokyo takes three hours.

▶ Sendai *209D3*

The largest city in Tohoku was flattened in World War II and has since been rebuilt along the lines of any modern Japanese city. It is a good base from which to explore the area of Tohoku, Matsushima (see panel) and the neighbouring Yamagata prefecture, a rural district where life follows the traditional Tohoku style. Sendai is two hours by Tohoku Shinkansen from Tokyo's Ueno station.

▶▶ Towada-Hachimantai National Park *209D4*

Lying northwest of Morioka, this area is divided into southern and northern sections. Hachimantai, in the south, is a mountainous area of volcanic activity, better known for its *onsen* (hot springs) and thermal resorts than for scenic beauty. Goshogake Onsen and Toshichi Onsen are two centres where people go to soothe away city stress and other ailments. Mixed bathing is the norm. The eastern entrance to the park is via Obuke, 40 minutes on the JR Hanawa line from Morioka (tour buses operate from here). The Lake Towada area, which lies to the north, is a region of exceptional scenic beauty. The lake itself occupies a giant crater, and the gentle mountain ranges around it provide plenty of good hiking and skiing. There are many *onsen* near by. Sukayu Onsen, to the north, which has a 1,000-person bath, is one of the best known. The pretty Oirase-keiryu (Oirase Valley) district, to the northeast, is also very popular with walkers, particularly in the autumn, when the valley is especially beautiful. There is a frequent bus service from April to October directly from Morioka to Lake Towada.

Matsushima Bay
Matsushima Kaigan station is 40 minutes by Senseki line from Sendai. This is the main stopping point for the famed Matsushima Bay (a very popular Japanese resort destination), which is dotted with small, pine-covered islands, some inhabited and others no more than tiny islets. The bay is regarded as one of Japan's 'Three Famous Views' (the other two are Amanohashidate, north of Kyoto and Itsukushima, near Hiroshima), and as such has suffered from commercialism. The islands may be toured by cruiser from Matsushima Kaigan Pier.

Sendai shops

■ Flushed with fresh air, easy to clean and good to live in, traditional Japanese houses are healthy places, emphasising simplicity, regularity and refinement. Built of a small number of locally available materials, usually wood, bamboo, paper, woven straw and stone tiles, they sit on stilts above the ground, allowing ventilation and giving protection to the structure from the effects of mildew and dampness......■

***Tatami* rooms**
Slippers are worn on wooden floors, but the inner *tatami* matted rooms must be entered in bare or stockinged feet. The street, the *genkan*, the wooden corridors and the *tatami* matted rooms represent four levels of decreasing contamination between public and private places. The exclusion of dirt from the *tatami* rooms is important, as the floor is used both as an eating and as a sleeping surface.

A farmhouse lantern

Health and cleanliness The Japanese home contains several standard features for the maintenance of a clean and healthy house. The *genkan* is a paved area at the same level as the garden, with a raised wooden floor, where residents sit to remove their shoes before donning slippers to move into the house. The *engawa*, or veranda, is a well-protected porch that affords shelter from the sun in the summer without blocking low winter rays. The opening onto it allows plenty of air to circulate through the house, even during heavy rain. Like the *genkan*, the veranda has easily maintained floor surfaces, whose proximity to the garden facilitates cleaning. Symbolically, the *engawa* is the link between house and garden. It is associated with meditation in monasteries, where it is the platform from which nature is contemplated.

Futons (Japanese bedding) are simple, warm, easily cleaned and unobtrusive. Essentially similar to the European duvet, futons are easily folded twice and placed in cupboards designed to contain them. Aired frequently in the *engawa*, futons reflect by their number and pattern the age, status and taste of their users.

Tatami (floor mats) are located in all major rooms. They are resilient and give good support for the back (residents sleep on the floor).

Seasonal living Rooms are arranged and re-arranged according to the way they are used. In the hot and humid summer, all room dividers made of sliding panels can be opened or removed, encouraging the flow of fresh air throughout the house. In the winter, the rather loose association of open rooms with large openings to the outdoors can be converted to an arrangement of isolated rooms, which can be closed off from each other and the outside by sliding panels and outside shutters. In cold weather, families gather about the *kotatsu*, a table placed over a *hibachi* (a small brazier), which sits below the floor. This feature is equivalent to the Western hearth, and is symbolic of the family unit.

To live well in the traditional Japanese house, considerable stress is placed on appropriate dress in summer and winter. The *yukata* is a lightweight, heavily starched, loose, cotton garment worn in the summer, which allows free circulation of air next to the skin. In the winter, however, it is traditional to wear layers of heavier garments. Their full sleeves allow hand warming and, in a sitting position, the surface area is reduced and body heat more efficiently retained. Clothing becomes a heavily insulated, personal tent.

Bath and toilet In a traditional Japanese house, the lavatory and bath tub are never in the same room. They are regarded as separate and distinct, requiring their own space. The bath is frequently associated with the garden and contains enough room for several people to dress in an atmosphere of natural beauty and social ease. It is designed to give comfort and to allow bathers to be exposed and to relax. The lavatory is sometimes entered only upon leaving the house. It is sited carefully in order to reduce odours and social embarrassment. The lavatory compartment is always very well ventilated and may contain a flower arrangement.

Genkan

Many visitors do not pass the *genkan*, thereby reducing the intrusion of dirt into private areas of the house. No animals are allowed past the *genkan*, although they may be allowed to sleep there. These customs ensure that most dirt is left in the *genkan*, where it can readily be removed to the street or garden.

Traditional houses at Ogimachi village

Tohoku West

▶▶ Hirosaki 209C4

Unlike nearby Aomori, this small, compact town escaped wartime bombing; despite this, post-war planners went on to destroy much of the town's architectural heritage. Fortunately, the city retains some of its old winding alleys and has an appeal enhanced by the friendliness of the townspeople, the thriving local craft traditions and some well-maintained sites of cultural interest. The tourist office by the station provides a map of the town and information in English.

Hirosaki is approximately four hours by train from Morioka and 30 minutes by train from Aomori, the busy port town that usurped Hirosaki's position as the cultural and political centre of Tohoku.

Tazawako Lake

Melting love
Despite being extremely deep and situated in the north of Tohoku, Tazawa-ko Lake never freezes over. According to local legend a great beauty, transformed into a dragon, sleeps in the lake. To keep warm, she and her dragon husband make passionate love all winter long and heat up the water.

▶▶ Kakunodate 209C4

The train journey to Kakunodate from Morioka (55 minutes, JR Tazawa line) passes fine mountain scenery on its way to this small and pretty town, which has one of the best-preserved collections of *samurai* houses in Japan. Found in the inner town (Uchimachi), the *samurai* neighbourhood has about half a dozen original houses and gardens open to the pubic (9–5), of which Aoyagi, with its turf roof, is especially renowned. Kakunodate's founding lords were originally from Kyoto. They imported with them many weeping cherry trees and the town and its river banks are generously planted, so that, in season, cherry blossom blows through the streets in clouds. The outer town (Tomachi) once the merchants' quarter, remains the commercial part of town. Kakunodate is well known for items made from cherry bark, a craft which was once the main source of livelihood for poorer *samurai*.

▶▶ Tazawa-ko Lake 209C4

This lovely crater lake, the deepest in Japan, has exceptionally clear water. The lake shore is being developed but still maintains a rustic atmosphere. Cruise boats operate from Tazawa-Kohan, where bicycles are also available for rent. In the surrounding countryside there are many isolated inns, with their own open-air hot-spring pools. Nyuto Onsen, connected by bus to Tazawako Lake, is the main resort and has smaller inns scattered around it. To get to Tazawako, take the JR Tazawa line from Kakunodate (16 minutes) or Morioka (40 minutes). Ths tourist office is to the left of the station. From the station it is a 15-minute bus ride to Tazawa-Kohan on the lake edge.

Tamagawa Onsen▶▶ is a very old spa town with a reputation for especially restorative and curative thermal springs. Many of its individual inns are of wooden construction and conditions are quite basic, but they provide an interesting experience and a change from Japan's usual over-commercialisation of natural resources. Reach the spa by bus from Tazawako (one and a half hours).

▶▶ Yamagata *209C3*

Yamagata city is the capital of Yamagata prefecture, a largely unspoiled region in the heart of Tohoku. The Japanese are promoting the area as one which 'remains largely undiscovered by the international tourist', and there is consequently much information available at the tourist office in Yamagata JR station, one hour, 15 minutes from Sendai by JR express train. Yamagata itself has few attractions and is mainly used by the Japanese as a base for summer hiking and winter skiing in the Dewa Sanzan and Mount Zao areas. Dewa Sanzan is composed of three peaks: Gassan, Yudono-san and Haguro-san; each one an important sacred site, and the setting for Shinto shrines. Mount Zao is a very popular skiing destination in the winter months. Zao Onsen is the region's centre of accommodation; a cable-car operates from there to the mountain summit. Winter snowfall is generally heavy. **Yamadera Temple▶▶▶** is a mountaintop monastery made famous by the *haiku* poet Basho. The ascent involves steep climbing, but is rewarded with wonderful views. The precincts are extensive and worth exploring.

Bandai-Asahi National Park
Occuping an area to the west and south of Fukushima and to the west of Yamagata, Bandai-Asahi includes some of the most pretty, interesting and accessible mountain and lake scenery in Japan. Azuma-san (the Azuma mountains), near Fukushima, are ideal for moderate hiking tours. Access to Azuma-san is from Jododaira bus station on the Bandai-Asahi Skyline road. Fukushima is one hour, 40 minutes on the Tohoku Shinkansen line from Ueno station in Tokyo. Bandai-Kogen, at the centre of Bandai Plateau, is 40 minutes from Fukushima on the Skyline road or three hours on the scenic Bandai-Asahi Lakeline road.

Yamadera Temple

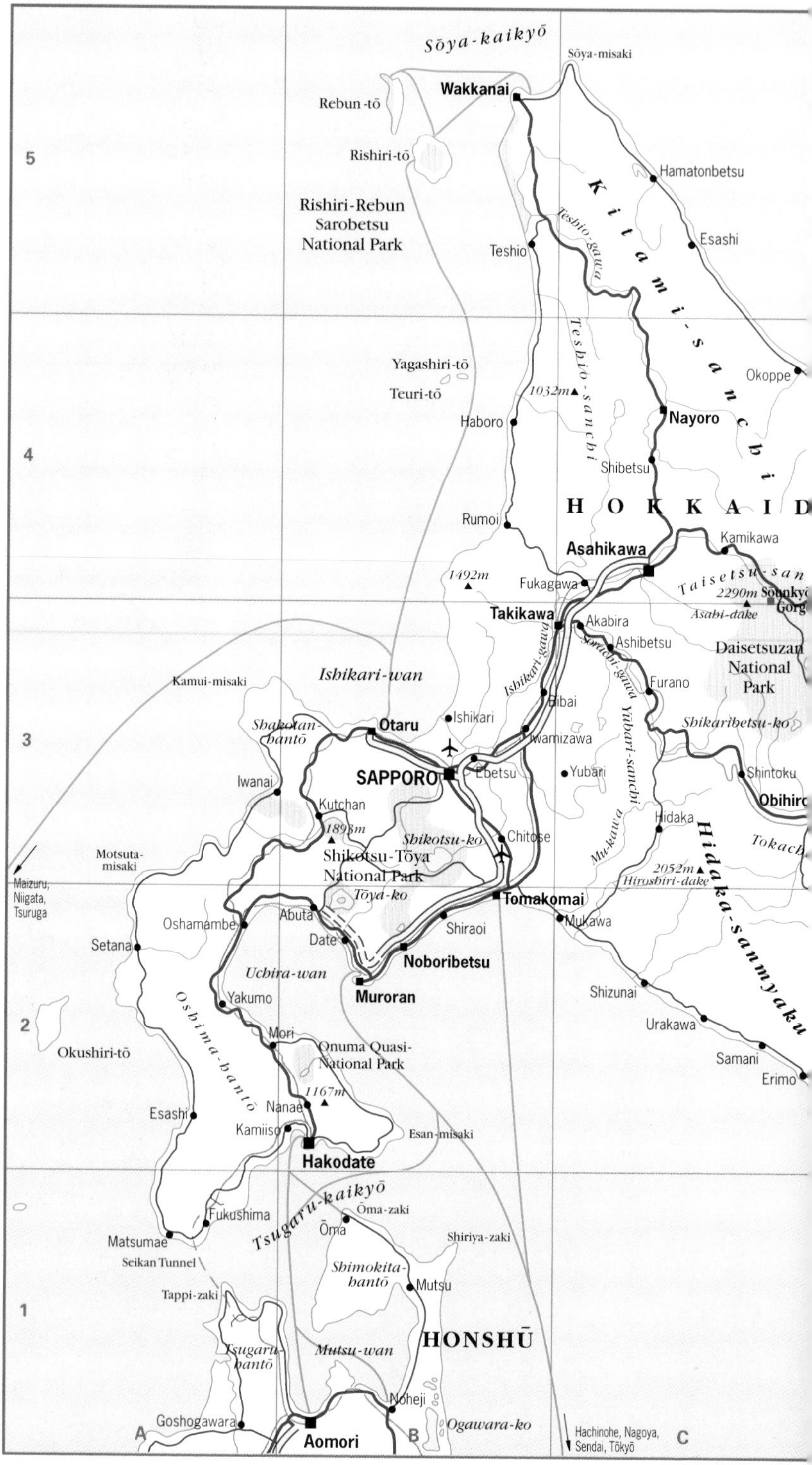
Sōya-kaikyō
Sōya-misaki
Wakkanai
Rebun-tō
Rishiri-tō
Rishiri-Rebun Sarobetsu National Park
Hamatonbetsu
Kitami-sanchi
Teshio-gawa
Esashi
Teshio
Teshio-sanchi
Okoppe
Yagashiri-tō
Teuri-tō
1032m
Nayoro
Haboro
Shibetsu
HOKKAIDO
Rumoi
Kamikawa
Asahikawa
1492m
Fukagawa
Taisetsu-san
2290m
Asahi-dake
Takikawa
Akabira
Ashibetsu
Daisetsuzan National Park
Kamui-misaki
Ishikari-wan
Ishikari-gawa
Sorachi-gawa
Furano
Bibai
Yūbari-sanchi
Ishikari
Shakotan-hantō
Otaru
Shikaribetsu-ko
Iwamizawa
SAPPORO
Ebetsu
Yubari
Shintoku
Iwanai
Obihiro
Kutchan
Hidaka
1893m
Shikotsu-ko
Chitose
Mu-kawa
Tokachi
Motsuta-misaki
Shikotsu-Tōya National Park
Hidaka-sanmyaku
2052m
Hiroshiri-dake
Maizuru, Niigata, Tsuruga
Tōya-ko
Tomakomai
Abuta
Mukawa
Oshamambe
Shiraoi
Date
Setana
Noboribetsu
Uchira-wan
Shizunai
Muroran
Oshima-hantō
Yakumo
Urakawa
Mori
Okushiri-tō
Onuma Quasi-National Park
Samani
Erimo
1167m
Nanae
Esashi
Kamiiso
Esan-misaki
Hakodate
Tsugaru-kaikyō
Ōma-zaki
Fukushima
Ōma
Shiriya-zaki
Matsumae
Seikan Tunnel
Shimokita-hantō
Mutsu
Tappi-zaki
HONSHŪ
Tsugaru-hantō
Mutsu-wan
Noheji
Goshogawara
Aomori
Ogawara-ko
Hachinohe, Nagoya, Sendai, Tōkyō
A
B
C
1
2
3
4
5

HOKKAIDO

Mombetsu
Yūbetsu
Saroma-ko
Notoro-ko
Abashiri
Abashiri-ko
Memambetsu
Bihoro
Rubeshibe
Kitami
Shiretoko-misaki
Shiretoko National Park
1660m
Rausu
Shari
Nemuro-kaikyō
SU
Notsuke-suidō
Kawayu
Kussharo-ko
Mashū-ko
Akan-ko
Teshikaga
Naka-Shibetsu
Nemuro-wan
Akan Kohan
1499m
Akan National Park
Konsen-daichi
Fūren-ko
Nemuro
Ashoro
Kami-Shihoro
Kushiro-Shitsugen National Park
Akan
Kushiro-heiya
Akkeshi
Ikeda
Shiranuka
Kushiro
Tokachi-gawa
heiya
Hiro'o
Erimo-misaki
0
50
100 km
Sendai, Tōkyō
D
E

Hakodate viewpoint, Hokkaido

Hokkaido This northernmost and second largest of the four main Japanese islands is the least populous region of Japan. There are few cultural or historical reasons to visit Hokkaido, but for those who enjoy the outdoors it offers forests, mountain ranges, lakes, volcanoes, hot springs, open landscapes and the chance to hike, ski and cycle.

Hokkaido is connected to Honshu by the 53km-long Seikan Tunnel, the world's longest, which runs under the Tsugaru Straits. The island is bordered by the Pacific Ocean to the south and north, by the Sea of Japan to the west and by the Sea of Okhotsk to the northeast. Possession of four of the Kuril Islands in the Sea of Okhotsk is acrimoniously disputed by Japan and Russia. Hokkaido offers rich agricultural, fishing and mineral resources.

Japanese colonists Until the beginning of this century Hokkaido, a wild and inhospitable place, was not considered an inhabitable area by the Japanese. They visited and settled only the island's coastal regions, to fish and collect seaweed. Some Ainu, Japan's original indigenous people, lived in the interior, but there were no inland Japanese settlements or agriculture. Shortage of space on the other main islands, coupled with the return after 1945 of many Japanese colonists from abroad, led to the first real development of the island and today over five million people live there.

Sapporo The large, modern capital city, laid out on a grid system, has many parks, but is not a place to visit for tourist attractions. It does, however, have an active and famous nightlife – the Susukino district is as exciting and *risqué* as anything in Tokyo – and it provides a good base from which to explore the wilderness areas of Hokkaido. The tourist information office is at Sapporo station.

National Parks The national parks of Hokkaido are large, wild and scenic and perhaps the main reason for visiting this remote region of Japan. Three of the major parks are listed here. **Daisetsuzan National Park** is the largest

Snow festivals
Snow festivals (*Yuki Matsuri*) are held throughout the winter in the parts of northern Japan that have heavy snowfalls. The most famous is held in Sapporo for four days, from the first Wednesday in February. The festival began by chance when in 1950 some high school students made six ice sculptures in Odori-Koen Park. Today two million visitors attend the festival each year. Over 200 elaborate ice carvings are displayed in the park, which is, in fact, a broad avenue, running east to west, bisecting the city centre.

national park in Japan and one of the most unspoiled. A network of hiking paths gives access to most areas of the park and to many of the mountain peaks, none of which rises much above 2,133m. Most of the accommodation available in the park includes access to hot-spring baths. **Akan National Park** is well known for its beauty and wildlife. It is dominated by volcanic peaks, but lakes and vast forests add variety. Akan lies in the east of Hokkaido and can be reached from Kushiro to the south. Kussharo-ko is the largest volcanic lake in Japan and a focal point of the national park. **Shikotsu-Toya National Park** lies in southwest Hokkaido, not far from Sapporo, and is known for its caldera lakes, volcanoes, hot springs and forests. Lakes Toya and Shikotsu (the second deepest in Japan) give the park its name.

Getting there Sapporo is 10 and a half hours by train from Tokyo. Chitose, 40km south of Sapporo, is Hokkaido's main airport. The approximate flight time from Tokyo is 1 hour and 20 minutes. There are frequent train connections with Sapporo. Japan Air Lines (JAL) flights are scheduled to Chitose from Tokyo, Osaka and Fukuoka. All Nippon Airways (ANA) and JAL also run services from many other Japanese cities.

There are ferry services from Tokyo to Tomakomai or Kushiro and from many towns on the coast of Tohoku, such as Oma-Hakodate, Aomori-Muroran and Noheji-Hakodate. There is a rail network on Hokkaido and internal flights between major cities.

Food
One of the unexpected surprises of visiting Hokkaido is the quality of the regional food. Restaurants tend to be reasonably priced and without pretension. Specialities include shellfish, salmon, herring, squid, sea urchin, corn on the cob, potatoes and Chinese noodles (*ramen*). Genghis Khan, a Mongolian-inspired mutton or lamb barbecue cooked by the guest (or a chef) at the table, is another great favourite.

The unspoiled serenity of Daisetsuzan National Park

Abashiri

Duckweed
Lake Akan is famous for its rare spherical duckweed, called *marimo*, which is found only in a few lakes around the world. The green spheres absorb oxygen from the water and then float to the surface, where they exhale and sink. Examples of *marimo* may be seen in shops and information centres and in the *marimo* museum on a small island in the lake. A boat trip on the lake lasts one and a half hours and calls in at the museum.

Kushiro Great Marsh
This is the home of the *tancho* (red-crested crane), brought back from the brink of extinction and now forming a colony of around 400. They are shy birds who live deep in the marshes, but visitors may see them at the Red-Crested Crane Natural Park, south of Akan, where some are kept behind high mesh fences. A bus to the Crane Park from Akan Kohan bus terminal takes one hour, 15 minutes (get off at the Tsuru-koen bus stop).

►► Abashiri *231D4*

Although a small town, this is the main settlement on the Sea of Okhotsk. During the winter the sea is ice-bound and the floes reach up to the beach. The inhabitants make their living from fishing in the summer months, when the local delicacies of shrimp and 'hairy crab' are taken from the icy seas. Abashiri is the terminus of the JR Sekihoku line; the limited express takes five hours, 40 minutes from Sapporo. There is a tourist information office in the station. Flights from Sapporo's Chitose airport to Memambetsu (near Abashiri) take 55 minutes by JAS.

The **Municipal Museum►►** houses a collection of genuine Ainu artefacts and pre-Ainu material discovered in the Moyoro Shell Mound, site of an ancient Ainu dwelling place. One part of the Municipal Museum is the Abashiri Prison Museum (Abashiri Kangoku), which records the grim conditions suffered by the convicts who were used to develop the region (open 8:30–5).

Oroke Kinenkan► is a museum dedicated to preserving the heritage of a small tribe of nomadic reindeer herders who live on Sakhalin island (open 8:30–5).

About 3km southwest of Abashiri, on route 39, is **Tento-zan►►** hill. From its observation tower there are views of the Sea of Okhotsk and nearby mountain peaks.

►► Akan National Park *231D4*

Set in eastern Hokkaido, Akan National Park features three major caldera lakes, volcanic mountains, numerous hot springs and extensive forests of primeval trees. Towns near the park are Bihoro (in the north) and Kushiro (in the south). Buses for the park leave from both towns (neither is of particular interest in its own right). Kushiro has an airport and there are flights there from Tokyo (one hour, 35 minutes) and Sapporo (40 minutes). Bihoro is five hours, 20 minutes from Sapporo by JR Sekihoku line limited express. Kushiro is three and a half hours on the same line from Bihoro. Within the park the town of Akan Kohan is the most important resort area. There is a tourist information office near the town's bus terminal.

The easiest way to travel around the park is by sightseeing buses, although those who wish for more freedom may prefer to hire a car for a few days. The tour buses are noisy and do not stop long at any of the sights; it is worth getting off at one, exploring on foot and then catching another tour bus later (this is allowed if you hold on to your ticket).

Ainu Kotan Village►, a 10-minute walk west of the bus terminal in Akan Kohan spa town, is a street of souvenir shops and a thatched-roofed centre where displays of Ainu dancing are held six times a day from May to the end of October.

About 14km from Lake Mashu, **Kawayu Onsen**►► is a hot-spring resort near Io-san, an active volcano which vents steam from two ravines. Visitors often buy fresh eggs from the grocery store near the car park and boil them in the small pools of hot water.

Lake Akan►► lies in the western part of the park, surrounded by dense forests and two volcanoes: O-Akandake to the east (dormant) and Me-Akandake to the south (active). Both mountains may be climbed and are popular with hikers.

Lake Kussharo►► is the park's largest lake, and attracts campers and water sports enthusiasts. The lake is at its most attractive in the autumn when the leaves of the surrounding trees change colour.

Lake Mashu►►, a 20-minute drive from Teshikaga (one hour, 15 minutes by JR express from Kushiro), is almost 213m deep and ringed by high rock walls with little or no footholds. The lake is best examined from two viewing spots on the western side.

Boiling mud at Akan National Park

Lake Akan

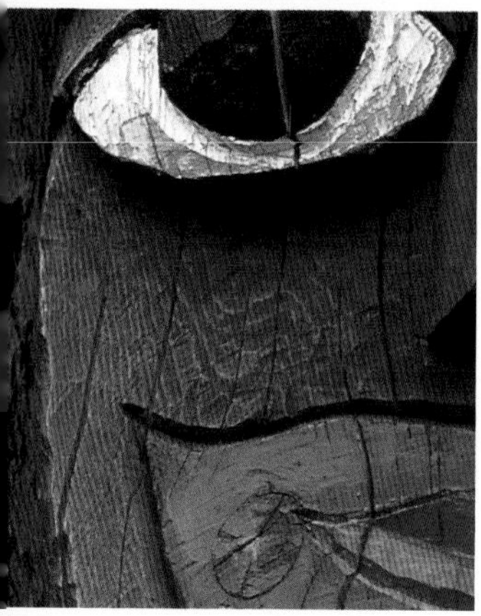

■ The ancestors of the Ainu were the original inhabitants of Japan. Organised into nomadic tribes who lived by hunting, fishing and gathering, they roamed freely over the central and northern parts of Japan, but as waves of aggressive invaders and settlers moved in from the Asian mainland, they were gradually pushed northwards. The Ainu were formidable warriors, and constant fighting between them and the Japanese put a great strain on the resources of the emerging Japanese state. However, over the centuries the Ainu were pacified and controlled until, by the 19th century, they were restricted to their present settlements in Hokkaido......■

Prayer sticks
Kotan-kara-kamui, the Spirit of the World, came from the skies to establish the land of the Ainu. On his return he forgot his chopsticks, and to prevent them rotting he turned them into willow trees. The Ainu still use willow to carve their *inau*, or prayer sticks.

Above: detail of an Ainu totem
Below: Ainu village

Racially the Ainu are related to the peoples of Siberia. Generally they have lighter skins than the Japanese and the men exhibit a much greater growth of hair. According to custom only `men strong in wisdom' are allowed to wear beards. Traditionally young Ainu women were heavily tattooed on the mouth, on the arms and on the backs of the hands before marriage, but this custom has now almost died out, due to the legal ban on Ainu tattooing established by the Japanese government. In the 19th century the Victorian traveller Isabella Bird visited the Ainu and described the women as: 'universally tattooed, not only with the broad band above and below the mouth, but with a band across the knuckles, succeeded by an elaborate pattern on the back of the hand, and a series of bracelets extending to the elbow. This process of disfigurement begins at the age of five, when some of the sufferers are yet unweaned. They expressed themselves as very much grieved and tormented by the recent prohibition of tattooing. They say the gods will be angry, and that the women can't marry unless they are tattooed'.

Traditional houses Most Ainu now live in Japanese-style homes, but traditionally Ainu houses were rectangular wood-framed buildings, with dirt floors covered in reed mats, and thatched walls and roofs. Raised wooden platforms covered in mats or animal (often bear) skins were used for sleeping and an open-fire pit, placed in the centre of the house, was used for cooking, heating and religious purposes. Fire was sacred to the Ainu, and the hearth would often be decorated with *inau*, specially carved wooden prayer sticks, which are still found wherever the Ainu honour the

The Ainu

spiritual beings they called *kamui* (similar to the Japanese *kami*).

Bear spirits Bears were and still are held in high regard by the Ainu, and an important part of Ainu culture is the festival known as *iomante*, through which they pay their respects to the *kamui* of the bear. In times past, when the bears awoke from their winter's hibernation, the men went into the woods and captured a cub, which would be taken to the village and cared for until it was about two years old. The animal was then sacrificed either by strangulation or by being shot with arrows. The head was removed and placed on a pole, and the flesh eaten at a feast which featured dancing by the men and gifts of *saké* to the bear's head as gratitude for its sacrifice. By sending the spirit of the bear back to its ancestors the Ainu showed their appreciation for its strength and courage, attributes they hoped would become theirs, as they believed the spirit of the bear would be reborn as an Ainu.

Today, traditional Ainu culture is almost dead, although there has been a recent resurgence of interest among younger members. The Ainu are often said to be the 'American Indians' of Japan, and in the same way Ainu culture is now mainly displayed in 'Ainu villages' built specially for the tourist trade. For the tourist, perhaps the best exposition of genuine Ainu traditions is to be found in the Ainu Museum in Shiraoi, Hokkaido, housed in the former home of an English minister who collected Ainu artefacts in the late 19th century.

Top: Ainu festival
Above: an Ainu couple

Exorcism of evil spirits
According to Ainu belief, sickness is caused by evil spirits and healed by driving them away. A crippled man has his legs and arms bound with bulrush stems and cloth and is gently beaten with branches. The bindings are then cut away and thrown into a river, while the Ainu shout at the spirits to flee.

Hakodate by night

Daisetsuzan hiking trails
Access to many of Japan's national parks seems to have been considered only in terms of the motorist or tour bus. Daisetsuzan is an exception, providing a network of hiking trails. With adequate maps, equipment and provisions, it is possible to explore this remote and beautiful region on foot. Tomuraushi Onsen, deep in the interior of the park, is a good base, and information is available from the Hokkaido Tourist Association, Keizai Centre Building, Nishi-1-Chome, Kita 2, Chuo-ku, Sapporo (tel: 011 231 0941; open 9–5, Saturday 9–1; closed Sunday).

►►► Daisetsuzan National Park *230C3*

Located in the centre of Hokkaido, this is Japan's largest national park. Its scenery is spectacular, with lakes, high mountains, deep gorges, waterfalls, forests, hiking trails and the highest mountain in Hokkaido, Mount Asahidake (2,290m). Sounkyo Onsen, at the edge of the spectacular Sounkyo Gorge is one of the best places to stay (see also Asahidake Onsen, below) while exploring the park, as long as you can ignore the spa hotels, which seem to be designed to clash with the natural beauty of the surroundings. The only way to travel to Sounkyo Onsen is by bus. If you are travelling from Sapporo, leave the train at Kamikawa (two and half hours by JR Sekihoku line) and transfer to the local bus service (35 minutes to Sounkyo Onsen). A tourist information office, called the PC Centre, is located near the bus station.

Asahidake Onsen►►► is a quiet, remote village, one hour, 40 minutes by bus from Asahikawa which is reached from Sapporo on the JR Sekihoku line. It gives access to a two-hour ascent of Mount Asahidake and other mountain trails.

A cable-car travels from Sounkyo Onsen to the terminal on **Kurodake Mountain►►**. Change here for the chair-lift, which travels up the mountain to the beginning of the hiking trails. An hour's steady walking will take you to the peak where you will be rewarded by spectacular views of the surrounding mountains. Be sure to wear sturdy shoes or boots.

Lake Daisetsu►► was created by a rock and earth dam across the Ishikawa River, which flows through the Sounkyo Gorge. An enjoyable way to visit the lake is to hire a bicycle from Sounkyo's bus terminal and pedal along the path which skirts the edge of the gorge. **Sounkyo Gorge►►** itself is 20km long and extends into the park from its northeast entrance. The valley is hemmed in by rocky cliffs almost 190m high and features tremendous views at each turn of the road. Beyond Sounkyo Onsen the gorge is renowned for its waterfalls; Ryuei-no-taki (Shooting Star) and Ginga-no-taki (Milky Way) are particularly recommended.

►► Hakodate *230B2*

Situated on the southwest coast of Hokkaido, Hakodate has been a fishing port since the 18th century, and was one of the first to be opened to trade with the West by the Treaty of Kanagawa in 1854. Hokkaido is connected to Honshu by the longest underwater tunnel in the world, the 54km Seikan Railroad Tunnel.

A tourist information office is located to the right of JR Hakodate station. The Hokato Kotsu bus company runs a four-hour sightseeing tour of the city, which leaves from the railway station.

A three-minute walk south of the JR station leads to **Asa Ichi►►**, a fish and vegetable market open 5am–noon, but at its peak at 8am. Over 400 shops sell a range of food, including *kegani* ('hairy crab'), generally considered to be one of the best delicacies of Hokkaido.

Goryokaku►►, a Western-style fortress, was built in 1864 in the centre of the city and designed as a five-pointed star, allowing the defenders to concentrate a murderous crossfire on attackers. Seized by supporters of the Tokugawa family, it fell to troops loyal to the Emperor Meiji in 1868. All that remain are the outer walls; the grounds have been turned into a park of 4,000 cherry trees. A small museum contains relics of the battle (open May–October 8–8, November–April 9–6).

The foreigners' **Motomachi District▶▶** features several Western-style buildings, including a Greek Orthodox Church founded in 1862. To get there take a street car from the JR station to Jujigai stop (five minutes).

Mount Hakodate▶▶ is a small volcanic hill, 335m high, with famous views over the city and a restaurant on the summit. A bus leaves from the JR station for the 20-minute drive to the top.

See also pages 240–1.

Igloo weddings
Lake Shikaribetsu is Daisetsuzan park's only natural lake. In the winter the lake freezes over and local people build a village of igloos on the ice, where they hold winter weddings. In March the igloo village becomes the site of the local Shikaribetsu Kotan Festival.

Hakodate fishing boats

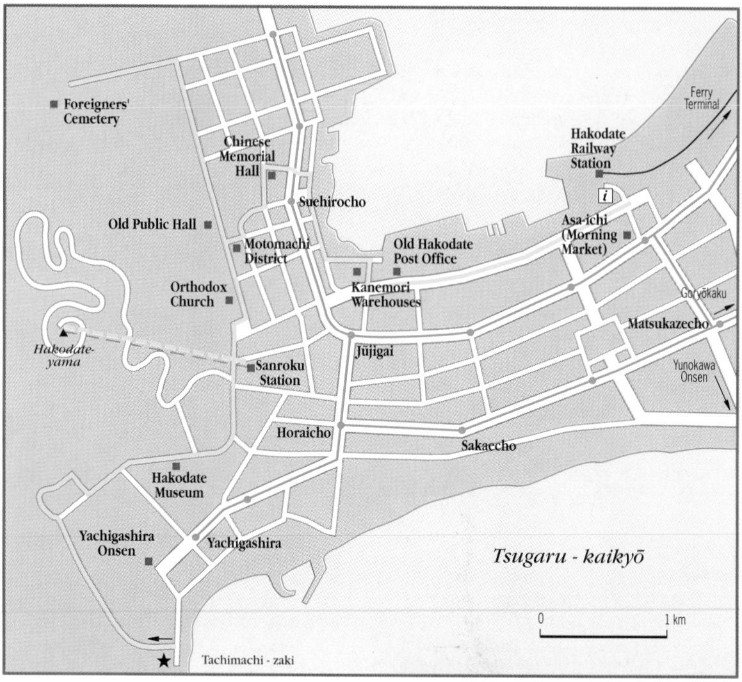

Walk Hakodate

Distance: 5km; time: three to four hours.

Hakodate occupies a strategic site on a fine harbour, backed by Mount Hakodate and overlooking the Tsugaru Straits. This walk starts at Cape Tachimachi on the Pacific Ocean, passes around the base of Mount Hakodate, through the old Western community of Motomachi and ends at the Foreign Cemetery. There is also a possible detour to the Kanamori Warehouse district with its shops, cafés and restaurants.

Start at Hakodate station (south of the station there is a large **produce market▶▶**, held Monday to Saturday 5am–noon, which is worth visiting). Take a cab to **Cape Tachimachi▶▶**, an Ainu word meaning 'a place on the rocks where you wait for fish and catch them with a spear',or take the tram to the **Yachigashira Spa▶** stop (20 minutes). There is a huge public baths

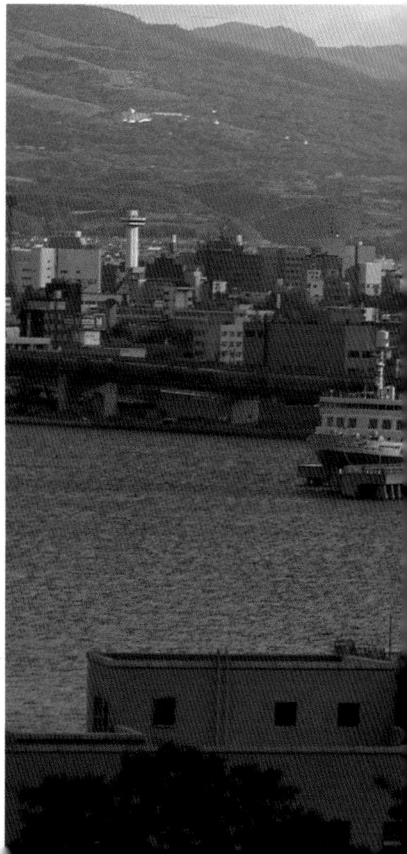

here. Then it is a 15-minute walk south. To the east, in the distance, is Yunokawa Spa, the oldest hot-spring resort in Hakodate.

Follow the route northwest and then northeast passing **Hakodate Museum▶▶**, which houses Ainu relics, before reaching Sanroku station. Here you can take a tram to the top of **Mount Hakodate▶▶▶**. The night view from the summit is rated among Japan's 'best three'. Few Japanese come to Hakodate without visiting the mountain at night to enjoy the spectacular view over the city. There is a café on the summit.

Continuing north, past the green onion domes of the **Greek Orthodox Church▶** on your left, go through the old foreign community area of **Motomachi** (see page 239), a district of Western buildings that developed during Hakodate's period as a treaty port. The **Old Public Hall▶▶**, completed in 1910, is representative of the Western-style architecture of the Meiji period, and has the feel of a British colonial structure.

Continue north along the road to the **Foreigners' Cemetery▶▶**, which is laid out on a hill overlooking the port, and is filled with the graves of Russians, Chinese, English, French and Americans. The oldest graves are those of two American sailors who fell ill and died during Admiral Perry's mission in 1854.

Take a cab back to Hakodate station or retrace your steps to the Old Public Hall. From here it is a 15-minute walk to the Suehirocho tram stop, where you can catch a tram. Alternatively, walk on to the **Kanamori Warehouse District▶**, a waterfront development of shops and cafés. From here you can walk back along the waterfront to the railway station.

Hakodate Harbour, one of the first ports to be opened to foreign trading following the end of Japan's self-imposed period of isolation

Sapporo restaurants

Oodles of noodles
Sapporo is famous for its Chinese noodles, or *ramen*. The most popular place to eat them is the Ramen Yokocho, an alleyway of 16 noodle shops situated one block east of the Susukino subway station.

▶▶ Sapporo 230B3

The capital of Hokkaido has a population of 1.6 million and is the largest city on the island. Just over a century ago it was no more than a collection of Ainu huts, but at the beginning of the Meiji Period the Japanese government decided to colonise the island. Following the advice of American experts, construction of the new city of Sapporo (from the Ainu meaning 'big, dry river') was started in 1871. Streets were laid out on a 100m grid system, with wide avenues and parks. There are few interesting buildings, but the grid design is easy to negotiate. The Sapporo transportation information office, in the underground concourse of Odori station, supplies information on the comprehensive and efficient city bus and subway networks (see page 232 for details of how to get to Sapporo).

Information in English about Sapporo and Hokkaido is available from the Sapporo City Tourism Department, Nishi-2-chome, Kita 2, Chuo-ku, (tel: 011 211 2376), open 9–5, Saturday 9–1, closed Sunday; or from the tourist office in Sapporo station (closed on the second and fourth Wednesdays of every month). Sapporo International Communication Plaza, Kita 1, Nishi 3, Chuo-ku, open 9–9, has a reading room with newspapers and books in English.

The **Batchelor Memorial Museum▶▶** is in the grounds of the Botanical Gardens, which grow over 5,000 plant varieties. It houses the collection of an Englishman, John Batchelor, who was deeply interested in Ainu culture and people (open 9–4, 1 October–3 November 9–3; closed Monday 4 November–29 April).

Sapporo's most famous landmark is its **Clock Tower▶▶**, built in 1878 as part of Sapporo Agricultural College (now Hokkaido University) and is now open to the public. Inside is a small museum illustrating the local history of Sapporo.

In 1876, Western influence established the first brewery in Japan; the **Sapporo Beer Garden and Museum▶▶** is built on the site of that original Sapporo Brewery. Free tours of the museum last about an hour, and run daily between 9am and 3:40pm. The Beer Garden is open for the consumption of beer and food from 11:30am to 9pm.

Nakajima-koen Park▶▶ lies about 3km from Sapporo station and features a rose garden, boating lake, Nakajima Sports Centre and two buildings classified as national cultural treasures: the Hasso-an tea house and gardens, and the Hohei-kan, a Western-style building originally built as an Imperial guesthouse.

▶▶▶ Shikotsu-Toya National Park *230B3*

See map on page 246.

This 1,000 sq km park near Sapporo is the setting for lakes, volcanoes and the hot-spring spas of Toyako Onsen and Noboribetsu Onsen. Access is via the JR Sapporo–Hakodate line. For Lake Toya leave the train at JR Toya station (2 hours, 10 minutes) and take the bus to Toyako Onsen. For Noboribetsu Onsen disembark at Noboribetsu Station (1½ hours) and take the bus from there (20 minutes).

Abuta Volcano Science Museum▶▶, above the Toyako Onsen bus terminal, features photographs and lava displays of the huge eruption of Mount Usu in August 1977, which covered 80 per cent of Hokkaido with volcanic ash. The most interesting feature is the 350-seat 'experience room', which duplicates some of the effects of a volcanic eruption (open 9–5).

Jigokudani▶▶ ('Hell Valley'), at the northern edge of Noboribetsu Onsen, is a volcanic crater 450m in diameter full of boiling water and mineral formations caused by the volcanic activity. A concrete path (Hell Valley Promenade) follows the left side of the crater, and leads to a lookout point over a large pond of boiling water called Ohyunuma. *(Continued on page 246.)*

Sapporo Snow Festival
The Snow Festival started in 1950 as a way to entertain the citizens of Sapporo, depressed in the aftermath of World War II. It takes place in the first week of February and features over 300 huge statues made of snow, distributed in three sections of the city: Odori-koen Park, Makomanai and Susukino.

Shikotsu-Toya National Park

FOCUS ON *Soapland districts*

■ Every large Japanese city has a 'soapland' – an area of bars, massage parlours, night clubs, restaurants and striptease joints. They used to be called 'Turkoland', but the name was changed after complaints from the Turkish Embassy. The new name derives from the practice in Japanese massage parlours of soaping the customer all over, while he lies on a rubber mattress......■

Pachinko
Bright, garish, noisy and smoke-filled, *pachinko* pinball parlours are always found in soapland districts. There are over 10,000 of these establishments in Japan and more than half the population admits to playing *pachinko* pinball machines on a regular basis. Punters win tokens which they swap for prizes ranging from cigarettes to hi-fi equipment. Apparently *pachinko* was invented by a Korean in Nagoya who, after World War II, wanted to find a use for surplus ball bearings.

Soaping is for a basic fee. For an extra payment the masseuse uses her hands and body to work the soap into a lather. The cost continues to rise depending on the customer's requirements. Outside, massage parlours are generally garishly illuminated with bright neon lighting, and tough-looking individuals by the entrances trying to persuade passers-by to go in. They tend to cater for company men, usually drunk, socialising after work.

Soapland areas are quite safe for men and women to walk around and the experience can be instructive about Japanese sensibilities. For example, Japanese men are not at all sheepish about their enjoyment of the services on offer, and there is none of the furtiveness found in similar districts elsewhere in the world, such as Soho in London or Times Square in New York.

The Yakuza (the Japanese mafia) are usually involved in the soapland business, and can sometimes be seen cruising through the streets in the large American Cadillacs favoured by top Yakuza men. (Japanese import taxes have raised the prices of these cars, giving them extra kudos in their owners' eyes.)

The girls who work in soapland districts often come from country areas or distant towns. They tend to earn as much money as they can for four or five years and then return home. Family or friends need not know what they have been doing, and there is no loss of face; many go on to set up businesses or find eligible husbands and often do well. Japanese newspapers occasionally carry stories revealing that a well-known company boss or politician is married to a 'soapland girl'.

The practice and licensing of particular soapland areas by the government is part of a long tradition in Japanese society. In the 17th and 18th centuries, entertainment for townsmen and for visitors alike (and often the main reason for going to town) was the brothel and the theatre. In large towns and at post stations along main roads, such as the Tokaido, red-light districts were established and licensed by

Patchinko *player*

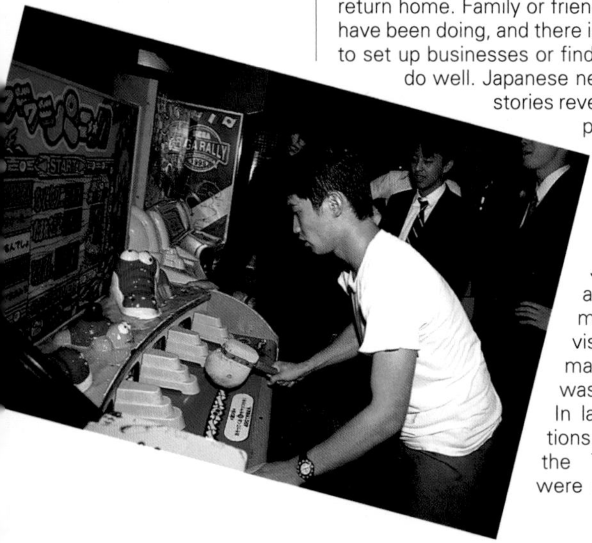

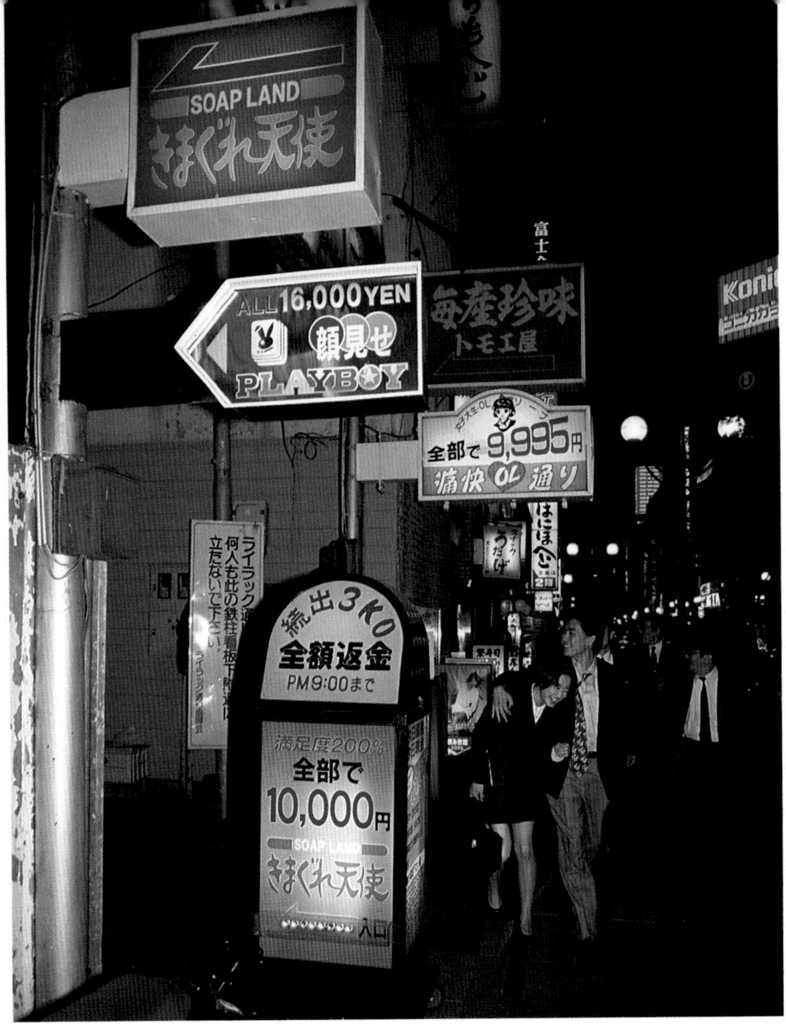

Signs for soapland

the government. Girls in brothels were graded and priced according to their class and background and their skills in such arts as singing, dancing, the tea ceremony, music and dress. Those of the highest rank were entitled to reject a customer they did not like. All, however, were controlled by pimps and were virtual slaves.

Nowadays visiting a prostitute is not freely condoned in Japanese society, although there is still much less stigma attached to doing so than there is in the West. Paid sex in Japan is very expensive, and a new wave of package trips has now emerged for businessmen taking 'golfing holidays' in Manila or Bangkok; the golf clubs never leave their bags and may even be left at a special depository at Narita Airport.

For Japanese women attitudes are gradually changing. It was recently reported in a respectable Japanese newspaper that some soapland districts now have Adonis bars staffed by handsome waiters and barmen available to their female customers to hire for sex. Apocryphal or not, such a story would certainly have failed to make it into print only a few years ago.

Alcohol
For the Japanese there is no shame in getting drunk; in fact, in some circumstances, your hosts may expect you to drink too much. Beer and/or *saké* are the usual accompaniments to a meal. Guests do not pour their own drinks but allow their companions to do it, and are expected to pour theirs. An empty cup or glass is a signal that a fill-up is required.

Jigokudani (Hell Valley)

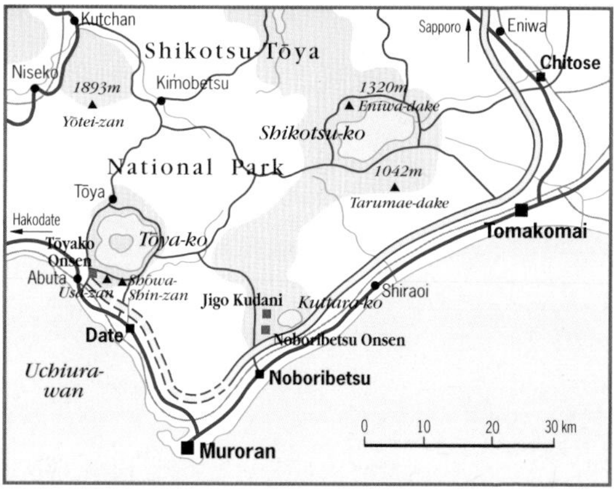

(Continued from page 243.) **Noboribetsu Onsen**►► is a resort famous for its variety of hot-water springs. Eleven different types of mineral-saturated hot water, ranging in temperature from 45°C to 91.5°C and totalling over 10,000 tonnes a day, spring from the ground. Though not a sophisticated resort, this is the most popular spa town in Hokkaido, and is always crowded during holiday periods.

Toyako Onsen►►, the main holiday centre for the park, is a typical Japanese holiday resort with many hotels, inns and souvenir shops. Lake Toya is near by and boat trips across the lake are available. The hot-spring waters are famous for their curative qualities, and Toyako Onsen can be very busy in the summer months.

TRAVEL FACTS

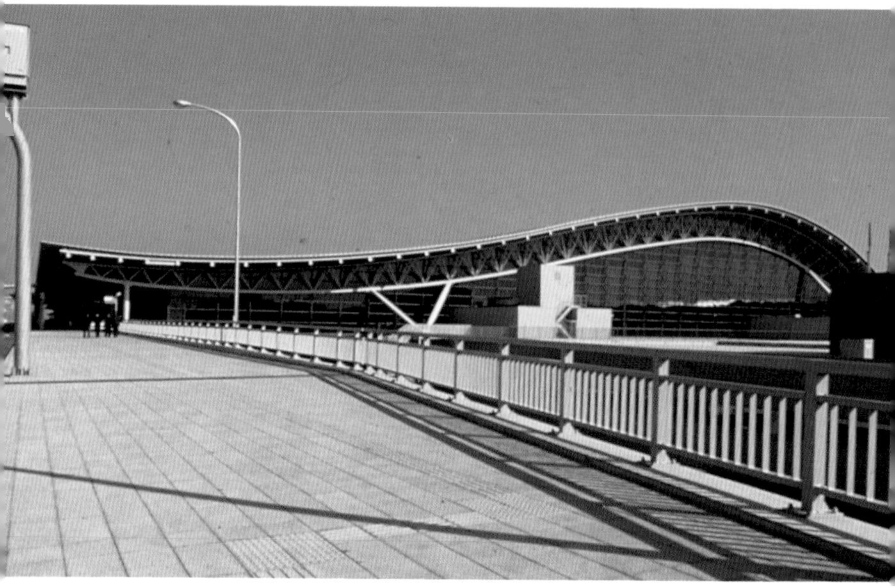

Kansai International airport

By air Narita, officially called New Tokyo International Airport, is the arrival and departure point for international flights to and from Tokyo.The best ways to get to and from the airport, which is 66km from the city centre, are by bus or train. The airport limousine bus information and ticket office is in the arrivals lobby just outside the exit from the customs hall. There are limousine bus services to Tokyo City Air Terminal (TCAT), Tokyo station and all the major hotels (the coach goes from one hotel to the next in a circular route). Depending on the traffic, the journey can take between one and a half and two hours. For travel back to the airport, take the bus at least three hours before departure time. If you leave from TCAT you can book in for your flight and hand in your luggage, which is taken to the airport and put on your flight. (Some airlines do not provide this service.)

JR offers two services from Narita to Tokyo station: the Narita Express (53 minutes) runs at least once every hour from 9:13am to 9:43pm; Airport Narita (1 hour, 24 minutes) runs every hour on the hour. Keisei Line Skyliner is a privately operated express train between Narita Airport and Keisei-Ueno station in Tokyo. It runs every 40 minutes between 6am and 8pm, and takes exactly 61 minutes. From Ueno station you can take a taxi or subway (not recommended for your first visit) to your destination. There is a shuttle bus from the arrival hall at the airport to Keisei station, which is a short distance away. The Keisei information counter and ticket office is near the exit from the customs hall. You will have to pay airport tax on departure from Narita; buy a ticket at TCAT or at a tax counter at the airport (before entering the departure lounge).

The new Kansai International airport is Japan's latest plunge into state-of-the-art construction work. In response to ever-growing demands for international and internal flight services, especially in the Kansai area, national government and private investors have spent 1.5 trillion yen building the airport of the future. The airport is a huge man-made island, lying 5km off the Senshu Coast at the southern end of Osaka Bay, with air connections to 44 countries and 22 areas within Japan. It is joined to the land by a double-layer access bridge, which brings both rail and road services.

The airport is serviced by two rail lines, JR West and Nankai Electric RR. JR's Haruka Express runs directly to Kyoto through Shin-Osaka and Tennoji stations. Nankai runs two limited express trains from Namba. The first, the rapi:t α, runs non-stop between Namba and the airport (29 minutes). The second, rapi:t β, stops at Sakai (11 minutes) and other express points along the way. It is also possible to take non-express trains from other points to the airport.

High-speed sea services exploit the airport's marine location. The Jet Foil service to K-CAT on Port Island (Kobe) runs from 5AM to 11:15PM daily, taking only 30 minutes. The high-speed catamarans to Awaji and Tokushima take 34 and 90 minutes respectively.

Limousine bus services are available to and from most areas in Kansai.

Customs regulations Clear passport control and collect your luggage before moving on to the 'non-resident' customs counters. Drugs, pornography and firearms are strictly prohibited. Non-residents are allowed to bring in the following duty free: 400 cigarettes *or* 100 cigars *or* 500g tobacco; 3 bottles (760cc each) alcohol; 50gm/2fl oz perfume; other goods up to ¥200,000 in value.

Travel insurance Standard travel insurance is advisable, including cover for medical care. Japanese hospitals have high standards but they are expensive, as are dental surgeries. (English- and, to a lesser extent, German-speaking doctors and dentists are not uncommon.)

Travel phones The travel phone is a service provided by the Japanese government to help tourists. If you get into difficulties or need information you can use the travel phone anywhere in Japan and speak to somebody in English. Find a yellow or blue phone (not a red one) or use a private phone. In a public phone, insert ¥10 and dial 106, and ask the operator in English for 'collect call TIC'. The ¥10 coin is returned with the call. Alternatively, dial 0088 222 800 for information on Eastern Japan, 0088 224 800 for information on Western Japan (both calls free). In Tokyo and Kyoto insert a ¥10 coin and dial 3503 4400 for Tokyo and 371 5649 for Kyoto. The coin is returned on connection.

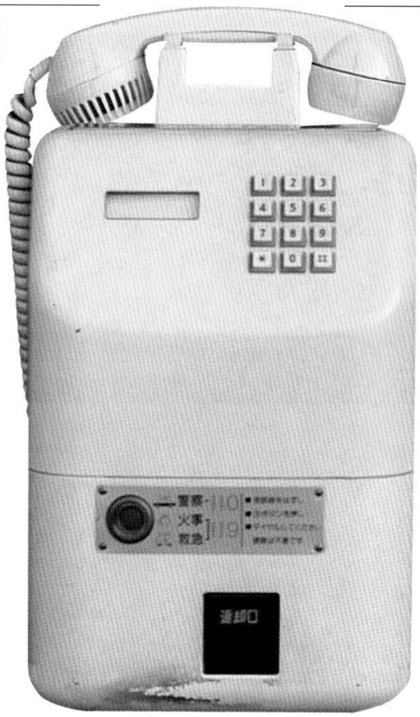

A public telephone: the colour tells you its function

Visas and vaccinations Citizens of most European countries do not need a visa to visit Japan and they may stay for upto 90 or, in some cases, 180 days without applying for one. Visitors from the US, Canada and New Zealand need a visa only for visits of over 90 days; they are readily given and are free of charge. Apply to the Japanese Embassy in your own country for details (see page 264) and check requirements before you leave. Visitors from Australia need a visa for any visit to Japan. Visitors from Europe, New Zealand, Canada, Australia or America do not need any vaccination certificates to get into Japan. Once there, you do not need to take any special health precautions.

Old and new walk side by side

Climate In general the climate of Japan resembles the temperate climate of the East Coast of the US, although the subtropical, southern island of Kyushu is warmer and the snowy, northern island of Hokkaido is colder. The best times to travel are in the spring and autumn. There are four distinct seasons. Spring begins in March (early April in northern Honshu and Hokkaido) and lasts until the beginning of June. April and May are warm and dry months, good for travelling. From late March to mid-April the cherry blossom ripens northwards from Kyushu to Hokkaido. The summer and rainy seasons start in early June – a hot and humid time (except in Hokkaido). From mid-July to early September it remains hot but not wet. Mountain areas are refreshing at this time of the year. Autumn is a time of clear skies and comfortable temperatures, although late September can be wet. Winter in the north and at high altitudes is cold, snowy and beautiful. In other areas temperatures rarely drop below freezing.

WEATHER CHARTS

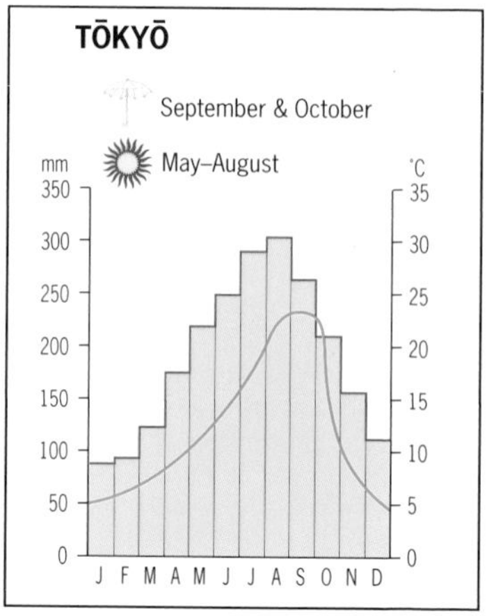

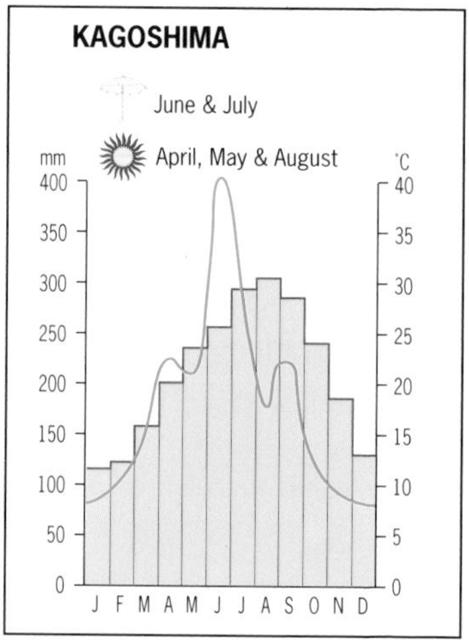

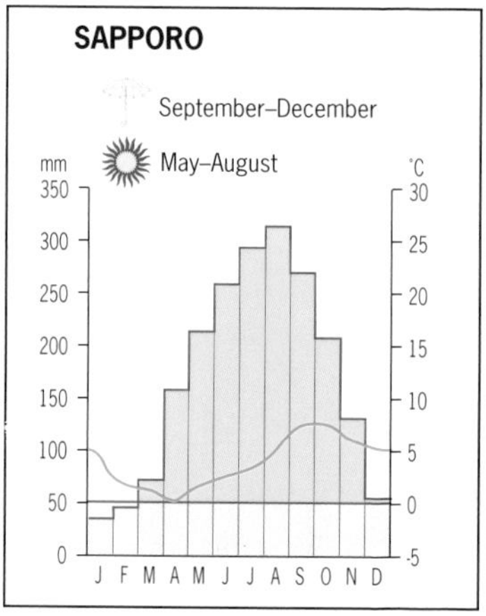

Money matters Credit cards are widely accepted in Japan, but cash is still the preferred way of paying bills in normal transactions and the Japanese often carry huge wads of money around with them (a reflection of their safe society). Japanese currency is the yen and there are three types of paper notes and six different coins: 1,000, 5,000 and 10,000 yen bills; and 1, 5, 10, 50, 100 and 500 yen coins. Visa, Diners Club, MasterCard and American Express are the major credit cards. Access is not very well known or widely accepted. Travellers' cheques in yen or dollars are easily exchanged for cash at the banks but are not readily accepted at small shops and restaurants. The rates of exchange at banks for cash and travellers' cheques are invariably higher than in hotels.

Regions of Japan There are eight 'official' regions in Japan, as follows: Hokkaido, Kyushu and Shikoku, and the five regions of Honshu, the largest island: Tohoku, the mountainous rural northeastern region; Kanto, east central Honshu, Japan's most urban region (includes Tokyo); Chubu, the mountainous central region of Honshu, including the Japan Alps; Kinki, lying to the west and including Japan's second largest industrialised area, centring on the cities of Osaka and Kobe, and the historical capitals of Kyoto and Nara; and finally, Chugoku on west Honshu, an agricultural and fishing region.

Time differences All of the islands of Japan are in the same time zone. London is nine hours behind (eight hours during British Summer Time), New York and Los Angeles 14 and 17 hours behind, respectively. Australia is one or two hours earlier; New Zealand is three hours earlier; Canada is 12 and a half to 18 hours later.

Tipping Tips are neither given nor expected. Large hotels and restaurants may, however, add a 10 to 15 per cent service charge on to your bill. There is also a government tax of 10 per cent on food or accommodation accounts of 2,500 yen or more and 5,000 yen or more respectively. If the charge is added to your bill you will pay an extra 10 per cent tax. A government tax of 3 per cent is added to food bills of ¥7,500 or less and 6 per cent to bills over that sum; the same applies to accommodation bills of ¥15,000 or less and over ¥15,000.

When to go The Japanese all tend to take their holidays between similar dates and it is best for foreign travellers to avoid these vacation times. The three major holiday periods are: two or three days before and after New Year's Day; the week following Greenery Day (29 April), known as Golden Week; and the week that includes 13–16 August, the Obon Festival, when many Japanese return to their home towns.

The torii *gate at Itsukushima Shrine, Hiroshima*

Buses Japan has an excellent network of local city and rural buses and the bus terminal is often adjacent to the train station, so it is easy to make use of both buses and trains. For long journeys buses are slower and less comfortable than trains but they are somewhat cheaper. Japanese Railways provides a service of overnight long-distance buses on which the Japan Rail Pass (see pages 254–5) is valid.

Buses come into their own for local journeys. Unfortunately many do not show their destination in *Romaji* (Japanese Roman script), so it is important to be sure of the number you wish to take, in which direction you want to take it, and where, if at all, you need to change buses. This information can be obtained from tourist offices. Once you know your bus number and destination, write them on a piece of paper so that people can help you. Knowing how much to pay once you are on board is much easier than catching the right bus. As you enter the bus (at the back) take a ticket from the dispensing machine inside the door. It has a number on the back. A meter above the driver's head matches the cost of the fares against the numbers on the backs of the tickets. It rotates during the bus journey, increasing the fare against the ticket numbers accordingly. As you get off, put your fare into the collecting machine by the driver's side. There is box attached to the machine that will give change for coins and notes.

Car rental Cars can be reserved through Hertz-Japan (tel: 03 3356 8002) and other major companies including Nippon (tel: 03 3485 7196, English-speaking operator available) and Nissan Car Lease (tel: 03 5424 4123, English-speaking operator). An international driving licence is required. Traffic drives on the left and speed limits vary, but generally the limit is 80kph on highways and 40kph in urban areas.Renting a car locally to explore the immediate area can be a sensible proposition, but for travelling through the country, driving is not the best option. Train services are comprehensive, fast and frequent; the roads, by contrast, are congested and not particularly well signposted and, off the major roads, signs are given only in *Kanji* (Chinese characters).

Travellers with disabilities In many towns and cities plastic raised markers are embedded in the pavements at traffic crossing points to assist the blind, and bird song is broadcast to

A driver's-eye view of tram-travel in Matsuyama, on Shikoku Island

help the blind know when to cross. JR stations have similar raised studs a small distance from platform edges and before stairs. In larger cities, public lavatories often provide special facilities and some hotels can provide rooms for the disabled. In Tokyo these include the Imperial Hotel, the Hotel New Otani, Tokyo Prince Hotel and Miyako Hotel. With advance warning help is available at Narita airport for disabled passengers, and the limousine bus service (see page 248) is also accessible.

Written enquiries can be sent, well in advance of travel, to the Physically Handicapped Lifestyle Centre, 1-44-2 Umegaoka, Setagaya-ku, Tokyo 154.

Ferries Frequent ferry services connect the main islands of Japan and local ferries connect all populated small islands to the nearest main ports as well as to other islands in the same group. Tokyo or Osaka to Kyushu or Shikoku or Hokkaido are popular main routes. Ferries are less expensive than air or rail although obviously slower. Economy travellers occupy one large *tatami* mat room where they eat, sit and sleep together. On longer routes, a small Japanese public bath is situated on the same deck. Private cabins also are available. Tickets and information can be obtained from travel agents based in Japan.

Subways Many large Japanese cities have subway systems, most providing the quickest and cheapest way of moving about town. Subway maps are provided at station information counters or local tourist offices.

Taxis Taxis are quite expensive but the fare shown on the meter is exactly what you pay: tipping is not the custom. It is a good idea to carry the address and telephone number of your destination in *Romaji* and to show the taxi-driver. After hailing a cab do not try to open the taxi door. The driver will open the kerbside door by remote control. Similarly, do not try to close the door on leaving. A red light on the dashboard indicates an available taxi; a green light means it is occupied.

The International Student Identity card, available in many countries from student organisations, entitles the holder to discounts at several art galleries, museums, theatres and so on, plus youth rail passes and reductions on some local transport networks.

Trains Trains are the quickest way of exploring Japan. Japan Railways (JR) run 28,000 trains daily and there are also numerous private railway lines. The fare system is complex and needs to be understood to avoid paying the highest prices. There is a basic fare for any train, calculated by the distance travelled. Added to this fare are various surcharges, mainly dependent on how fast the train is, but also on whether you reserve a seat or not and on the class of travel. There are four categories of train; the slower they are, the less you pay. The Shinkansen are the fastest; limited stop express (Tokkyu or Cho-tokkyu) next to fastest; express (Kyuko) next to slowest; and local trains (Futsu) the slowest.

For people with limited time and no restrictions on their expenses, Shinkansen are the trains to use. For the budget traveller in no rush the best trains are a combination of the limited express for long journeys and the local trains for exploring a particular area. If you wish to stop at places *en route* to your destination, purchase a ticket for the whole journey; you are allowed to make as many stops as you wish, as long as the date on your ticket remains valid for the whole journey. The period of validity is one day for 100km, two days for 200km and then one day for each additional 200km. Some restrictions may apply on Shinkansen routes; an information line is available on 03 3423 0111. You can get refunds on unused tickets and also change your routing once without any handling charge. If you are not sure how much your fare is or where you are going, buy the cheapest ticket from a ticket machine or ticket office and pay any balance due at your destination; most stations have a fare adjustment counter. (Reserved tickets are purchased in the 'green window' counters, called *midori-no-madoguchi* in Japanese.)

For foreign visitors to Japan who intend to make a reasonable number of train journeys it is worth buying a Japan Rail Pass. These are valid for one to three weeks and can save the traveller quite a lot of money. They may only be purchased outside Japan, and they allow the user unlimited travel on all JR rail, bus and boat services. Get a voucher from an authorised sales agent (lists available from JNTO) in your own country and exchange it for a rail pass at Tokyo or Osaka stations on your arrival, or better still from the JR counter at Narita Airport (open 7am–11pm every day).

Do not carry a lot of luggage; busy trains usually have space for only one medium-sized suitcase. Most trains have buffet cars and/or food and drink available from trolleys which are pushed up and down the aisles. They also sell *eki-ben* (lunchboxes), but those sold on stalls at the station are usually cheaper and fresher. All reasonably sized stations and all those on JR lines display station names in *Kanji* and *Romaji* letters. The name of the station is in the middle of the nameboard with the preceding and following stations above and beneath it. Keep a careful watch for these nameboards when approaching a station.

Right: Tokyo rush hour

Sometimes there is only one and it can flash past before you have seen it. Try to avoid travelling during the rush hours (7–9am and 5–7pm). All of the major railway stations are equipped with an information counter where you can get maps, accommodation advice and assistance with your train-travel from English-speaking assistants.

The following Japanese phrases may be useful for visitors who are travelling by train.

At what time does the train for Tokyo leave? *Tokyo yuki no densha wa nanji ni demasu ka?*
From which platform? *Nanban sen kara demasu ka?*
Where is platform 1? *Ichi ban sen wa doko desuka?*
Does the train for Osaka leave from here? *Osaka yuki no densha wa koko kara demasu ka?*
I want to get off at Tokyo station. *Tokyo eki de oritai desu.*
Will you tell me when to get off? *Itsu oritara yoi ka oshiete kudasai?*
How many stations (before) I get off? *Koko kara nanbanme no eki de oriruno desu-ka?*

Boarding a Shinkansen train

Making contact

Uniformity is an early lesson for Japanese school children

Language The Japanese spend many years at school learning English but very few are confident of speaking it, though it is probable that their English is better than most visitors' Japanese. The following Japanese phrases are among those that are likely to be most helpful to a foreign visitor.

Mr or Mrs *san* after the surname (but don't ever append it to your own name)
Yes *hai*
Yes, I am listening *hai, hai*
Yes, I agree *hai, so des*
Thank you *(domo) arigato*
Yes please *hai onegaishimasu*
No (rarely used) *iie*
No, I disagree *chigaimas*
I am sorry *gomen-nasai*
Excuse me (also used to call waiter) *sumimasen...*
Good morning *o-haiyo-gozaimasu*
Good afternoon *konnichi-wa*
Good evening *konban-wa*
Good night *oya-sumi-nasai*
Goodbye *sayonara*
Excuse me, do you speak English? *sumimasen, Eigo hanashimasu-ka?*
Yes, just a little *hai, sukoshi dake*
No, I can't *iie, dame desu*
(On starting a meal) *itadakimas*
Cheers! *kampai!*
Thank you (for kindness) *domo arigato gozaimash'ta*
Thank you (after a meal) *gochiso-sama desh'ta*
What is your name? *o-namae-wa?*
My name is 'Smith' *watashi wa 'Smith' desu*
(I'm) ill *(watashi wa) byooki desu*
Help! *tasukete (kudasai)!*
hospital *byooin*
Police *Keisatsu*
How much is it? *ikura desu ka?*
for bed and breakfast *choshokutsuki*
for full board *sanshokutsuki*
excluding meals *sudomari desu*
does that include...? *wa tsuite imasu-ka?*
meals *shokuji*
service *saabisu*
Have you anything cheaper? *Nani ka motto yasui no wa (arimasen ka?)*
Menu, please *menu o kudasai*
Bill, please *kanjo onegaishimasu*
Do you accept credit cards? *credit cardo tsukaemasu ka?*
coffee-shop *kissaten*
restaurant *restoran*
beer *biru*
water *mizu*
milk *milku*
coffee *kohee*
Indian tea *kocha*
Japanese or Chinese tea *ocha*
sugar, please *satoh, kudasai*

For details of the Japanese writing system, see pages 20–1.

Hokkaido sign: beware of bears

Emergencies

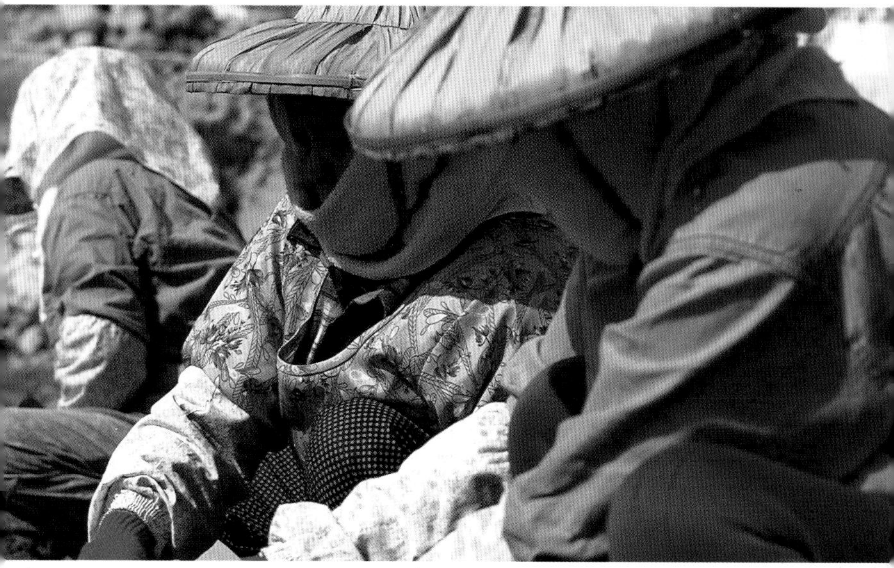

Archaeologists excavating a site on Ishigaki Island

Emergency telephone numbers Police: 110; Ambulance/Fire: 119. Press the red button on the telephone and dial. No money is required. The operator will answer in Japanese so you will probably need the assistance of a Japanese-speaker. See pages 248–9 for details of English-speaking operators.

Health The Japanese have the highest life expectancy in the world. Japan is a clean, hygienic country and doctors are highly trained. Health insurance is recommended for travellers. Clinics with English-speaking doctors include: Hibiya Clinic, Hibiya Mitsui Building, 1-1-2 Yurakucho Chiyoda-ku, Tokyo (tel: 03 3502 2681) and Japan Baptist Hospital, 14 Yamanomotocho Kitashirakawa, Kyoto, Sakyo-ku (tel: 075 781 5191). English is spoken at the following hospitals: Ginza area: St Luke's International Hospital (Sei Roka Byoin), 9-1 Akashi-cho, Chuo-ku (tel: (03) 3541 5151); Shinjuku area: International Catholic Hospital (Seibo Byoin), 2-5-1 Naka Ochai, Shinjuku-ku, (tel: 03 3951-1111).

Lost property If you forget something or leave it in a public place there is every chance it will still be there when you return. All public transport systems, including taxi companies, have a lost and found service. In Tokyo:
Taxis (tel: 03 3648 0300)
JR (tel: 03 3231 1880)
Subway (tel: 03 3834 5577)
Buses (tel: 03 3815 7229)
The Tokyo Central Lost and Found Police Office is at 1-9-11, Koraku, Bunkyo-ku (tel: 03 3814 4151)

Pharmacies Japanese pharmacies sell the same range of goods as Western chemist shops. Pharmacies are easily found in any town. In Tokyo there is an English-speaking chemist at the American Pharmacy, Hibiya Park Building, 1-8-1, Yurakucho, Chiyoda-ku (tel: 03 3271-4034/5), open 9–7 Monday to Saturday, 11–7 Sunday and holidays.

Police Robbery is very rare in Japan and violent crime is even less likely. Japanese policemen and women are helpful and approachable, but very few speak any English. Every Japanese district has its own police box (*koban*), usually near a busy road junction or station. The police on duty will help you find an address if you can show them a map of its location.

Media Japan has four daily English-language newspapers on sale in hotels or at major railway stations. There are English editions of the *Asahi*, *Yomiuri*, and *Mainichi*, and the fourth is the independent *Japan Times*. The monthly English-language *Tokyo Journal* gives comprehensive reviews and listings of theatre, film, art shows and restaurants.

Japanese newspapers differ from their Western counterparts in two main areas: a clear-cut stance in articles is avoided, and the publisher, not the reporter, assumes responsibility for the content of a story. A journalist is always expected to work closely within the framework of the newspaper's editorial policy.

English-language television and radio programming is available at most large hotels.

Post offices The Japanese postal service is very efficient in delivering both domestic and foreign mail. Post offices are open 9–5 Monday–Friday, with cash deposits or withdrawal until 3pm; Saturday 9–12:30 (main offices only); closed on Sunday and national holidays. The Central Post Office next to Tokyo station is open 24 hours a day. Small neighbourhood post offices close on the second Saturday of each month. Mail boxes are red.

The distinctive red post boxes are easy to spot

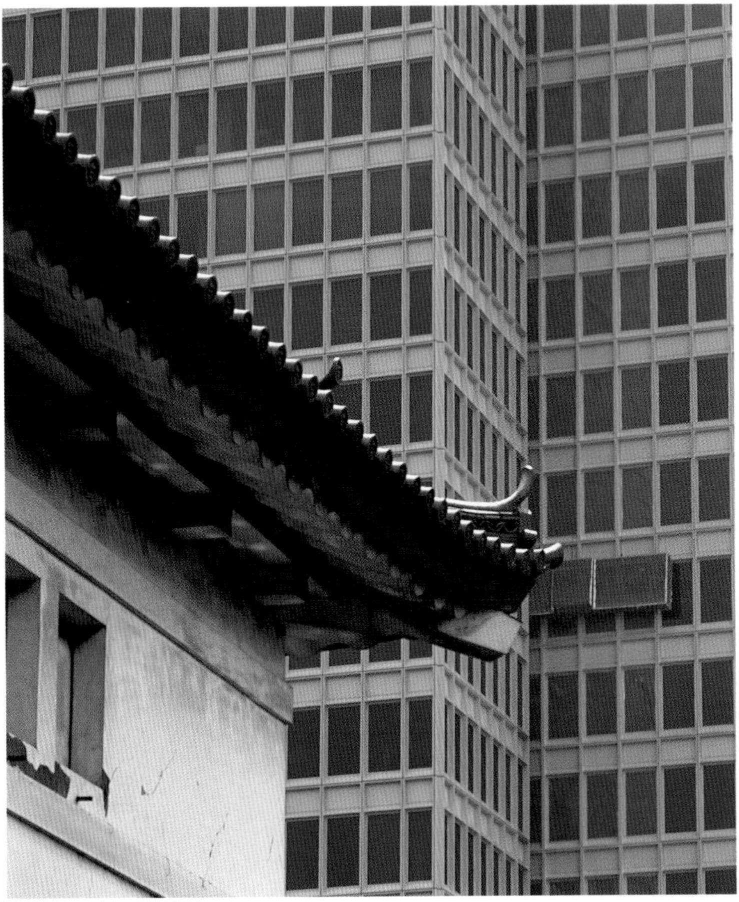

The urban architecture of Tokyo, ancient and modern

Letters addressed in *Romaji*, sent to Japan or within Japan, should have the address printed in large, bold print to make it easier for the Japanese sorter to read. To post a letter or card in Japan, take it to the post office and have it weighed. Post office clerks read *Romaji*. Large post offices may be used as *poste restante* addresses.

Telephones Picture diagrams inside public telephone booths show the dialling procedure. Pay phones are different colours depending on their function. International calls are possible from card phones, most green phones and some grey phones, but not from pink phones. One minute costs ¥10. International calls may be dialled direct or through the operator. To get the international information service dial 0057; for the international operator, dial 0051. Dial direct international calls as follows: 001 + the national number of the country being called + area code + local phone number. The national number of Australia is 61; Canada is 1; Ireland is 353; New Zealand is 64; the UK is 44 and the US is 1. If the area code starts with an 0, omit it. To call Japan from Australia dial 0011 81; from Canada 01181; from the UK and Ireland 0081; New Zealand 0081 and the US 011 81. Again, omit the area code's initial 0. Fax is widely used in Japan and most offices and hotels have their own fax machines.

Bottles of saké *ready to be enjoyed*

Camping and self-catering organisations There are some campsites in Japan, but they tend to be difficult to find and primitive. Camping is not a popular or common pastime. People on a tight budget who wish to cater for themselves would be better advised to stay in youth hostels. The Japan Youth Hostel Association is at Hoken Kaikan, 1-1 Ichigaya Sadohara-cho, Shinjuku-ku, Tokyo (tel: 03 3269 5831).

Children Young visitors are well catered for in Japan and there are theme parks, aquariums, zoos, video display exhibitions and other child-orientated events readily available throughout the country. There is also a Disneyland on the outskirts of Tokyo. Local tourist information centres have full details of their area's amenities.

Children in Japan are allowed to walk, cycle and travel on public transport on their own from a very early age, and family homes and schools are still found in city centres.

Japanese children really enjoy meeting foreign boys and girls and later becoming pen friends with them. If you do take children with you to Japan they will have no difficulty in making friends, despite the language differences.

CONVERSION CHARTS

FROM	TO	MULTIPLY BY
Inches	Centimetres	2.54
Centimetres	Inches	0.3937
Feet	Metres	0.3048
Metres	Feet	3.2810
Yards	Metres	0.9144
Metres	Yards	1.0940
Miles	Kilometres	1.6090
Kilometres	Miles	0.6214
Acres	Hectares	0.4047
Hectares	Acres	2.4710
Gallons	Litres	4.5460
Litres	Gallons	0.2200
Ounces	Grams	28.35
Grams	Ounces	0.0353
Pounds	Grams	453.6
Grams	Pounds	0.0022
Pounds	Kilograms	0.4536
Kilograms	Pounds	2.205
Tons	Tonnes	1.0160
Tonnes	Tons	0.9842

MEN'S SUITS

UK	36	38	40	42	44	46	48
Rest of Europe	46	48	50	52	54	56	58
US	36	38	40	42	44	46	48

DRESS SIZES

UK	8	10	12	14	16	18
France	36	38	40	42	44	46
Italy	38	40	42	44	46	48
Rest of Europe	34	36	38	40	42	44
US	6	8	10	12	14	16

MEN'S SHIRTS

UK	14	14.5	15	15.5	16	16.5	17
Rest of Europe	36	37	38	39/40	41	42	43
US	14	14.5	15	15.5	16	16.5	17

MEN'S SHOES

UK	7	7.5	8.5	9.5	10.5	11
Rest of Europe	41	42	43	44	45	46
US	8	8.5	9.5	10.5	11.5	12

WOMEN'S SHOES

UK	4.5	5	5.5	6	6.5	7
Rest of Europe	38	38	39	39	40	41
US	6	6.5	7	7.5	8	8.5

Electricity From Tokyo east to Hokkaido the current is 100 volts at 50 cycles. Western Japan operates on 100 volts at 60 cycles. North Americans with electronic equipment that operates at 110/60 will have no problems. Europeans using devices designed to operate at 240/50 cycles will need to adjust them or, if they are not convertible, use a transformer. Some of the major hotels have 240/50 outputs.

Entrance fees Most Japanese museums, galleries, monuments and nationally known temples and gardens charge entrance fees, which usually fall in the ¥300–¥600 range .

Opening times
Banks open Monday–Friday 9–3, Saturday 9–noon; closed Saturday, Sunday and national holidays.
Museums usually April–October 9–5, November–March 9–4:30; closed Monday and 29 December–3 January. Most museums stop letting people in half an hour before closing time. If a national holiday falls on a museum's weekly closing day, it closes on the following day instead.

Shops open from around 10am. Some close at around 6pm; others stay open until much later. Many, but not all, in the central business district are open on Sundays and holidays.

Department stores all open six days a week at 10am. Some stay open to 8pm, although most close at 6pm on Saturday and Sunday and holidays. Some are closed on Mondays, and others on Wednesdays and Thursdays.

Photography A huge array of cameras, processing facilities and film of every sort is available in even the smallest Japanese town.

Places of worship The following places of worship in Tokyo hold services in English:
Anglican: St Alban's, 3-6-25 Shibakoen, Minato-ku (tel: 03 3431-8534).
Baptist: Tokyo Baptist Church, 9-2 Hachiyama-cho, Shibuya-ku (tel: 03 3461 8425).
Catholic: St Ignatius, 6-5 Kojimachi, Chiyoda-ku (tel: 03 3263-4584).
Jewish: Jewish Community of Japan, 3-8-8 Hiro, Shibuya-ku (tel: 03 3400-2559).

Toilets Most modern facilities in large towns provide Western-style toilets but in rural areas Japanese squat-style toilets are still quite common. There are public lavatories in railway stations and public parks (they do not provide paper) but those in department stores and coffee shops are always cleaner.

Information on hand at the Grand Shrines of Ise-Jingu

However Westernised modern Japan may appear, traditional etiquette continues to be very important. Most Japanese expect that as a foreigner you will not understand the complexities of their social behaviour, and that you will behave according to Western rules. However, evidence of a basic understanding of Japanese values and a respect for them will certainly be appreciated, enjoyed and acknowledged by the people you meet.

Status Japanese society is even today hierarchical and spoken Japanese contains a battery of expressions which, used appropriately, set both the relative social positions and the sex of the speaker and the person spoken to. Both parties immediately know where they stand on the ladder of inferiority, equality or superiority. Visitors especially on business, are accorded a relatively high status, and may respond to this by being polite and effusive in expressing thanks even for minor favours. For receivers of hospitality – be it drinks, a meal or a gift – it is customary to say *Arigato gozaimasu*, a polite 'Thank you', at the time of receiving and at the next meeting. Saying 'Thank you' several times symbolises a long-term rather than a transitory relationship.

Groups versus individuals The Japanese have a tendency to think in terms of the social group they belong to, rather than as individuals. This leads to an intrinsic acknowledgement of the rights of the group over those of an individual member, and a close observance of family morals and taboos. Social harmony (*wa*) is highly valued in the workplace and at home. In business and politics consensus opinion is vital before decisions or policies are made public, and an open display of conflict is viewed as deeply embarrassing.

Thinking ahead Forethought is another distinctive feature of Japanese behaviour. It is always best to do things for others before being asked. For example, a host will try and anticipate what a guest might want or need. Tea or coffee and even a meal may be served without you asking for it. Room dividers (*fusuma* and *shoji*) in a traditional Japanese house are not fitted with locks. If the *fusuma* is closed a person wishing to enter needs to choose correctly between knocking, calling out or just going away.

Bowing The Japanese bow a lot to each other on meeting or departing. The depth and frequency of the bows depends on the status of the people involved. To be on the safe side imitate any bows you receive. Hold both

Bid for good luck at Motsuji Temple

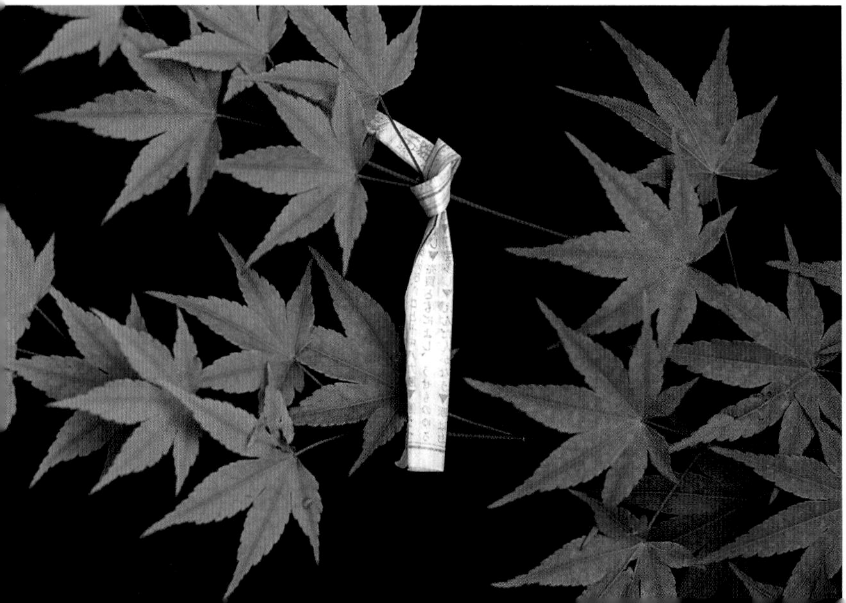

arms straight and bow with the upper body. Shaking hands is an alternative way of introducing yourself and still a novelty to the Japanese. However, a strong handshake is not needed and would not be understood.

Conversation and smiling In conversation, it is common for the listener to nod and utter approving sounds. These do not, however, necessarily mean consent or agreement. In fact, in most cases they signal only that the listener is concentrating on what you are saying. Another possible source of misunderstanding is smiling. For a Japanese smiling may be a way of hiding embarrassment; don't take it to mean assent all the time. Smiling may even disguise inner sadness. Genuine happiness is indicated more accurately by creases in the corners of the eye. According to Japanese thinking, disclosing such emotions would be to foist off one's problems onto another, to burden the listener and thereby show a lack of consideration.

A monk with a cold signs pilgrims' log books at Koya-san Temple

Nose-blowing It is normal in Japan to clear your throat or sniff if you have a cold or a running nose (and even acceptable to spit discreetly in the street). However, it is not done to blow your nose in public. The people you see wearing masks over the mouth and nose do so because they have a cold, not because of pollution. It is best to go to the toilet or to some other private place if you need to blow your nose.

Tourist offices

Embassies and consulates in Tokyo
The following countries have embassies and/or consulates based in Tokyo.
Australia: 2-1-19 Mita, Minato-ku (tel: 03 5232 4111).
Canada: 7-3-38 Akasaka, Minato-ku (tel: 03 3408 2101).
Ireland: 25 Kowa Building, 8-7, Sanbancho, Chiyoda-ku (tel: 03 3263 0695).
New Zealand: 20–40 Kamiyama-cho, Shibuya-ku (tel: 03 3467 2271).
UK: 1 Ichiban-cho, Chiyoda-ku (tel: 03 3265 5511).
US: 1-10-5 Akasaka, Minato-ku (tel: 03 3224 5000).

Japanese embassies and consulates abroad
Australia: 112 Empire Circuit, Yarralumla, Canberra, ACT 2600 (tel: 06 273 3244).
Canada: 255 Sussex Drive, Ottawa, Ontario K1N 9E6 (tel: 613 236 8541).
New Zealand: Norwich Insurance House, 3-11 Hunter Street, Wellington 1 (tel: 04 731 540).
UK: 101–104 Piccadilly, London W1V 9FN (tel: 0171 465 6500).
US: 2520 Massachusetts Avenue NW, Washington DC 20008 (tel: 202 939 6800).

Tourist offices The Japanese National Tourist Office (JNTO) operates three main Tourist Information Centres (TIC) in Japan. They give advice on travel arrangements and accommodation and stock lots of useful free literature. Most towns of any size in Japan operate their own tourist offices, normally within or near the main railway station.

Tokyo office: Kotani Building, 1-6-6 Yurakucho, Chiyoda-ku (tel: 03 3502 1461). Open weekdays 9–5, Saturday 9–noon; closed Sunday and national holidays.
Tokyo International Airport office: Airport No 2 Terminal Building, Narita Airport, Chiba Prefecture (tel: 0476 34 6251). Open 9–8.
Kyoto office: Kyoto Tower Building, Higashi-Shiokojicho, Shimogyo-ku (tel: 075 371 5649). Open weekdays 9–5, Saturday 9–noon; closed Sunday and national holidays.
JNTO also operates a main office in Tokyo and others abroad.
Japan (main office): Tokyo Kotsu Kaikan Building, 2-10-1 Yurakucho, Chiyoda-ku, Tokyo 100 (tel: 03 3216 2905).
Australia: Level 33, The Chiffley Tower, 2 Chiffley Sq, Sydney, NSW 2000 (tel: 02 232 4522).
Canada: 165 University Avenue, Toronto, Ontario M5H 3B8 (tel: 416 366 7140).
UK: Heathcoat House, 20 Savile Row, London W1X 1AE (tel: 0171 734 9638).
US: One Rockefeller Plaza, Suite 1250, New York, NY 10020 (tel: 212 757 5640).

Seeing how the land lies, with help from a tourist information office

HOTELS AND RESTAURANTS

ACCOMMODATION

There is no shortage of accommodation for the traveller in Japan. In the cities there is a wide variety of options while in rural areas there are usually *minshuku* (see pages 80–1), small inns and hotels and sometimes *ryokan* (see pages 220–1). The range of average prices for different categories of accommodation is as follows:

Hotel accommodation:
Expensive (£££)
¥27,000–40,000
Moderate (££)
¥17,000–26,000
Budget (£) ¥6,000–11,000

Other accommodation:
Ryokan ¥20,000–40,000 (includes breakfast and dinner)
Business hotels
¥8,000–12,000
Minshuku ¥6,000–8,000
Japanese inns
¥5,000–7,000
Youth hostels
¥1,000–3,000

TOKYO

Akasaka Prince Hotel (£££) 1-2 Kioi-cho, Chiyoda-ku (tel: 03 3234 1111). First-class service, excellent views, quality post-war architecture and tasteful modern room furnishings.
Akasaka Tokyu Hotel (££/£) 2-14-3 Nagata-cho, Chiyoda-ku (tel: 03 3580 2311). Excellent central location, rooms not big but with all facilities, wide variety of restaurants. Popular: book well ahead.
Ana Hotel Tokyo (£££) 1-12-33 Akasaka, Minato-ku (tel: 03 3505 1111). In the Ark Hills area, between Roppongi and Akasaka, a 37-storey, 903-room block with a sober exterior and vast areas of marble inside. Facilities include a health club and pool, executive floor and several restaurants.
Atamiso (££) 4-14-3 Ginza, Chuo-ku (tel: 03 3541 3621). This small hotel (74 rooms) offers a friendly personal service. It is located close to central Ginza's nightlife and shopping.
Elegant Inn Yasuda (£) 1-56-28 Matsubara, Setagaya-ku (tel: 03 3322 5546). Japanese inn offering Western- and Japanese-style rooms, air conditioned. Good value.
Fairmont Hotel (££/£) 2-1-17 Kudan Minami, Chiyoda-ku (tel: 03 3262 1151). For Tokyo this is an older style hotel (built in 1952). Small and quietly positioned near the Imperial Palace. Highly recommended during the cherry blossom season in spring.
Ginza Capitol (££) 2-1-4 Tsukiji, Chuo-ku (tel: 03 3543 8211). A basic business hotel with compact rooms, close to Tsukiji subway station, reasonably convenient for Ginza.
Ginza Ocean (££) 7-18-15 Ginza, Chuo-ku (tel: 03 3545 1221). The Ginza Ocean is a cut above the usual business hotel, with a friendly staff and a good Japanese restaurant.
Holiday Inn Tokyo (££) 1-13-7 Hatchobori, Chuo-ku (tel: 03 3553 6161). Similar to any other Holiday Inn but with smaller rooms (relatively large for Tokyo, however). Western-style restaurant. Convenient for Tokyo station.
Hotel Ohgaiso (£) 3-3-21 Ikenohata, Taito-ku 110 (tel: 03 3822 4611). Good location opposite Ueno Park. Reasonable, well-equipped rooms for the price. The windows can be opened (not common in Tokyo). Japanese- and Western-style food in restaurants. Doors close at 2am.
Hotel Okura (£££) 2-10-4 Toranomon, Minato-ku (tel: 03 3582 0111). Traditional atmosphere, spacious rooms, quietly sophisticated, popular with diplomats and businessmen.
Hotel Seiyo Ginza (£££) 1-11-2 Ginza, Chuo-ku (tel: 03 3535 1111). Very expensive, small and luxurious hotel with highly personalised service. Staff to guest ratio is three to one! Reservations a must.
Imperial (£££) 1-1-1 Uchisaiwaicho, Chiyoda-ku (tel: 03 3504 1111). On the edge of Ginza, facing Hibiya Park, this is a city-within-a-city, with 1,059 rooms, over 20 restaurants, dozens of shops, a health club and pool. Rooms are beautifully appointed, with superb views from the upper storeys.
Keihin Hotel (££) 4-10-20 Takanawa, Minato-ku (tel: 03 3449 5711). Slightly out of the way in Shinagawa district, but an excellent value, straightforward modest hotel. There is usually somebody at the desk who can speak English.
Kikuya Ryokan (£) 2-18-9 Nishi-Asakusa, Taito-ku (tel: 03 3841 6404). Very small, with eight Japanese-style rooms, some with private bathroom. Just off Kappabashi-dori.
Kimi Ryokan (£) 2-36-8 Ikebukuro, Toshima-ku (tel: 03 3971 3766). A friendly little place with Japanese-style rooms, it is popular with Westerners and often full. Seven minutes' walk northwest of Ikebukuro station.
Mikawaya Bekkan Ryokan (£) 1-31-11 Asakusa, Taito-ku (tel: 03 3843 2345). Friendly, inexpensive Japanese inn, almost on the doorstep of Asakusa Kannon Temple.

Miyako Hotel (££/£) 1-1-50 Shirokanedai, Minato-ku (tel: 03 3447 3111). Large rooms with big windows, some overlooking hotel's own gardens. Good facilities and Japanese cuisine. Free bus service to nearest station and Ginza.
New Otani Hotel (£££) 4-1 Kioi-cho, Chiyoda-ku (tel: 03 3265 1111). Huge hotel complex, largest in Japan but offers restaurants and services to match. Attractive feature is its surprisingly large garden.
Okura (£££) 2-10-4 Toranomon, Minato-ku (tel: 03 3582 0111). Stately, formal, one of the first of the post-war grand hotels, with 883 rooms, many restaurants, an art gallery and indoor and outdoor pools.
Palace (£££) 1-1-1 Marunouchi, Chiyoda-ku (tel: 03 3211 5211). Overlooks the moats of the Imperial Palace, and a subway stop from Ginza. Elegant public areas and 394 beautifully appointed guest rooms.
President Hotel (££) 2-2-3 Minami Aoyama, Minatu-ku (tel: 03 3497 0111). The only small, moderately priced hotel, located in the expensive Aoyama district. Rooms equipped to a high standard and the in-house restaurants are recommended.
Roppongi Prince (£££) 3-2-7 Roppongi, Minato-ku (tel: 03 3587 1111). Compact 216-room hotel close to Roppongi's entertainments. The courtyard with a café and swimming-pool is an asset.
Sakura Ryokan (£) 2-6-2 Iriya, Taito-ku (tel: 03 3876 8118). Close to Ueno and Asakusa, with Western- and Japanese-style rooms.
Shiba Daimon (££) 2-3-6 Shiba-Daimon, Minato-ku (tel: 03 3431 3716). This friendly hotel, which sees few Western guests, is located in the Tokyo Tower area. It has a good Chinese restaurant.
Shinagawa Prince Hotel (£) 4-10-30 Takanawa, Minato-ku (tel: 03 3440 1111). Acceptable budget accommodation with reasonably sized rooms. Part of a sports complex; mainly young clients; 24-hour coffee bar.
Shinjuku Prince Hotel (££) 1-9-1 Marunouchi, Chiyoda-ku (tel: 031 3205 1111). A business hotel with atmosphere. Central location on the edge of Kabukicho, Shinjuku's red-light district. Twenty-four hour room service, reasonably priced restaurants, small rooms but good value for money.
Shinjuku Washington (££) 3-2-9 Nishi-Shinjuku, Shinjuku-ku (tel: 03 3343 3111). A shiny modern business hotel near the Shinjuku skyscrapers, with 1,310 compact rooms and largely impersonal or automated services. Five minutes' walk from Shinjuku station.
Star (££) 7-10-5 Nishi-Shinjuku, Shinjuku-ku (tel: 03 3361 1111). A small, functional but friendly hotel with 80 rooms, only a couple of minutes' walk from Shinjuku station and the entertainment district.
Tokiwa Hotel (££) 7-27-9 Shinjuku, Shinjuku-ku (tel: 03 3202 4321). A good-value *ryokan*-style hotel with character. Western- and Japanese-style rooms. Good location in the heart of Shinjuku.
Tokyo Hilton International (£££) 6-6-2 Nishi-Shinjuku, Shinjuku-ku (tel: 03 3344 5111). One of the high-rises of Shinjuku, with great views from the upper floors, 807 rooms, 5 restaurants, indoor and outdoor pools and tennis courts.
Tokyo Kokusai International Youth Hostel (£) Central Plaza 18F, 2-1-1 Kagurazaka, Shinjuku-ku (tel: 03 3235 1107). Simple accommodation in a modern tower-block. Reservations in advance are required. Send a letter with a self-addressed postcard for reply.
Tokyo Station Hotel (££) 1-9-1 Marunouchi, Chiyoda-ku (tel: 03 3231 2511). Built in 1915, this hotel occupies much of the distinctive red-brick section of Tokyo station. Spacious, comfortable rooms with a rather faded elegance. Has a slightly eccentric air.
Tokyo YMCA Sadowara Hostel (£) 3-1-1 Ichigaya, Sadowara-cho (tel: 03 3268 7313). Men and women welcome. Well-run, modern building. Wash basins are provided in every room. Doors close 11pm.
Westin Tokyo (£££) Yebisu Garden Place, 1-4-1 Mita, Meguro-ku (tel: 03 5423 7000). A stylish hotel with richly decorated public areas and 445 guest rooms, part of a new leisure development on the former Sapporo Brewery site.
Yaesu-Ryumeikan (££) 1-3-22 Yaesu, Chuo-ku (tel: 03 3271 0971). Japanese inn offering Western- and Japanese-style rooms, air conditioned. Good value for money.
YMCA Asia Youth Centre (£) 2-5-5 Saragaku-cho, Chiyoda-ku (tel: 03 3233 0631). Men and women welcome. Rooms basic. Western and Japanese breakfasts served, indoor pool available. Doors close at midnight. Seven or eight minutes' walk from Suidobashi or Jinbocho stations.
YWCA Sadohara (£) 3-1-1 Ichigaya-Sadoharacho,

Shinjuku-ku (tel: 03 3268 7313). Pleasant but very small, so early reservation is essential. A few rooms are available for couples. A few minutes' walk from Ichigaya station.

Kamakura
Kamakura is so close to Tokyo that relatively few people stay overnight. Most hotels tend to be decorated in Japanese style and room charges may include dinner and breakfast.
Kamakura Hotel (££) 2-22-29 Hase (tel: 0467 22 0029). Close to Hase station and Yuigahawa beach. Old established hotel. Western and Japanese rooms. Price incudes dinner and breakfast.

Nikko
A tour of Nikko can be undertaken on a day trip from Tokyo. Most accommodation is in Japanese-style inns.
Pension Hillside Terrace (£) 2441 Nikko (tel: 0288 54 3235). Friendly, clean place with good food.
Pension Turtle (£) 2-16 Takumi-cho (tel: 0288 53 3168). Good location near Toshogu Shrine. Comfortable rooms. Recommended.

CENTRAL HONSHU

Hakone
Fuji-Hakone Guest House (£) 912, Sengokuhara, Kanagawa 250-06 (tel: 0460 4 6577). A simple but clean Japanese inn in quiet surroundings. The owners speak English. Worth a couple of nights' stay (two nights minimum) to explore the region.
Fujiya Hotel (££/£) 359 Miyanoshita, Hakone-machi, Ashigarashimogun 250-04 (tel: 0460 2 2211). Built in 1878 – one of the oldest Western-style hotels in Japan. Charming character and traditional Japanese service. Fine gardens.
Naraya Ryokan (£££) 162 Miyanoshita, Hakone-machi, Ashigarashimogun 250-04 (tel: 0460 2 2411). Opposite the Fujiya Hotel. A *ryokan* that has been in the same family for many generations. Elegant, *tatami* rooms with mountain views. First-class Japanese cuisine and hot-spring baths.

Fuji Five Lakes
Hotel Ashiwada (££) 395 Nagahama, Ashiwada-mura, Minami-Isuru-gun, Yamanashi 401-4 (tel: 0555 82 2321). On the shore of Lake Kawaguchi, a new, functional Japanese-style hotel; good base for climbing Mount Fuji in season.
Kawaguchiko Youth Hostel (£) near Kawaguchiko station (tel: 0555 72 1431). Busy during Fuji climbing season, otherwise quiet. Closed November–late March.

Ise Shima National Park
Futamikan Ryokan (£££) 569-1, Futami-cho, Mie Prefecture 519 (tel: 05964 3 2003). An old, very traditional Japanese inn on the coast, five minutes from the Wedded Rocks of Futamigaura. Excellent food, sea and garden views.
Hoshide Ryokan (£) 2-15-2 Kawasaki, Iseshi, Mie Prefecture 516 (tel: 0596 28 2377). A simple, traditional *ryokan*. The owners serve macrobiotic food for breakfast and dinner. Close to Ujiyamada and Iseshi stations.
Ise City Hotel (££) 1-11-31 Fukiage, Iseshi, Mie Prefecture 516 (tel: 0596 28 2111). Close to the Hoshide *roykan*, a conveniently situated business hotel offering friendly service and quite small but comfortable rooms.

Izu Peninsula
Ginsuiso Hotel (£££) 2977-1 Nishina, Nishi Izucho, Dogashima (tel: 0558 52 1211). Very expensive, classy resort; *ryokan*-style hotel with superb clifftop location. Book well in advance.
Haji Minshuku (£) 708 Sotoura-Kaigan, Shimoda City (tel: 05582 2 2597). A friendly *minshuku*. The owner speaks English. Close to the beach. Price includes two meals.
Kaikomaru Minshuku (£) Nishi-Izu-cho, Sawada, Dogashima (tel: 0558 52 1054). At the opposite end of the scale to Ginsuiso: a simple, family-run *minshuku*, with its own hot-spring bath. No English spoken.
New Fujiya Hotel (££) 1-16 Ginzacho, Atami, Shizuoka 413 (tel: 0557 81 0111). A straightforward, efficiently run, resort hotel. Indoor and outdoor hot-spring baths. A functional base for exploring Izu Peninsula.
Shimoda Tokyu Hotel (££/£) 5-12-1 Shimoda, Shimoda, Shizuoka 415 (tel: 05582 2 2411). Located on a hill overlooking Shimoda Bay, with sea and mountain views. Outdoor swimming pool, hot-spring baths. Large and impersonal but very practical.

Kobe
Hotel Okura Kobe (£££) 2-1 Hatobacho, Chuo-ku, Kobe 650 (tel: 078 333 0111). Good location in Merikan Park and close to downtown shopping areas; 35-storey hotel with elegantly furnished rooms and impeccable service.
Kobe Washington Hotel (££) 2-11-5 Shimoyamate-dori, Chuo-ku, Kobe 650 (tel: 078 331 6111). An effi-

ciently run business hotel with an atmosphere more pleasant than is usually found in such establishments. Convenient for a one-night stop.

Oriental Hotel (££/£) 25 Kyomachi Street, Chuo-ku, Kobe 650 (tel: 078 331 8111). A well-established, red-brick city hotel, part of old Kobe. Service is good and the small rooms well equipped and comfortable.

Ryokan Takayama-so (£) 400-1, Arima-cho, Kita-ku, Kobe, Hyogo Prefecture 651-14 (tel: 078 904 0744). Set in one of the oldest spas in Japan. Manager speaks English. Good food, and a hot-spring spa on the premises.

Tor Ryokan (£) 3-12-1 Kitanagasa-dori, Chuo-ku, Kobe 650 (tel: 078 331 3590). An inexpensive Japanese-style inn located in the centre of Kobe. Convenient.

Nagoya

Hotel Sunroute Nagoya (££) 2-35-24 Meieki, Nakamura-ku, Nagoya 450 (tel: 052 571 2221). An unexpectedly bright and cheerful business hotel. Public areas quite spacious, rooms small. Located very close to Nagoya station.

International Hotel Nagoya (££/£) 3-23-3 Nishiki, Naka-ku, Nagoya 460 (tel: 052 961 3111). High-quality, long established popular hotel with a European feel. Western and Japanese restaurants available.

Nagoya Miyako Hotel (££) 4-9-10 Meieki, Nakamura-ku, Nagoya 450 (tel: 052 571 3211). A medium-priced hotel offering good service and convenient central location.

Osaka

Holiday Inn Nankai (££) 2-5-15 Shinsaibashisuji, Chuo-ku, Osaka 542 (tel: 06 213 8281). Close to Namba station, shopping and nightlife areas. Spacious rooms; children under 12 are accommodated free. Western and Japanese restaurants available.

Hotel New Otani (£££) 1-4-1 Shiromi, Chuo-ku, Osaka 540 (tel: 06 941 1111). One of the best hotels in Osaka, set in a new, futuristic building that towers over Osaka Castle. Services are comprehensive, prices are steep. Excellent fitness club.

Osaka Terminal Hotel (££) 3-1-1 Umeda, Kita-ku, Osaka 530 (tel: 06 344 1234). Within the Osaka station complex – the lobby opens on to the station. Busy location but very convenient for a one night stop. Fortunately, the hotel rooms are soundproofed. Some have fine views over the city.

Shin-Osaka Sen-1 City Hotel (£) 2-2-17 Nishi-Miyahara, Yodogawa-ku, Osaka 532 (tel: 06 394 3331). A basic but adequate business hotel for the budget traveller. Some rooms have private baths; otherwise, there are public baths. Rooms reasonably well equipped. The hotel lobby is found on the sixth floor of the building.

KYOTO

Higashiyama Youth Hostel (£) 112 Shirakawabashi-goken-cho, Sanjo-dori, Higashiyama-ku (tel: 075 761 8135). Well-situated for Kyoto station. Guests obliged to take dinner and breakfast. Book ahead in season.

Hiiragiya Ryokan (£££) Anekoji-agaru, Fuyacho, Nagagyo-ku (tel: 075 221 1136) Expensive; extremely distinguished guests.

Hiraiwa Ryokan (£) 314, Hayao-cho, Kaminoguchi-agaru, Ninomiyacho-dori, Shimogyo-ku (tel: 075 351 6748). Popular, central Japanese inn. Showers only.

Hotel Alpha (££) Kawaramachi, Sango-agaru, Nakagyo-ku (tel: 075 241 2000). Excellent location in central Kyoto. Comfortable, business-style hotel. Deluxe rooms brighter and bigger, worth the extra outlay. Restaurant serves classic Japanese cuisine.

Koto Utane Youth Hostel (£) 29 Nakayama-cho, Uzumasa, Ukeyo-ku (tel: 075 462 2288). Near Ryoan-ji Temple. Simple concrete structure offering basic accommodation. Cycle hire and laundry facilities.

Kyoto Century Hotel (££) 680 Higashishiokoji-cho, Shiokoji-sagaru, Higashinotoin-dori, Shimogyo-ku (tel: 075 351 0111). Near Kyoto station. Good-value Japanese-style rooms available.

Kyoto Holiday Inn (££) 36 Nishihiraki-cho, Tekano, Sakyo-ku (tel: 075 721 3131). Inconveniently located in northeast residential area, but provides good facilities and the best sports hotel complex (including an ice rink) in Kyoto. Shuttle bus to town centre. Rooms for the disabled.

Kyoto Park Hotel (££) Sanjusangendo Side, Higashiyama-ku (tel: 075 525 3111). In eastern Kyoto opposite National Museum. Combines Western and Japanese features.

Kyoto Royal Hotel (££) Sanjo-agaru Kawaramachi, Nakagyo-ku (tel: 075 223 1234). Prime location on central Kawamachi-dori. Service is good and location convenient.

Matsuba-ya Ryokan (£) Nishiiru Higashinotoin, Kamijuzuyamachi-dori, Shimogyo-ku (tel: 075 351 3727). Inexpensive Japanese inn close to Kyoto station and Sanjusangendo Temple. Homely atmosphere, no private facilities.
Miyako Hotel (£££) Sanjo-Keage, Higashiyama-ku (tel: 075 771 7111). Well-established hotel with first-class reputation. Western- and Japanese-style rooms.
Nashinoki Inn (£) Agaru Imadegawa, Nashinoki-dori, Kamigyo-ku (tel: 075 241 1543). North of Imperial Palace; a family-run *ryokan* in a quiet district.
New Miyako Hotel (££) Hachijo-guchi, Kyoto Station (tel: 075 661 7111). Sister hotel to the classier and more expensive Miyako Hotel. Opposite Kyoto station. Rooms small but many restaurants and bars. Popular with younger Japanese travellers and tour groups.
Ohara Nenbutsuji Kaikan (£) Raigoincho, Ohara, Sakyo-ku (tel: 075 744 2540). One hour by bus from Kyoto station. Take bus from stop 1 in front of Kyoto Central Post Office to Ohara.
Pension Higashiyama (£) Sanjo-sagaru, Shirakawa-zuji, Higashiyama-ku (tel: 075 882 1181). Located in eastern Kyoto, by the Shirakawa canal. Clean, small hotel, constructed in 1985. Western- and Japanese-style rooms available. Doors close at 11:30pm.
Takaragaike Prince Hotel (£££) Takaragaike, Sakyo-ku (tel: 075 712 1111). Located in the north of the city. Large rooms, views of mountains and forests.
Tani House (£) 8 Daitokuji-cho, Murasakino, Kita-ku (tel: 075 492 5489). Japanese-style inn run by friendly Japanese couple. Popular with foreign visitors on a tight budget. Near Koto-In Temple.
Tawaraya Ryokan (£££) Fuyacho, Oike-Sagaru, Nakagyo-ku (tel: 075 211 5566). Very expensive, traditional *ryokan*, generally acknowledged as one of the finest in Japan. Booked months in advance.
Temple Accommodation The following temples accept foreign guests; book in advance by letter. Vegetarian breakfast is usually included in the price. Dormitory-style accommodation is the norm.
Hiden-In Temple (£) 35 Sennyuji Sandai-cho, Higashiyama-ku (tel: 075 561 8781). From Kyoto station take bus 208 to Sennyuji-michi stop.
Myokenji Temple (£) Teranouchi Horikawa, Kamigyo-ku (tel: 075 414 0808). From Kyoto station take bus 9 to Horikawa Teranouchi stop.
Myorenji Temple (£) Teranouchi Horikana, Kamigyo-ku (tel: 075 451 3527). As for Myokenji Temple.
Three Sisters Inn Annex (££) Heian Jingu, Higashi Kita Kado, Sakyo-ku (tel: 075 761 6333). A traditional Kyoto *ryokan*-style inn accustomed to foreigners. Quiet and comfortable accommodation.

WESTERN HONSHU

Hagi
Hokumon Yashiki Ryokan (££/£) 210 Horiuchi, Hagi-shi, Yamaguchi Prefecture 758 (tel: 08382 2 7521). *Ryokan* inn, with spacious rooms and traditional service, in old *samurai* neighbourhood near castle grounds.
Tomoe Ryokan (££) 608 Hijiwara, Hagi-shi, Yamaguchi Prefecture 758 (tel: 08382 2 0150). An elegant old inn with lovely gardens. Food excellent. Bath and toilets shared.

Himeji
Himeji Castle Hotel (££) 210 Hojyo, Himeji 670 (tel: 0792 84 3311). Near the station and the castle. Outdoor swimming-pool and Western-style restaurant.

Hiroshima
ANA Hotel Hiroshima (££/£) 7-20 Nakamachi, Naka-ku, Hiroshima (tel: 082 241 1111). One of Hiroshima's best hotels, five minutes' walk from the Peace Park and business district. Rooms spacious and well equipped.
Hiroshima City Hotel (££) 1-4 Kyobashi-cho, Minami-ku, Hiroshima (tel: 082 263 5111). Regular business hotel right opposite the station. Recently renovated. Convenient for a one-night stop.
Ikedaya Minshuku (£) 6-36 Dobashi, Naka-ku, Hiroshima (tel: 082 231 3329). Good accommodation near Peace Park. Dinner and breakfast included in the price.

Kurashiki
Ryokan Kurashiki (££/£) 4-1 Honmachi, Kurashiki 710 (tel: 0864 22 0730). Splendid *ryokan* in the heart of old Kurashiki. Constructed from an old merchant's house and connecting rice and sugar warehouses. Excellent restaurant attached which serves classic *Kaisaki* Japanese food.

Matsue
Horaiso Ryokan (££) Tonomachi, Matsue 690 (tel: 0852 21 4337). Pleasing *ryokan* in private location near the castle.
Tokyu Inn (££) 590 Asahimachi, Matsue 690 (tel: 0852 27 0109). Handy

location across the street from Matsue station. Part of a business hotel chain. Reasonably sized rooms and most facilities that the traveller will require.

Miyajima

Jyukeiso Ryokan (££) Miyajima, Saeki-gun 739-05 (tel: 0829 44 0300). A family run *ryokan*, on a small hill east of the pier. English spoken; Western breakfast available on request.

Okayama

Culture Hotel (££) 1-3-2 Gankunan-cho, Okayama City 700 (tel: 0862 55 1122). Imaginatively designed hotel with cheerful rooms and a friendly staff. Western-style restaurant.

Tsuwano

Meigetsu Ryokan (££) Tsuwano-cho, Kanoashi-gun 699-56 (tel: 08567 2 0685). Excellent traditional *ryokan* located in the middle of town.

Wakasagi no Yado Minshuku (£) Tsuwano-cho, Kanoashi-gun 699-56, Shimane-ken (tel: 08567 2 1146). Small, family-run *minshuku*. Japanese and Western breakfast. Japanese dinner.

SHIKOKU

Kochi

Hotel Takasago (££) 2-1 Ekimae-cho, Kochi-shi, Kochi 780 (tel: 0888 22 1288). Slightly scruffy *ryokan* but food is fine and price reasonable.

Washington Hotel (££) 1-8-25 Otesuji, Kochi-shi, Kochi 780 (tel: 0888 23 6111). Near the castle. Fairly large rooms, friendly staff.

Matsuyama

ANA Hotel Matsuyama (£££) 3-2-1 Ichiban-cho, Matsuyama 790 (tel: 0899 335511). Matsuyama's best hotel, in the city centre. Near the cable-car for Matsuyamaji Castle and streetcar stop for Dogo Onsen. Variety of bars and restaurants.

Shinsen-en Youth Hostel (£) 22-3 Dogohimezaka Otsu, Matsuyama 790 (tel: 0899 336366). Near Dogo Onsen, busy in season. Laundry and bicycle hire facilities.

Taikei Business Hotel (££) 3-1-15 Heiwa Dori, Matsuyama 790 (tel: 0899 43 3560). Cheerful business hotel with more character than most. Public baths on the premises.

Shodo island

There are numerous *minshuku* on the island. Book when you get there in Tonosho, or at the tourist office in Takamatsu before you leave (see pages 182–3).

Takamatsu

Hotel Kawaroku (££) 1-2 Hyakken-cho, Takamatsu 760 (tel: 0878 21 5666). A combination of *ryokan* and ordinary hotel. Western- and Japanese-style rooms, Japanese food served in your room or Western food in the hotel restaurant. In the heart of the city.

Takamatsu Grand Hotel (££) 1-5-10 Kotobuki-cho, Takamatsu 760 (tel: 0878 51 5757). Near the station, shopping arcades and the pier. Rooms recently given long-overdue renovation. Lobby on third floor with views over Tamamo Park.

KYUSHU

Aso National Park

Pension Flower Garden (£) Takamori-machi, Ozu, Takamori 3096-4, Kyushu (tel: 09676 2 3012). Western-style pension in pretty setting. Good food. Cab ride from Takamori station, or call and the hotel will arrange to collect you.

Yamaguchi Ryokan (££) Tarutama Onsen, Choyo-son, Kyushu (tel: 09676 7 0006). Mountain *onsen* set in delightful countryside. Cab ride from Aso-Shimoda station.

Beppu

Sakaeya Minshuku (£) Ida, Kannawa, Beppu 874 (tel: 0977 66 6234). Well-established *minshuku* with its own hot-spring baths. House is old and has character. Food basic but well cooked. Book ahead.

Suginoi Hotel (£££) Kankaiji, Beppu 874 (tel: 0977 24 1141). Beppu's best known, largest and most opulent hotel, more like a mini resort. Gigantic baths. Not the ideal place for those seeking peace and quiet.

Tamanoyu (£££) Yufin-cho, Oita-ken (tel: 9077 84 2158). Yufin hot-spring resort is one hour by bus from Beppu and an elegant, fashionable and sophisticated alternative to it. The Tamanoyu is very expensive but an exceptionally refined and charming traditional inn. Despite this, the atmosphere is relaxed, and if you can afford one night here it is highly recommended.

Fukuoka/Hakata

Clio Court Hotel (££) 5-3 Hakataeki-Chuogai, Hakata-ku 812 (tel: 092 472 1111). Modern, chic hotel designed by Rei Kurokawa. Rooms are decorated in a variety of styles; you can choose when you book. Western and Japanese restaurants and cheaper food bars. Lack of single rooms, however.

Hotel New Otani (£££) 1-1-2 Watanabe-dori, Chuo-ku, Fukuoka 810 (tel: 092 714 1111). First-class hotel

with services to match. Rooms large and very tastefully decorated.
Suehiro Inn (£) 2-1-9 Minamihonmachi, Hakata-ku, Fukuoka 816 (tel: 092 581 0306). Inexpensive Japanese inn. *Tatami* rooms small but clean, some with private baths. In front of Nishitetsu Zasshonokuma station on the overhead line from Fukuoka station.
Toyo Hotel (££) 1-9-36 Hakata-eki, Higashi, Haikata-ku 812 (tel: 092 474 1121). Business hotel conveniently located by Hakata station. Functional but comfortable enough. Rooms on top floors have more light.

Kagoshima
Kagoshima Hayashida Hotel (££) 12-22 Higashisengoku-cho, Kagoshima 892 (tel: 0992 24 4111). In the centre of town. Rather eccentric, space-age theme in the décor.
Shigetomiso Ryokan (£££) 31-7 Shimazu-cho, Kagoshima 890 (tel: 0992 47 3155). Very expensive *ryokan* which is set in a former villa once belonging to the Shimazu ruling clan.

Kumamoto
Kumamoto Shiritsu Youth Hostel (£) 5-15-55, Shimazaki-machi, Kumamoto 860 (tel: 096 352 2441). Efficiently run youth hostel, open to both male and female residents. Proprietor can speak English.
Maruko Hotel (££) 11-10 Kamitori-cho, Kumamoto 860 (tel: 096 353 1241). Japanese inn-style hotel with mainly *tatami* rooms, which are comfortable and air conditioned. Western and Japanese meals are available.
New Sky Hotel (££) 2 Higashiamidaji-cho, Kumamoto 860 (tel: 096 354 2111). Modern, large and attractive hotel which offers excellent amenities at a reasonable price. Enjoys a convenient location – near Kumamoto Castle and Suizenji Garden.

Miyazaki
Seaside Hotel Phoenix (££) 3083 Hamayama Shioji, Miyazaki 880-01 (tel: 0985 39 1111). Mix of Japanese- and Western-style rooms. Relaxing and cheerful. Facilities of the more expensive sister Sun Hotel Phoenix are available.

Nagasaki
Nagasaki Grand Hotel (£££) 5-3 Manzai-machi, Nagasaki 850 (tel: 0958 23 1234). Well-established, small and discreet hotel, which has a beer garden. Laid out in a tropical setting and open in the spring and summer months.
Nagasaki Kenritsu Youth Hostel (£) 2 Tateyama-cho, Nagasaki 850 (tel: 0952 23 5032). Located near Nagasaki station. Open to non-members. This is only basic accommodation, but laundry facilities are provided for residents.
Nagasaki Washington Hotel (££) 9-1 Shinchi-machi, Nagasaki 850 (tel: 0958 28 1211). Part of a dependable chain of business hotels. Unusually, the rooms are fitted with Japanese-style bath tubs. Located in the Hamanomachi shopping district and close to Chinatown.
Sakamoto-ya Ryokan (£££) 2-13 Kanaya-machi, Nagasaki 850 (tel: 0958 26 8211). An elegant wooden *ryokan* which provides a personalised service to its guests. *Shippoku* (a Nagasaki meal of various dishes) served on request.
Tanpopo Minshuku (£) 21-7 Hoeicho, Nagasaki 852 (tel: 0958 61 6230). Basic *tatami* rooms at budget prices. The concrete building is ugly but within walking distance of Peace Park. The nearest station is Urakami; call from there and the hotel will arrange to pick you up.

OKINAWA

Central Okinawa
Sheraton Okinawa Hotel (££/£) 1478 Kishaba, Kitagusuku-son, Nakagami-gun, Okinawa (tel: 098 935 4321). On a hill in central Okinawa; fine views and a comprehensive service. Outdoor swimming-pool is surrounded by tropical plants.

Naha
Okinawa Harbour View Hotel (£££) 2-46 Izumizaki, Naha-shi, Okinawa (tel: 098 853 2111). Set on the island, providing a combination of the best city and resort hotel.
Pacific Hotel Okinawa (££) 3-6-1 Nishi, Naha-shi, Okinawa (tel: 098 868 5162). Good, comfortable and slightly less expensive than the Harbour View.

NORTHERN HONSHU

Kakunodate
Hyakusuien Minshuku (£) 31 Shimonaka-machi, Kakunodate, Senboku-gun (tel: 0187 55 5715). Central *minshuku* in a converted 19th-century warehouse. Old-fashioned *irori* hearth and mini museum included on the premises.
Ishikawa Ryokan (£/£) 32 Iwase-machi, Kakunodate, Senboku-gun (tel: 0187 54 2030). Modern but quite unpretentious and welcoming Japanese inn, run by friendly family who serve good food.

Kamikochi

Kamikochi Imperial Hotel (£££) Kamikochi, Azumi-mura, Nagano-ken (tel: 0263 95 2001). Modern, high-class lounge hotel run by the Imperial Hotel of Tokyo.

Nishi-Itoya Sanso Inn (££) Kamikochi, Azumi-mura, Nagano-ken (tel: 0263 95 2206). Traditional wooden inn. Accommodation with meals. Near Kappabashi Bridge.

Kanazawa

Garden Hotel (££) 2-16-16 Honcho, Kanazawa 920 (tel: 0762 63 3333). A rather welcoming business hotel located close to the station. The rooms are small, but the beds are a comfortable size and the windows open. Practical for a short stay.

Kanazawa Tokyu Hotel (££/£) 2-1-1 Kohrinbo, Kanazawa 920 (tel: 0762 31 2411). New hotel in the centre. Public areas spacious. Guest rooms are small but rooms on the higher floors have good views.

Miyabo Ryokan (£££) 3 Shimo-Kakinokibatake, Kanazawa 920 (tel: 0762 31 4228). Traditional and very expensive inn surrounded by the oldest private garden in the city. The best rooms open on to the garden.

Murataya Ryokan (£) 1-5-2 Katamachi, Kanazawa 920 (tel: 0762 63 0455). Relaxed Japanese inn in the middle of town. No private baths but *tatami* rooms comfortable.

Matsumoto

Hotel New Station (££/£) 1-1-11 Chuo, Matsumoto 390 (tel: 0263 35 3850). Convenient location near railway station. Friendly business hotel offering good value. In-house food delicious.

Matsumoto Tokyu Inn (££) 1-3-21 Fukashi, Matsumoto 390 (tel: 0263 36 0109). Better class of business hotel, close to the railway station. Cheaper rooms are very small, bigger rooms rather expensive but a pleasant place to stay if you are using it as a base for exploring the area.

Morioka

Hotel Metropolitan Morioka (££/£) 1-44 Morioka, Ekimae-dori, Morioka, Iwate 020 (tel: 0196 25 1211). Within the station complex. The rooms are designed for sleeping rather than lingering but there is a good Chinese restaurant on the premises.

Ogimachi

Accommodation in Ogimachi is restricted to thatched farmhouse, *minshuku* bed, breakfast and dinner accommodation. Book at the village tourist office (0576 96 1751).

Sado Island

Sado Seaside Hotel (£) Ryotsu-shi, Sado Island (tel: 0259 27 7211). Cheerful, inexpensive hotel. A short cab ride away from the Ryotsu ferry port. Japanese-style rooms with private bath.

San Kei Kan Minshuku (£) Ryotsu-shi, Negai 260, Sado Island (tel: 0259 26 2440). Very friendly, family-run *minshuku* by the beach. No English spoken.

Sendai

Dochuan Youth Hostel (£) 31 Kitayashiki, Onoda, Taihaku-ku, Sendai, Miyagi 980 (tel: 022 247 0511). Thirty minutes by bus or cab from the station, this is the best youth hostel in the region. A converted thatched-roofed farmhouse set on the edge of the countryside.

Sendai Hotel (££) 1-10-25 Chuo, Sendai, Miyagi 980 (tel: 022 225 5171). Modern, but well-established, reputable hotel, located close to the station.

Takayama

Hishuya Ryokan (££/£) 2581 Kami Okamotocho, Takayama 506 (tel: 0577 33 4001). Good traditional inn near Hida-no-sato village outside Takayama. Quiet and refined atmosphere.

Kinnikan Ryokan (££/£) 48 Asahimachi, Takayama 506 (tel: 0577 32 3131). First-class traditional Japanese inn in the heart of old Takayama. Small and popular; best to book ahead.

Yamakyu Minshuku (£) 58 Tenshoji, Takayama 506 (tel: 0577 32 3756). A cross between a *minshuku* and a *ryokan*. Reputations for good food and a delightful public bath.

Yamagata

Goto Matabei Ryokan (££) 2-2-30 Ryumachi, Yamagata 990 (tel: 0236 22 0357). Old, fairly comfortable Japanese inn. Plenty of character and simple but well-cooked food.

Washington Hotel (££) 1-4-31 Nanoka-cho, Yamagata 990 (tel: 0236 24 1515). Straightforward functional business hotel, part of a reliable chain that generally provides good service.

HOKKAIDO

Abashiri

Sakura-so Minshuku (£) 27-41 Omagari, Abashiri-shi, Hokkaido (tel: 0152 44 2337). Helpful, friendly owners.

Akan kohan
Akan Angel Youth Hostel (£) 5-1 Shuri Komanbetsu–Akan-Kohan, Akan 085, Hokkaido (tel: 0154 67 2309). Well-run youth hostel. Busy in season.
Nibushi no Sato Minshuku (£) Kussharo-Kohan, Teshikaga-machi, Kawakami-gun, Hokkaido (tel: 0154 83 2294). A cab ride out of Akan-Kohan village. Has its own hot-spring baths. No English spoken.
Yamoura Hotel (££) Akan-Kohan, Akan 085, Hokkaido (tel: 0154 67 2311). Small hotel on the lakeside at the southern end of Akan-Kohan village. Mainly Japanese-style *tatami* rooms. Western-style rooms tend to look away from the lake.

Hakodate
Akai Boshi Minshuku (£) 3-22 Asahi-cho, Hakodate 040 (tel: 0138 26 4035). Small, family-run establishment ten minutes' walk from the station.
Hotel Hakodate Royal (££) 10-9 Omori-cho, Hakodate 040 (tel: 0138 26 8181). Western-style hotel. Efficient, cheerful staff. Cab ride from the station.

Noboribetsu Onsen
Akiyoshi Hotel (££/£) Noribetsu Onsen, Norietsu 059, Hokkaido (tel: 01438 4 2661). *Ryokan*-style hotel, friendly, efficient service. Central location. One of the best places to stay in the area.
Kiyomizu Ryokan (£) 60 Noribetsu, Onsen-cho, Noribetsu 059, Hokkaido (tel: 01438 4 2145). Japanese inn a short walk from the bus terminal serving good *tempura*.
Suzuki Ryokan (££) Karurusu Onsen, Noribetsu-shi, Hokkaido (tel: 01438 4 2285). A 30-minute cab ride out of Noribetsu Onsen in a quiet mountain location. Large old inn equipped with a traditional hot-spring bath.

Sapporo
Fujiya Santus Hotel (££) Nishi 7, Kita 3, Chuo-ku, Sapporo 060 (tel: 011 271 3344). Small hotel offering a warm welcome and very good value for money. Located near JR Sapporo station and shopping district.
Hotel Alpha Sapporo (££/£) Nishi 5, Minami 1, Chuo-ku, Sapporo 060 (tel: 011 221 2333). Classy city hotel near shopping district and the Susukino nightlife area. Good service, friendly staff.
Nakamuraya Ryokan (£) Nishi 7, Kita 3, Chuo-ku, Sapporo 060 (tel: 011 241 2111). Japanese inn with modern facilities and local food. Near station and city centre.
Sapporo Washington Hotel II (££) Nishi 6, Kita 5, Chuo-ku, Sapporo 060 (tel: 011 222 3311). Better class of business hotel. Part of a reputable chain.

Sounkyo Onsen
Daisetsu zan Shirakaba-so Youth Hostel (£) 1418 Higashikawa-machi, Kamikawa-gun, Hokkaido (tel: 0166 97 2246). Accessible by bus from Asahigawa or Sounkyo Onsen. Scenically located hostel with its own hot-spring baths and good food.
Kumoi Ryokan (££) Sounkyo, Kamikawa-gun, Hokkaido (tel: 01658 5 3553). New Japanese inn with its own hot-spring bath and some rooms with private bath. Western breakfast is provided on request.
Sounkyo Grand Hotel (££) Sounkyo, Kamikawa-gun, Hokkaido (tel: 01658 5 3111). A *ryokan*-style hotel. One of the better and more reasonably priced of the many resort establishments in the area. Always busy in the summer.

Toyaku Onsen
Ikosio Minshuku (£) 83 Sobetsu-cho, Sobetsu-Onsen, Hokkaido (tel: 01427 5 2522). In a small *onsen* district 2km west of Toyaku Onsen. Good, clean establishment serving fine food.
Shawa Shinzan Youth Hostel (£) 103 Sobetsu-cho, Sobetsu-Onsen, Hokkaido (tel: 01427 5 2283). The hostel is slightly shabby but has a good hot-spring bath.
Toya Park Hotel (££) Toyako Onsen, Hokkaido (tel: 01427 5 2445). Small hotel offering attractive views of the lake. Excellent service provided. Manager speaks English.

RESTAURANTS

Almost all large Japanese towns and cities have an abundance of restaurants to suit every imaginable taste and budget. At home, space is usually too limited for socialising – and eating and drinking out is very much a part of the Japanese way of life. Whether you are buying street food or dining in an expensive restaurant, service and hygiene standards are first class. With such a choice available, the Japanese tend to dine out in their own neighbourhoods and to travel only to establishments with a particular reputation or a special style of food. There is also the strategic problem of finding a restaurant in a strange district. The Japanese address system is complex and even cab drivers often have to stop and ring a place on the

way there. If you see a likely establishment during the day, ask for a business card: they usually have a map on the back, which can be shown to the cab driver. Cash is preferred to credit cards especially in smaller establishments. Price categories per person without drinks:
Expensive (£££) over ¥8,500
Moderate (££) ¥2,500–8,500
Budget (£) under ¥2,500

TOKYO

Ajanta (£)
3-11 Nibancho, Chiyoda-ku (tel: 03 3264 6955). Subway: Kojimachi. This Indian restaurant is an old favourite, with the simplest of settings but one of the most comprehensive menus in Tokyo. The vegetarian and non-vegetarian, south and north Indian dishes are as authentic as you will find.
Bengawan Solo (££) 7-18-13 Roppongi, Minato-ku (tel: 3408 5698). Subway: Roppongi. Indonesian restaurant serving good *rijsttafel* (a variety of dishes served on one tray) at a reasonable price.
Benjarong (££) Miyata Building 2F, 1-4-12 Kabukicho, Shinjuku-ku (tel: 03 3209 7064). Subway: Shinjuku. An elegant Thai restaurant with cuisine to match, beautifully prepared by the former chef of a top Bangkok hotel. The menu is fully explained in English. Lunch prices are much less than dinner.
Bougainvillea (££) Romanee Building 2F, 2-25-9 Dogenzaka, Shibuya-ku (tel: 03 3496 5537). Subway: Shibuya. Vietnamese food may yet challenge Thai for the 'ethnic' crown. This popular place has a wide choice of authentic dishes: noodle soups, crab with coriander, spring rolls, sweet-and-sour pork or chicken, meatballs, crisp salads.
Cafeteria Caft (£) 2-1-1 Nishi-Shinjuku, Shinjuku-ku (tel: 03 3344 6969). Subway: Shinjuku. A plain and simple self-service counter but the offerings include budget-priced set menus centred around noodles, curry and rice, and even *sushi*.
Chotoku (£) 1-10-5 Shibuya, Shibuya-ku (tel: 3407 8891). Subway: Shibuya. The best of handmade Udon noodles offered in a huge variety of dishes.
Don-Don (£) 3-6-9 Akasaka, Minato-ku (tel: 03 3585 8920). Subway: Akasaka-mitsuke. An all-day, all-night economy diner, serving basic rice-bowl dishes: rice and beef, rice and curry, at budget prices.
Edo-Gin (££) 4-5-1 Tsukiji, Chuo-ku (tel: 03 3543 4401). Subway: Tsukiji. Well-established and popular, serving *sashimi* and *sushi* made from the freshest fish from the nearby market. You can see some of it still swimming in a tank.
Fukuzushi (££) 5-7-8 Roppongi, Minato-ku (tel: 3402 4116). Subway: Roppongi. Fashionable *sushi* restaurant serving excellent *sushi* despite modern trappings.
Furosato (££) 3-4-1 Aobadai Meguro-ku (tel: 03 3463 2310). Subway: Nakameguro, Shibuya. Traditional country food in a reconstructed, picturesque old mountain farmhouse. Fish, chicken and vegetables grilled over a *hibachi* (small charcoal grill) are a speciality.
Futaba (£) 2-8-11 Ueno, Taito-ku (tel: 03 3831 6483). Subway: Ueno. Ueno is well known for *tonkatsu* (fried pork cutlet), eaten with rice, soup and pickled vegetables; this is one of the oldest restaurants serving the dish.
Genrokuzushi (£) 5-8-5 Jingumae, Shibuya-ku (tel: 03 3498 3968). Subway: Meijijingu-mae. An economical way to eat *sushi*: little dishes, each containing a pair of pieces, circle past you on a conveyor belt and you pick the dishes that take your fancy. The chefs work to replace the *sushi* while they chat to the customers. (Another branch is in the Asakusa area at 1-2-3 Hanakawado, Taito-ku.)
Gold Leaf (£££) Taisei Koki Building B1F, 5-4-12 Hiroo, Shibuya-ku (tel: 03 3447 1212). Subway: Hiroo. In Tokyo Thai food is booming. This is one of the most attractive places in the city to eat it, with a décor of teak wood and black lacquer complementing the colourful dishes. Bangkok-trained chefs prepare subtly spiced salads, soups laced with the quintessential Thai ingredients of lemon-grass, coriander, chilli and coconut milk, and delicious curries. Service is polished and the menu explains it all in English.
Gonin Byakusho (££) 4th Floor Roppongi Square Building, 3-10-3 Roppongi (tel: 3470 1675). Subway: Roppongi. The name means 'five farmers' and the restaurant has an authentic country atmosphere. Food is grilled around a large clay oven.
Han (££) 4-3-20 Toranomon, Minato-ku (tel: 03 3578 8293). Subway: Kamiyacho. One of a chain, with real Japanese atmosphere and traditional cooking. A keen young man kneels to take your order, tapping it into his hand-held termi-

nal. Lots of small dishes give you a chance to try new experiences or old favourites.

Hard Rock Café (££) 5-4-20 Roppongi, Minato-ku (tel: 03 3408 7018). Subway: Roppongi. Hamburgers, salads and snacks, ice-creams and pie, to the sound of loud music. Long lines form at weekends.

Hassan (££) 6-1-20 Roppongi B1F, Minato-ku (tel: 03 3403 8333). Subway: Roppongi. A busy traditional restaurant with a choice of *tatami* (straw mats) or chairs. The set menus of *tempura, sukiyaki* and *shabu-shabu* include all-you-can-eat options, at a higher price, for the very hungry.

Hayashi (££/£) 4th Floor, Sanno Kaikan Building, 2-14-1 Akasaka (tel: 3582 4078). Serves the dishes of Hida, a mountainous region in central Honshu. Old farmhouse atmosphere. Specialises in food grilled over *hibachi* at your table.

Higo Batten (££) AG Building 1F, 3-18-17 Minami-Aoyama, Minato-ku (tel: 03 3423 4462). Subway: Omotesando. Tasty combinations of fish and shellfish, vegetables and meats grilled on bamboo skewers. Traditional décor of black wood and white screens.

Honke Ponta (£) 3-23-3, Ueno, Taito-ku (tel: 3831 2351). Subway: Ueno-hirokoji. The oldest *tonkatsu* (pork) restaurant in Tokyo. Famous for its thick and tender cuts of pork. Pre-war décor.

Inakaya (£££) 3-12-7 Akasaka, Minato-ku (tel: 3586 3054). Subway: Akasaka. Lots of noise and atmosphere. Mounds of various types of food; select whatever you wish and the chef, on a raised platform behind the counter, will cook it to order.

Jinya (££) My City Building 7F, Shinjuku Station, 3-38-1 Shinjuku-ku (tel: 03 3352 0018). Subway: Shinjuku. Family-style Japanese cooking, beautifully presented. There is a choice of *tatami* or conventional table and chairs.

Johnny Rockets (£) Coco Roppongi Building 2F, 3-11-10 Roppongi, Minato-ku (tel: 03 3423 1955). Subway: Roppongi. Good, freshly made hamburgers, french fries and salads, and other fast food staples.

Kisoji (£) Ginza Jujiya Building 5F, 3-5-4 Ginza, Chuo-ku (tel: 03 3567 0406). Subway: Ginza. A convenient Ginza spot for budget set-menu lunches of soup and rice with fish or chicken.

Komagata Dojo (££) 1-7-12 Komagata, Taito-ku (tel: 3842 4001). Subway: Asakusa. *Dojo* are small river fish and this establishment has been serving them in a variety of dishes for nearly 200 years. *Tatami* mat seating.

Konomi (£££) 1-7-2 Nishi-Asakusa, Taito-ku (tel: 03 3843 7773). Subway: Tawaramachi. A small restaurant in the Kappabashi district, specialising in the cuisine of Kyoto. *Kyobento*, a double-decker lacquered box lunch of two dozen beautiful little seasonal dishes, is an aesthetic treat.

Kyubei (£££) 8-5-23 Ginza, Chuo-ku (tel: 03 3571 6523). Subway: Higashi-Ginza. Founded many years ago, and still going strong, this restaurant specialises in some of the most expertly made *sushi* to be found anywhere in Japan.

La Tour d'Argent (£££) New Otami Hotel, 4-1 Kioi-cho, Chiyoda-ku (tel: 03 3239 3111). Subway: Akasakamitsuke. The first branch outside Paris of the famous La Tour d'Argent. Absolutely the finest French and Japanese-inspired dishes in opulent surroundings. Very expensive.

Lintaro (££) 5-9-15 Ginza, Chuo-ku (tel: 03 3571 2037). Subway: Ginza. Lintaro Mizuhama is the friendly owner of the restauant which bears his name, and he is often to be found chatting to the diners or directing the service. He's a Ginza native and expert: his family has been here for centuries. The deep basement room is a surprise, with its high ceiling and Italian Renaissance pictures. The food is Italian but with an added Japanese flair in its presentation and some of the flavours. Superbly fresh salads and vegetables come from the restaurant's special gardens.

Mai-Thai (££) 1-18-16 Ebisu, Shibuya-ku (tel: 03 3280 1155). Subway: Ebisu. This is a small, cheerful and popular spot in a side street, serving a typical Thai menu at reasonable prices. One of a growing choice of eating places in the fast-developing Ebisu area.

Mominoki House (£) 2-18-5 Jingumae, Harajuku (tel: 3405 9144). Subway: Harajuku. Excellent natural foods restaurant serving idiosyncratic menu inspired by macrobiotic/ French/Japanese foods and cooking styles. Good-value fixed-lunch.

Nakase (£££) 1-39-13 Asakusa, Taito-ku (tel: 03 3841 4015). Subway: Asakusa. A famous and long-established *tempura* restaurant near Nakamise-dori. Follow your nose to the delicious smells, but be prepared to wait. Often

the line forms outside the door well before opening time. Lunch is the best – for economy and because the area shuts early.
Nanbantei (££) 4-5-6 Roppongi, Minato-ku (tel: 03 3402 0606). Subway: Roppongi. A popular *yakitori* (grilled food) restaurant. Friendly atmosphere.
Rice Terrace (££) 2-7-9 Nishi-Azabu, Minato-ku (tel: 03 3498 6271). Subway: Nogizaka. A relaxed setting for enjoying some of the best Thai food in Tokyo. The service is friendly but polished. Try to get a table downstairs; the upper level is cramped.
Robata (££/£) 1-3-8 Yurakucho, Chiyoda-ku (tel: 03 3591 1905). Subway: Yurakucho. Set in a replica of an old Japanese farmhouse with authentic rustic-style interior. Serves good regional cuisine.
Rock 'n' Roll Diner (£) Big Ben Building B1F, 2-5-2 Kitazawa, Setagaya-ku (tel: 03 3411 6565). Subway: Yoyogi-uehara. American-style salads, hamburgers and sandwiches in a big, busy '60s environment.
Roppongi Sumida (£££) Aoda Roppongi Building B1F, 3-16-33 Roppongi, Minato-ku (tel: 03 5570 5777). Subway: Roppongi. *Teppanyaki* grilled delicacies expertly prepared from fresh crab, abalone, prawns and other seafoods and steak.
Ryu Sushi (£) 5-2-1 Tsukiji, Chuo-ku (tel: 03 3541 9517). Subway: Tsukiji. It is hard to get any nearer to the source of supply than this little *sushi* bar next to the market halls. Unusual for the Tsukiji location, the owner is not the senior chef but another sort of artist, the painter Ryutaro Shiina. He is normally in attendance from an early hour, greeting the customers who mostly work in the market. It's a great place to satisfy your hunger after a pre-dawn visit there.
Sakafuji (£) 1-6-1 Asakusa, Taito-ku (tel: 03 3843 1122). Subway: Asakusa. A bright and friendly modern restaurant on three floors, next to Hotel TOP. *Yakitori, kushiage, tempura* and *teppanyaki* are among the many choices.
Samovar (££) 2-22-5 Dogenzaka, Shibuya-ku (tel: 03 3462 0648). Subway: Shibuya. Authentic Russian stews and soups, kebabs, rye bread, beers and vodkas.
Samrat (£) Shojikiya Building 3F, 4-10-10 Roppongi, Minato-ku (tel: 03 3478 5877). Subway: Roppongi. One of the first of the Indian wave and still popular, serving *tandoori* dishes and curries on the milder side. The all-day buffet represents good value for money. (Samrat has other branches including: Koyas One Building 6F, 13-7 Udagawacho, Shibuya-ku.)
Sanjugo Danya (£) B1F, Shibuya City Hotel, 1-1 Maruyama-cho, Shibuya-ku (tel: 03 3770 9835). Subway: Shibuya. The '35 Steps' is a Japanese-style bistro, with East-West country cooking to suit local and European tastes. Take your shoes off and choose a seat at the counter or one of the low tables. The staff don't speak much English but a few words go a long way.
Sasanoyuki Restaurant (££) 2-15-10, Negishi, Taito-ku (tel: 03 3873 1145). Near JR station Uguisudani. Specialises in *tofu* dishes. A good selection of vegetarian dishes available.
Shabu Zen (££) 5-7-16 Roppongi, Minato-ku (tel: 03 3585 5600). Subway: Roppongi. A big restaurant specialising in *shabu-shabu*, including 'all-you-can-eat' deals. The American beef is less costly than the local. (Another branch is at Ginza Core Building, 5-8-20 Ginza, Chuo-ku.)
Shakey's (£) 3-18-2 Shinjuku, Shinjuku-ku (tel: 03 3352 7473). Pizza, pasta, seafood place. At lunchtime you can eat as much as you wish for a very reasonable sum from a pizza buffet bar. Other Shakey's branches offer the same deal.
Shigeyoshi (£££) Olympia Co-op B1F, 6-35-3 Jingumae, Shibuya-ku (tel: 03 3400 4044). Subway: Meijijingu-mae. A small counter and a few tables, with the chefs in full view. The style of cooking is utterly traditional, from the Nagoya area. Lunch prices are reasonable.
The Siam (£) World Town Building 8F, 5-8-17 Ginza, Chuo-ku (tel: 03 3572 4101). Subway: Higashi-Ginza. This one has been around for years, and it is still serving tasty Thai standards at economical prices, for Ginza, especially at lunchtime.
Takeno (£££) 6-21-2 Tsukiji, Chuo-ku (tel: 03 3541 8698). Subway: Tsukiji. Fine quality *sashimi* and *sushi;* fish fresh from the market. Most of the lunchtime customers are market professionals: the evening crowd comes from far and wide, drawn by the Takeno's reputation. At the *sushi* counter, the chefs keep their jewel-like creations coming until you reluctantly call a halt.
Tamazushi (£) B2F Ginza Core Building, 5-8-20 Ginza, Chuo-ku (tel: 03 3573 0057). Subway:

Higashi-Ginza. Quick service of good *sushi*, with economical set menus and *à la carte*, depending on what is in season. At lunchtime, you may have to wait for the business crowd to clear.
Ten-Ichi (££) 6-6-5 Ginza, Chuo-ku (tel: 03 3571 1949). Subway: Ginza. Well-known *tempura* establishment originally founded in 1930 by Isao Yabuki who raised the standard of *tempura*-making to an art form.
Tokai-en (£) 1-6-3 Kabukicho, Shinjuku-ku (tel: 03 3200 2934). Subway: Shinjuku. An enormous Korean operation, with all-you-can-eat bargain lunches. Spicy seafood, stews and bulgogi barbecues are specialities. It can get boisterous in the late evening.
Tokyo Kaisen Restaurant (££) 36-1 Kabukicho, 2-chome, Shinjuku-ku (tel: 03 5273 8301). Relatively new establishment above a 24-hour fish market. Choose from a huge variety of fish downstairs, take it upstairs and the staff will prepare it for you.
Tomoca (££) 1-7-27 Yotsuya, Shinjuku-ku (tel: 03 3353 7945). Subway: Shinjukugyoen-mae. This is an agreeable, relaxed Sri Lankan restaurant where you select your curry, choosing from shrimp, fish, chicken or beef, and specify the degree of spiciness. (Don't ask for the hottest unless your digestive system is made from Teflon.) A whole range of extras comes with it: poppadums, salads, fried eggplant, *dal* and tangy *sambals*.
Tsukiji (££) Miyuki Building B1F, 5-6-12 Ginza, Chuo-ku (tel: 03 3571 0071). Subway: Higashi-Ginza. A bright and busy all-day restaurant in the heart of Ginza. The set menus at lunchtime are attractive and reasonably priced.
Tsunahachi (£) 3-31-8 Shinjuku (tel: 3352 1012). Subway: Shinjuku (east exit). This is the largest of a chain of inexpensive *tempura* restaurants. Helpful and popular with young people. Set meals represent the best value.
Yabu Soba (£) 2-10 Awajicho, Kanda (tel: 3251 0287). Subway: Awajicho. Established in 1880, this is one of the most famous *soba* noodle shops in Tokyo. English menu available.
Zakuro (££) basement TSB Kaikan Building, 5-3-3 Akasaka (tel: 3582 6841). Subway: Akasaka. Popular *shabu-shabu* restaurant, which also offers inexpensive *sukiyaki* and *obento* (lunchboxes). English menu available.

CENTRAL HONSHU

Hakone
Fujiya Hotel Dining Room (££) Fujiya Hotel, 359 Miyanoshita, Hakone (tel: 0460 2 2211). Classic period hotel in Miyanoshita on the Hakone Tozen railway. Good service provided in the graceful old dining room.

Kobe
Gaylord (££) Basement, Meiji Seimei Building, 8-3-7 Isogami-dori, Kobe (tel: 078 251 4359). Good Indian food, especially Tandoori dishes, in upmarket Indian restaurant surroundings. Lunchtime specials are excellent value. Popular with local foreign residents.
Masaya Honten (£) 1-8-21 Nakayamate-dori, Kobe (tel: 078 331 2890). A popular noodle restaurant. Fast, cheap, quality food.
Misono (£££) 1-7-6 Kitanagasa-dori, Kobe (tel: 078 331 2890). One of Kobe's oldest steakhouses. Beef comes from local cattle reared in traditional pampered style and is cooked at your table.

Nagoya
Kishimen-tei (£) 3-20-4 Nishiki, Naka-ku, Nagoya (tel: 052 951 3481). Tiny place with a reputation for serving the best *kishimen* noodles (a Nagoya speciality) in town.
Yaegaki Tempura Restaurant (££) 3-17-28 Nishiki, Naka-ku, Nagoya (tel: 052 951 3250). Long-established restaurant serving fresh fish and vegetable *tempura* in one of Nagoya's few wooden buildings. English menu available.

Osaka
Fuguhisa (££) 3-14-24 Higashi-ohashi, Higashinari-ku, Osaka (tel: 06 972 5029). Specialises in *fugu ryori* (blowfish cuisine). Unpretentious, good-quality cooking at a price difficult to beat.
Hankyu Grand Building Restaurants £/££ 32 Bangai, Osaka. The top four floors of this building near Osaka station have a wide range of eating establishments serving Japanese and Western food.
Kuidaore (££) 1-8-25 Dotonbori, Osaka (tel: 06 211 5300). A popular restaurant serving a variety of Japanese food. Four floors, prices rise as you go up. Easily recognised by the mechanical clown outside the entrance.
Mimiu (££) 6-18 Hiranomachi 4 chome, Chuo-ku, Osaka (tel: 06 231 5770). Old teahouse-style establishment, the home of *udon-suki*, noodles simmered at your table in a pot with seasonal ingredients.
The Seasons (£££) Hilton International, Osaka, 8-8

Umeda 1-chome, Kita-ku (tel: 06 347 7111). Elegant European food in plush but friendly surroundings. Very close to Osaka station.

KYOTO

Agatha (££) 2nd floor, Yurika Building, Kiyamachi-dori, Sanjo-agaru, Nakagyo-ku (tel: 223 2379). *Robatayaki* (charcoal grill) restaurant with Agatha Christie-style 1940s décor. Creative cooking, fun atmosphere and popular, especially with the fashion crowd.
Ajiro (££) Myoshinji Minamimon-mae, Hanazono, Sakyo-ku (tel: 463 0221). *Shojin ryori*-style temple cooking in a restaurant setting. Meals served in private rooms. Near south gate of Myoshinji Temple. Open to 6pm only.
Ashiya Steak House (££/£) 172–13 Kyjomizu 4-chome, Higashiyama-ku (tel: 541 7961). Friendly establishment serving excellent Kobe beef in charming traditional house.
Hirano-ya (££) Maruyama Koen, Chion-in, Minami-mon-mae, Higashiyama-ku (tel: 561 1603). Attractive tea-house specialising in traditional Kyoto dish, a simmered dish made from yams or potatoes and dried cod. Recipe 300 years old.
Hyotei (£££) Kusakawa-cho 35, Nanzenji (tel: 771 4116). One of the best *kaiseki* restaurants in Kyoto. Beautifully presented meals served in a small but handsome house opening onto a lovely garden. *Tatami* mat seating in private rooms.
Izeki (££) Pontocho Shijo Agaru, Nakagyo-ku (tel: 221 2080). Beautifully arranged *kaiseki*-style set menus in tasteful restaurant at moderate prices.
Izusen (£) Daijiin-nai, Daitokuji-cho, Murasakino, Kita-ku (tel: 491 6665). Fast service, inexpensive temple food in a sub-temple of Daitokuji. Open to 5pm only.
Kalhoji (££) Masamune 20, Momoyama-cho, Fushimi-ku (tel: 611 1672). Unusual Chinese-style *shojin ryori* food from Zen temple of the Obaku sect. Shared dishes. Open to 5pm only.
Mankamero (£££) Inokuma-dori, Demizu-agaru, Kamigyo-ku (tel: 441 5020). Very expensive, traditional, old establishment (1716) serving food of the Yusoku-ryori style, once the cuisine of the imperial court. If you can afford it, it is a very special night out. To try the food at a more reasonable price, eat there for lunch and order the fixed price *take-kago-bento*.
Minokichi (££/£) Sanjo-agaru, Dobutsuen-mae dori, Sakyo-ku (tel: 771 4185). Established in 1735, one of Kyoto's best-known restaurants. Variety of menus served in a complex of buildings. Delightful garden. The restaurant's speciality is *Kyo-kaiseki* meal of eight dishes.
Misoka-ankawamichiya (£) Fuyacho-dori, Sanjo-agaru (tel: 221 2525). Perhaps the most famous *soba* noodle shop in Kyoto. Small, with tiny rooms, opens out on to a central courtyard. Located at this premises in old Kyoto for the past 300 years.
Nishiki (££) Nakano-shima, Koen-uchi, Arashiyama, Ukyo-ku (tel: 075 871 8888). Set on an island right in the middle of the Oi River. The tea house serves excellent *Kyo-ryori*.
Oiwa (£) Nijo-sagaru, Kiyamachi-dori, Nakagyo-ku (tel: 231 7667). A variety of deep-fried kebabs served in a renovated treasure house.
Okutan (££) 86-30 Fukuchi-cho, Nanzenji (tel: 771 8709). Founded over 300 years ago as a vegetarian restaurant; one of the oldest and best *tofu* places in Kyoto. Beautiful garden.
Rokusei (££) 71 Nishitenno-cho, Okazaki, Sakyo-ku (tel: 751 6171). Good Kyoto cuisine served in a tasteful modern restaurant overlooking tree-lined canal.
Takasebune (£) Nishikana, Chiyamachisagaru, Shijo-nishi, Shimogyo-ku (tel: 351 4032). Excellent *tempura* and *sashimi* dishes served at very reasonable prices.

WESTERN HONSHU AND SHIKOKU

Hagi
Fujita Soba-ten (£) Kumagai-cho, Hagi (tel: 08382 2 1086). Friendly hand-made *soba* restaurant. Also sells *tempura*. Closes 7pm and second and fourth Wednesday of each month.

Hiroshima
Okononi-mura (£) 5-21 Shin-tenchi, Hiroshima (tel: 082 241 8758). Two floors of stalls each selling their own versions of *okonomiyaki*, a Japanese-style pancake with a variety of fillings.
Suishin (££) 6-7 Tatemachi, Naka-ku, Hiroshima (tel: 082 247 4411). Specialises in *kamameshi*, a rice casserole cooked with various ingredients, especially fresh fish. Very busy, in the middle of town. Five floors of dining rooms.

Kurashiki
Kamoi Sabo (£) 1-3-17 Chuo, Kurashiki (tel: 0864 22 0606). Very reasonably priced *sushi* in a grand old

rice granary. *Nuku-sushi*, a steamed rice and fish dish, is the house speciality.

Matsue

Minami-kan (££/£) 14 Suetsugu Honmachi Matsue (tel: 0852 21 5131). Excellent *kaiseki* cuisine and local seasonal specialities in modern surroundings.

Matsuyama

Shin-Hamasku (££) Sanbancho-4-chome, Matsuyama (tel: 0899 33 3030). Spacious restaurant in the middle of town. Serves fresh Inland Sea fish dishes, local dishes and a variety of other Japanese fare.

Unkai (££/£) 6th floor, ANA Zenniku Hotel, 3-2-1 Ichiban-cho, Matsuyama (tel: 0899 33 5511). Near the city centre and castle. Excellent service, sophisticated surroundings.

Takamatsu

Maimai-tei (££) Nakahonmachi, Takamatsu (tel: 0878 33 3360). Extremely good *sanuki-udon* (thick, white, wheat-flour noodle) dishes. Small, unpretentious restaurant. The owner/chef makes some of his own utensils.

Takamatsu Grand Hotel (££) 1-5-10 Kotobukicho, Takamatsu (tel: 0878 51 5757). Near the station and port. Nine Japanese restaurants on its second floor.

Tenkatsu (££) Hyogomachi, Takamatsu (tel: 0878 21 5380). Popular *tempura* and *sushi* restaurant in the Hyogomachi shopping arcade near the station. The *sashimi* is prepared from fish that swim around, oblivious, in a tank in the restaurant. Seating is on *tatami* mats or there is the option of sitting on stools at the counter.

KYUSHU AND OKINAWA

Beppu

Amamijaya (£) 1-4 Jissoji, Beppu (tel: 0977 67 6024). Specialises in hand-made flat noodle dishes. *Fugu* also available. Wall display of local crafts.

Fugumatsu (££) 3-6-14 Kitahama, Beppu (tel: 0977 21 1717). Blowfish (*fugu*) restaurant. Simple, straightforward Japanese-style restaurant. *Fugu* and other fresh fish dishes are of good quality.

Fukuoka

Gourmet City (£) Basement, Hotel Centraza, 4-23 Hakataeki-Chuogai, Fukuoko (tel: 092 461 0111). Collection of about 10 restaurants offering variety, economy and convenience (near Shinkansen exit of Hakata station).

Gyosai (££) 3-chome Hakata-Ekimae, Fukuoka (tel: 092 441 9780). One of four Gyosai restaurants in Fukuoka. Good seafood dishes in amenable surroundings.

Hemmingway's (£) 2718 Maizuru, Tenjin (tel: 092 714 0986). Late bar/pizza house with friendly relaxed atmosphere. Good value.

Tsukushino (£££) 15th Floor, ANA Hotel, 3-3-3 Hakata-Ekimae, Fukuoka (tel: 092 471 7111). The best classic Japanese food. Impressive views over the city. English menu available.

Kagoshima

Satsuma (£) 10-4 Chuo-chu, Kagoshima (tel: 0992 52 2661). Local cuisine; try the *Satsuma-age*, deep fried fish sausage and sweet yams.

Kumamoto

Mutsugoro (££) Basement, Kumamoto Green Hotel, 12-11 Hanabata-cho, Kumamoto (tel: 096 325 2222). Small restaurant serving local dishes (mainly horse meat) and various seafood.

Senri (££) Suizenji Koen Park, Kumamoto (tel: 096 384 1824). Within Suizenji Park. Local dishes, including horse meat, eel and river fish. Western and *tatami* seating.

Miyazaki

Kuretake (£) Basement, Nikko Building, Tachibana-Dori, Miyazaki (tel: 0985 24 2818). Local specialities. Try *hiyajiru*, a cold fish soup served over hot rice.

Nagasaki

Fukiro (£££) 146 Kami Nishiyama-machi, Nagasaki (tel: 0958 22 0253). Old wooden Japanese-style building with *shoji* screens and *tatami* mats, set on a clifftop stone staircase near Suwa Shrine. Specialises in *shippoku* meals, a Nagasaki speciality in which a variety of small dishes are served all together. Four or more diners are usually required for a *shippoku* feast to be served.

Hamakatsu (££) 1-14 Kajiya-machi, Nagasaki (tel: 0958 23 2316). Modern restaurant serving reasonably priced *shippoku* (minimum two people) and a variety of set menus that feature local dishes. This is a good place to try the local cuisine.

Shikai-ro (£) 4-5 Matsugae-machi, Nagasaki (tel: 0958 822 1296). Four floors seating over 1,500 people. Popular restaurant that was responsible for inventing *champon* two centuries ago – a Chinese-inspired, thick noodle dish. English menu available.

Naha
Heiwa Dori Shopping Arcade (£) Heiwa Dori, Naha, Okinawa. Food stalls in the arcade sell a very wide variety of Japanese dishes. You can eat your meal there without ceremony or take away.
Restaurant Naha (££/£) 2-4-4 Tsuji, Naha, Okinawa (tel: 098 868 2548). Good local cuisine combined with a floorshow of authentic Okinawa folk dance.
Sam's by the Sea (££) 10th floor, Naha Shopping Centre, Naha Port, Okinawa (tel: 098 862 6660). The Sam's chain is run by an American ex-military family and their restaurants combine Western and Japanese cooking. Large portions, good service. Lighting may be a little dim for some tastes.

NORTHERN HONSHU

Kanazawa
Kaga Tobi (£) Kohrinbo 109, 2-1 Kohrinbo, Kanazawa (tel: 0762 62 0535). Set on a back street just behind the Kohrinbo 109 department store, the Kaga Tobi serves a wide variety of good Japanese dishes.
Kanko Bussankan (£) 2-20 Kenrokumachi, Kanazawa (tel: 0762 22 7788). In the Ishikawa Prefectural Products Centre, near the Kenrokuen Garden main entrance. Open during the daytime only (10am-6pm), serving *sashumi*, noodles and the local cuisine, *kaga-ryori*, which uses mountain vegetables, shellfish (particularly tiny sweet shrimps) and river fish.
Miyoshian (££) 1-11 Kenrokumachi, Kanazawa (tel: 0762 21 0127). In the Kenrokuen Garden; established for over a century. *Tatami* mats and views over the pond. *Kaga-ryori* considered to be the best in Japan.

Matsumoto
Kura (££) Ko-Kudesai, Matsumoto (tel: 0263 33 6444). *Sushi* and *tempura* restaurant in a mud-walled, moated old house located right in the heart of town.
Naja (£) 4-3-20 Ote, Matsumoto (tel: 0263 36 9096). Vegetarian establishment with English menu available. Food well prepared.
Taiman (££/£) 4-2-4 Ote, Matsumoto (tel: 0263 32 0882). Deservedly well-known French restaurant serving excellent food in rustic Japanese setting. Furnished with Matsumoto *mingei* furniture. Located close to the castle.

Sendai
Iwashiya (££/£) 4-5-42 Ichiban-cho, Sendai (tel: 022 222 6645). This is probably the best seafood restaurant in town. *Tatami* seating.

Takayama
Kakusho (££/£) 2-98 Babacho, Takayama (tel: 0577 32 0174). Old mansion house in the eastern part of town near Tenshoji Temple. A nationally known restaurant with a reputation for top-class *shojin-ryori*, the vegetarian fare served at Buddhist temples.
Kofune (£) Hanasato-cho 6-6, Takayama (tel: 0577 32 2106. A noodle shop close to the station. Convenient and inexpensive. English-language menu available – which is unusual in an establishment such as this.
Suzuya (££) 24 Hanakawa-cho, Takayama (tel: 0577 32 2484). Small restaurant, decorated in rustic Takayama style, serving local specialities. Try *sansai-ryori*, mountain vegetables and *ayu*, a river fish grilled with soy sauce or salt.

HOKKAIDO

Hakodate
Bay Restaurant (££) 11-5 Toyokawa-cho, Hakodate (tel: 0138 22 1300). Housed in a waterfront warehouse. Seafood dishes are served in unusual combinations, such as tuna fish in coconut milk.
Chat Noir (£) Union Square, Meijikan (1st Floor), Hakodate (tel: 0138 27 1200). Elegant designer restaurant serving simple Japanese food.

Sapporo
Ramen Yokocho (£) A small alley in Susukino (one block south and running vertical to Susukino Avenue) packed with Sapporo *ramen* (Chinese noodles, the local speciality) shops. For the current favourite join the longest queue.
Sapporo Biru-en (££) N6, E9 Sapporo (tel: 011 742 1531). Sapporo's original brewery, now converted into a German-style beer garden. The house speciality is a cook-it-yourself lamb and vegetable barbecue called Genghis Khan, washed down with lots of beer.
Silo (££) 5 Minamo, 3 Nishi Chou-ku, Susukino, Sapporo (tel: 011 531 5837). Located in a rustic old building, serving Hokkaido specialities including smoked deer meat, sliced frozen salmon, bear meat, corn and potatoes.

Index

N

O

P

PICTURE CREDITS AND CONTRIBUTORS

Picture credits

The Automobile Association would like to thank the following photographers, libraries and associations for their assistance in the preparation of this book.

BRITISH MUSEUM 40a Battle of Yaskina, 41b Courtesans; **MARY EVANS PICTURE LIBRARY** 33a Courtesan, 34b Amaterasu (sun goddess), 42b Commodore Perry, 42c Perry's expedition, 45a Emperor Meiji, 104/5a Daimo & Suite, 110a Yokohama earthquake 1923, 110b Earthquake cartoon; **M GOSTELOW** 51a Tokyo Asakusa, 61 Sengakuji, 64b Market Tsukiji, 65 Marking tuna (Tsukiji), 66 Yasakuni Shrine war memorial museum, 248b Tokyo Ikebukuro; **ROBERT HARDING PICTURE LIBRARY** 24b Preparing for *sumo* wrestling, 237a Ainu 'Marimo' festival Hokkaido; **MICHAEL HOLFORD** 38b Akita armour; **HULTON DEUTSCH COLLECTION LTD** 46b US Marines, Okinawa, 47 Pearl Harbor; **THE IMAGE BANK** Cover Kyoto Zen Garden Temple, Spine Jitzo stone images Nikko, B/flap Ueno, good luck plaques; **JAPAN NATIONAL TOURIST ORGANIZATION** 16 & 17a Kansai International Airport, 32b Okutsu Onsen, 80b Minshuku, 99 L Yamanaka, 220a Ryokan; **KOBE CITY MUSEUM** 112 Painted screen; **KYOTO NATIONAL MUSEUM** 36b Clay farmer; **THE MANSELL COLLECTION** 39 *Samurai* warrior, 40b Iyeyasu, 41a Hideyoshi, 43 Emperor Meiji & Empress, 237b Ainu man & wife; **OTA MEMORIAL MUSEUM OF ART** 60b Kataoka Nizaemon VII in role of Ki-no-Natora; **PICTURES COLOUR LIBRARY LTD** 3 *Saké* barrells, 4a Tokyo, 265a Tokyo snack stall; **POPPERFOTO** 111a & 111b Kobe earthquake; **REX FEATURES LTD** 44b Emperor Hirohito; **D SCOTT** 104 Kanbara stage sixteen of the Tokaido, 104/5 Shono stage forty-six of the Tokaido, 105 Fukuroi stage twenty-eight of the Tokaido; **SPECTRUM COLOUR LIBRARY** 5c Cherry blossom (Ueno Park), 9a Sanja festival, 12a Robots, 13b Assembly line, 16b Bullet train, 18a Yushima shrine, 24a *Sumo* wrestlers, 25 *Sumo* wrestling, 31 Karatsu festival, 36a Kasuga shrine Nara, 93 Shinkansen bullet train, 94/5 Mt Fuji, 98 Mt Fuji & Kawaguchi Lake, 101b Mt Fuji & Hakone Komagatake ropeway, 103 Hakone Mt Fuji & L Ashi, 124 Zen Garden Daitokuji Temple, 135a Daisen-in-Zen Garden, 162 Himeji Castle, 175a Wakayama Mt Koya Ryn Onsen, 207a Naginata Martial Art, 220b Tsumago interior of Waki Hojin, 225 Miyagi Sendai shopping centre, 247a Tokyo Shibuya; **TOKYO NATIONAL MUSEUM** 34a Clay human mask; **VICTORIA & ALBERT MUSEUM** 76a & 76/7 Sword; **ZEFA PICTURES LTD** 10b Ibukushima shrine, 11 Mnt Fuji, 20a Calligraphy, 26a Sign, 27 Shinjùku, 44a 'Kansei Three Beauties', 45b Kuntsada Cherry blossom viewing, 46a Hiroshima ruins, 51b, 58a, 58b & 59 'Kabuki Theatre', 89a Portrait face.

All remaining pictures are held in the Association's own library (AA PHOTO LIBRARY) and were taken by JIM HOLMES with the exception of pages 2, 18b, 19a, 20b, 28a, 29b, 30b, 50, 52a, 55, 56, 62a, 63, 64a, 68/9, 73a, 78/9, 84b, 88a, 91a, 92a, 117, 131a, 137, 142a, 143, 158, 159a, 159b, 167b, 201, 219, 249, 251, 255, 256a, 264 which were taken by D Corrence.

The Automobile Association would also like to thank Nicolas Soames of Naxos Audiobooks and the Japan National Tourist Organization (JNTO) in London for their help during the preparation of this book.

The author would particularly like to thank Harry Cook and Simon Halewood for their assistance with the research for some sections of this book, and Helen Morgan for her expert typing of the manuscript. The author would also like to thank Terry Randsley, Philip Quirk and Glen Walford.

Contributors

Series adviser: Christopher Catling **Joint series editor:** Susi Bailey
Copy editor: Nia Williams **Designer:** Tony Truscott Designs
Verifiers: Martin Gostelow and Patrick Wilson **Indexer:** Marie Lorimer